The Being of the Phenomenon

Renaud Barbaras, c. 1998. Photo by Emmanuelle Barbaras.

RENAUD BARBARAS

The Being
of the
Phenomenon

Merleau-Ponty's Ontology

TRANSLATED BY TED TOADVINE AND LEONARD LAWLOR

INDIANA UNIVERSITY PRESS

Bloomington and Indianapolis

This book is a publication of

Indiana University Press
601 North Morton Street
Bloomington, IN 47404-3797 USA

http://iupress.indiana.edu

Telephone orders 800-842-6796
Fax orders 812-855-7931
Orders by e-mail iuporder@indiana.edu

Published in French as *De l'être du phénomène: l'ontologie de Merleau-Ponty* by Editions Jérôme Millon, Grenoble, France.
© 1991 by Editions Jérôme Millon
© 2004 by Indiana University Press

Manufactured in the United States of America

Library of Congress Cataloging-in-Publication Data

Barbaras, Renaud.
[De l'être du phénomène. English]
    The being of the phenomenon : Merleau-Ponty's ontology / Renaud Barbaras ; translated by Ted Toadvine and Leonard Lawlor.
        p. cm. — (Studies in Continental thought)
Includes bibliographical references and index.
    ISBN 0-253-34355-0 (cloth : alk. paper) — ISBN 0-253-21645-1 (pbk. : alk. paper)
    1. Merleau-Ponty, Maurice, 1908–1961. I. Title. II. Series.
    B2430.M3764B3413 2004
    111'.092—dc22
                                                            2003015583

1 2 3 4 5   09 08 07 06 05 04

Contents

Translators' Introduction

Originally published in France in 1991, *The Being of the Phenomenon: Merleau-Ponty's Ontology* is Renaud Barbaras's first major work.[1] It aims to restore the development of Merleau-Ponty's thought in its coherence. Thus, proceeding diachronically from Merleau-Ponty's earliest works to his last, Barbaras's reading is teleological. The *telos* that oriented all of Merleau-Ponty's work, for Barbaras, is the ontology that we find in Merleau-Ponty's last and unfinished masterpiece, *The Visible and the Invisible*. Being is understood as an intertwined relation between silent vision and linguistic expression—in a word, as the flesh. *The Being of the Phenomenon* attempts to reconstruct this carnal ontology. We might even say that it is an attempt to complete *The Visible and the Invisible*. Of course, such a project then concerns the transformation of Merleau-Ponty's phenomenology into ontology. Thus one of the main thrusts of the book is to confront Husserl's phenomenology, or, more precisely, to present the idea that Merleau-Ponty's perspective starts precisely where Husserl's perspective ends. As the initial reception of *The Being of the Phenomenon* in France shows, Barbaras accomplishes his project with great clarity, profundity, and richness.[2] Indeed, Françoise Dastur has said that *The Being of the Phenomenon* provides us with a "complete and powerful analysis of the Merleau-Pontian 'ontology of the visible.'"[3] Thus, an English translation of *The Being of the Phenomenon* has to be seen as an invaluable study of Merleau-Ponty's thought, one that complements and perhaps even exceeds other existing secondary sources in English.[4]

1. Barbaras is currently Professor of Contemporary Philosophy at the Université de Paris I, Panthéon-Sorbonne.
2. See the reviews of *De l'être du phénomène* by N. Depraz and J. M. Mouille-Arévant in *Revue de métaphysique et de morale,* no. 3 (1992); J. Ch. Margelidon, in *Etudes philosophiques,* no. 1 (January–March 1993); J. C. Pinson, in *Revue: recueil,* no. 2 (1992); and P. Trotignon, in *Revue philosophique,* no. 1 (1993).
3. F. Dastur, "Perceptual Faith and the Invisible," *Journal of the British Society for Phenomenology* 25, no. 1 (January 1994): 52 n. 47.
4. See G. B. Madison, *The Phenomenology of Merleau-Ponty: A Search for the Limits of Consciousness* (Athens: Ohio University Press, 1981), and M. C. Dillon, *Merleau-*

The Being of the Phenomenon consists of four parts, corresponding roughly to the four stages, as Barbaras sees them, of the development of Merleau-Ponty's ontology. In the first part, "Toward Ontology," Barbaras treats Merleau-Ponty's writings prior to *The Visible and the Invisible* "as an introduction to ontology in the strict sense." Barbaras shows the way into Merleau-Ponty's final ontology by determining the limitations of his early phenomenological thought. In particular, Merleau-Ponty's symmetrical critique of intellectualism and realism in *Phenomenology of Perception* does not result in a positive characterization of the perceptual field. Mired in traditional dichotomies, the description of perception here ends up oscillating between intellectualism and realism. The body, Merleau-Ponty's great discovery in the early works, is, according to Barbaras, an attempt to mediate between subject and object through an ambiguity that culminates in "pre-personal consciousness." The "tacit *cogito*" in turn re-institutes the dependence of sense on consciousness, although this consciousness can be defined only negatively. So far, a positive description of the phenomenal is still missing. Yet for Barbaras, Merleau-Ponty's philosophy of expression opens the way for a positive characterization. Rather than subordinating expression to perception, Merleau-Ponty describes perception on the basis of expression. On this account, just as Gestalt psychology had allowed Merleau-Ponty to rediscover behavior, so Saussure's linguistics allows him, in *The Prose of the World*, to rediscover the primordial experience of expression below the level of oppositional categories. The body comes now to be understood positively as primordial expression. Through diacritical difference, language, as Merleau-Ponty is able to show, cannot be understood through the opposition between matter and form. It is the "soil" of all genesis. This soil makes us understand subjectivity not as consciousness but as a point of passage in the genesis of sense, and it already points in the direction of ontology. If, like the phenomenological reduction, painting reveals the primordial layer of the world's "mute" self-expression, then for Merleau-Ponty phenomenology's

<hr />

Ponty's Ontology (Bloomington: Indiana University Press, 1988). We says "perhaps exceeds" because of Barbaras's attempt to integrate the working notes to *The Visible and the Invisible* into the ontology he is reconstructing. Moreover, it is clear that *The Being of the Phenomenon* functions as the foundation of an original philosophical position that Barbaras is currently developing. We shall return to this point of originality at the end of our introduction.

famous "return to the things themselves" means, according to Barbaras, a return to "brute," unconstituted being, to "the being of the world as the veiling of sense, as wild *logos.*"

Barbaras's second part examines the method by which Merleau-Ponty gains access to being in *The Visible and the Invisible*. "Interrogation" attempts to take stock of the "ontological diplopia," the "to-and-fro" movement of fact and essence. Accordingly, Barbaras investigates the critical chapters of *The Visible and the Invisible*, where Merleau-Ponty tries to situate himself between Husserl—who continues to confront the problem of the fact after believing himself to have overcome it by reducing the world to essence—and Sartre, who falls prey to the "bad dialectic" that absorbs the duality back into an identity of opposites. The strength of a philosophy of essence lies in its equation of being with appearing, an appearing that realism could never explain. Nevertheless, the laws of appearance do not exhaust the being of what appears, and the pure essence—which would require a total eidetic variation—is not a possible object of experience. While the return to essence claims to rest on experience, it in fact conceives existence as the negation of nothingness, thereby transforming what appears into a clear and distinct positivity. Sartre's bad dialectic of pure positivity and pure negativity is therefore abstract. Thus, Sartre closes himself off from any recognition of phenomenality, of the "something" beyond the positive and negative.

For Merleau-Ponty, as Barbaras points out, purity eliminates the possibility of being experienced. For Barbaras, Merleau-Ponty's own methodological approach, his "hyperdialectic," is a response to the ambiguity of dialectic. The hyperdialectic must be conceived as a thought that knows that it cannot complete itself; it is constantly aware of its inescapable rootedness in being. How does philosophy itself come to be generated from being, from this soil? It must rediscover itself as the pure interrogation that has the being of the question as its own being. Sense is interrogative since, like a question, it involves the possibility of an answer and yet precludes a final answer. Philosophy as interrogation, then, is the ultimate openness to being; being itself, now understood as self-interrogation, does away with the ontological diplopia. Thus, the central issue of *The Visible and the Invisible* is to reconceive the continuity of perception, speech, and thought within this ontology of interrogation.

Having traced out Merleau-Ponty's philosophical development from his early works to the critical chapters of *The Visible and the Invisible,* in parts III and IV of *The Being of the Phenomenon* Barbaras examines this ontology in its own right: first, "The Visible," the primordial articulation of the sensible, followed by "The Invisible," the primordial articulation of sense. As Barbaras points out, the focus on the visible stems not from any prioritization of visual experience, but rather from vision's quality of crystallizing the paradox of all sensibility through its tendency to efface itself before the object and thereby forget itself as vision. Vision (as well as touch) reveals a corporeal reflexivity that is essentially incomplete. As is well known, I cannot see myself seeing without becoming the object of vision and therefore no longer the one who sees. This essential structure of vision is due to embodiment, and embodiment indicates an inseparability from or ontological kinship with the world. The intertwining of subject and world as revealed through the reflexivity of sensibility is the very meaning of *chiasm*. By using the terms *visible* and *invisible*, Merleau-Ponty wants to reconceive fact and essence "chiasmatically," as intertwined and prior to their opposition. This chiasm of fact and essence, of sense and sensible, means that Merleau-Ponty (unlike the early Sartre) conceives being as its own negation and vice versa. Invisibility is a "fold" of the visible. The name for the relation to being that forms within being, then, is flesh.

Flesh, as Barbaras observes, is Merleau-Ponty's answer to the problem of intentionality. Importantly, within this context of the philosophy of flesh, Barbaras argues that the thing is no longer exterior to its manifestations, no longer based on an infinite (as in modern philosophy) that would be opposed to finite experience. Rather, the infinite is understood as openness; and the lived present, appearance itself, appears against a horizon—a distance—that it cannot encompass. For Barbaras, then, perceiver and perceived are abstract moments of perception as dimension. Dimension turns out to be the link that joins perception to language, since dimension reveals the diacritical structure itself of the world. The difference or distance between the appearance and the horizon makes language possible—or even *is* language. Poetry, playing the same role as painting has with respect to the visible, leads us back to the ultimate ontological texture. This ultimate texture is, of course, the flesh itself, which is not simply the body in the literal sense. Rather, since the body and the world are variants of a single dimension, they are also variants of each other. Nevertheless, the body is distinct due to its role as "dimension of all dimensions," as universal dimensionality. The body, in Barbaras's view, is the culmination of materiality as well as of subjectivity; the body's incarnation within the world rests on the very dimensionality that opens it to the world and makes the world appear before it. If flesh can be characterized by dimensionality, then this dimensionality must itself be understood in terms of a primordial temporality and spatiality, as the point where space and time cross. Here we return with Barbaras to the problem of distance. Depth is the primordial experience of spatiality, the first dimension, which Descartes missed by transforming it into an objective and measurable distance. But distance does not unfold *between* me and the thing; rather, distance remains interior to the thing, synonymous with its resistance to or refusal of my approach. Here it even seems that for Barbaras, time is understood in terms of distance. According to him, Merleau-Ponty rejects the traditional idea that the present is a point, instead understanding the present as a passage in which the past is an irreducible alterity, in which the present therefore always involves a distance.

Although the analysis thus far has considered only the sensible aspect of being, in the book's final part, "The Invisible," Barbaras takes on the most difficult problem confronting Merleau-Ponty's ontology: the relation between the sensible and the rational or ideal, the world opened by signification. Because the sensible has a sense, the perceived maintains an ideality within itself. Yet this "wild essence" is not the same as the more transparent meaning of ideality (such as a geometrical object). The difficulty thus lies in respecting the phenomenal difference between sense and meaning while maintaining their ontological continuity. While the visible and the invisible do not separate off as positive entities, Merleau-Ponty must nevertheless offer a means of preventing them from simply merging into an ontological monism of the sensible. The problem is to make the transition from the sensible in the strict sense to the objective in the strict sense. In response, following Merleau-Ponty, Barbaras embarks on a long analysis of intersubjectivity. The other operates at the conjunction between the two "planes" of sensible and object. Of course, the other must be understood on the basis of the flesh. Thus the world and the other turn out to be ontologically co-primordial, a chiasm. This chiasm is Merleau-Ponty's famous idea of syncretism, a generalized anonymous carnal existence in which every person is interwoven with everyone else. Nevertheless, it is necessary that the generality of flesh sustain itself by individuating itself. Hence, the other appears within the sensible world as an individual; and as an individual, the other appears as a certain "presentation of the unpresentable." Here, as Barbaras shows, Merleau-Ponty recognizes the fundamental phenomenological insight that the interiority of another can never be made present and therefore maintains a certain distance. The other is just as much absence as presence. But this absence makes the other desirable. For Barbaras, desire is the self's expressive response to its separation from itself as given in the appearance of the other. Desire is thus fundamentally narcissistic, but this narcissism is not yet that of an ego. Desire precedes the separation of self and other—or rather, through sexualization, it is the first moment of self-identity.

Mediating between the givenness of the other in the flesh and the relation of language in the strict sense, desire is the mute language of the body that strives to rediscover itself in the invisible of which the other's body is the trace. This attempt is always frustrated, despite the possibility of a temporary harmony within the embrace. Yet for Barbaras, the failure of desire exhibits desire's role within the expressive teleology. What desire seeks is not mastery of or submission to the other, but the relation of expression that only language as such can come to fulfill. Desire understood as primordial expression thus paves the way for expression proper in speech. The illusion of the self-subsistent idea has its phenomenal basis in the auto-affection of the voice, the element of the flesh that apparently erases its own materiality in its movement toward a meaning. Vocal expression represents a step beyond the visible precisely insofar as it offers the possibility of a true reversibility. Nevertheless, even the self-return of the voice carries a moment of non-coincidence, and the body of speech, the condition of its expressivity, attests to its essential incarnation. Even better than touch or vision, speech shows us the irreducibility of sensibility to facticity, while its own rootedness in sensibility guarantees its inability to close itself off into a realm of pure supra-sensible signification. The diacritical nature of the sign also receives its foundation in this incarnation, once we grasp expression as the articulation of signs and understand sense as the relation uniting and differentiating them. The transition of this articulation from the dense body of the visible to the lighter flesh of language fulfills the expressive teleology of being. In speech, the subject finds self-expression only by exteriorizing itself in a body, a body that opens itself to the listener just as much as to the speaker. Within this relation, the world no longer comes to interpose itself between us, as did our visible and tangible bodies in the advent of desire. Still, the division from the other remains. The other comes to me only as the inaccessible other side of this spoken being. In a sense, as Barbaras proclaims, "speech is the genuine body of the other," since it is truly in speech that the other's presence and absence are fused. Hence, speech opens a cultural world, fulfilling the universality that remained latent in the sensible world, but it does so as a modality of the sensible world itself.

The flesh, then, as a "structural identity" between the sensible and linguistic expression, answers the most difficult problem that organizes *The Visible and the Invisible*. The inchoative speech of the visible, its silent *logos,* cannot be opposed to expression. Expression is a "sublimation" of sensibility and maintains itself only as incarnated. Every perception is a primordial expression, but only insofar as it remains buried in the world's depths and calls for the efforts of linguistic expression. Hence Merleau-Ponty finds, as Barbaras puts it, "an analogy or a parallelism between perception and expression" that nevertheless refuses to identify them purely and simply. Perception and expression "both proceed from flesh," but "they do not refer to the same flesh"; they "cannot be confused, but neither can they be opposed." Thus we arrive at the final chiasm, the "ultimate truth." While perception and expression are ultimate dimensions, from the perspective of the phenomenal field they are facts to be ordered by the final dimension, that of being. Being, then, is the principle of openness or proliferation that allows the intercommunication of all the interlocking chiasms that compose it. But since being cannot be distinguished from the beings that manifest it, its absolute difference from beings is at the same time their absolute identity. The absolute makes sense, Barbaras concludes, only as human contingency; and being, the invisible ultimate dimension of this world, presents itself only in its irreducible absence.

In his closing chapter, Barbaras reflects on the implication that this ontology and Merleau-Ponty's philosophical approach hold for his relationship to Husserl and Heidegger. Indeed, Barbaras reflects on the future of phenomenological philosophy. He shows that Merleau-Ponty's specific path arises as the fulfillment of what remains "unthought" in both Husserl and Heidegger. Merleau-Ponty's philosophy therefore functions both as their definitive critique and as their continuation. By returning to the *Lebenswelt* without the baggage of a philosophy of consciousness, by approaching the ontological difference as a chiasmic relation between being and beings rather than as their absolute difference, Merleau-Ponty carves out a future for phenomenology, a future within which philosophy might construct itself around the awareness of its own rootedness, within which spirit might have the humility to recognize the sensible world as its other side, and within which our questioning of the world might first thematize itself as a moment of the world that it questions. This future, as Barbaras invites us to recognize at the close of *The Being of the Phenomenon*, remains our own possibility.

To conclude, we would like to point out that Barbaras himself has started to actualize this possibility. His most recent book, *Le désir et la distance* (*Desire and Distance*),[5] demonstrates, we think, a remarkable originality. Perhaps Barbaras is the first new voice in France since the 1960s. In *Desire and Distance,* Barbaras presents a critique of the phenomenological concept of perception. Husserl had defined perception in terms of fulfillment, of a bringing close, and intentionality in terms of need. Thus the phenomenological concept of perception for Barbaras involves no distance. In order to be able to understand the distance that defines perception, intentionality, in turn, must be redefined through desire. This idea— desire and distance—opens the way for a reconsideration of the concept of life, a "cosmobiology," as Barbaras says.[6] Yet such a cosmobiology "is rooted" in a reflection on Merleau-Ponty's philosophy,[7] a reflection presented precisely in *The Being of the Phenomenon*. If we are right, therefore, about the originality of Barbaras's recent thinking, then it is important not to read *The Being of the Phenomenon* as if it were merely another "secondary source" about Merleau-Ponty.

The Being of the Phenomenon is really a book about the development of an original "phenomenological ontology"—desire and distance—that takes Merleau-Ponty's work as its guiding clue.

Leonard Lawlor and Ted Toadvine

5. Renaud Barbaras, *Le désir et la distance* (Paris: Vrin, 1999); Stanford University Press is preparing an English translation. His other works include *La perception* (Paris: Hatier, 1994), *Merleau-Ponty* (Paris: Ellipses, 1997), and *Le tournant de l'expérience* (Paris: Vrin, 1998).

6. Barbaras, *Le désir et la distance,* p. 163.

7. See the "Preface to the English Translation." Barbaras himself would probably disagree with this comment, that is, that all of his thought results from a reflection on Merleau-Ponty, since Jan Patočka, more recently, has had an increasing influence on him. Yet, since Barbaras's thought always begins with perception, it remains inextricably connected to that of Merleau-Ponty.

Note on the Translation

In translating phenomenological terminology and Merleau-Ponty's own vocabulary, we have generally followed the conventions of available English translations. A few terminological decisions are worth noting, however. First, we have consistently translated *sens* as "sense" and *signification* as "meaning," except in a few obvious cases in which the context entailed rendering the latter as "signification." For *le sentir,* which the English translation of *Phenomenology of Perception* renders as "sense experience," we have used "sensibility." In the few cases in which Barbaras has used *sensibilité,* also rendered here as "sensibility," we have indicated the French term in brackets. Lastly, we have chosen to translate *membrure* by "inner frame" rather than the "inner framework" familiar to readers of *The Visible and the Invisible,* both to distinguish it from *cadre* and to maintain the reference of the French term to the bodily "frame."

We would like to thank, first of all, Emporia State University and the University of Memphis for their support during the completion of this translation. Its publication was made possible in part by grants from both universities. We are grateful that Marda Kaiser could proofread and index the manuscript. Elizabeth Locey of the Department of Foreign Languages at Emporia State University deserves much credit for her generous proofreading and helpful translation suggestions. We must thank Hugh J. Silverman, who suggested in 1995 that we translate *De l'être du phénomène* into English. We are also grateful to John Sallis for accepting this volume into his prestigious series at Indiana University Press. We are especially grateful to Dee Mortensen at Indiana University Press for guiding this project to its completion. And, finally, we must thank Renaud Barbaras for his support and assistance throughout our work on this translation.

Ted Toadvine and Leonard Lawlor

List of Abbreviations

The following abbreviations are used to refer to works by Merleau-Ponty. For translated texts, French precedes English page numbers in citations. Available English translations have been used whenever possible, although these have been altered when necessary for accuracy or consistency. Complete publication information is included in the bibliography.

CAL "La Conscience et l'acquisition du langage"; *Consciousness and the Acquisition of Language.*

CCF "Un inédit de Maurice Merleau-Ponty"; "An Unpublished Text by Maurice Merleau-Ponty: A Prospectus of His Work."

HN "Husserl et la notion de Nature"; "Husserl's Concept of Nature."

OE *L'œil et l'esprit;* "Eye and Mind."

PHP *Phénoménologie de la perception; Phenomenology of Perception.*

PM *La prose du monde; The Prose of the World.*

PRI "Le primat de la perception et ses conséquences philosophiques"; "The Primacy of Perception and Its Philosophical Consequences."

RC *Résumé de cours, Collège de France 1952–1960;* "Themes from the Lectures at the Collège de France, 1952–1960."

S *Signes; Signs.*

SC *La Structure du Comportment; The Structure of Behavior.*

SHP *Les sciences de l'homme et la phénoménologie;* "Phenomenology and the Sciences of Man."

SNS *Sens et Non-Sens; Sense and Non-Sense.*

UAC *L'union de l'âme et du corps chez Malebranche, Biran et Bergson; The Incarnate Subject: Malebranche, Biran, and Bergson on the Union of Body and Soul.*

VI *Le visible et l'invisible; The Visible and the Invisible.*

Preface to the English Translation

In general, ten years represent little in the history of the reception of and commentary on an author. But as far as Merleau-Ponty is concerned, the ten years that separate the French publication of this book from its American translation are an exception. In fact, the situation of Merleau-Ponty studies has changed considerably—at least in Europe; in the United States, in contrast, the Merleau-Ponty Circle has existed for twenty-five years. Within a few years, Merleau-Ponty's status has gone from that of a neglected author, little known and little studied, to that of a classic author. It is striking to note that in the eyes of students and young scholars born after his death, Merleau-Ponty is almost as remote as Bergson or Kant, having that at once infinite and distanceless remoteness characteristic of the authors who have once and for all joined the small group of philosophers making up the tradition. This change is undoubtedly due to the inevitable effect of the passing of time. But for the many people who knew him and associated with him—and they are still numerous—it is more difficult to think of Merleau-Ponty as a classic author, that is, as reduced to his oeuvre. The younger generation has not had to make this effort, since Merleau-Ponty was never their contemporary.

But we cannot stop here. The temporal distance alone cannot explain this revival of interest, beginning in the 1980s and becoming apparent in the 1990s, which is confirmed by the importance of recent publications. We could mention the relative decline of Heideggerian phenomenology's influence on the younger generations, along with a certain return to Husserl, leading naturally to a turn toward Merleau-Ponty, since he certainly represents the most eminent Husserlian legacy in France. More generally, a new attention paid to French philosophy and its legacy has played a role: thus we begin to realize that Merleau-Ponty was immersed in a precise context, marked by the figures of Maine de Biran, Ravaisson, and Bergson—but also by those of Alain, Léon Brunschvicg, and Maurice Pradines, authors cited less often precisely to the degree that they are part of the surrounding milieu. While, as a consequence of his main interests, Merleau-Ponty turned to German authors very early on, it is hardly debatable that he read them according to this context: that is, according to questions, themes, and a philosophical posture, so to speak, which were French. To account for this revival of interest, we could just as easily refer to the growing attention to various aspects of Merleau-Ponty's philosophy paid by those in other disciplines—for example, psychology, neuroscience, aesthetics, or the history of art. But this is because, for constitutive reasons, Merleau-Ponty's thought owed its very livelihood to the contributions of other fields (psychology, psychoanalysis, sociology, history, aesthetics, etc.) toward which he generally showed a great perceptiveness. We could multiply these hypotheses in trying to explain what some call a return of Merleau-Ponty, and it is certain that the French philosophical context of recent years has played a role. But the only true explanation is the intrinsic importance of Merleau-Ponty's philosophy, an importance that, in the end, should have become obvious to sincere readers, as occurs with every thought worthy of the name. From this point of view, causes are no more than occasions, the best proof being that in countries such as the United States, Italy, or Japan, where Merleau-Ponty has never known a true "time in the wilderness," one witnesses the same intensification of research. This is general evidence for the discovery of a thought whose full import we have not yet measured.

The recent publications are both the sign and the cause of this upsurge of interest, and it is undeniable that having the unpublished manuscripts (mainly the Collège de France course notes and the preparatory notes for *The Visible and the Invisible*) available to the public constitutes a turning point in Merleau-Ponty research. The publication of the courses, those on nature and those from 1959 to 1961, is a major event. While it certainly does not lead us to change our view of Merleau-Ponty's philosophy as a whole, it does allow us to reevaluate the importance of certain authors or certain themes for the elaboration of his ontology. The course on nature, and particularly the reflection on life, appears henceforth as an essential step in the constitution of the ontology and also reveals the influence on Merleau-Ponty of his reading of such thinkers as Bergson and Schelling. The 1959–61 courses likewise allow us to determine more clearly the depth of his reading of Heidegger and the importance of his confrontation with literature. In parallel with these publications, one must emphasize the relative abundance, and especially the quality, of works published on Merleau-Ponty; the multiplication of colloquia and seminars dedicated to him; and—an incontestable sign—the growing number of theses concerned with his work. The clearest manifestation of this intense activity is the trilingual journal of Merleau-Ponty studies, *Chiasmi International*. Thus, what was treated as an exigency in my introduction to this work, namely the need to read Merleau-Ponty as a classic, now appears obvious.

Looking back over this work on the occasion of its translation, I do not have the peculiar feeling that is typical in these situations. This work has never been truly distant from me, since all of my later works, whether or not they deal with Merleau-Ponty, are rooted in it. I should admit then, at the risk of seeming presumptuous, that for the most part I would write the same thing today. The investigations that I have carried out since have led me to complete and develop certain points rather than to correct them. As for the interpretation of the evolution of Merleau-Ponty's thought as a whole, I believe that I can maintain my developmental hypothesis starting from the problem of ideality and truth, that is, from the necessity of passing from a phenomenology of perception—open to the reproach of being nothing other than a psychology of perception—to a *philosophy* of perception, discovering in perception a mode of being that holds good for every possible being. Hence the importance of the theory of expression, particularly linguistic expression, where significations properly speaking are constituted. The ontological "turn" arises from this phenomenology of expression. The question of ideality's mode of rootedness in the perceived opens onto a profound reworking of categories: by a sort of inversion, perception itself is conceived as primordial expression and the perceived as a wild *logos*. The depth of Being is not negation but much rather the reserve and thus the source of every possible meaning, starting with perceptual meaning.

I do believe, however, that the importance of *The Structure of Behavior* and the use made of the Gestalt, an importance attested to throughout his work and particularly in the working notes, must be emphasized more than I did here: this allows us to point out, on the one hand, the considerable influence of Kurt Goldstein, while not neglecting, on the other hand, the deep continuity of Merleau-Ponty's thought. In this respect, the course on nature seems to be an essential link, since we see there how the concepts of form and totality are reelaborated within the context of a phenomenology of life. It would not be an exaggeration to say that the ontological turn is also driven by a concern, manifest since the beginning, for granting a satisfactory status to the concept of form by weighing all of its phenomenological implications. In fact, Merleau-Ponty does not hesitate to affirm that "the Gestalt contains the key to the problem of the mind" (VI 246/192). In the first works, it looks as though when Merleau-Ponty tried to provide an account of the fundamental event of perception, described by the concept of form, he started from concepts that remain inadequate because they are caught in oppositional systems. Hence, the solutions that could be described as *dialectical,* either by way of an explicit reference to Hegel in *The Structure of Behavior* or with recourse to the Husserlian theory of the living present in *Phenomenology of Perception.* But the solution remains merely verbal in both cases: it tries to fill in a gap [*écart*] between an experience and categories that are inadequate to it. In this sense, we can also understand the long text devoted to dialectic in *The Visible and the Invisible* as a self-clarification. Thus, the continuity of the theme of form and the necessity that it represents lead to a fracture at the heart of Merleau-Ponty's thought on the question of dialectic. *The Visible and the Invisible* is, in my eyes, an extraordinary example of non-dialectical thought, and it is not surprising that many readers recognize in Gilles Deleuze what they find in Merleau-Ponty and vice versa.

The reference to Bergson is fundamental in the later Merleau-Ponty, and I have not been able to give it its proper due here. An accurate reading of *The Visible and the Invisible,* one that respects its balances and symmetries, must grant Bergson a place comparable to that occupied by the other great interlocutors, such as Husserl and Sartre. In the chapter on intuition, Husserl and Bergson occupy an exactly symmetrical position and are then situated, if we may say so, on an equal critical footing. Merleau-Ponty brushes aside factual coincidence just as much as intellectual adequation; he seeks a philosophy of intuition that would be an equal distance from both Husserl and Bergson and that would take strict account of negativity. This does not mean, however, that he reduces Bergsonian intuition to the naive version of a pure and simple fusion. On the contrary, he was one of the first, even before Deleuze, to show the complexity of the Bergsonian theory of intuition and the role it gives to negativity—that is, of the distance or wrenching that it allows as soon as it is originarily the experience of duration. More generally, the critique of Sartre in the "Interrogation and Dialectic" chapter would need to be relocated within a general reflection on nothingness, a reflection that would integrate the famous critique of nothingness in the third chapter of *Creative Evolution,* and also the just as famous passages of "What Is Metaphysics?" Here the 1959–61 course and the unpublished materials from *The Visible and the Invisible* come to our assistance. The Sartrean dialectic appears there as a sort of dramatized subjectivation of the precession of nothingness around Being—the source, as Bergson shows, of the principle of sufficient reason. In the last analysis, then, the unity beyond all differences that characterizes objective thought (in the Merleau-Pontian sense) lies in the fact of approaching Being on the ground of nothingness and then of folding it down onto the essence, since the essence is alone suited to resist the threat of nothingness. Inversely, an authentic ontology must integrate nothingness into its definition of being, and it is here that the debate with Heidegger makes sense. The problem of nothingness indisputably constitutes one of the major lines of force of Merleau-Ponty's thought.

Finally, this book has led me to study the question of motility more thoroughly. On the authority of both Husserl and psycho-physiological research, Merleau-Ponty emphasizes early on the motor character of intentionality. In *Phenomenology of Perception,* for example, he writes that "Our bodily experience of movement is not a particular case of knowledge; it provides us with a way of access to the world and the object, with a 'praktognosia,' which has to be recognized as original and perhaps as originary" (PHP 164/140). The subject is situated in the world, and its perception is inseparable from an approach, in Erwin Straus's sense of the term. Or rather, since this formulation is still dependent on the duality of thought and extension, intentionality must be understood as a specific dynamism, a "movement" in a sense that precedes the distinction between literal and metaphorical, between local displacement and meaningful apprehension. The "I think," and then straightaway the "I perceive," is truly an "I can," as Husserl had already anticipated. Merleau-Ponty writes that "no *Wahrnehmen perceives* except on condition of being a *Self of movement*" (VI 310/257), which amounts to saying that the Self is constituted in living movement; it is in this movement that the identity of the retiring-into-oneself and the leaving-of-oneself by which Merleau-Ponty defines incarnated subjectivity is realized. Therefore, the problem of perception as posed by Merleau-Ponty opens the horizon of a subject whose ontological sense definitively escapes the distinction between *res cogitans* and *res extensa.* Now, it seems to me that Merleau-Ponty never tapped into the reserves expressed by the sentence "no *Wahrnehmen perceives* except on condition of being a *Self of movement*"; he never took the step that leads from the original to the originary. A theory of the motor body, or rather of movement as an originary mode of the perceiving body, is still required. As I have tried to show, moreover, such movement refers ultimately to desire as the living subject's ultimate ontological sense. If Merleau-Ponty does not explicitly go this far—even though his admirable theory of phenomenality, summed up in the differentiated identity of the visible and the invisible, called for a radical revision of the body's ontological sense—

it is undoubtedly because he still remains prisoner of a philosophy of consciousness inherited from Husserl. This appears clearly in the final analysis of the body in terms of sensing and sensed, touching and touched, subject of the world and part of the world. Such conceptual pairs are just so many displaced modalities of the duality of consciousness and object. The chiasm, then, appears as a means of filling in the gap [*écart*] between these dual categories and the originary experience, of recombining what was split apart beforehand, rather than as a truly innovative concept. Thus, I am inclined more and more to think of Merleau-Ponty's final philosophy as not having fully cast off the presuppositions of the philosophy of consciousness and as faltering because of a lack, rather than an excess, of radicality. In this sense, the famous notes on the necessity of leaving behind the consciousness–object duality should be read as the expression of an exigency rather than as a final report. As the state of the texts reveals, Merleau-Ponty's philosophy was still a philosophy in a state of becoming, and it was certainly not fully completed when death interrupted the work. This justifies our constantly returning to it.

Renaud Barbaras
August 2000

Acknowledgments

I would like to thank in particular Bernard Bourgeois, who showed his confidence in me and supported me throughout the development of this work, but also Jacques Garelli, who gave me the benefit of his great knowledge of Merleau-Ponty and warmly encouraged me, and finally Marc Richir, who, through the depth of his comments, allowed me to focus this work definitively.

Renaud Barbaras, 1991

I would like to offer my warm and sincere thanks to Leonard Lawlor and Ted Toadvine for their remarkable translation, as I know the enormous amount of work that it represents. It is a joy and, above all, an honor to be translated by two philosophers who are among the best current specialists in Merleau-Ponty's thought.

Renaud Barbaras, 2000

Introduction to
the French Edition

[9] The destiny of Merleau-Ponty's philosophy is marked by ambiguity. It is a part of our contemporary inheritance; it is cited frequently, and has become a classic of sorts. And yet, it is still absent. No one ignores it, but few have read it, as if Merleau-Ponty's thought had the virtue of excusing us from studying it, as if it were summed up in an intuition or a style which it would be a matter merely of taking up on its own account. There are many reasons for this. First, one has to recognize the audience that German philosophy found in France with Husserl and Heidegger. Merleau-Ponty is most often considered through a confrontation with them. Of course, this is justified. It is incontestable that Merleau-Ponty pursues an uninterrupted debate with Husserl and that the period of *The Visible and the Invisible* corresponds if not to a reconciliation, then at least to an encounter with Heidegger's thought. It is still nevertheless the case that against the background of this reference to German philosophy, Merleau-Ponty traces a singular path that at once integrates and overcomes the philosophy of constitution as well as that of *Dasein* (RC 148/173, 156/179–80). But because this separation from Husserl and Heidegger is still the prerequisite for beginning to undertake any phenomenological philosophy, a thought trying to gather up the truth of Husserl and Heidegger, a thought trying to sketch the place of their convergence, could not find its own place. In the end, it is the very rigor with which Merleau-Ponty defines his proximity and distance in relation to Husserl in particular—a rigor that excludes any boisterous taking of sides—which makes him stand out against the philosophical landscape. It is true, as we shall see, that Merleau-Ponty's philosophy takes up Husserl's way of proceeding, which is itself open and unfinished. But, as he himself has shown, to take something up does not mean to repeat it; indeed, his relation to Husserl is beyond the alternative of an objective reading or an arbitrary commentary. As is always the case when thought submits itself to the imperative of rigor, Merleau-Ponty distinguishes himself and comes into his own philosophy [10] by placing himself as close as possible to Husserl, by taking up his movement of thought with a clairvoy-

ance shown by few commentators. Some believed that they could dispense with reading Merleau-Ponty because he looked to be so close to Husserl, even though this proximity, as soon as it was not confused with piety, was the best guarantee that a phenomenology worthy of this name was in the process of being born in Merleau-Ponty.

This misunderstanding has been aggravated, at least until the seventies, by his assimilation into the French existentialist movement dominated by Sartre. Once again, it is true that his relationship with Sartre remained ambiguous for a long time; it is true that *Phenomenology of Perception* testifies to a deep inspiration common to the two thinkers. However, in *The Visible and the Invisible,* Merleau-Ponty determines what separates him from Sartre with an incomparable precision. A careful reading of *Phenomenology of Perception* gave us a sense of the fact that the apparent proximity of the two ways of thinking conceals an insurmountable distance; this distance separates an authentically phenomenological philosophy, dedicated to the description of our openness to Being in opposition to the abstractions of idealism and realism, from a philosophy that substitutes for the presence to the world the identity of Being and Nothingness, an identity that is itself achieved by means of the abstract opposition of Being and Nothingness. At best, this assimilation to French existentialism has made the investigations of Merleau-Ponty insipid by reducing them to the confused themes of existence and engagement. We can say "at best" here, because by his rejection of simplifications, by his care to espouse "wild" experience without any presuppositions, Merleau-Ponty was discouraging any reading that sought to find an echo of Sartre's rallying cries. What seems to have happened is that since Merleau-Ponty was considered too demanding and, in a word, too philosophical to be read as an existentialist, he was also deemed not innovative enough to deserve to be read as an interlocutor with German phenomenology. Undoubtedly this is why, in the 1960s and 1970s, Italian philosophers numbered among the best commentators on Merleau-Ponty; their distance from the French intellectual context allowed them to study him on his own terms.[1]

However, there is another reason for this erasure that refers to the very history of Merleau-Ponty's thought. We do not [11] have any one text that gathers together the final state of his philosophy. In a sense, such a requirement hardly seems to conform to the essence of a phenomenological way of proceeding. Above all else, Merleau-Ponty's philosophy is valuable be-

1. For example, G. Derossi, G. L. Brenna, E. Paci, and E. Caruso.

cause of its power of interrogation, because of this constant and in principle unachievable demand to return to experience in its brute state, in opposition to the idealizations sedimented on top of it. The novel character of his writings stems from this demand; Merleau-Ponty's writings have often been criticized for being "metaphorical" without anyone ever wondering about what concept of metaphor or, finally, what concept of speech is supporting such a denunciation. Merleau-Ponty notes in *The Visible and the Invisible* that "it is a question of whether philosophy as reconquest of brute or wild being can be accomplished by the resources of eloquent language, or whether it would not be necessary for philosophy to use language in a way that takes from it its power of immediate or direct signification in order to equal it with what it wishes all the same to say" (VI 139/102–103). Merleau-Ponty showed a long time ago that what defines speech is its forgetfulness of itself as a production, its naive understanding of itself as the mark of a thought transparent to itself, and, consequently, its unawareness of its being rooted in the perceived world. What is really at issue then—and this explains the originality of his writing—is to proceed to a reduction of language, and to develop a language that neutralizes conceptual sedimentations and consequently makes it possible for language to be revealed as belonging to a "wild *logos*." Insofar as it is a return to the originary field of experience, philosophy must provide itself with a way of speaking that allows to appear both that about which it is speaking and that which is speaking in it. However, if Merleau-Ponty's project truly calls for the invention of a way of speaking, it is never at the price of a renunciation of eloquence and pedagogical requirements. In Merleau-Ponty's eyes, a way of speaking that would not testify to its originary inscription would certainly not be philosophical, but neither would a reflection that would not first submit itself to the imperative of the natural light. This tension runs throughout Merleau-Ponty's writings. It seems to us that this is not the case in certain of Heidegger's texts where, in the grip of Being and Saying, the dimension of sense is almost lost.

Nevertheless, Merleau-Ponty's thought remains unfinished. Based on the results of Gestalt psychology, the unveiling of the field of perception [12] is still dependent—as we shall try to show—on categories derived from reflective philosophy, categories that Merleau-Ponty nevertheless denounces. It quickly became obvious in his mind that *Phenomenology of Perception* would be only a preliminary work, whose philosophical significance was not clearly established; it was essentially devoted to the description of perceptual experience and to the symmetrical critique of intellectualism and realism. This is why many texts from the period of 1945 to 1959 are concerned to take up and ground the achievements of *Phenomenology of Perception;* in other words, they are concerned with figuring out how much philosophical reorganization is called for by the discovery of the perceptual field. According to a movement whose steps we shall attempt to explicate, this way of proceeding leads to a project of radical reformulation of the categories at work until then; it results in the awareness of the necessity of bringing the results of *Phenomenology of Perception* to an ontological explication (VI 237/183). This was the purpose of the work originally titled *The Origin of Truth* but published under the title that Merleau-Ponty had adopted in the end, *The Visible and the Invisible.* It is incontestable, for those who are familiar with Merleau-Ponty's work, that it is only in this later work and in some contemporaneous texts that what was announced in the earlier investigations is genuinely realized and that Merleau-Ponty's philosophy is laid out in a complete form. It seems to us that the earlier works acquire coherence and consistency in light of *The Visible and the Invisible,* ensuring that we can read them only by means of the reformulation to which they finally give way. For us, Merleau-Ponty's philosophy coincides with his ontology, and it seems to us that the texts which precede it must be invoked only as the path which leads up to it. This is why, as many commentators have noted, there is nothing to be gained in choosing between continuity and rupture. Merleau-Ponty's thought is profoundly unified. First, *The Visible and the Invisible* gathers up all of what had been thought before; thus, there is no rupture. But that does not mean that his philosophy had been given to him in one fell swoop; precisely because of the project which animates it, it had to be won in a struggle against the rigidity of inherited concepts, that is, first of all against itself. This is why its unity is truly accomplished at the heart of a becoming. Merleau-Ponty's philosophy is no different [13] from any other on this point. The difference lies rather in the fact that *The Visible and the Invisible* remains largely unfinished. Even though one could not confine oneself to the works already published—even Merleau-Ponty himself admitted that they were unsatisfactory—one does not have at one's disposal one text in which Merleau-Ponty finally finds his position, one text that allows us to resolve everything.

For all these reasons, both because of the very nature of his philosophy —which sought to be an interrogation or a task rather than a doctrine— and because of the incompleteness of his thought, Merleau-Ponty survives, in the words of Char, as an inheritance without last will and testament. In fact, then, the only thing we can do is take it up on its own account and pursue the path that his thought opened. Merleau-Ponty remains simultaneously present and absent, as this thought which founds, or at least inseminates, numerous contemporary reflections, without its own contours ever being clearly outlined. As Paul Ricoeur notes, "our relation to the greatest of French phenomenologists has perhaps already become what his was to Husserl: not a repetition but an appropriation of the very movement of his reflection."[2] This explains the state of the commentaries. Most of them prior to the 1970s are concerned mainly with *Phenomenology of Perception* and recount the evolution of his thought without trying either to grasp its necessity or to explicate its end point. On the other hand, however, many authors who, without being commentators, base themselves more or less explicitly on Merleau-Ponty's later thought allow us to illuminate his ontology, which reaches us by means of its echo.[3]

Our wish here was to restore the missing link. Our intention is neither to take up the movement of his thought from one end to the other in order to grasp *The Visible and the Invisible* as its end point, nor to evaluate his heritage as developed elsewhere. Our intention is to reconceive Merleau-Ponty's ontology on its own terms—which is, in our eyes, the key to his entire thought as well as to numerous contemporary reflections. In fact, it seems to us that *The Visible and the Invisible* and some of the texts connected with it give a very precise idea of this ontology, provided that we do not ignore the works where the ontology is already announced—works such as *The Prose of the World* and especially [14] the working notes, which are numerous and very often precise and brilliant. To us, it looks as though we have here at our disposal material whose richness justifies the attempt to explicate this never-completed work.

We could characterize the spirit in which we have considered these texts by saying that we have read them as if they were *classics*. Assuredly, Merleau-Ponty situates himself consciously in this tradition when he outlines his ontology, and it seems to us that the heritage in which his thought is rooted is still more Cartesian than Husserlian. It is true, he notes, that "for the past fifty years, metaphysical thought has sought its way outside the physico-mathematical coordination of the world, and its role in rela-

2. P. Ricoeur, *Le conflit des interprétations* (Paris: Seuil, 1969), p. 243n; trans. D. Ihde as *The Conflict of Interpretations* (Evanston, Ill.: Northwestern University Press, 1974), 247n7.
3. We cite, among others, P. Ricoeur, H. Maldiney, G. Granel, J. Garelli, M. Richir.

tion to science seems to be to awaken us to the 'non-relational background' that science thinks about and does not think about" (S 190/151). This is what opposes our philosophical situation to what he calls "major rationalism." However, Merleau-Ponty adds,

> major rationalism is still of major importance for us and is even close to us in that it is the indispensable way toward the philosophies which reject it, for they reject it in the name of the same exigency which gave it life. At the very moment when it was creating natural science, it showed by the same movement that it was not the measure of being and carried consciousness of the ontological problem to its highest point. In this respect, it is not *past*. As it did, we seek not to restrict or discredit the initiatives of science but to situate science as an intentional system in the total field of our relationships to Being; and the only reason why passing to the infinitely infinite does not seem to us to be the answer is that we are appropriating again in a more radical way the task that that intrepid century had believed itself rid of forever.
> (S 191/151–52)

Merleau-Ponty's force and rigor seem to us to reside in this acknowledged continuity with the spirit of classical metaphysics. For him, it is a question of recognizing the fact of Reason without remaining silent about our being rooted in a world which from the start does not lend itself to the lucidity of intellectual knowledge, of preserving the metaphysical consciousness of transcendence without descending into an irrationalism or mysticism—that is, without renouncing the requirements of consciousness, knowledge, and ultimately of action. We could therefore have called this work *Merleau-Ponty and Ontology*: for him it is less a question of innovation than of appropriating [15] in a novel way the problems that confront classical ontology, that is, of thinking "the fundamental metaphysical fact" which is "this double sense of *cogito:* I am sure that there is being—on the condition that I do not seek another sort of being than being-for-me" (SNS 114/93). It seems to us that precisely because of the sense that he, following Husserl, assigns to tradition—"*the power to forget origins* and to give to the past not a survival, which is the hypocritical form of forgetfulness, but a new life, which is the noble form of memory" (S 74/59)—we can appreciate Merleau-Ponty's richness and singularity most by considering him without neglecting the relation he maintains with a tradition.

When we speak of classicism, we also mean that we want to read Merleau-

Ponty just as one reads a classic author. Commentators insist on the fact that Merleau-Ponty teaches us the way in which he must be read. Because the truth of an author is not an object that can be circumscribed, because it resides in an unthought which inhabits it through and through without being formulated anywhere, the reading must be an interpretive appropriation, an active intersubjectivity, an echo. If this means simply that no interpretation is a mere repetition, that the reader reconceives the work on the basis of its own difference without anyone being able to say that this is an arbitrary projection, this is obvious. But the risk is that by means of the authority of this obvious fact, we dispense with a scrupulous reading and go straight to an "intuition" of Merleau-Ponty that would only need to be reactivated differentially, instead of paying careful attention to the movement and concepts across which this intuition is elaborated. In our eyes, Merleau-Ponty's always luminous thought is still arduous, sinuous, and dense. By remaining as attentive as possible to the text, we propose simply to try to explicate it, just as one explicates a classic author; no one would think of exercising this dimension of active appropriation first in relation to a classic author. It seems to us not only that the richness of the texts at our disposal justifies a work of reconstitution but also, because of their density and their incompleteness, that they require such a work of reconstitution.

If *The Visible and the Invisible* marks a turn in Merleau-Ponty's thought, both by the radicality of its questioning and the novelty of its concepts, it is still the case that this mutation was called for by the development of Merleau-Ponty's entire [16] earlier reflection. *The Visible and the Invisible* comes to fulfill an interrogation at work since *The Structure of Behavior*. The significance of this ontological turn can then be truly measured only by reconstructing the movement of thought that it comes to fulfill. While *The Visible and the Invisible* attests to a continuity of concerns in relation to the earlier works, the problems encountered in them are truly the ones that motivate the final deepening. We must therefore first follow the path that leads up to the ontology by emphasizing what demands or anticipates the development of the reflection and the overcoming of the philosophic framework of the first works. We must consider the totality of the work as an introduction to ontology in the strict sense.

By basing themselves on Gestalt psychology, the first two works try to return to the authentic figure of the perceived and thus to clarify a phenomenal order that escapes the thematizations of realism and intellectualism. During this period, the status of philosophical interrogation is not itself being interrogated; the possibility of a philosophy that allows experience itself to speak is taken for granted. The status of discourse and knowledge and their capacity to be related to a ground that exceeds them are not themselves questioned. In contrast, *The Visible and the Invisible* opens with an interrogation of philosophical interrogation itself: the question "What is philosophy?" appears as the precondition of the later exploration of Being. The world is not considered in an immediate way—immediacy is often the reverse side of naiveté, the means of submitting experience to an implicit, prior framework—and the mediation of Gestalt psychology does not give us access to it; the world is grasped by means of the fact of interrogation and of discourse. The fact of interrogation and discourse is precisely what can be said and questioned, and, as we shall see, the overcoming of the phenomenon toward its being is based on this mutation of method. It is therefore necessary to reconceive the status of philosophical interrogation by bringing it into confrontation, as Merleau-Ponty does in the completed part of *The Visible and the Invisible,* with the different figures of reflective philosophy, in particular with Husserlian eidetics and Sartrean dialectics. The movement that leads us from *Phenomenology of Perception* to the world of interrogation, that is, to the wild essence, is *regressive.* The consideration of the problem of speech and ideality, which is secondary in *Phenomenology of Perception,* and the interrogation [17] of the rootedness of ideality within the perceived lead Merleau-Ponty to supersede the constrictive framework of a phenomenology of perception in favor of an ontology. This descending movement, which leads from expression to Being and from being-in-the-world to flesh, must be accompanied by an ascending movement which, starting from the originary ground that is finally brought to light, allows us to examine and ground all the dimensions of experience, to ascend again from "solipsistic" sensibility to ideality itself. In order to show this, we will respect the order envisioned by Merleau-Ponty for constructing his ontology by considering first the visible and then the invisible. But though these two moments may respond to a concern for being faithful to experience, it will still be necessary to interrogate the genuine significance of this duality. In a sense, Merleau-Ponty's ontology is, in its entirety, an attempt to gain access to an idea of Being that will allow us to restore an originary articulation of the sensible and of sense.

Part One.
Toward Ontology

1 The Dualism of
Phenomenology of Perception

1. The Symmetrical Critique of Intellectualism and Realism

[21] Expressed as early as the introduction to *The Structure of Behavior,* Merleau-Ponty's purpose lies in understanding the relation between consciousness and nature. The situation of psychology, which attempts to conceive this relation, is characterized by the juxtaposition of a critical philosophy that turns all of nature into an objective unity constituted before consciousness and a science that places consciousness in nature and conceives the relation between them in terms of causality. The question then lies in determining the extent to which this relation between consciousness and nature can be adequately defined by one of the terms of the alternative. To apprehend this question directly, without recourse to the results of science, assuredly exposes us to the risk of intellectualism and keeps us a prisoner of these alternatives. What is at issue therefore is to enter into the question "by starting from below" (SC 2/4), through an analysis of the notion of behavior, which has the advantage of being neutral in regard to the distinction between the psychic and the organic. This analysis of behavior amounts to relying on the descriptions that psychology provides of behavior, while risking taking up its naturalistic presuppositions. Thus, "in order not to prejudge the issue, we shall take objective thought on its own terms and not ask it any questions which it does not ask itself. If we are led to rediscover experience behind it, this transition will be motivated only by objective thought's own difficulties" (PHP 86/72). The way of proceeding which leads back to experience [22] develops in two moments. First, the study of Gestalt psychology leads us to question again the naturalistic ontology that is still the presupposition of all psychology. Gestalt psychology allows us to characterize the relation between the organism and its environment as one of understanding, as a certain way of intending the surrounding world, which cannot be reduced to the constancy hypothesis, that is, to the causal and univocal relation of stimuli

and response. The organism does not respond to the stimulus insofar as the stimulus is endowed with objective properties, but only insofar as the stimulus has a value in regard to the animal's vital *a prioris*. The role of the philosopher then lies in going along with this movement that overcomes the causal hypothesis by taking it to its ultimate consequences, consequences that Gestalt psychology does not notice. Gestalt psychology tends to keep the form within the framework of objectivistic ontology; in other words, it subordinates the "world of behavior" to the "geographical world." Now, as soon as the transition from the physical order to the phenomenal order appears motivated, the subordination of one to the other can only be total. One cannot assert simultaneously that the world is given to the animal as a meaningful environment rather than as a set of physicochemical individuals *and* that the relation of animal behavior to this environment is based on nature in-itself. In short, the "geographical world" no longer makes any sense; in fact, it is confused with the observer's "world of behavior." If Merleau-Ponty here is turned toward science, it is to the extent that science is made from phenomenology. Understood in this significant way, the notion of the form liberates a transcendental perspective.

This detour through Gestalt psychology would, however, be unnecessary if it did not allow us to conceive transcendental consciousness differently. If the issue were only to show that the "world of behavior" and behavior itself are only objects for a consciousness,

> a moment of reflection would have provided us with a certitude in principle. Does not the *cogito* teach us once and for all that we would have no knowledge of any *thing* if we did not first have a knowledge of our thinking and that even the escape into the world and the resolution to ignore interiority or to never leave things, which is the essential feature of behaviorism, cannot be [23] formulated without being transformed into consciousness and without presupposing existence for-itself [*pour-soi*]? But by following this short route we would have missed the paradox that is constitutive of it: behavior is not a thing, but neither is it an idea. It is not the envelope of a pure consciousness and, as the witness of behavior, I am not a pure consciousness. (SC 138/127)

This is why Merleau-Ponty must show in a descending movement that if the notion of form grounds a critique of naturalism, it allows us just as much, and for the same reasons, to call intellectualism into question. The meaningful relation of the organism to its environment is still a relation to a reality, to a transcendence, and is not therefore based on a consciousness transparent to itself; it is not based on an act of knowledge. The study of behavior reveals rather what Merleau-Ponty already calls an existence, a being-in-the-world, a tacit relation to a presence rather than a possession of something in a representation. *The Structure of Behavior* therefore concludes: "The natural 'thing,' the organism, the behaviors of others and my own behavior exist only by their sense; but this sense which springs forth in them is not yet a Kantian object; the intentional life which constitutes them is not yet a representation; and the 'understanding' which gives access to them is not yet an intellection" (SC 241/225).

This new meaning of transcendental consciousness—only sketched in *The Structure of Behavior*, where Merleau-Ponty is still bothered by the Kantian reference—is the object of *Phenomenology of Perception*. What is at issue then is to confirm and to deepen, by means of perceptual experience just as it is lived, the perspective opened by the first work, to explore the domain that had been explicated in *The Structure of Behavior* only at the level of animal behavior. While *The Structure of Behavior* was situated essentially on the terrain of objectivity in order to make the failure of naturalistic ontologies obvious and in order to free up the constitutive dimension of consciousness, *Phenomenology of Perception* is developed on the terrain of lived consciousness in order to make apparent the impossibility of conceiving its constituting work in terms of an intellectual possession. The study of lived consciousness comes about in order to confirm on the human level this self-exteriority, this obscurity which the analysis of animal behavior revealed. By adopting an external viewpoint, by observing behavior [24] as a mundane object, the first work was aiming primarily at denouncing realism; by adopting the internal viewpoint of perceptual experience, liberated by Gestalt psychology, the second work aims its critique rather at intellectualism.

2. The *Phenomenology of Perception*'s Dualistic Presupposition

This double critique cuts across the entire *Phenomenology of Perception*, whose every chapter is organized according to an immutable rhythm. After describing a field of determinate experience while taking into account the results of Gestalt psychology, Merleau-Ponty denounces the inadequacy of the intellectualist hypothesis and makes us take note of the irreducibility of lived experience to the acts of a constituting consciousness. Then, in a second moment, he shows that the results of the description can nevertheless not be reinterpreted in the framework of a realist philosophy. As it consists in dismissing two successive concepts of experience as unacceptable presuppositions, this approach poses a problem. In order "not to be prejudiced," Merleau-Ponty refuses to begin by adopting a philosophic position, whether realist or intellectualist. On this condition, the pure domain of experience will be describable precisely insofar as it escapes from these two directions of thought. But his approach then consists not so much in reconceiving the originality of the perceptive field as in making its irreducibility to realism and intellectualism obvious. The result is that its description in the end remains dependent on this double presupposition. Or rather, the originality of the perceptual field is reconceived not so much in a positive way, which would invite us to invent new concepts, as negatively, like a kind of critical beam pivoting from one side of objective philosophy back to the other. Thus, because he does not directly consider the question of the philosophical status of experience, Merleau-Ponty remains negatively dependent on the reference to these two antagonistic philosophies of experience. The domain of perception is not truly thought in its own right; rather, it is thought as a sort of place where the insufficiency of the two incriminated solutions is revealed. The rejection of every presupposition certainly allows Merleau-Ponty to open up a new theoretical space, but this space is not thought through to the end. By symmetrically dismissing realism and intellectualism, he is content with circumscribing the new space; in this way, [25] he is still a prisoner of the terminology belonging to these two philosophies. Realism and intellectualism are not so much overcome as pushed to the side, with the result finally that the double negation tends to turn itself into a double affirmation. Far from giving way to a radical reevaluation of the concepts of objective philosophy, the description is actualized in a terminology that is *simultaneously* realist and intellectualist. *Phenomenology of Perception* is characterized by this divergence between the philosophic terrain that it circumscribes and the categories by means of which we enter into it.[1] This is why we can say that this text is more descriptive than philosophical. It does not conceive the terrain of perception in a radical way; and insofar as *Phenomenology of Perception* does conceive perception, it falls short of what it discovers.

First, then, we have the experience of one's own body. This experience,

1. This point is made quite clearly by Bernard Sichère in *Merleau-Ponty ou le corps de la philosophie* (Paris: Grasset, 1982), 83f.

which reveals an irreducible opening of the subject to the world or a rooted-ness of consciousness which would not be able to be a rootedness *for* consciousness, gives rise to two types of formulations. On the one hand, the body is brought to the foreground, and its description allows us to see clearly the irreducibility of experience to the duality of subject and object, to the duality of fact and sense. It "*has* its world or understands its world without having to pass through representations"; it "*is* the potentiality of a certain world," so that finally "the body is a *natural ego,* and, as it were, the *subject* of perception" (PHP 164/140–41, 124/106, 239/206). With the word "body," a new concept of experience seems to be announced, a new concept which makes no recourse to the notion of consciousness, or rather, a new concept which brings forward another definition of the subject. Nevertheless, this "potentiality" and this "having" of the world are not thought through to the end, with the result that Merleau-Ponty slides back toward a realist conception, a conception implied by his recourse to psychology that always grasps the body in a movement of objectification. Implicitly, then, the body is considered by means of the duality of the organic and the psychic. The body becomes "the mediator of the world," mediator for a consciousness which is itself only "the being-toward-the-thing through the intermediary of the body" (PHP 169/145, 161/138–39). The body comes to mediate the opposition between the subject and the object, thereby forbidding one from conceiving, in an intellectualist way, the belonging of the object to the subject. The body allows one to unveil an originary layer of the perceived in which sense [26] cannot be separated from its factual incarnation. The very terms of the opposition, however, are not called into question. While, in a first moment, the body seemed to designate an original existential mode that is *beyond* facticity and ideality, in fact it appears as something divided by means of the subject–object opposition; it appears as the still mysterious place where the subject–object relation is tied together. This is why finally the body can be described only across the symmetrical exclusion of the two terms of the opposition. The body is neither the subject nor the object, but the mediation of the subject and object. And this mediation is not thought all the way through, precisely because it is thought as mediation. Merleau-Ponty oscillates therefore between a unitary conception of the body and a dualistic vision which turns the body into the "means" of consciousness. Merleau-Ponty never reaches the point of conceiving the identity *and* the difference of consciousness and its body *together;* in other words, he never reaches the point of describing *positively* the fact that the body belongs neither to the domain of the object nor to that of the subject. Ultimately, Merleau-Ponty's analysis assumes here the Cartesian ambiguity to which he never stops returning. Just as Descartes valued, beyond the real distinctions of substances, a kind of union which can be known only by means of this union —that is, by the practice of life—Merleau-Ponty posits, *beside* the real duality of the body and spirit, a substantial union (PHP 232/199) which is revealed only at the heart of perceptual experience. It is true that he contests, in Descartes, the possibility of adopting this double attitude, and that he asserts the necessity of distinguishing between its parts: "If we take the methods of the First Meditation seriously, are we not led to consider the Sixth as an aberration? And conversely, if we take the Sixth Meditation seriously, how were the methods of the First possible? . . . If the union of the soul and the body is a confused thought, how was I able to discover the *cogito*? And, if I discovered the *cogito*, how can I be the unreflective subject of the Sixth Meditation?" (UAC 15–16/35). Nevertheless, in *Phenomenology of Perception,* Merleau-Ponty does not distinguish them. This does not mean that he refers the union, as Descartes finally does, to the level of the irrational, or at least to what is inaccessible to the knowledge of the understanding: since we live it, there must really be a way of conceiving it. Nevertheless, he does not work through the reversal that would be consistent with conceiving this "irrational" [27] as the very place of rationality and with reducing the real distinction to the rank of being a simple appearance.

The difficulty appears as well with the notion of *existence,* which is omnipresent in *Phenomenology of Perception* and absent in the works that follow. Existence designates the movement by which the body, which is irreducible, as we have seen, to a pure object, gives sense. In fact, "the human body is defined in terms of its property of appropriating, in an indefinite series of discontinuous acts, meaningful kernels which overcome and transfigure its natural abilities" (PHP 226/193). Existence is thus "this open and indefinite power of meaning—that is, simultaneously of grasping and communicating a sense—by which man transcends himself toward a new behavior or toward others, or toward his own thought, across his body and his speech" (PHP 226/194). The central intention of *Phenomenology of Perception* is this power of meaning, of escape, this sense always already at work, which is not distinguished from its own accomplishment, and which, in this way, cannot be opposed to the factical foundation from which it would emerge. But by grasping this power by means of the notion of existence, Merleau-Ponty does not allow himself in *Phenomenology of*

Perception to understand what he has discovered, for existence is conceived as human existence, that is, as the *subject* of the movement of transcendence rather than as the very advent of sense. It is finally "*man*" who "transcends himself toward a new behavior." Existence is grasped as man's facticity, even though the experience to which it refers leads us to overcome the frontal relation of man to being, to overcome the duality of subject and object. Prisoner of a dualist framework, Merleau-Ponty can therefore describe it only in a negative way: it coincides neither with the passivity of the anthropological subject situated in the objective world nor with the pure activity of the constituting subject. But existence is still really that of a subject, or rather is the subject itself, so that the fullness of the experience to which it refers cannot be attained. The notion of *pre-personal consciousness,* which is a term synonymous with existence, crystallizes the ambiguity. Even though Merleau-Ponty discovers an experience that is no longer personal, an experience in which the category of the person finds itself contested, he grasps it still on the basis of the personal subject, as a negation that is already its affirmation.

The attempt to force this experience into categories that in reality it contests takes place, of course, at the level of the description of the perceived world, a description that follows from that of the body. [28] It is sufficient to show this on the basis of the chapter devoted to space, which is exemplary in this regard. Contrary to objective thought, what is at issue is to bring to light an existential, anthropological space that is prior to objective space, making objective space therefore only one determination of space. In this way Merleau-Ponty shows, following Binswanger, that the expression "to fall from the clouds" does not refer to an analogical relation, that is, does not consist in designating an emotion through a spatial relation under the pretext that a gesture of prostration accompanies this emotion. This expression conceals an existential direction, a "direction of meaning" that traverses the different regional spheres and receives a particular specification in each of them. Therefore, there is a kind of spatiality prior to objective perception. This claim is confirmed by the description of specific, anthropological spaces, such as those of the "primitives," for whom the left is first experienced as the place of evil or the place of bad omens. As always in Merleau-Ponty, pathology or primitiveness reveals the originary experience on which the "normal" is based. In pathology or primitiveness, the presence of the world to the body is not that of the spatial object—or rather, the spatiality of the object is inseparable from its "physiognomy," from the meaning that it has for existence, a meaning that is indistinctly spatial, perceptive, and emotive. Merleau-Ponty concludes, "We must recognize as prior to 'acts of meaning' (*Bedeutungsgebende Akten*) of theoretical and thetic thought, 'expressive experiences' (*Ausdruckerlebnisse*); as prior to the signified sense (*Zeichen-Sinn*), the expressive sense (*Ausdrucks-Sinn*); and finally as prior to any subsumption of content under the form, the symbolic 'pregnancy' of the form in the content" (PHP 337/291). Here, Merleau-Ponty succeeds in reaching the properly descriptive moment. The risk of empiricism is present here, and a qualification turns out to be necessary. In fact,

> Since there are as many spaces as there are distinct spatial experiences, and since we do not allow ourselves to anticipate, in infantile, diseased or primitive experience, the forms of adult, normal and civilized experience, are we not imprisoning each type of subjectivity, and ultimately each consciousness, in its own private life? Have we not substituted for the rationalist *cogito* which discovers a universal constituting consciousness in myself, the psychologist's *cogito,* which remains incommunicable within the experience of its life? Are we not defining subjectivity as the identity of each person with that experience? Is it not the case that inquiry into the nature of space and, generally speaking, into nascent experience, prior to their objectification, and the [29] decision to scrutinize experience itself for its sense, in short, phenomenology, ends with the negation of being and sense? Are not mere appearance and opinion being brought back under the name of the phenomenon? (PHP 337–38/291–92)

Merleau-Ponty says that there are still equivocations involved here that need to be dissipated. The critique of intellectualism—which constitutes the essential part of the chapter on space—is therefore followed by a move to negate the empiricist interpretation. If the "primitive" or the schizophrenic have *their* world, it is still the case that their experience is that of a *world.* Experience could not be an incommunicable psychic event, precisely because it is an experience. Merleau-Ponty explains it in this way: originary experience, here mythical consciousness, "is not borne away by each of its pulsations, otherwise it would not be conscious of anything at all. It does not distance itself from its noemata. But, if it passed away with each one of them, if it did not outline the movement of objectification, it would not crystallize itself into myths" (PHP 338/292). We can see the problem clearly: the rejection of empiricism, enacted by means of the presupposition of consciousness, leads inevitably back to intellectualism and makes us lose the understanding of the initial experience. Of course, Merleau-Ponty also tries to keep himself from the intellectualist side, but we cannot help asking ourselves what a noema that is not distant or abstract means, what an objectification that is only "sketched" means. A few lines later, Merleau-Ponty concludes finally in terms that are strictly the *reverse* of those with which the description came to a close: "Human spaces present themselves as built on the basis of natural space, and 'non-objectifying acts,' to speak the language of Husserl, present themselves as based on 'objectifying acts'" (PHP 340/294). Again Merleau-Ponty warns us against an intellectualist interpretation of the formula; but since the opposite of intellectualism is empiricism (which this analysis is challenging), this warning can only take the form of an empty and incomprehensible negation: "The objectifying acts are not representations" (PHP 340/294). We find ourselves still asking here what is meant by an objectification which does not pass through representations, or a consciousness which, not passing away with each one of its noemata, nevertheless does not represent them [30]. The problem finally comes into focus in the conclusion of the whole analysis: "We must understand how, at a stroke, existence projects around itself worlds that mask objectivity from me, at the same time fastening upon it as the aim of the teleology of consciousness, by picking out these 'worlds' against the background of one single natural world" (PHP 340/294). How can there be a teleology of consciousness if these worlds are picked out against the background of one single natural world? Does not this nature destroy in advance their non-objective, ontic sense of worldhood? Objectivity cannot be *masked* by experience and simultaneously constitute the *telos* of experience. If it is masked, it is given in a dimension of being "already-there" which absorbs all teleology; and the worlds then are *really* only masks—that is, appearances, experiences that are deprived of full status and thereby are destined to be absorbed back into this nature, which they dissimulate and which is their truth. It seems therefore that we have to make a choice. Objectivity can be assigned as the aim of the teleology of consciousness—but then the perceptual world against whose background objectification takes place can no longer be characterized as a nature, and the "consciousness" that makes the perceptual world appear can no longer be defined as objectifying. Or the perceptual world can already be this nature against which the anthropological worlds that cover it over stand out—but then to speak of a *teleology* of objectivity no longer makes sense, and the anthropological spaces lose their whole constitutive validity. The tension that runs throughout *Phenomenology of Perception* is clearly seen here. On the one hand, Merleau-Ponty unveils a universe of originary experience such that objectivity can have there only a teleological status, that is, objectivity can constitute only a genuinely derived dimension. But, on the other hand, we get to this experience by means of categories that have not been criticized—in particular, that of consciousness. The result is that in order to avoid empiricism and therefore to remain on the phenomenological level, Merleau-Ponty is led to subordinate the world to a nature, to conceive the subject of experience as transcendental consciousness and teleology as something always already accomplished. The formula that he uses—"teleology of consciousness"—crystallizes the entire problem. Merleau-Ponty's ambiguity lies here, in the attempts to subordinate the teleological dimension of objectivity to consciousness. Now, this consciousness, which is presupposed instead of being reconceived on the basis of the teleology, determines a precession of the *telos* at the heart of the world, which is then thrust back upon a nature. We can speak therefore [31] of the teleology of consciousness only insofar as consciousness is not the subject but the other name of this teleology, insofar as consciousness is produced in or as this teleology. And if objectivity must still be an "aim," it is so on the condition that the worlds no longer stand out from "one single natural world" but from Being itself.

It seems that Merleau-Ponty did not concede enough to intellectualism and failed to appreciate its hold on the philosophy of consciousness, since he claims to conceive the appearance of the phenomenon on the basis of consciousness while avoiding the intellectualist determination of this consciousness—that is, the dimension of representation and objectification. The failure of this way of proceeding lies in the fact that it ultimately makes intellectualism look like the truth of consciousness; a philosophy which aims at describing originary experience without involving itself in intellectualism or in a way opposite from it must ipso facto renounce the very perspective of consciousness. What Merleau-Ponty seems to lack in *Phenomenology of Perception* is this lucidity, and that is why the description, which first moves against intellectualism, finally goes back to it, since it aims to avoid the symmetrical risk of empiricism. However, to renounce intellectual consciousness does not in any way imply that we have to give up objectivity. Respect for the phenomena makes sense only if it is respect for objectivity as well. The only thing that is at issue is to understand objectivity itself as phenomenon, as a moment of the givenness of the world instead of subordinating the world to an objectifying consciousness. We are taking stock of the difficulty before which Merleau-Ponty must have found himself at the threshold of *The Visible and the Invisible:* in fact, the project in *The Visible and the Invisible* lies in conceiving the inscription of the subject in the world in such a way as to ensure that when we discard the category of consciousness, we do not return to realism, and we do not in any way compromise the possibility of giving an account of objectivity.

With the help of the notion of the *tacit cogito,* Merleau-Ponty attempts in the third part of *Phenomenology of Perception* to grasp the genuine meaning of being-in-the-world. We must therefore expect to rediscover the same problems that we have already evoked. Against the intellectualist reduction of the world to a pure object, Merleau-Ponty attempts to bring to light the irreducible figure of the perceived; the originary fact is that "something shows itself, there is phenomenon." This fact means "there is an absolute certainty of the world in general, but not [32] of any one thing in particular" (PHP 344/297). *Phenomenology of Perception* does not allow us to conceive this situation on the exact level where it is established. It immediately translates the "there is phenomenon" into "there is consciousness of something" (PHP 342/296). Instead of this certainty being grasped on the basis of what it is certain of, namely, the world itself, it is immediately explicated in terms of self-certainty. The subordination of this certainty to a *cogito* is considered obvious, while actually this certainty is first a positing of the world itself. This primacy of the *cogito* corresponds to an insufficient determination of the notion of the world. The world is explicated neither in its own terms nor on its own basis: as the originary and irreducible unity of being and appearing, as the identity of "self-showing" and the being that shows itself. The world is implicitly understood as a reality in itself, and a consciousness becomes necessary then in order to support phenomenality. We do not really find empiricism and intellectualism being overcome; rather, the implicit positing of a reality in itself calls for the determination of the phenomenon on the basis of the *cogito.* The *cogito* can be defined only negatively, by excluding the transcendental interpretation. Such is the meaning of the tacit *cogito:* "Consciousness is neither the positing of oneself, nor ignorance of oneself, it is *not concealed* from itself, which means that there is nothing in it which does not in some way announce itself to it, although it does not need to know this explicitly" (PHP 342/296). What we are finding here is the double negation that leads us to determine the place of perception as a non-place. Since we have to avoid empiricism, it is necessary to concede a *cogito*, "an experience of the self by the self"; but this self-presence is not a knowing—"this indeclinable subject has upon itself and upon the world only a slippery hold" (PHP 462/403–404). The question that has not been raised here is precisely whether it is necessary to avoid empiricism; perceptual experience is not explicated in its own terms but on the basis of, and against, the realist interpretation. Thus, because he first confronts experience with the realist hypothesis, that is, because he first conceives experience as falling short of itself insofar as it is *experience* of the world, Merleau-Ponty is led to grasp experience beyond itself as experience *of the world*—in other words, he is led to submit it to a *cogito*. Therefore, the [33] distance he then takes in relation to intellectualism when he defines this *cogito* as tacit takes the shape of a negation that is void of sense. We have to wonder, in fact, what could be meant by a *cogito* not defined by self-presence, a *cogito* that nevertheless makes the world spring forth without knowing it, a *cogito* that divines the world instead of constituting it. Merleau-Ponty cannot really maintain the *cogito* and *simultaneously* dismiss the intellectualist interpretation: the negations by which Merleau-Ponty characterizes the tacit *cogito* in order to distance himself from intellectualism would be consistent only if they led to a negation of the *cogito* itself.

3. Merleau-Ponty's Idealism

Most commentators have criticized Merleau-Ponty for going too far in his critique of intellectualism. Merleau-Ponty would have dissolved reflection into unreflective life, with the result that he would be prohibited from giving an account of reflection and objectification, and he thereby would even have exempted himself from grounding the possibility of his own discourse. In the end, such a philosophy would be coherent only on the condition of coinciding with the silence of the lived world, that is, of abolishing itself as philosophy (cf. PRI 138/30). In contrast to this view, it seems to us that guided by the presupposition of consciousness, *Phenomenology of Perception* remains profoundly dependent on the intellectualism that it denounces. The affirmation of the *cogito*, which is correlative to the transcendental perspective already relinquished in *The Structure of Behavior*, weighs heavily on the description of the lived world, which is in the end always already understood as a nature. Because he determines teleology on the basis of consciousness and not consciousness as teleology, because he therefore does not conceive teleology as such, Merleau-Ponty remains somehow caught up in teleology, dependent on its objectifying direction: the phenomenon is always already subordinated to consciousness, the world is always already identified with nature, and finally perception is always already identified with reason, instead of explicating the inscription of reason in the world—that is, instead of explicating teleology itself. Thus, what Beaufret says in the discussion of Merleau-Ponty's presentation of "The Primacy of Perception" seems in a way prescient:

> To say that Merleau-Ponty stops at a phenomenology without any means of going beyond it is to fail to understand that the phenomenon itself, in the phenomenological sense of the term, goes beyond the realm of the empirical. [34] The phenomenon in this sense is not empirical but that which manifests itself really, that which we can really experience, in opposition to what would be only a construction of concepts. Phenomenology is not a falling back into phenomenalism but the maintenance of contact with "the thing itself." If phenomenology rejects "intellectualist" explanations of perception, it is not to open the door to the irrational but to close it to verbalism. Nothing appears to me less pernicious than the *Phenomenology of Perception.* The only reproach I would make to the author is not that he has gone "too far," but rather that he has not been sufficiently radical. The phenomenological descriptions which he uses in fact maintain the vocabulary of idealism. In this they are in accord with Husserlian descriptions. But the whole problem is precisely to know whether phenomenology, fully developed, does not require the abandonment of subjectivity and the vocabulary of subjective idealism as, beginning with Husserl, Heidegger has done. (PRI151/41–42)

But we must not conclude from this that the objection that commentators make is groundless. Truly, there is no need to choose between objecting to Merleau-Ponty's intellectualist presuppositions and denouncing in him an irrationalism of the lived. In fact, it is *because* he does not go far enough in the description of the lived world that he is led, at the same time, to go too far. As soon as the vocabulary of intellectualism is preserved, one can describe the world only in the form of a pure and simple negation of intellectual consciousness; the description can appear then only as a return to the irrationality of the lived or rather as an identification of the lived with the empirical. In other words, Beaufret's objection that Merleau-

Ponty's detractors misunderstand phenomenology is in a way valid for Merleau-Ponty himself. Because he gains access to the phenomenon by means of the categories of idealism, because he situates himself therefore upstream of or beyond phenomenality, the return to the phenomenon takes place by an immediate negation of this idealism and appears then to be really a flowing back toward the empirical, this side or downstream of the phenomenon. As soon as the phenomenon is not apprehended positively but situated at the crossing of a double negation, it is inevitable that this non-place be read as a return to the intellectual subject, since the phenomenon *is not* the empirical, and also as a return to the empirical [35], since the phenomenon *is not* an intellectual object. Simply put, the two critiques are not situated on the same level. There is a straightforward reading, attentive to the description of the perceived world, which takes the critique of intellectualism literally and which results in the objection of irrationalism. And, in fact, because *Phenomenology of Perception* does not bring the problem of reflection and reason to the forefront, it does not contain the means of deflecting the interpretation in which the phenomenal and the empirical are assimilated to one another. There is a phenomenological reading—that of Beaufret, for example—which situates itself immediately on the level of the phenomenon as distinguished from the empirical and which is then attentive to Merleau-Ponty's incapacity to bring the phenomenon's originality to light because he is dependent on the vocabulary of subjectivity.

In the end, Merleau-Ponty remains a prisoner of the duality between reflection and the unreflective; dominated by the presupposition of the primacy of an autonomous, reflective order, he can characterize the phenomenal only as the unreflective itself, in the sense of a negation of all reflection. Conversely—and this testifies to the complicity of the two critiques—by putting the autonomy of the reflective order in question, that is, by interrogating the way intellectual consciousness is rooted in perceptual life, Merleau-Ponty will be led to overcome the very notion of the unreflective. For if reflection must be able to root itself in the unreflective, the unreflective is not the other of reflection but its birthplace, inchoative reflection. The uncritical positing of a reflective order led to apprehending the phenomenon as its immediate negation, namely, as the unreflective; conversely, a genuine critique of reflection, which would consist in grasping reflection in its very phenomenon, forces on us a critique of the unreflective. By denouncing the autonomy of reflection entirely, that is, by profoundly recognizing its character as reflection *on* the unreflective, Merleau-Ponty must thereby also discover that the unreflective makes sense only as unreflective *for* reflection. One has to substitute another sense of negation for the idea of immediate negation: "negation-reference (zero of . . .)" (VI 311/257), which exists only as the beginning (on the side of the unreflective) or as the conservation (on the side of reflection) of what it negates. Then, the notion of consciousness, far from being obvious, becomes the name of a problem, that of phenomenality, that is, the problem of the world; and consciousness will have to be grasped as a moment of the world rather than as its opposite.

[36] It is still the case that in *Phenomenology of Perception*, Merleau-Ponty does not reach these conclusions. He gains access to the phenomenal terrain by means of categories that conceal its originality and that then call forth contradictory interpretations. It seems that Merleau-Ponty becomes aware of this rather quickly. In the statement he provided for his candidacy to the Collège de France, he begins by establishing the necessity of fixing the philosophic sense of his first investigations, for, as he concludes, "The study of perception could only teach us a 'bad ambiguity,' a mixture of finitude and universality, of interiority and exteriority" (CCF 409/11). In Merleau-Ponty's eyes, this does not mean that we have to renounce the results of *Phenomenology of Perception;* its sole mistake is that it remains on the descriptive level, being content with bringing to light this domain which still must be thought out. This revision, which will ultimately consist in passing from a description of the perceived world to the philosophy of perception for which it calls, will be the objective of the later works. However, the full scope of reorganization that this revision imposes becomes apparent only with *The Visible and the Invisible.* Thus, he specifies in a working note, "Results of *Ph.P.*—Necessity of bringing them to ontological explicitation" (VI 237/183). And the failure of *Phenomenology of Perception,* in Merleau-Ponty's eyes, is undoubtedly due to the categories by means of which its results are explicated: "The problems that remain after this first description: they are due to the fact that in part I retained the philosophy of 'consciousness'" (VI 237/183); and still more clearly, "The problems posed in *Ph.P.* are insoluble because I start there from the 'consciousness'–'object' distinction" (VI 253/200). Now, what is valid for *Phenomenology of Perception* as a whole is particularly valid for the part that concerns the problem of others [*autrui*]. It is therefore necessary to devote a chapter to this question, not only because it drives Merleau-

Ponty's thought from beginning to end but also because, more than any other, it reveals the tension that cuts across *Phenomenology of Perception*. More than any other description, the description of the experience of the other demonstrates the failure of the perspective adopted in this work, and therefore the necessity of a passage to ontology.

2 The Other (*Autrui*)

1. The Problem

[37] It is impossible to exaggerate the importance of the question of the other throughout Merleau-Ponty's work. In fact, Merleau-Ponty's work can be read entirely as a meditation on what this incontestable experience of others implies.[1] Instead of the other being considered only as a moment of the world, the other from the start informs the description of the perceived world. The perceived world is first what responds to the possibility of the other, the place where others are liable to appear. Therefore, we must distinguish between the order of exposition and the heuristic order. Of course, in *Phenomenology of Perception,* the study of the world as perceived closes with a chapter devoted to the human world. There the human world is reconceived as a dimension added on top of that of the thing, a dimension whose givenness is rooted in that of the perceived world. However, this original experience of the human world orients the analysis from the beginning; throughout *Phenomenology of Perception,* the description of the sensible and of the object borrows its vocabulary from the experience of the other, as if the characteristics of every experience were crystallized in this one.[2] There is not one chapter in this work where Merleau-Ponty does not test his conclusions by showing how they agree with the experience of intersubjectivity. In short, from the start, the explication of the perceived world is guided by the horizon of the perception of the other. Its way of proceeding therefore is finally circular. Because the other secretly informs the study [38] of the sensible world, because the perceived world is approached from the possibility of intersubjectivity, the conclusions produced on the level of the sensible world reinform the descriptions of the other. This is why, when Merleau-Ponty finally enters

1. See Merleau-Ponty's radio broadcasts with G. Charbonnier, "Douze entretiens avec Maurice Merleau-Ponty," recorded for the R.T.F. between May 25 and August 7, 1959.
2. Sensation is "coexistence" (PHP 216/185, 247/213, 255/221), "communion" (247/213, 370/320), "coition" (370/320). The sensor "sympathizes" (247/214) with the qualities of the object. Things are defined by their "behavior" (318/275).

into the question of the other explicitly, his analysis essentially consists in referring the reader to the conclusion he reached on the level of the sensible and of the thing. The analysis of the other in a way precedes itself. According to the constitutive order, the analysis of the other follows from that of the world, but the world has always already been understood as a universe where other humans can appear.

In any case, starting with *The Structure of Behavior,* the viewpoint of this experience guides the symmetrical challenge to realism and intellectualism, that is, to objective thought. Merleau-Ponty explains this in a working note:

> One can claim that the order of the phenomenal is second by reference to the objective order, is but a province of it, when one considers only intra-mundane relations between objects. But as soon as one introduces the other and even the living body, the work of art, the historical milieu, one realizes that the order of the phenomenal must be considered as autonomous and that, if one does not recognize this autonomy in it, it is definitively *impenetrable.* (VI 263/209)

As we have seen, we enter into the study of behavior, in Merleau-Ponty's first work, from an external viewpoint; the point is to relate behavior to the descriptions of psychology that are implicitly or explicitly guided by the presupposition of a naturalist ontology, that is, to consider behavior as an object. Thus, the irreducibility of behavior to the constancy hypothesis is made clear as much at the level of the relation of the observer to the observed behavior as at the level of the behavior to its world. Perception is at first reconceived by means of the test that the psychologist performs in relation to meaningful behavior. The external viewpoint, which considers behavior as an event in the world and not as it is lived, conceals an internal viewpoint, that of the observer who lives and understands the behavior. The inadequacy of the stimulus-response schema is verified first at the level of this unique intersubjectivity rather than at the objective level of the relation between the behavior and its world. The organism testifies to an irreducible unity, which can only be the object of an *understanding;* it is a *perceived* reality:

> The significance and value of vital processes [39] which science, as we have seen, is obliged to take into account are assuredly attributes of the *perceived* organism, but they are not extrinsic denominations with respect to the true organism; for the true organism, the one which sci-

ence considers, is the concrete totality of the perceived organism, that which supports all the correlations which analysis discovers in it but which is not decomposable into them. (SC 169/156)

As soon as experience is reconceived as the experience of another organism and, in a general way, as the experience of another existence, its object can no longer be characterized as a reality in-itself; the organism is "a whole which is significant for a consciousness which knows it, not a thing which rests in itself" (SC 172/159). Here Merleau-Ponty initiates a way of proceeding that will structure all of his works: the experience of the other imposes, better than any other, a *phenomenological reduction;* it calls for a radical critique of realism. By conceiving consciousness as an empirical subjectivity, by reducing it to the property of existing for itself that certain natural beings possess, and correlatively by determining perception as a real relation, we are unable to account for the immediate and irreducible character of the perception of the other. What defines the other is in fact its reference to me, its merging with the meaning that it presents to a consciousness. The alterity of the other therefore first means its difference vis-à-vis the world understood in the realist sense; the other exceeds all sensible content, escapes from the in-itself, and merges with the sense that it offers to a subjectivity. This is why, in *The Structure of Behavior,* Merleau-Ponty reconceives the other by means of the notion of form—that is, as an indecomposable unity, as a totality irreducible to the sum of its parts (SC 182/168). More than that of the thing, the experience of the other establishes the evidence of the *cogito* as true.

Of course, realist philosophy attempts to reconstitute the certainty of the other in an indirect way, by recourse to reasoning by analogy. The consciousness of the other, which in principle is impenetrable, will be inferred from a resemblance between the only thing from the other that is given to me, namely, its objective body, and my own body. Taking up Scheler's argumentation, Merleau-Ponty relentlessly returns to the fact that reasoning from analogy is impossible (see, for example, SC 169/156; PHP 404/352). The critique is developed [40] simultaneously on the level of fact and on the level of principle, both de facto and de jure. First, child psychology makes clear the originary character of the experience of the human world, an originality that seems hardly compatible with the elements that reasoning from analogy requires. In fact, the body of the child and that of the other with which it finds itself related exhibit only a slight objective resemblance; moreover, they cannot be compared insofar as the child does not possess an objective image of its own body; and finally, the child cannot perform such reasoning from analogy since a child does not yet possess discursive thought. The relation to the other is immediate; far from the relation to the other being inferred from sensible contents, the other is already present in and as this content, that is, as its own body. The originary quality of the perception of the other truly excludes the possibility that this perception rests on an inference. The genetic priority demonstrated by psychological observation has transcendental validity here. The experience of the other testifies to the essentially significant character of consciousness. But even if we assume that the elements on which this reasoning would be based are available, such a reasoning from the objective resemblance of bodies would not, in any case, allow us to infer the existence of *another* consciousness; it would allow us to infer only the presence of *my* consciousness in the other (PHP 68/55–56). Thus, the presupposition that motivates the recourse to analogical inference—namely, the duality between the other's consciousness, which is closed in on itself, and the sensible content—makes this inference fail. If what was really at issue were to infer *conclusively* that there is an other, nothing would be sufficient to convince me of its presence; no sign could lead me to this meaning once separated from it, that is, as soon as the sign is not given to me from the start as the very presence of the other. In other words, every theory of projection assumes what it claims to demonstrate: we would not be able to project our own lived experiences into a sensible appearance if something in the appearance did not suggest it to us. But then, the inference becomes unnecessary at the moment that it turns out to be possible. In fact, the analogy does not found the experience of the other but proceeds from it. The analogy only confirms the experience and nourishes a methodical knowledge of the other. We could be mistaken concerning the sense of an expression, but we could not be mistaken that it is a human expression. Thus, the perception of the other is in Merleau-Ponty's eyes [41] an essential argument against realism. Insofar as it is also, perhaps above all else, an experience of others, my experience cannot be understood as a real contact, as a coincidence with a reality subsisting in itself. The other is given to me as an irreducible meaning. The objectivity of the world rests on this immediate presence of the other. It is not the case that I am enclosed in a private subjectivity; rather, the world manifests itself to me as what is immediately accessible to others. It involves the requirement that what is offered to me be offered equally to them. The consciousness that the expe-

rience of the other makes clear appears, from the start, to open on an objective reality, rather than objective reality being explained by means of an
incomprehensible intermonadic relation between private subjectivities. It
is here, at the very heart of this objective reality, that the possibility of the
other must be sought.

The insistence on the problem of the other, however, does not first have
the function of discovering what we would have been convinced of with
"a moment of reflection." Actually, above all Merleau-Ponty invokes this
dimension of experience in order to challenge intellectualism. This dimension could not have a status within transcendental idealism. As other,
as belonging to the world, the other can only be an object. And yet, since
consciousness defines itself through the identity of being and appearing,
the appearance of another consciousness in the world is unthinkable. The
alter ego finds itself dismembered by the division that intellectualism inaugurates. As other, the other is on the side of the object; as ego, it merges
with me. Thus, if the ontological sense of what is consists in its presentation to a consciousness in the form of a unity of sense, the appearance of a
being whose ontological sense is to be other turns out to be incomprehensible. The immanence that defines sense forbids in principle the givenness
of a being that is transcendent. The experience of the other is distributed
between a world that no subjectivity can hollow out and a subjectivity that
is not in any way worldly, since it makes the world appear. Realism missed
the communication of consciousnesses *by a lack;* it conceived subjectivity
as an insular reality and sensibility as a mundane event, with the result that
subjectivity was in principle cut off from every other consciousness; realism's fault was that it lacked a givenness of sense, a meaningful unity of
the world in which an agreement could be produced. This is why only the
givenness of an objective world allows us to understand the possibility of
the appearance [42] of the other. But idealism misses this communication
by excess. Because objectivity is from the start determined as ideality and
world stripped clean of its facticity, the alterity of subjectivity becomes
unthinkable and the communication of consciousnesses is reduced to their
identity within a unique constituting subject:

> Reflective analysis knows nothing of the problem of the other, or that
> of the world, because it insists that with the first glimmer of conscious-
> ness there appears in me the power to go in principle to a universal
> truth, and that the other, being without thisness as well as without loca-

tion and body, the Alter and the Ego are one and the same in the true world which is a connection of minds. There is no difficulty in understanding how I can conceive the Other, because the I and consequently the Other are not taken into the cloth of phenomena; they have validity rather than existence. (PHP vi/xii)

Realism understands facticity in the form of an objective belonging to the world, so that failing to think the order of truth, it misses intersubjectivity; but idealism dispossesses consciousness of its alterity, of the facticity which allows it be pluralized, so that it misses intersubjectivity just as much by absorbing it immediately back into the unity of truth. This is why if, on the one hand, the experience of the other assumes that the possibility of an objective reality be emphasized, this objective reality must, on the other hand, be reconceived from the incontestably true fact of intersubjectivity.

Intellectualism must then also rely on analogy. It is again a matter of seeking the marks of a unique transcendental subjectivity within the objective world. Consequently, it stumbles upon the aporias that already confronted realism. Since there are only objects in front of a pure consciousness, we must discover the signs of a transcendental subjectivity within the objects. But, as we have seen, nothing in this appearance can motivate such an inference. Situated before subjectivity, the object is in some fashion too far away for a presence to be able to manifest itself in it. The life of subjectivity takes refuge entirely on the side of the unique transcendental consciousness, while what is in front of transcendental consciousness finds itself deprived of any subjectivity—it becomes a pure object. The scission between constituting and constituted that intellectualism enacts hollows out an abyss between the other's consciousness and its body. Insofar as it is consciousness, the other cannot be other; it merges with me. Insofar as it is body, nothing distinguishes it from other objects. Finally, therefore, we have to choose. Intellectualism can maintain [43] its interpretation of the donation of sense as intellectual possession, but then it is forbidden from giving an account of the experience of the other. The plurality of consciousnesses is postulated, but it is not established as true. Consciousness cannot simultaneously be itself, pure self-presence, and many. Or intellectualism can acknowledge the irreducibility of the experience of the other, but it must admit then that a body can signify a subjectivity, that the relation between a body and a subjectivity does not refer to an inference, and that, consequently, the immediate opposition between the body—situated on the side of the object—and consciousness is found to be blurred. In order for a subjectivity to make its appearance in the world, consciousness must, essentially, be outside of itself; it must escape from the place of self-possession in immanence. Just as it allows us to denounce realism in favor of a consciousness that donates sense, the experience of the other leads therefore to the rejection of an idealism that would reconceive this donation of sense in the form of an intellectual possession, that would assert the transparency of perception to the truth. Let us note that the two perspectives that have been evoked are profoundly connected. It is by the very same move that, on the one hand, reflection gives itself a world in itself within which consciousnesses are situated as natural realities and consequently are cut off from one another and that, on the other hand, reflection subordinates this world to a pure transcendental subjectivity that has the spectacle of empirical subjects unfolding before itself. The relation to the other is then missed in two ways. Belonging to the natural world, consciousness is not in a position to unfold an objective universe within which a communication with others could be established; but pure transcendental subjectivity absorbs all alterity back into itself, and the world loses the transcendence that made it possible for the other, as such, to appear. In other words,

> The naturalism of science and the spiritualism of the universal constituting subject, to which reflection on science led, had this in common, that they leveled out experience: in the face of the constituting I, the empirical selves are objects. The empirical Self is a hybrid notion, a mixture of in-itself and for-itself, to which reflective philosophy could give no status. Insofar as it has a concrete content it is inserted in the system of experience and is therefore not a subject; insofar as it is a subject, it is empty and resolves itself into the transcendental subject. (PHP 68/56)

Thus, as soon as it transcends the subjective sphere, the other becomes an obstacle to the idealist interpretation of [44] perception, and Merleau-Ponty invokes the experience of the other against this interpretation.[3] The other appears; its transcendence, therefore, could not correspond to the factual presence of something transcendent. But it appears in such a way as not to give *itself* in this appearing; it remains transcendent to its given-

3. See, for example, PHP 401/349; S 117/93; VI 67/43, 73/48.

ness. Or rather, it gives itself as this very transcendence. It is precisely the presence of a non-presence. This claim does not mean that the other's absence conceals another presence—that would be to fall back into the aporias of objective thought and to look for the signs of a consciousness in a corporeal presence—it means instead that the other presents itself as absent, that manifestation and withdrawal are identical in it. Therefore, as soon as we take stock of what the experience of the other implies, we see ourselves being forced to overcome the opposition, which is also a kind of complicity, between the empirical subject and the transcendental subject, between fact and essence. The relation to the other requires a signifying unity of the perceived; it assumes that the perceived is situated "higher" than the existent that is spread out on the plane of pure multiplicity. Consequently, it assumes that consciousness is to be grasped as something other than the place of a sensible passivity. But this signifying unity cannot be reduced to the pure identity of ideality; the relation to the other requires that the perceived be situated "lower" than an essence, that is, apprehended in such a way that consciousnesses can remain situated in it, so that consciousnesses can remain capable of alterity. With the other, what is at issue is to think the world in such as a way as to sketch in it the possibility of a communication of consciousnesses, and therefore the principle of unity which founds a rational horizon—without this communication abolishing the difference between consciousnesses, that is, their rootedness in the world. Consequently, what has to be done is to conceive the world in such a way as to keep rationality on the horizon, to make it subsist as the world's own horizon. Obviously, correctly posed, the problem of the other carries reflection beyond the alternatives of objectivism and calls for a reorganization of its categories.

2. The Confrontation with Husserl

In the examination of this problem, Merleau-Ponty's path crosses that of Husserl. While it is undeniable that Merleau-Ponty targets Husserl in the denunciation of transcendental idealism, Merleau-Ponty nevertheless pays [45] homage to Husserl for having been the first to define the difficulty. This distinguishes him from the classical idealist, for whom the experience of the other did not even raise a specific problem: "For Husserl, on the contrary, it is well known that there is a problem of the other, and the alter ego is a paradox" (PHP vi/xii). For Merleau-Ponty, the point is to take up this paradox, that is, to develop everything implied by Husserl's description of the alter ego. Since it is performed from the viewpoint of the closure of the ego—every object is a unity of sense constituted in me—constitutive analysis leads to the objection of solipsism. As long as it does not give an account of the other, constitutive analysis cannot claim to reach the ontological sense of the world again in its full scope. For the world is not given merely as a private world, but indeed as alien to my sphere, as an intersubjective world. A phenomenology that would claim by itself to form a philosophy would be exposed to the objection of transcendental solipsism. Since the objective tenor of the world is based on the experience of others, what is at issue is to give an account of this new "layer" of sense without renouncing the principle of the closure of the ego—that is, consequently, to constitute *in me* the sense "alter ego." Hence the decision to proceed to a second reduction, which consists in abstracting from all intentionality that which is directed to the alien, thereby opening a "sphere of ownness." This new reduction is at first surprising. Are we not already situated in the sphere of the pure "I" owing to the disconnection of all transcendence? Of course. But the world of what is for me involves several dimensions and, in particular, a tenor of sense that defines it as alien. It is necessary therefore to take an extra step by attempting to constitute, at the very heart of the reduced world, this "layer" of sense. This amounts to unveiling a more originary level of the "I," which embraces what is proper to me rather than the phenomenal field in its entirety. On the basis of this new delimitation, we will be able to gain access to the non-I in its genuine sense. Then it is a matter of tracing a line of division within consciousness, between what is proper to it and what is not, in order to free up the intentional threads which lead from consciousness to the other. Husserl states the problem in the following way: "*How* can my ego, within his peculiar ownness, constitute under the name, 'experience of the alien,' precisely something *alien*—something, that is, with [46] a sense that excludes the constituted from the concrete make-up of the sense constituting I-myself, as somehow the latter's analogue?"[4] Here we are at the maximal point of tension of the constitutive way of proceeding, since what is at issue is to constitute "within" the ego a being whose sense is to transcend this ego. As Ricoeur notes, this tension ultimately puts into play phenomenology's two constitutive dimensions: the idealist requirement by virtue of which the other, *like the thing*, must appear as a unity of sense;

4. E. Husserl, *Cartesian Meditations*, trans. D. Cairns (The Hague: Martinus Nijhoff, 1977), paragraph 44, 94.

and the fidelity to experience which requires that the other transgress the sphere of ownness and "make a *surplus* of presence arise at the limits of my lived experience, a surplus which is incompatible with the inclusion of all sense in my lived experience."[5] To Merleau-Ponty, this tension looks like an insurmountable contradiction: "This difficulty of principle, posited as a limit at the beginning of the fifth *Cartesian Meditation,* is nowhere eliminated. Husserl *disregards* it: since I have the idea of others, it follows that in some way the difficulty mentioned *has in fact been overcome*" (S 117/94).[6] As soon as it must be constituted within the sphere of ownness, the other cannot be constituted as other. Husserl certainly tries, by means of the notion of analogical appresentation, to reconcile the donation of the other as a unity of sense with its transcendence. But, to appropriate Ricoeur's expression, we have to say that the ontic validity that is connected with the appresentation of the other in the presentation of its body seems irreducible to the validity that is connected with the unities of sense at work in the constitution of things. How, within what first presents itself as an object, can the wrenching be produced by whose means this object becomes the place of another consciousness? The abyss between the objective presentation of the body of the other and the appresentation of the other itself appears unbridgeable. Situated before a consciousness, the other cannot appear as the consciousness that it is. As soon as the other is examined on the basis of the opposition of the own and the alien, that is, as [47] an alter ego before an ego, its transcendence is inexorably missed. When Husserl, examining the experience of the other in the fullness of its sense, finds himself in a position to break out of the framework of "egology," he performs a reduction to the sphere of ownness which betrays the closure of the ego, a closure which keeps Hus-

5. P. Ricoeur, "Sympathie et respect," in *A l'école de la phénoménologie* (Paris: Vrin, 1986), 268.
6. When Merleau-Ponty examines the question of the constitution of the other in Husserl, he relies essentially on the Fifth Cartesian Meditation. It seems that he was unaware of a number of unpublished texts devoted to intersubjectivity; these were not part of the group of transcribed manuscripts available in Paris starting in April of 1944 (see H. L. Van Breda, "Merleau-Ponty and the Husserl Archives in Louvain," trans. S. Michelman, in *Texts and Dialogues,* by M. Merleau-Ponty, ed. H. J. Silverman and J. Barry, Jr., 150–61 [Atlantic Highlands, N.J.: Humanities Press, 1992]). His critique therefore stems from a relative misunderstanding of the development of Husserl's thought concerning this question.

serl from freeing up the intentional threads that lead from me to the other. As Merleau-Ponty says, "the passage to intersubjectivity is contradictory only with regard to an insufficient reduction, Husserl was right to say. But a sufficient reduction leads beyond the alleged transcendental 'immanence,' it leads to the absolute spirit understood as *Weltlichkeit*, to *Geist* as the *Ineinander* of the spontaneities" (VI 226/172). By means of a reduction to the sphere of ownness, Husserl tries to free himself from a naiveté in regard to intersubjectivity, that is, to overcome the implicit position of a plurality of empirical consciousnesses. But he is still prisoner of this naiveté insofar as he stays on the level of immanence instead of orienting himself toward the ultimate layer of a "consciousness" which would be openness to transcendence, of an "own" which is already a "non-own," or rather which stops short of the opposition between the own and the alien. In fact, "the transcendental, being a resolute overcoming of the *mens sive anima* and the psychological, *goes beyond subjectivity* in the direction of counter-transcendence and immanence" (VI 226/172). While Husserl tries to keep the experience of the other within the framework of this "counter-transcendence," that is, within the framework of an egology, for Merleau-Ponty it is a matter of recognizing this experience as the place where a more originary dimension is revealed, freed from the naive position of an intuitive ego situated in opposition vis-à-vis what is alien to it. This is why he notes that the reduction to the sphere of ownness, reconceived in its truth, "is only a test of primordial bonds, a way of following them into their final prolongations" (S 221/175). Thus, "the difficulty of principle" which opens the Fifth Cartesian Meditation can be overcome

> only because the one within me who perceives the other is capable of ignoring the radical contradiction which makes theoretical conception of the other impossible. Or rather (since if the one within me ignored it, he would no longer be dealing with the other), only because he is able to live that contradiction as the very definition of the presence of the other. This subject [48] which experiences itself as constituted at the moment that it functions as constituting is my body. We remember that Husserl ended up basing my perception of a way of behaving (*Gebaren*) which appears in the space surrounding me upon what he calls the "pairing phenomenon" and "intentional transgression." It happens that my gaze stumbles against certain sights (those of other humans and, by extension, animal bodies) and is thwarted by them. (S 117/94)

In contrast to Husserl, who tries to reach the other again on the basis of the "I," Merleau-Ponty's way of proceeding actually starts from the irreducibility of the experience of the other. Following Husserl, Merleau-Ponty clarifies this experience with the help of the concept of pairing. However, instead of subjecting pairing to the tension of the own and the alien, Merleau-Ponty reconceives the flesh (which, for Husserl, was synonymous with ownness) *on the basis of the fact of transgression,* that is, as the actual identity of a possession and a dispossession, of a closure and an opening. Far from being the origin-pole of an intentionality which carries itself toward the other, the flesh is the originary unity of the own and the non-own—an ownness, that is, a consciousness, which sustains itself only by transgressing its own limits, by opening itself to another. To summarize, we have to say that Merleau-Ponty's starting point is Husserl's ending point, namely, this phenomenon of pairing, a phenomenon on the basis of which one must rethink the status of the corporeal subject.

In Merleau-Ponty, what follows from this is that the problem of the other does not occupy the same place in the economy of the constitutive method. All of what we have seen, in fact, amounts to saying that the other cannot be considered the response to the problem of the transcendence of the world. In Husserl, the constitution of the other carries the weight of the constitution of a world endowed with objective transcendence. Now, the egological viewpoint, which makes the transcendence of the world re-emerge as a problem, leads nevertheless to the impossibility of accounting for the other. Why would consciousness be capable, with the other, of opening itself to a transcendence that escapes from it at the level of the world? Is it not on the condition of its being given within a world that is *already* transcendent that the other can be reconceived in its alterity? Transcendence must be understood in a univocal way. Cut off from the world, consciousness is ipso facto cut off from all transcendence and, consequently, from its alter ego. Thus, by taking its starting point in the solitude of the ego [49], that is, on the basis of an absence from the world, the constitution of the other can only reactivate the tension between immanence and transcendence; it cannot resolve the tension. In contrast, the problem of the other can be resolved only on the condition that consciousness is reconceived as originarily capable of transcendence. To pose the problem of the other is to determine it as a moment of the problem of the world: not as what must carry the transcendence of the world but as what is carried by this transcendence. Only insofar as the subject is grasped as the openness to the world can the experience of the other be given its due, no longer as the experience of an alter ego for an ego, but as the experience by one flesh of another flesh, of another perception, and finally of a dimension of the world itself. The other is itself only if it borrows from the world its alterity, if it proceeds from the world's depth. There is not therefore a plurality of consciousnesses to be constituted, but a plurality to be acknowledged and described as what is given with the transcendence of the world:

> the objective transcendence is not *posterior* to the position of the other: the world is already there, in its objective transcendence, before this analysis, and it is its very meaning that will be rendered explicit as meaning. . . . [Hence the introduction of the other is not what produces the "objective transcendence": the other is one of its indexes, a moment of it, but it is in the world itself that the possibility of the other will be found.] (VI 226/172)

One can move through Husserl's enterprise in two directions. On the one hand, as all commentators have noted, Husserl is dependent on the primacy that he gives to Nature: the thing holds then the place of the model, of the guiding thread for the exposition of constitution. But, on the other hand, the fidelity to experience and the profoundly philosophical ambition of phenomenology lead it to neglect no field of experience and, consequently, to confront the experience of the human world. Trân Duc Thao brings this duality to light very clearly:

> Transcendental idealism had two entirely different goals. On the one hand, the explication of the *Dinglichkeit* as *ideal correlate* enabled one to bypass the concept of nature *in itself*, in the sense in which nature in itself would prevent the comprehension of a strictly human existence whereby being *is* only inasmuch as it is *for me*. But, on the other hand, it was necessary to disengage the meaning of the world of persons, inasmuch as its *being for me* implies *existence* itself, in the full sense of the term, since I [50] perceive the world precisely as a collection of *subjects*; i.e., of other "*me's*." The same concept of "constitution" now refers to the positing and recognition of an *absolute reality*. . . . The theory of the world of spirit was inserted into the general project of the *Weltkonstitution*, interpreted according to the concept of *Dingkonstitution*. But the originality of the domain should have produced a new framework

wherein the very notion of the "thing" would have had an entirely new meaning.[7]

It is clear that all the problems of the Fifth Cartesian Meditation come from maintaining the framework of the *Dingkonstitution* at the level of the explication of the donation of the other. Merleau-Ponty's project can then be understood as the fulfillment of a program called for by Trân Duc Thao, namely, as the attempt *to invent a new meaning of the thing on the basis of characteristics of experience clearly seen on the level of the intersubjective world.* It is a matter of grasping the thing not as a unity of sense but as something that even while appearing is still endowed with the transcendence inherent in the fact that the thing is given in common—that is, that the transcendence of the other is inscribed in it. The thing is precisely the correlate of the intersubjective universe. While Husserl's analysis unfolds essentially on the plane of the naturalistic attitude, Merleau-Ponty's analysis proceeds from a consciousness of the originality of the personalistic attitude:

> What is false in the ontology of *blosse Sachen* is that it makes a purely theoretical or idealizing attitude absolute, neglecting or taking as understood a relation with being which founds the purely theoretical attitude and measures its value. Relative to this scientific *naturalism*, the *natural* attitude involves a higher truth that we must regain. For the natural attitude is nothing less than naturalistic. We do not live naturally in the universe of *blosse Sachen*. Prior to all reflection, in conversation and the practices of life, we maintain a "personalistic attitude" that naturalism cannot account for, and here things are not nature in itself for us but "our surroundings." Our most natural life as men intends an ontological milieu which is different from that of being in itself, and which consequently cannot be derived from it in the constitutive order. (S 206/163)

In the personalistic attitude,

> We are in a relation to a common surrounding world—we are in a personal association: these belong together. We [51] could not be persons for others if a common surrounding did not stand there for us in a community, in an intentional linkage of our lives. Correlatively spoken,

7. Trân Duc Thao, *Phenomenology and Dialectical Materialism*, trans. D. J. Herman and D. V. Morano, ed. R. L. Armstrong (Dordrecht: Kluwer Academic Publishers, 1986), 49.

the one is constituted with the other. Each ego can, for himself and for others, become a person in the normal sense, a person in a personal association, only if comprehension brings about the relation to a common surrounding world.[8]

The thing does not rest in itself; it participates in the surroundings, it is given to a community of persons, it is engaged on the basis of this collective experience. But, at the same time and to this extent, the experience that I have of others and of my belonging to a community is based on the depth of the perceived thing and is inscribed in it. Strictly speaking, we perceive neither the other itself nor pure things—these two abstractions are interdependent—but rather somehow we perceive the articulation of the one on the basis of the other. We perceive the world as correlate of a community, the thing as "mounted" on the dimensions of interpersonal experience. The thing is offered to everyone, but in such a way that this totality is still differentiated and is not overcome in an identity or in an ideality; therefore the thing is just as much absent from each of us and is transcendent. The other, then, is given not as an alter ego in front of me, but as a relation to a world that is also mine, or rather as inscribed in an anonymous relation to the world, that is, as a dimension of the visibility of the world.

3. The Failure of *Phenomenology of Perception*

If the awareness of the "paradox" of the other orients Merleau-Ponty's whole way of proceeding, one can nonetheless ask whether the solution that he provides on the level of *Phenomenology of Perception* is satisfactory. Does he really manage to overcome the Husserlian perspective, which, as we have seen, does not permit the problem to be resolved? The chapter devoted to the other brings together the results of the previous descriptions. The discovery of one's own body as an openness to the world, an openness that cannot be reduced to the positing of a noema, allows Merleau-Ponty to overcome the aporias of objective thought. Thus, the earlier series of analyses is gathered together in this idea that "I *have* the [52] world as an incomplete individual, through the agency of my body as

8. E. Husserl, *Ideas Pertaining to a Pure Phenomenology and to a Phenomenological Philosophy, Second Book: Studies in the Phenomenology of Constitution,* trans. R. Rojcewicz and A. Schuwer (Dordrecht: Kluwer Academic Publishers, 1989), §51, 201.

the potentiality of this world" (PHP 402/350). Therefore, since the world is not entirely unfolded in the form of a definite object, other behaviors can arise in it. Since my perception is incarnated, and therefore opaque to itself, it no longer excludes the appearance of another perception. Since I am not a pure subject, the body of the other will no longer be a pure object; a consciousness will be able to inhabit it. It is only a matter of "decompressing" the immediate opposition of consciousness and the body. As soon as my consciousness is mundanized, as soon as it "descends" into the world, the world can "ascend" to consciousness, gather itself into consciousness's visibility, and another existence can appear within it. Everything is based therefore on the discovery of the "anonymous" character of the perceptual subject:

> If I find in myself, through reflection, along with the perceiving subject, a pre-personal subject given to itself, and if my perceptions are centered outside me as sources of initiative and judgment, if the perceived world remains in a state of neutrality, being neither verified as an object nor recognized as a dream, then it is not the case that everything that appears in the world is arrayed before me, and so the behavior of the other can have its place there. (PHP 405/352–53)

The possibility of the other really comes from this behavior that, insofar as it is initiation to the world *itself,* is not from the start divided up into insular consciousnesses. The results of Gestalt psychology here converge with Husserl's descriptions: originarily incarnated, consciousness can no longer be situated in a frontal relation with alien consciousnesses, but rather is from the start decentered in relation to itself and can, consequently, be coupled with those alien consciousnesses; it can transgress its world toward this other world that the life of the other represents. Despite this connection to Husserl and Gestalt psychology, Merleau-Ponty's analyses in *Phenomenology of Perception* are developed instead within the context of Scheler's philosophy. In fact, Scheler examines the question of the other not on the basis of the *cogito* but on the basis of an "undifferentiated" psychic current which is realized in an emotive evidence and which precedes subjective differences. Moreover, Merleau-Ponty finds the confirmation of this psychic undifferentiation in child psychology, which clearly exhibits a "transitivism" during the first intersubjective relations. This proximity to Scheler is not, however, unqualified. In fact, it is not a question of [53] holding on to a pure and simple undifferentiation in which alterity would no longer make sense. If we situate ourselves strictly at the level of the anonymity of being-in-the-world, or, rather, if we define being-in-the-world by this anonymity, "we level down the I and the Thou in an experience shared by a plurality, thus introducing the impersonal into the heart of subjectivity and eliminating the individuality of perspectives. But have we not, in this general confusion, done away with the alter Ego as well as the Ego?" (PHP 408/355–56; see CAL 240/48). The other appears *as such,* and, to this extent, its givenness does not refer to an insular consciousness; however, if the relation to the other were based truly on an anonymous subjectivity, it would lose all meaning because there would be no distinction within this anonymity, that is, because finally there would be no consciousness to which the other could appear. The ego and the alter ego have parallel destinies: the moment the ego vanishes into the anonymity of being-in-the-world, the other undergoes the same fate and stops being *other* because it is not a consciousness. Just when the experience of the other appears possible, since the abyss between insular subjectivities can be bridged, the experience loses all meaning, for along with their differences, the consciousnesses themselves disappear. Alterity and egoity are not opposed. On the contrary, because a consciousness is endowed with identity, because it is self-consciousness, it can be other, that is, differ from an other. Therefore, if the relation to the other excludes self-transparent consciousnesses, the relation also challenges the idea of an undifferentiated psychic current—only a consciousness, a self-relation, can engender a difference, a divergence in the heart of this current. The move critical of Husserl's egology, which is based on the discovery of the anonymity of being-in-the-world and which eventually converges with Scheler's perspective, calls now for an opposite move that leads to a revindication of one of Husserl's truths against Scheler. The existence of the other makes sense only insofar as it is reconceived from the viewpoint of an ego, to which it can appear and from which it can be distinguished as an alter ego. At this point, the problem is posed in a way that conforms to all the dimensions of the experience. There is certainly an originary anonymity, but this anonymity must at the same time be rejected since it is *experienced* and consequently divided up by the consciousnesses which are fused in it. There is [54], then, a solipsism which cannot be overcome, and yet this solipsism must also be rejected, since the experience that consciousness has of its solitude presupposes a prior background of communication with the other. In fact, the solitude of consciousness is the experience of the *absence* of others, and it refers consequently to an originary relation with them against whose background this absence can be experienced as such. All absence is a modality of presence. Let us note, on the other hand, that insofar as it is *formulated,* this solipsism destroys itself, since it is situated thereby within a horizon of intersubjectivity. Negated by discourse, the other always reappears as the implicit pole of the vocation of discourse. Thus, in *Phenomenology of Perception,* the problem of the other is posed negatively in the form of a double exclusion of Scheler and of Husserl: "By minimizing self-consciousness, Scheler also compromises consciousness of the other. Husserl, on the contrary, wanting to retain the originality of the ego, can introduce the other only as destroyer of this ego" (CAL 241/48).

From a certain perspective, Merleau-Ponty goes no farther: the problem of the other is posed, but it is not genuinely resolved. In fact, he is content to invoke the experience: "Since we live through this situation, there must be some way of making it explicit. Solitude and communication cannot be the two horns of a dilemma, but two moments of one phenomenon, since in fact the other exists for me" (PHP 412/359). And when it is a question of clarifying this experience, Merleau-Ponty abandons, in a rather abrupt way, the terrain of intersubjectivity and refers the reader to his earlier conclusions:

> The problem of the existential modality of the social is here at one
> with all problems of transcendence. Whether we are concerned with
> my body, the natural world, the past, birth or death, the question is
> always how I can be open to phenomena which transcend me, and
> which nevertheless exist only to the extent that I take them up and live
> them; *how the presence to myself (*Urpräsenz*) which establishes my own
> limits and conditions every alien presence is at the same time depresenta-
> tion (*Entgegenwärtigung*) and throws me outside myself.* (PHP 417/363)

Although, as we said, the experience of the other determines the critique of the idealism of the Fifth Cartesian Meditation and the orientation toward a phenomenology of perception, we have to acknowledge [55] that in *Phenomenology of Perception,* Merleau-Ponty does not entirely take stock of the problem and stops short of thinking through this experience. Better than any other, the experience of the other reveals how much Merleau-Ponty is still dependent on the dualities of the objective philosophy that he denounces. Everything depends on how one's own body, on which intentional transgression is based, is apprehended. As in the preceding chapters, the ever-present duality between consciousness and its body is carried away toward the unity of perceptual life. Instead of taking note of the experience of the other, that is, instead of reconceiving the body on the basis of this experience, Merleau-Ponty continues to explain it within a framework that remains idealistic, the framework within which the body had been considered up to this point. The essentially negative character of his description follows from this. Through incarnation, consciousness "loses its transparency," and to this extent the other is "not impossible." If the world is not a pure object, the behavior of the other can figure there; "if my consciousness has a body, why should other bodies not 'have' consciousnesses?" (PHP 403/351). Merleau-Ponty puts the obstacle to the appearance of the other on the level of intellectual consciousness with the result that by freeing himself from this condition of impossibility, he claims thereby to liberate a condition of possibility. Now, a negation of the negation, that is, the rejection of the intellectualism at whose heart the perception of the other cannot find a place, does not result in the establishment of a position. While Merleau-Ponty aims at describing the body as the place of an originary coexistence with the world and with others, the categories that he calls forth lead him to regress toward a perspective in which the body is grasped as what eventually obscures consciousness and not as what radically contests its insularity. As the use of the negative term *obscurity*—but also the term *pre-personal* consciousness—reveals, just when the terrain of the experience of others is freed up, at the same time it is concealed, since the openness to the other remains a possibility of consciousness and therefore is just as much a negation of the other. Perceptual consciousness, in its opacity, is still a deficient mode of intellectual consciousness rather than a specific dimension of experience. Therefore, it does not manage to transform itself into the clarity of an experience that genuinely gives the other. In the end, the body is still understood as *one's own* body, instead of being conceived in a way that would surmount in it the opposition between the own and the alien, an opposition [56] which retains pure and simple undifferentiation in the form of anonymity as one of its figures. In fact, because he is still dependent on the framework of a philosophy of consciousness, Merleau-Ponty oscillates between the requirement of an immediate negation of this philosophy by means of an impersonal consciousness, by means of a night in which all consciousnesses are one and the same, and the requirement of an immediate affirmation of consciousness, an affirmation which leads nevertheless to the impossibility of the other. This is why his analysis essentially reduces itself to a symmetrical exclusion of both Husserl's and Scheler's positions. He can overcome the intellectual consciousness from which he starts only by having recourse to an undifferentiated psychic current which, through its very excess, leads back to its contrary, namely, the abyss between insular subjectivities. What one has to do then is reconcile the irreconcilable—identity and difference, fusion and separation. But because the experience of the other is from the start subjected to a presupposition, it is missed simultaneously by excess and by lack: by excess in the hypothesis of an anonymity in which all alterity finds itself dissolved; by lack in the maintenance of a consciousness in front of which no alter ego can appear. The experience of the other is situated precisely short of the opposition of identity and difference, fusion and distance; this is why a change of philosophical terrain is required. In truth, the other is other only insofar as it remains on my side; it is accessible only insofar as it remains other. The existence of the other must be considered beyond the opposition of the one and the many, an opposition which proceeds always from the positing of consciousness as *mens sive anima* or—and this amounts to the same thing—as transcendental immanence. To the extent that consciousness is not closed in on itself, intersubjectivity will no longer be understood as the pure multiplicity for which a unity becomes unthinkable; to the extent that intersubjectivity is established short of plurality, the consciousnesses in relation stop short of pure identity and can then be open to others. Merleau-Ponty therefore cannot get beyond Husserl's perspective. He is content to develop and describe intentional transgression; he does not draw from it the consequences for the status of subjectivity. In other words, solipsism is not overcome: corporeal anonymity is finally subordinated to an insular consciousness, into which the alterity of the other is seen to be absorbed. The corporeality upon which the relation to the other is supposed to be founded is still understood as what mediates the relation of consciousness to the world. The moment of [57] mediation is subordinated to the terms that it mediates, and the other is subordinated to the consciousness that, through the intermediary of its body, must confer existence on it. Insofar as it proceeds from an anonymous corporeality, consciousness overcomes itself toward the other, but it is still *consciousness* that overcomes itself in the other, with the result that it is not the *other* that is attained. In reality, only a reflection that manages to grasp the radical unity of consciousness and "its" body is capable of giving an account of the openness to the other.[9]

The hasty assimilation of the problem of the other to that of the world

9. Concerning the problem of solipsism in *Phenomenology of Perception,* see P. Caruso, "Il problema dell'esistenza altrui in Merleau-Ponty," *Aut aut,* no. 66 (1961).

determines the failure of the analysis. Just as in the case of the object, Merleau-Ponty puts intellectual consciousness forward as the obstacle to the experience of the other. Since the lived experiences of consciousness are not "*cogitationes* shut up in their own immanence," since consciousnesses are "beings which are overcome by their world," they "can be overcome by each other" (PHP 405/353). By liberating the transcendence of the world, perceptual consciousness is supposed to liberate the transcendence of the other. However, the transcendence of the other *precisely does not have the same meaning as that of the world;* rather, it is by means of the meaning of the transcendence of the world that the genuine sense of transcendence, as *ontological* transcendence, is revealed. While the world remains, in *Phenomenology of Perception,* a *transcendence in immanence,* the other exists only as a transcendence "to the second power," a transcendence that requires a depth of the world that the description of *Phenomenology of Perception* does not manage to restore. Because the thing is different from me, it is not radically other; it does not need this transcendence in order to be opposed to me. In contrast, by virtue of its identity with me, the other can be other only if it is absolutely other; its transcendence is an exteriority without immanence, without return. As long as the openness to the world is subordinated to a consciousness, it cannot take account of the presence of the other, which is not so much transcendent *for* consciousness as transcendent *to* consciousness. In order to found the experience of the other, it is not enough to denounce intellectual consciousness. This procedure can only be negative and preparatory. If it is still a consciousness which is overcome by the world, it cannot be overcome by the other whose transcendence exceeds that of the world or, rather, gathers up [58] the world's truth as radical transcendence. In order for the appearance of the other to be possible, it is necessary that "consciousness" be its own overcoming, that it accomplish itself in and as this overcoming. The experience of the other indeed leads to a radicalization of the problem of perception. If perception excludes a real transcendence, an in-itself ready to be turned back into the pure object of a ubiquitous consciousness, at the same time it excludes subjective immanence and prohibits the recourse to an egological pole. The plurality of "consciousnesses" makes sense only if the being of consciousness is not pure being for-itself. In *Phenomenology of Perception,* the originary unity of the "for-itself" and the openness to the world is subordinated to their difference, and the inscription of consciousness in the world is subordinated to the presencing of the world: the transcendence of the world is a phenomenal transcendence rather than an ontological one. In other words, consciousness does not possess the weight of reality that would allow it to be actually pluralized. It is too close to itself, and consequently too far from the world in order to be open to others. Since it is not other to itself, it cannot present itself as other, and the presence of the other then becomes incomprehensible. Thus, at the close of this examination of *Phenomenology of Perception,* it looks as though the experience of the other can truly be reconceived only from an ontological perspective. In fact, what is at issue is to conceive a subject that has access to itself only by being other than itself, that possesses itself only by being dispossessed, a belonging of the subject to the world that is just as much a belonging of the world to the subject, an immanence that is accomplished only as an openness to the transcendence of the world. The experience of the other indeed reveals the genuine implications of the experience of a world; and insofar as Merleau-Ponty explicates perception in terms that are still dependent on idealism, he does not manage in *Phenomenology of Perception* to take stock of this experience. Nevertheless, it seems to us that the attention that Merleau-Ponty gives afterward to this experience contributes to the liberation of his ontological perspective: the other is a being who is present only as absent, is given only as its own withdrawal, and, because of that, is not given to a consciousness. The experience of the other is, par excellence, the "presentation of the unpresentable." However, between *Phenomenology of Perception* and this ontological perspective, there is a growing awareness whose stages we must now evoke.

3   The Problem of Expression

1. The Natural World and the Cultural Landscape

[59] *The Structure of Behavior* and *Phenomenology of Perception* can be characterized as archaeological works. What is at issue is to bring to light the figure of the perceived world in contrast to the idealizations that have been sedimented on top of it and that lead to an idealistic philosophy of perception. It is in this way that Merleau-Ponty summarizes his first works in the statement he provided for his candidacy to the Collège de France:

> The perceiving mind is an incarnated mind. I have tried, first of all, to reestablish the roots of the mind in its body and in its world, going against doctrines that treat perception as a simple result of the action of external things on our body as well as against those that insist on the autonomy of consciousness. (CCF 402/3–4)

In the same text, Merleau-Ponty acknowledges that this investigation is open to an objection that he had formulated already in his presentation on the primacy of perception:

> If we consider, above the perceived world, the field of knowledge properly so-called—i.e., the field in which the mind seeks to possess the truth, to define its objects itself, and thus to attain to a universal wisdom, not tied to the particularities of our situation—we must ask: does not the realm of the perceived world take on the form of a mere appearance? Is not pure understanding a new source of knowledge, in comparison with which our perceptual familiarity with the world is only a rough, unformed sketch? (CCF 405/6)

Here, Merleau-Ponty is pointing out not only a lacuna—it is true in fact that the problem of knowledge is hardly considered in *Phenomenology of Perception*—but also a problem that corresponds to this very lacuna, a problem which it raises but of which it is [60] also the symptom. As long as the problem of truth is not considered, as long as the consequences of the description of the perceived world are not established on the plane of intellectual knowledge, in other words, finally, as long as this description of the perceived is not transformed into a philosophy of perception, the return to the perceived can be interpreted as a provisional stage, interesting from the viewpoint of psychological knowledge but destined to be overcome, since it will be defined as a mere appearance when it is considered on the level of the understanding. Being content with criticizing intellectualism instead of questioning it, and instead of making the genesis of the true appear within the perceived, amounts to leaving the terrain free for intellectualism and consequently opening oneself to the accusation of empiricism. The archaeological movement of the return to the originary figure of the perceived will therefore have philosophical value, and the critique of intellectualism to which it corresponds can be genuinely founded, only if a teleology—that is, a truth already at work in the perceived—is clearly seen. Consequently the perceived must be understood not as the other of truth but as its birthplace, its birthplace not only as background but even more as the source of truth. Of course, Merleau-Ponty has never conceived perception in any other way; but despite the accent put on the critique of intellectualism in *Phenomenology of Perception,* it has never been for him a question of conceiving the perceived as an autonomous layer from which it would be necessary to *derive* the order of the true. As we have seen, the analysis of perception made it possible, on the contrary, to make clear a movement of transcendence or meaning at all levels of behavior, from which the truth must proceed as well. The body is not the subject of sensible receptivity but the "trace of an existence": a point of passage of an expressive dynamic rather than a substrate of consciousness. Nevertheless, the fact that Merleau-Ponty insists only weakly on this aspect is significant, as it is this point which requires revision immediately following the publication of *Phenomenology of Perception.* He is not sure that the way in which perception is explicated in this work allows him to take account of expression, or rather he is not sure that the phenomenon of expression is grasped at a level that will allow him to integrate it with the phenomenon of truth, that is, at a level that will allow him to safeguard simultaneously both its specificity and its corporeal roots.

This is what appears when one reads the chapter titled "The Body as Expression and Speech." The analysis of language closes part 1, devoted to the body. The point then is [61] to confirm at the level of rational behavior what had been disclosed on the plane of motility and sexuality, namely, the irreducibility of behavior to the intellectual possession of a noema and therefore the attestation of an original significatory power at the level of the body. Nevertheless, the study of language has a privileged status, since this significatory power of the body unfolds in language the domain of ideality, which could not be identified with the lived world. This is why the analysis of language constitutes a sort of putting to the test of the philosophical fecundity of an archaeology of the perceived. Also, Merleau-Ponty begins by declaring: "In trying to describe the phenomenon of speech and the specific act of meaning [*signification*] we shall have the opportunity to leave behind us, once and for all, the traditional subject–object dichotomy" (PHP 203/174). According to an immutable rhythm, the demonstration consists first in challenging the empiricist and intellectualist interpretations of language, both of which posit the sign and the meaning as separate from each other. In other words, both empiricism and intellectualism are unaware of the fact that the word *has* a sense. One must acknowledge, on the contrary, that the word possesses a gestural or existential meaning from which the constituted meaning proceeds, that "the process of expression brings the meaning into being or makes it effective, and does not merely translate it" (PHP 213/183). Therefore, one must reject the exteriority of the sense vis-à-vis the sign: the sense must be identified with the sign, understood no longer as vocal matter but as a gesture which, like all the others, surpasses itself toward its sense, presents itself as always already significant. However, the assertion according to which this gesture itself, which is speech, traces out its sense appears to pose a problem:

> It seems at first impossible to concede to either words or gestures an immanent meaning, because the gesture is limited to showing a certain relationship between man and the perceptible world, because this world is presented to the spectator by natural perception, and because in this way the intentional object is offered to the spectator at the same time as the gesture itself. Verbal "gesticulation," on the other hand, aims at a mental landscape which is not given to everyone, and which it is its task to communicate. (PHP 217/186)

But culture provides here what nature does not give: there is a common world constituted by sedimented meanings, that is, by earlier acts of expression. Speech aims at this world just as the gesture refers to the sensible world. The [62] response is surprising. Even though what was at issue was to found ideality in transcendence or in corporeal expressivity, that is, to make speech appear as the place in which the opposition between fact and sense is genuinely surpassed, Merleau-Ponty begins by treating as parallel corporeal gesture and speech, the perceived world and the cultural landscape that speech deposits. Still under the control of the nature–culture opposition, the analysis describes the ideality of the "world," but it does not show how this analysis connects with the world itself, with the perceived. This orientation is determined by the earlier analyses. If it is true that the whole purpose of *Phenomenology of Perception* is really to make us see clearly the irreducibility of the body to the objective order, to accentuate its expressive power, it is still the case that this expressive power is first disclosed through the example of natural behaviors, notably motor behaviors, such as they are described in Gestalt psychology. Merleau-Ponty remains dependent, then, on the fixation of the natural dimensions of the body, and the progress vis-à-vis naturalism does not consist so much in surpassing the body toward expression as in surmounting the objective body in favor of the living body. He does not genuinely conceive this body *as* expression, which would suppose that one consider the body *starting from* the phenomenon of expression, that is (as he will do it later), by grasping speech as an originary phenomenon; what he is doing here is apprehending expression starting from the body conceived as the subject of natural behaviors. Reduced to corporeal transcendence implicitly understood as the power to unfold an *Umwelt*, understood as perception, expression cannot be treated as equivalent to the phenomenon of speech. The order of ideality appears therefore as a specific world being superimposed on the perceptual world with no possibility of genuine continuity between the two. This is why, beyond the still vague unity of the notion of expression, the subject–object duality reappears in the displaced form of an opposition between the natural world and the cultural world, despite the fact that the notion of expression was aiming to overcome such duality. The description of the expressive body remains stuck in the presupposition of a naturality that makes the world of culture appear as an autonomous and finally problematic reality. We are dealing with two distinct orders, and expression is not grasped at a level deep enough for the duality to be reabsorbed. The clarification of their connection, then, is essentially realized metaphorically. We can certainly describe speech as "gesture," but we [63] still have to understand how speech can actually be a gesture, that is, how a gesture can become something that speaks. We can certainly speak of mental or cultural "landscape," but we still have to understand how ideality can exist as a world, that is, how the perceived world can produce meanings. It is clear that beyond the metaphors, the phenomenon of speech is not genuinely thought through. Insofar as speech is a gesture, it is reduced to the body as the vector of natural behaviors and then stops being meaningful; insofar as speech is speaking, it arises within an autonomous cultural world and we can no longer then understand how it can still be a power of the body and still be inscribed in the perceived world.

2. The Motivation of the Sign

However, Merleau-Ponty does not stay at this position. The description of the linguistic gesture as relation to a cultural universe can only be provisional. He is indeed going to have to come to the question of the "first speech": "It is true that the problem has been merely shifted one stage further back: how did the available meanings themselves come to be constituted?" (PHP 217/186). Linguistics emphasizes the unmotivated character of the connection between the verbal sign and meaning, a characteristic that corresponds to the mode of significance specific to language. How then can one reconcile the arbitrariness of the sign with the gestural dimension of speech? Dominated by a notion of gesture inherited from the study of natural behaviors, the analysis of language leads necessarily back to the question of its origin, which is itself conceived in an empirical and non-transcendental sense. What is at issue is to understand how a linguistic or conceptual meaning has been able to emerge within a gestural silence. The response can only be inspired by naturalism: the conceptual sense proceeds from an emotive sense that poetry, literally, allows us to hear. Thus,

> If we consider only the conceptual and terminal sense of words, it is
> true that the verbal form—with the exception of endings—appears
> arbitrary. But it would no longer appear so if we took into account
> the emotional content of the word, which we have called above its "ges-
> tural" sense, which is all-important in poetry, for example. It would
> then be found that the [64] words, vowels and phonemes are so many
> ways of "singing" the world, and that their function is to represent
> things not, as the naive onomatopoeic theory had it, by reason of an
> objective resemblance, but because they extract, and literally express,
> their emotional essence. (PHP 218/187)

Merleau-Ponty adds, however, "there is here nothing resembling the famous naturalistic conceptions which equate the artificial sign with the natural one, and try to reduce language to emotional expression" (PHP

219/188). What distinguishes Merleau-Ponty's solution from a naturalistic reduction of language to the expression of emotions? How can one reconcile the transcendence of meaning in the sign, again asserted here, with the inscription of language in the body that reveals the emotional sense? The response consists in rejecting the pertinence of the opposition between natural and conventional, invoking the originary characteristic of expression:

> The artificial sign is not reducible to the natural one, because in man there is no natural sign, and in assimilating language to emotional expressions, we leave untouched its specific quality, if it is true that emotion, viewed as a variation of our being in the world, is contingent in relation to the mechanical resources contained in our body, and shows the same power of giving shape to stimuli and situations which is at its most striking at the level of language. (PHP 220/188)

The assertion that there is no purely natural sign will not allow us to take account of the eminently conventional behavior which defines language. The specificity of language, the new type of transcendence that it represents, is not being conceived in its own terms but, on the contrary, is being diluted as one among all of the non-natural signs. While Merleau-Ponty shows that language is not impossible by saying that every gesture is conventional, he does not show how it is possible. The assertion that emotion is contingent in regard to the objective mechanisms of the body will not allow us to understand that emotion can surpass itself toward linguistic meanings. Merleau-Ponty can claim to reconcile the gestural and the conventional, to identify emotive expression with a meaning and thus claim to found the possibility of language, only by means of an assimilation of the natural to the mechanical. But actually, by asserting that the smallest gesture is already no longer [65] mechanical, he nevertheless does not explain how certain gestures can become genuinely meaningful. The duality of nature and culture is dissolved in the notion of convention, understood as what is not mechanical; but this duality is not truly overcome. Merleau-Ponty invokes "as an ultimate fact this open and indefinite power of signifying" (PHP 226/194), but he does not think it all the way through. Insofar as he attempts to do so, he makes the duality between a cultural world and nature reemerge, and in the end he attempts to derive one from the other in a naturalistic way.

Ultimately, the maintenance of this dualist presupposition affects existence and expression with an ambiguous meaning. Expression is not so much thought as the signifying power of the body as it is thought as *life*. Or, rather, this signifying power is still assigned to a body understood in an objective sense so that the power is mainly conceived as vital power:

> biological existence is synchronized with human existence and is never indifferent to its distinctive rhythm. Nevertheless, we shall now add, "living" (*leben*) is a primary process from which, as a starting point, it becomes possible to "live" (*erleben*) this or that world, and we must eat and breathe before perceiving and awakening to relational living, belonging to colors and lights through sight, to sounds through hearing, to the body of another through sexuality, before arriving at the life of human relations. (PHP 186/159–60)

Thus, in *Phenomenology of Perception,* the signifying body is a living body rather than life being a life of meanings; it is the vector of a life rather than a "body of spirit." The question of language really looks then like a test case for a phenomenology of perception. The rejection of intellectualism calls for a genesis of ideality and, consequently, a philosophy of the expressive body, but the dependence of the analysis of expression on a still naturalistic conception of the body forbids Merleau-Ponty from taking account of ideality in a satisfactory manner. The *Phenomenology of Perception*'s procedure is essentially archaeological, that is, simultaneously descriptive and negative. It is a question not so much of showing how the genesis of ideality takes place in the perceived as of showing that the perceived is not reducible to ideality. This demonstration does not allow us to travel the opposite path [66] in a satisfactory way: expression is finally subordinated to perception, instead of perception being from the start described on the basis of the possibility of expression. The archaeological movement of returning to the figure of the perceived is fulfilled in categories that do not allow us to clarify, symmetrically, the inscription of ideality in the perceived. The ambition, asserted in the introduction to *Phenomenology of Perception,* of a reflection "equally capable of bringing to light the vital inherence and the rational intention" (PHP 65/53) of the phenomenon is not fulfilled. Perception appears as a distinct layer, correlative to a body that is the subject of behavior, and from the start separated from the order of meaning. The objection that Merleau-Ponty raised against himself, and that we evoked at the beginning of this chapter, is not merely rhetorical: the risk is in fact that the order of the perceived looks like a "mere appearance," the pure understanding appears as "a new source of knowledge" in relation to which our perceptual familiarity with the world would be only an "unformed sketch."

This explains the orientation of Merleau-Ponty's research after 1945. The issue then lies in responding to this objection, that is, in deepening the meaning of the perceived in order to make it appear no longer as a circumscribed domain, distinct from the world of ideality, but as the very place of rationality. We have to understand sensibility as the very beginning of knowledge rather than as its other, and show correlatively that there is no knowledge that does not have a sensible inscription. Thus perception makes sense only if "perception is everything because there is not one of our ideas or one of our reflections which does not carry a date, whose objective reality exhausts its formal reality, or which transcends time" (PRI 151/41). In short, it is a question of reconceiving the world according to the double requirement of *archē* and *telos*. It is only at this price—that is, on the condition of apprehending ideality as the very possibility of the perceived—that intellectualism will be able to be definitely constrained. But such a revision requires a reflection that will be oriented toward expression itself and expression in its eminent form, linguistic expression. Merleau-Ponty's explicit purpose then is to show that "knowledge and the communication with the other that it presupposes not only are original formations with respect to the perceptual life but also they preserve and continue our perceptual life [67] even while transforming it. Knowledge and communication sublimate rather than suppress our incarnation" (CCF 405/7). While, as he notes, the study of perception *was able* to teach us *only* a bad ambiguity, "there is a 'good ambiguity' in the phenomenon of expression, that is, a spontaneity which accomplishes what appeared to be impossible when we observed only the separate elements, a spontaneity which gathers together the plurality of monads, the past and the present, nature and culture into one sole cloth" (CCF 409/11). By reconsidering its own problems, the phenomenology of perception fulfills itself as a philosophy of expression. The germ of Merleau-Ponty's ontology lies in this reversal.

4 From Speech to Being

1. The Inscription of Meaning in Signs

[69] When Merleau-Ponty begins drafting *The Prose of the World*, he conceives this work as an extension of earlier investigations of symbolic behavior and knowledge. The purpose of these new investigations is to "definitively fix the philosophical significance of my earlier works" (namely, *Phenomenology of Perception*), but those earlier works still "determine the route and the method of these later studies" (CCF 404/6). In fact, a new type of relation between mind and truth is to be revealed at the level of sensible experience. Now, the drafting of *The Prose of the World* was interrupted. It is clear—we are referring here to Claude Lefort's preface to *The Prose of the World*—that the new investigation which is at first carried out in terms of the categories of *Phenomenology of Perception* brings about, through its very development, the necessity of a recasting. While, in 1952, Merleau-Ponty still emphasized the continuity with his earlier works, the working notes to *The Visible and the Invisible* refer to a radical rupture. Therefore, over the course of the drafting of *The Prose of the World*, Merleau-Ponty discovers the shortcomings of *Phenomenology of Perception*, and a new perspective arises which, confirming itself over the years that follow, will lead to *The Visible and the Invisible*. Conceived initially as an extension and fulfillment of the phenomenology of perception, the philosophy of expression actually frees up the space of an ontology. Understood completely, the phenomenon of expression upsets the duality that still imprisons Merleau-Ponty and reveals the limits of a philosophy of consciousness. The sense of the ontology then will lie in founding the phenomenon of expression so that it will be gradually [70] uncovered during this transitional period. This period is problematic for any interpreter of Merleau-Ponty. We cannot restore it in all of its detail. To do so would be to anticipate an ontology in the strict sense of the word, insofar as a number of analyses announce *The Visible and the Invisible*, even if these analysis find their genuine foundation only in this final work. But we cannot pass over this period in silence, since the necessity and significance of

the ontology will appear only if we understand the phenomenon of expression in its originality.

The question of language dominates the period that immediately follows *Phenomenology of Perception*. It is no longer a question of grasping language as a form of corporeal expressivity, or, in short, as a higher behavior. That would lead, as we have seen, to founding it in an obscure way on an emotional meaning. Rather, what is at issue is to locate ourselves at the very heart of the expressive operation without the prejudice of the categories by means of which we would have to describe it. By grasping the very event of expression instead of rooting it in a body whose status is predetermined, we will have the opportunity to deepen the meaning of the body. The approach here is parallel to the one adopted in *The Structure of Behavior*. An immediate reflection would run the risk of conceiving language in intellectualist terms, just as a direct approach to perception laid itself open to finding there nothing but the *cogito* of idealism. The risk is particularly acute at the level of language because the distinguishing feature of speech is the dissimulation of its signifying operation, a dissimulation that occurs by means of the signifying operation itself. The signifying operation occurs in order to be forgotten as an expressive act, in favor of the meaning that it institutes; the roles of expression and the expressed naturally reverse themselves, with the result that the expression looks like a set of signs adapted in a univocal way to meanings obtained from another source. What we first have to do therefore is rely on an objective description of language, as linguistics does; this detour through linguistics will lead us back to an authentic experience of expression, an experience freed from its intellectualist implications. This would take place just as the recourse to Gestalt psychology earlier had liberated the genuine status of perceptual experience by imposing the return to a consciousness which was not yet a kind of knowledge. Vis-à-vis the subject of expression, linguistics plays the role that Gestalt psychology played in regard to the subject of behavior. And just as there was no opposition between the objective knowledge of behavior and perceptual experience, so the [71] science of language is led, by means of it own movement, to overcome the scission between language conceived as an object and the experience of speech, as it could be collected together in a different way on the plane of literary creation.

In the study of language, we are about as close as possible to the problem of ideality, and consequently as close as possible to idealism. Because speech forgets itself as an operation by virtue of its very operation, because its work of signification leads to a dissimulation of the layer of primordial expression from which it proceeds, the experience of language itself leads to idealism and in any case reinforces idealism in its certainty of reaching preexisting meanings in themselves. That the world can be said means that its being is that of ideality and that the silence of perception is only the obscure underside of a meaning that is clear in itself. The return to speaking speech, to primordial expression, will allow us therefore not only to found a critique of idealism, a critique that determines simultaneously the limit and possibility of idealism, but also to reconceive the authentic figure of the world as that from which primordial expression proceeds, as what this expression simultaneously reveals and lacks. The classical conception of language consists in its reconstruction according to the univocal correspondence between sign and meaning. The relation of sign to sense is thus simultaneously immanence and transcendence:

> People usually think that sense transcends signs in principle, just as thought would transcend sonorous or visual indexes, and they think that it is immanent in signs in the sense that each one of them, having *its* sense once and for all, could not conceivably slip any opacity between itself and us, or even give us food for thought. Signs would have only one role, that of monition; they warn the hearer that he has to consider such and such of *his* thoughts. (S 53/42)

This description raises a problem, the very one that arises when we attempt to describe the perceived object in terms of a relation between form and matter. If the sign were truly transparent to the meaning, if it exhausted itself in its signifying function, then the efficacy of speech would be dissolved. If saying amounted to putting a word under each thought, "nothing would ever be said. We would not have the feeling of living in the language and we would remain silent, because the sign would be immediately obliterated by its own sense and because thought would never encounter anything but thought" (S 55/44). For the notion of the verbal sign [72] to preserve a sense, it is necessary to acknowledge that there is a signifying power of the sign that is its very work; consequently, the sign does not exhaust itself in the exhibition of a meaning. Speech preserves its specificity only if its relation to the meaning is not defined by possession, by transparency. Therefore we must return to the originary operation by which the meaning continues to be something intended by the sign, that is, as something still veiled or concealed within it. Insofar as the verbal matter is meaningful, it cannot be described on the basis of the form, namely, the form of the meaning that it helps bring into existence. The problem here is indeed comparable to the one that, in Merleau-Ponty's eyes, is present in Husserl's analysis of intentionality. What suitable reality can a *hylē* have, in fact, when it is described as the simple substrate of an apprehension which animates it and confers on it the function of figuration of the noema? Must we not reconceive this apprehension on the level of the very life of the *hylē,* which would amount to putting into question the definition of the noema as a unity of sense? Likewise, what can the notion of a sign mean if it is not the case that the sense proceeds from the sign's own life?

Described on the basis of the meaning, the sign looks like a discrete entity whose identity is based on the meaning that it exhibits. Conversely, as soon as the meaning is understood as the work of the sign, the latter can no longer be conceived as a positive entity—which was the only way the meaning had allowed it to be conceived. The sign is constituted as such in the very movement of signifying. Since the meaning is present to the sign only as its horizon, the sign is never completely determinate as a sign. The signifying operation is situated short of the opposition between meaning and sign; it is prior to their distinction, which is also their union. The signifying operation thus takes place at a level where the separation between the signs, on the one hand, and the meanings, on the other, has not yet been realized. Linguistics recognizes this when it stresses the *diacritical* character of the sign, a character to which Merleau-Ponty always returns. In a system of language, there are only differences, which are not based on positive terms, and in a parallel way both the signs and the meanings arise from these differences. The sense is given originarily in the form of oppositive principles, modes of discrimination; and by means of the ways in which these are put to work, signs are constituted as bearers of sense, that is, as discrete and definite beings. The operative sense must be defined as a configuration, [73] as a "lateral" relation among the signs. The sign signifies not as a mark of a sense, but insofar as it is traversed by a principle of variation that never itself appears; moreover, the signs cannot be abolished in favor of this principle, since it draws its identity from their difference. The operative sense "is not so much designated by words as it is implied by their edifice" (S 103/83); it can be described as this dimension or this theme that does not subsist outside of the variants in which it is given and thus resides somehow *between* the variants as the secret principle of their variation. The signs are therefore inhabited by a "principle of equivalence," because of which they are not pure matter. But this dimension subsists only as its own absence. It is retained in the thickness of signs in such a way that the transcendence of the sign toward the sense never abolishes the sign's materiality, never reaches a transparent meaning. The property language seems to possess of extracting the sense from the signs, of isolating it in a pure state, is in reality only "the simple presumption of embodying the sense in several formulas in which it remains the same" (PM 124/88). This "same" merges with the series of "others" through which it appears, that is, it appears with the very movement of differentiation. From the very moment when we reconceive it at the level of living speech, we discover that the sense of sense lies in never being present in person, of being implicated in this speech as a horizon which animates it, attracting it magnetically and soliciting therefore an indefinite appropriation: "Since the sign makes sense only insofar as it is profiled against other signs, its sense is entirely involved in language. Speech always comes into play against a background of speech; it is always only a fold in the immense fabric of language" (S 53/42).

This description should be generalized. However, at this stage of his reflection, Merleau-Ponty still apprehends language on the basis of categories at work in the analysis of perception. Perceptual sense informs linguistic sense. Also, he describes the movement of meaning by comparison with the profiles of things:

> Even though only *Abschattungen* of the meaning are given thematically, the fact is that once a certain point in discourse has been passed the *Abschattungen,* caught up in the movement of discourse outside of which they are nothing, suddenly contract into a single meaning. [74] And then we feel that *something has been said*—just as we perceive a thing once a minimum of sensory messages has been exceeded, even though the explanation of the thing extends as a matter of principle to infinity. (S 114/91)

Linguistic meaning and the thing are conceived in conformity with the solution that Husserl proposes in *Ideas I,* as "Ideas in the Kantian sense," as poles of expressive acts or of convergent sensations that animate the discourse or the perception without being actually given on their own. But if the dualities of *Phenomenology of Perception* still dominate the analysis, the results of linguistics, as Merleau-Ponty relates them, contain the seeds of the mutation of the modalities according to which perception is considered. The work of speech reveals a dimension prior to the opposition of sign and meaning, a dimension that contests the legitimacy of the analysis in terms of profiles and Idea. The "*Abschattungen*" of the meaning are not in reality thematically given and, insofar as this is the case, we cannot confer on sense the least positivity, the least unity, not even the unity of the Kantian Idea which is suited to an infinite process. If signs are truly diacritical, sense is simultaneously closer and farther from them: closer because the sense is always already implicated in them, because the signs are always caught in the element of sense; farther because *to this extent* the sense can no longer be distinguished from the signs and cannot therefore be determined as an infinite pole. The signs always already transcend themselves toward a sense which is not then different from them. This nevertheless does not mean that the being of the sign is exhausted in the sense; on the contrary, the plentitude of the sense requires that no sign exhaust it. Sense is non-present in principle, for it is synonymous with the quasi-materiality of the sign. The quasi-identity of sign and sense is just as much absolute distance, and meaning is pushed back toward an infinity that accepts no principle of totalization. Thus the being of language reveals a mode of infinity that does not allow the closure of the Kantian Idea and calls for the overcoming of the opposition between matter and form. The discovery of the infinite historicity of sense, of an open, non-totalizable infinity, will ultimately determine a thought of the world as pure transcendence, escaping from the category of sense as distinct unity of the multiple. We have to note, however, that this reversal can be seen from *The Prose of the World* on. In fact, the rhythm of this text is established by the [75] footnotes, a number of which represent an advance in relation to the course of the analysis. It seems that as he was drafting it, Merleau-Ponty was discovering the implications of an investigation that remained consciously held within the movement inaugurated by *Phenomenology of Perception*. At the end of the second part, for example, we find a note in which the analysis of language is put to good use on the plane of perception, in terms that contrast with contemporaneous texts, and in which all of *The Visible and the Invisible* is already present:

> Style as preconceptual generality—generality of the "axis" which is pre-objective and creates the *reality* of the world: the thing is there where I touch it; it is not a non-perspectival display of *Abschattungen;* it escapes *Erlebnisanalyse* . . . because there is a transtemporality which is not that of the *ideal* but that of the deepest wound, incurable. This nonconsti-

tuted rationality of the thing-axis . . . is possible only if the thing is nonfrontal, ob-ject, but what bites into me, and what I bite into through my body; if the thing is, itself too, given through an indirect grasp, lateral . . . (PM 63n/44–45n)

This description of the operative sense allows us to end up at an essential opacity of language. Concealed within the signs as the dimension of their active differentiation, as the principle of equivalence immanent to their variation, the sense always remains imminent, and thought is "haunted" by sense rather than exhibiting it. The intention proper to speech must be defined as a "qualified nothingness," a "determinate emptiness," and meaning is really only the determination *of* this emptiness, whose vacuity is sustained by the thickness of signs. Expression is such that, in principle, it cannot be complete; a thought possessed would thereby cease to be thought. Thought must essentially remain like "a tacking thread in the fabric of words" (VI 159/119). In reality, if we sought to transcend the signs toward a pure thought, we would fall back down into the verbal material. Meaning is given on the mode of a lack—not a lack such that meaning would still be a positive entity whose presence would need to be restored, but a lack such that its own mode of being consists in escaping from the very order of presence. Insofar as language can be compared to painting, beyond the illusion of a full meaning, sense is grasped in it as an insurmountable silence. If meaning is attached to its original state in speech, it [76] is not yet strictly "linguistic"; it merges with the "mute radiance of painting" (S 97/78). Expression reveals therefore a subject that possesses sense only insofar as the subject is dispossessed by it, a subject that reaches itself in speech only by escaping just as much from itself in speech. Now through the presence of sense, the self-presence by which consciousness is defined finds itself put into question. If meaning must be conceived as what magnetically attracts expression, as the dimension of variation and calling forth which inhabits expression but which expression does not possess, it seems that expression can no longer be sustained by a consciousness. Since meaning comes about within expression only in a deferred way, must we not then conceive the subject as what is won over and fulfilled in expression itself, rather than as the bearer of unities of sense? By rooting sense in expression, by making this mediation appear as primordial, Merleau-Ponty overcomes the presupposition of a confrontation of subject and sense, a confrontation from which both would draw their identity.

2. Synchrony and Diachrony

This is what the second part of the analysis confirms, which places us no longer at the level of the singular act of expression but at the level of the relation between language as a system [*langue*] and speech [*parole*]. Linguistics begins with the decision to treat language as an object, the project of explaining the facts of language by means of a set of laws. The present state of a system of language, the actual sense of words, would then be only the results of an external history, synchrony only a slice of diachrony. Now, "if we were enclosed in the irreconcilable meanings that words can acquire historically, we would not even have the idea of speaking; the will for expression would collapse" (PM 32/22). Linguistics cannot in reality economize on the viewpoint of the subject who, at each moment, speaks this language and overcomes in fact the accidents that history has incorporated into it. The subjective viewpoint envelops the objective viewpoint; synchrony envelops diachrony. The very possibility of speech, the fact that the subject lives his language as a coherent system immediately coordinated to expressive intentions, forbids us [77] from treating it as an object subjected to an external necessity. Historical accidents have perpetuity and can be integrated into a language only insofar as they are appropriated by a unique will for expression. If at each moment language manifests an internal logic, if one sole expressive power surmounts the disorder of facts that history bequeaths, then it is necessary to conclude that this logic also transcends the present, that it sketches a unity of language that is beyond each phase of synchrony: "if language is a system when it is considered according to a transversal slice, it must be a system in its development too" (S 108/86). By taking up and overcoming the historical past in the present expression, the speaking subject articulates this present into a future so that past, present, and future appear as moments of a unity, and history appears as the visible trace of a power that it does not cancel. Therefore, according to Merleau-Ponty, in addition to a linguistics of language which grasps it as a chaos of events, Saussure inaugurates a linguistics of speech which demonstrates a unity in each period, a totality without which communication and the linguistic community would be altogether impossible. The task of mediating between these two senses of linguistics will fall to Saussure's successors; thus, by means of the notion of "sublinguistic schema," Guillaume, for example, recovers in each language a law of equilibrium, a fundamental project, which orients and dominates the diachrony but without canceling it. The whole question then concerns this mode of unity, this cloth that reconnects the acts of speech and the speaking subjects, this signifying intention that transcends the present and appropriates the past simultaneously as a means and as a declaration of a future. Now, just as the analysis of behavior could have the function of revealing a *cogito* that would be sufficiently apparent from "a moment of reflection," the coherence and unity freed up by this linguistics of speech could not be confused with a transcendent reason. This unity is not distinct from its modes of advent, from acts of appropriation that it nevertheless animates and orients, and thus there is indeed a fundamental opacity within expression. What traverses and articulates the acts of speech cannot be conceived outside of exteriority, outside of the advent within which it commences. In fact, if synchrony envelops diachrony without absorbing it, one has to say as well that diachrony envelops synchrony from the perspective of another relation. [78] If "language allows random elements when it is considered according to a longitudinal slice, the system of synchrony must at every moment allow fissures where brute events can insert themselves" (S 108/86). The exteriority found within the acts of speech resonates within the very heart of each word spoken; as the analysis of the act of expression showed on another plane, speech must allow in its heart a weakness, an opacity, which exposes it to facticity. The interiority that speech reveals is not therefore that of the concept; if the system transcends the brute event, it is not however clearly possessed and spread out before a constituting consciousness. The facts have an effect and perpetuity only if they are appropriated by an intention to signify. Nevertheless, this intention is itself carried by the fact; it has no reality outside of the contingencies that it transforms into advents. Language looks therefore like an "equilibrium in movement" such that the equilibrium is realized only in and as the movement itself:

> Language is completely accidental and completely rational, because there is no expressive system that follows a plan or does not have its origin in some particular accident. Likewise, no accident becomes a linguistic instrument unless language breathes into it the value of a new mode of speech, by treating it as an example of a "rule" that in the future will apply to a whole sector of signs. (PM 50/35)

There is no question of establishing a dialectical relation between the two viewpoints, diachrony and synchrony, whose validity would be assumed from the start. The careful study of expression allows us to see the actual overcoming of the two viewpoints and opens up a plane where they become inoperative. Just as the analyses of Vendryes show, for example, language is subject to the two contrary requirements of expressivity and communication. In order to be understood, a way of speaking must be familiar—but not to the point of becoming indistinct; it must at the same time stand out against what is customary. The will for expression therefore does not come into contact with facts in order to turn them into its instrument; a necessity of facticity is at its heart, and its equilibrium calls for a disequilibrium. Expression does not use history: it makes itself history. As Merleau-Ponty says clearly, "The progress of psychology and linguistics consists precisely in that by revealing the *speaking subject* and speech in the present, they manage to ignore [79] the alternatives of the existing and the possible, of the constituted and the constituting, of facts and the conditions of possibility, of contingency and reason, of science and philosophy" (PM 54/37–38).

This analysis confirms and deepens that of the expressive act itself. The opacity of sense does not correspond to a failure, that is, to an absence of an ideally accessible pole; it is inherent within the very work of expression. The signifying intention that animates the acts of expression, synchronically and diachronically, does not subsist alongside the acts in which it is fulfilled. While each present act bears and reactivates the past by opening it to the future, it is true nevertheless that the past and future subsist only as the work that bears them. The coexistence of acts of expression is not founded on a transcendence of sense; the latter, strictly speaking, exists only as a task, the necessity that connects together all of the attempts. To recognize that the past and future envelop the present, that the present is traversed by a transcendent intention of unity, does not amount to locating this intention in the eternal, because it sustains itself only by being reactivated in each present. Meaning subsists only in the form of this necessity and call that traverse and animate the acts and consequently are not different from them. The intention gives life to the acts that intend it only because these acts breathe their life into it. Then, apprehended by means of the expressive sense, reason is not given as something hanging over history but as what merges with historicity itself; it is "reason in contingency." The unity of sense is identified with the difference of expressions; its eternity is an "existential eternity," which means—to use a word that Merleau-Ponty openly borrows from Husserl—that the mode of being of sense is that of *Stiftung*, of foundation. Foundation is the necessity of a future which fulfills itself only insofar as that future appropriates the foundation and in turn gives it meaning; this, however, does not mean that it closes it and achieves it but that it reactivates the foundation as a necessity. Incontestably, the study of expression reveals to Merleau-Ponty the dimension of historicity. Unambiguously, he recognizes it:

> We would undoubtedly recover the true sense of history if we acquired the habit of modeling it on the example of the arts and language. The close connection between each expression and every other within a single order instituted by the first act of expression effects the junction of the individual and the universal. [80] Expression—language, for example—is what most belongs to us as individuals, for while addressing itself to others, it simultaneously acquires a universal value. (PM 120/85)

Therefore, language allows us to think the entire order of culture as the order of the "advent."

During the years that follow the drafting of *The Prose of the World*, Merleau-Ponty devotes himself to clarifying the dimension of expression at all levels of culture. Throughout these levels, sense reveals itself in the form of a prepossession which precedes and orients only insofar as it is reactivated, in the form of a past which survives only by being thrown forward toward a future. Sense subsists only as its own imminence, as a horizon rather than as reason. As an infinite task, it is synonymous with transcendental or "fundamental historicity."

3. The Soil of Expression

These conclusions really call for a recasting of the categories used in *Phenomenology of Perception*. In that work, Merleau-Ponty's way of proceeding was in the end *progressive*; once the return to the body and to being-in-the-world was carried out, it was a matter of reconceiving the different levels of expression as higher modalities of being-in-the-world. Now this approach, as we have seen, could not be accomplished in a satisfactory way, for the body was still considered as an implicit duality between consciousness and object, with the result that being-in-the-world could not measure up to the dimension of expressivity—in particular, to its linguistic dimension. Therefore, there was still a tension between perception and expression. In contrast, the philosophy of expression brings forth a *regressive* approach that, starting from culture and language, interrogates their originary soil. The account of the body and the world must then be carried out on the basis of the phenomenon of expression, as what feeds their movement of transcendence. This is the path on which *The Prose of the World* strikes out. We can see its working sketch in the succession of courses offered by Merleau-Ponty at the Collège de France. After the series of presentations on speech and expression, there is a reflection on history, followed by the long course devoted to nature. Merleau-Ponty's ontology is born from this regressive movement: the point is to find some way of understanding the nature in which this culture, whose meaning [81] comes to be clarified, is rooted. While in his first period the analysis of language is carried out according to a parallel with perception, the development of the analysis and the discovery of historicity which emerges from it leads Merleau-Ponty, little by little, to question the categories which formerly presided over the description of the perceived. It is in this movement, by which expression comes to inform perception, that ontological interrogation is constituted.

Rather than trying to understand the work of expression, intellectualism assumes that it is finished. Its naiveté in regard to language, its unwarranted confidence in speech, leads it to ignore the fact of the world, to reduce it to transparent significations. In contrast, the discovery of expression, of the absence of closure, and of the infinity of sense implies the unveiling of the world in its authentic and originary figure. In *Phenomenology of Perception,* the negative critique of intellectualism, that is, the *immediate* return to the world, forbids Merleau-Ponty from putting this unveiling to work. On the contrary, by returning to the world from the phenomenon of expression, by grasping the very birth of sense instead of referring it straightaway to a perceptual ground, Merleau-Ponty gains access to the genuine figure of the world as soil or source of expression. Then, to the infinity of the *telos* brought to light in the expressive act, there *corresponds the infinity of an* archē. Insofar as it is the soil of the expressive movement, the world will have this infinite depth inherent in the fact that sense is never completely fulfilled. Because no expression erases itself in the face of a pure sense, because expression cannot claim to be nailed down in a full meaning, the world will be given only as withdrawal, as this "presence" which, through its obscurity, gives birth to expression without ever being absorbed into the expressed. Considered on the basis of expression, the world can no longer be defined through presence but as that whose being consists in exceeding every presentation. When it becomes the philosophy of expression, the phenomenology of perception is fulfilled as ontology. The discovery of an originary, operative sense that stops short of signification is ipso facto the discovery of a world which is before every presentation. The world is the infinite *archē* which corresponds to the infinite historicity expressing it. The universal is found no longer on the side of sense but on the side of the world; it is what feeds every expression while always missing from what reveals it. The world is what still *has to be* said within what expresses it and therefore is still withdrawn from what says it. While the approach to the world through the presupposition of the possibility of a presentation [82] determined a problematic of perception, the discovery of expression as infinite historicity entails on the contrary an approach to the world as that whose being exceeds all presence. To consider sense on the basis of expression is to consider the world on the basis of Being. Thus, Merleau-Ponty notes, the world is really what is "more than all painting, than all speech, than every 'attitude,' and which, apprehended by philosophy in its universality, appears as containing everything that will ever be said, and yet leaving us to create it" (VI 224/170).

No mistake, however, must be made about the meaning of this transcendence: in no way can it correspond to a return to some inaccessible ground, to some in-itself. If the world as infinite *archē* corresponds to the unfulfillment of the saying, it is still the case that it can be expressed; even if it is forever inaccessible as a pure signification, it is not of another order. It is precisely the place where the saying is rooted in its double dimension of conquest and incompleteness. Its withdrawal is not that of an in-itself, but its presence in the expression is not that of a for-itself. Insofar as it can be expressed, the world belongs to the order of sense; but insofar as the meaning is born in the expression only as its own imminence, this sense remains a captive of this world, and the world is in some way the very captivity of sense. Thus, to situate the world in the dimension of expression is not to dissolve it into ideality but to recognize, on the contrary, its transcendence. Because it is always already expression, the world is never fully expressed. One must say, along with Merleau-Ponty, that Being is "*what requires creation of us* for us to experience it" (VI 251/197); we can say this, however, only on the condition of adding that we experience Being only as what always transcends us. More than a rupture vis-à-vis the philosophy of expression, the ontology indeed seems to take into consideration what a philosophy of expression imposes when it is thoroughly understood. A philosophy of expression leads us to overcome the opposition of the given and meaning in favor of a unique teleology, in which the notion of the world designates only the moment of unfulfillment, the lack of every active *telos*.

This is why the field of language, which in the first period constituted only a privileged place for the study of expression, tends to be generalized. In fact, once the operant sense [83] is recognized under the constituted sense, the distinction between language in the strict sense and the layer from which it proceeds can no longer be made; the world is already in language, or rather is already language, primordial expression. It is this originary source that requires expression yet draws it back into its opacity. The silence of the world is already speech because language, even if it is fulfilled, is still silence. This is what causes the sliding of sense characteristic of this transitional period: going from language to the sense of a specific activity leads to language conceived as fundamental historicity, as *logos*. Language and perception, the difference between which dominated *Phenomenology of Perception*, appear only as two moments of one, more fundamental reality; they are distinguished only as a *logos* uttered from a "*logos* of the aesthetic world." Thus,

> the philosopher knows better than anyone that what is lived is lived-spoken, that, born at this depth, language is not a mask over Being, but—if one knows how to grasp it with all its roots and its foliation—the most valuable witness to Being, that it does not interrupt an immediation that would be perfect without it, that the vision itself, the thought itself, are, as has been said, "structured as a language," are *articulation* before the letter, apparition of something where there was nothing or something else. (VI 167/126)

What follows from this is that the problem of the origin of language, which presupposed an identification between language and the order of ideality, no longer makes any sense: grasped "with all its roots," language *is* the origin. The study of expression has therefore allowed us to situate the being of the world beyond the opposition of facticity and essentiality. If, as *archē* of an expressive teleology, the world could not be of the order of fact, nevertheless by virtue of the infinity of this *telos* neither can it belong to the domain of essence. *The Visible and the Invisible* will begin with the explicit critique of this opposition.

Along with the notion of the world, that of consciousness comes to be transformed. In fact, the notion of consciousness responds to the determination of sense as closure, positivity. Consciousness cannot be conceived otherwise than as the bringing to presence of *that of which* it is conscious. This is why the recourse to the notion of consciousness in *Phenomenology of Perception,* and then to the form–matter distinction, kept us from reaching the terrain of the world and led us to reconceive it always already as the object of a presentation, as a nature. The attention [84] paid to expression entails the explosion of the framework of a philosophy of consciousness and of the poles, empirical and transcendental, between which it was doomed to oscillate. Expression gives us access to the very place of their articulation and designates finally the transcendental power of the empirical as well as the efficacy of the empirical as the withdrawal or restraint of the transcendental. Being of the order of advent, expression is only the passage, never fully fulfilled, from the individual to the universal, the transcendental becoming of the empirical. Subjectivity thus is open and traversed by the expressive teleology: subjectivity no longer bears teleology; subjectivity is born in teleology. Aside from a number of indications of this mutation found over the course of articles that appear during this period, we have at our disposal one text in which the necessity of this mutation is asserted: the course taught at the Collège de France titled "Institution in Personal and Public History." Here Merleau-Ponty puts forward the problems that a philosophy of consciousness encounters. In particular, such a philosophy cannot account for the possibility of the other and coexistence. In such a philosophy, consciousness is assimilated to *constituting* consciousness. Merleau-Ponty recognizes what he did not fully take into account in *Phenomenology of Perception:* a philosophy of consciousness is always a philosophy of constitution—that is, in the end, an idealistic philosophy.

> For consciousness there are only the objects that it has itself constituted. Even if it is granted that certain of the objects are "never completely" so (Husserl), they are at each moment the exact reflection of the activity and faculties of consciousness. There is nothing in the object capable of throwing consciousness back toward other perspectives. There is no exchange, no interaction between consciousness and the object. (RC 59/107)

Therefore, we must substitute the notion of the *instituting* subject for that of the constituting subject:

> Thus what we understand by the concept of institution are those events in experience which endow it with durable dimensions, in relation to which a whole series of other experiences will acquire sense, will form

an intelligible series or a history—or again those events which sediment in me a sense, not just as survivals or residues, but as the invitation to a sequel, the requirement of a future. (RC 61/108–109)

Understood in this way as instituting, the subject is destined to be reconceived in an ontological perspective, that is, as instituted by its very institution. It will be the other name of the world understood as originary institution. As soon as [85] sense is understood as its own concealment in and as the world, the world can no longer be revealed as a bringing to presence, as being offered to a subject. As soon as it is the lack rather than the possession of ideality, the intention of the world in expression is just as much the birth of expression within the world, that is, the world's coming to itself and its withdrawal. It is clear that a teleology must be substituted for the confrontation of intellectual possession. The perspective of an infinite *subjectivation* takes the lead over the positing of a subject. Being and the subject have therefore parallel destinies. By "adventing" to sense in expression, the world fulfills itself as subject so that, although always already "subjective," it nonetheless is never *for* a subjectivity. In all strictness, "it is not we who perceive, it is the thing that perceives itself yonder—it is not we who speak, it is truth that speaks itself at the depths of speech" (VI 239/185). Overall, the project of bringing experience to the pure expression of its own sense, which Merleau-Ponty constantly reaffirms, finds its scope and fulfillment only with the ontological enterprise. This expression is conceivable only if it is the expression *of* the world itself, in the sense that expression proceeds from the world, in the sense that the world is its own expression. In other words, this expression is conceivable only if, consequently, we are not the subjects but the points of passage of this teleology.

Now, insofar as the subject is set aside in favor of teleology, the body loses its naturalistic, behavioral connotations. As soon as the subject gives up its constituting function, the body is stripped clean of its constituted dimension. In defining subjectivity by means of institution, Merleau-Ponty liberates the body from what stops it just short of expression, so that it can finally be thought as the very place of the teleology. This movement can be seen in "Indirect Language and the Voices of Silence." After having described at length the mute expression of painting, Merleau-Ponty is forced to go "to the other end of the problem": how does pictural expression, which announces that of language, root itself in the body? Can we be content with the body defined as "life" and the perceived as *Umwelt*? In reality, if the gestures of the painter are possible, this is first because "natural" gestures "already stylize." If the world can be painted, this is because a scattered sense that contains already all of what painting and language will unfold on their own account is gathered into it. Thus,

> All perception, all action which presupposes it, and in short, every human use of the body is already *primordial expression*. Not that derivative labor [86] which substitutes for what is expressed signs which are given elsewhere with their sense and rule of usage, but the primary operation which first constitutes signs as signs, makes that which is expressed dwell in them through the eloquence of their arrangement and configuration alone, imparts a sense in that which did not have one, and thus—far from exhausting itself in the instant at which it occurs—inaugurates an order and founds an institution or a tradition. (S 84/67)

The body alone brings to this order the destiny of expression, from the primordial layer up to its most sophisticated forms. And Merleau-Ponty notes in a striking way in *The Prose of the World* that "it is through our body that we have the first experience of the impalpable body of history prior to all initiation into art" (PM 117/83). Obviously, here the body is considered outside of any naturalistic dimension. The equivocations of *Phenomenology of Perception* have been removed; by liberating us from the subject–object duality, the philosophy of expression allows us to open up a notion of the body adequate to what had been glimpsed in *Phenomenology of Perception*. In a sense, ontology will merge with the explication of the body as primordial expression, as the body of history, that is, as *flesh*.

All the axes of Merleau-Ponty's ontology appear to be really the fulfillment of a consistent philosophy of expression, which is itself directed by the will to surmount the equivocations of the first works. By being generalized, in order to no longer run the risk of being interpreted as a mere appearance or as a "psychological anecdote," the description of the perceived is overcome by the philosophy of expression, and the philosophy of expression, grasped in all of its implications, is fulfilled in an ontological enterprise. Nevertheless, we still have to figure out the right path by which ontology succeeds in being constituted. Since the world is the very ground of the expressive teleology, that Being "that requires creation of us for us to experience it," the being of experience, cannot be apprehended outside of an expression that fulfills it. In fact, it is not a matter of returning to a veiled origin, of coinciding with a virginal world; the "brute" or "wild" world is in no way the site of the irrational. The role of reflection lies, on the contrary, in determining this impossibility of a coincidence that is correlative with the absence of an assignable origin: "the originary breaks up, and philosophy must accompany this break-up, [87] this non-coincidence, this differentiation" (VI 165/124). Expression is not a veil draped over the world but, insofar as it is the very becoming of the world, what can open us to it. Its creation is an unveiling; the divergence that it establishes is just as much coincidence. Therefore what is at issue for philosophy is to find a way of speaking that reaches the world again as mute expression, that grasps the birth of expression in its heart, or rather, that initiates us to the world as the birthplace of expression; rooted in the silence of the world, this speech will present itself as the speech of the things themselves. Of course, this speech can only be that of philosophy, but that does not stop it from feeding on other ways of speaking that put it on the path of the silence that it seeks. This is the central role of the reflection on painting. In "Indirect Language and the Voices of Silence," Merleau-Ponty is led to a reflection on painting by the very analysis of linguistic expression: "If we want to understand language as an originating operation, we must pretend to have never spoken, submit language to a reduction without which it would once more escape us by referring us to what it signifies for us, *look* at it as deaf people look at those who are speaking, compare the art of language to other arts of expression, and try to see it as one of these mute arts" (S 58/46). By means of painting, we will be able to open up the originary signifying of language, its inscription in the world before the world transmutes this signifying into ideality. As the mute expression of our contact with the world, painting lets us see the originary presence of the world; painting leads the world back to the silence of its first signifying. It truly plays the role of a reduction, in the phenomenological sense of the word; by going in the opposite direction of language, the opposite direction of the risk of idealization and of interiorization that language presents, painting makes a primordial layer appear, the place of a signifying which is not yet signification or meaning. Therefore, instead of covering over the world again, it frees it from sediments deposited by the objectifying activity of language: "when a stroke of the brush replaces a reorganization of appearances (in principle complete) which introduces us to wool or flesh, what replaces the object is not the subject—it is the allusive logic of the perceived world" (S 71/57). With painting, a genuine reduction can be carried out, no longer in the idealist sense of a return to transcendental subjectivity but in the ontological sense of an unveiling [88] of the primordial world. Ontology is a testimony to the will to gain access to an experience that is immediately philosophical, but painting alone can prepare the way of this immediacy. Philosophy fulfills itself as the speech of the world itself only by complying with painting as silent speech. "Indirect Language and the Voices of Silence" and especially "Eye and Mind" help free up the space of ontology, and a number of the categories at work in *The Visible and the Invisible* are borrowed from the description of pictorial expression.

The path that Merleau-Ponty follows from *The Structure of Behavior* to *The Visible and the Invisible* can thus be described according to the rhythm of a triple reference. Each stage of his thought corresponds to the consideration of an original field; the characteristics and limits of each phase of his reflection determine the choice of this domain just as they are determined by it. The psychology of behavior indeed allows the reduction of idealism, but it does this only in favor of what we have marked off as a form of naturalism; the analysis of the body is then traversed by the subject–object duality, and since it is essentially reconceived as living being-in-the-world, the body is thrown back onto the side of nature. Linguistics allows the liberation of the field of expression and, beyond the space of language, that of fundamental historicity; through a regressive movement, the subject–object duality is overcome in favor of a corporeality that is synonymous with teleology. However, this movement does not truly fulfill itself as long as Merleau-Ponty remains on the plane of a reflection concerning linguistics; during this period, which immediately follows *Phenomenology of Perception,* language is considered as an analogue of perceptual life rather than as transforming its meaning. It is only when the thought of expression turns itself back toward the operative sense at work in language, a sense that "precedes" its strictly linguistic expression—when the thought of expression turns into a phenomenology of painting—that it reaches the point where it can understand the insertion of expression into the world and, consequently, grasp the being of the world as the veiling of sense, as wild *logos.*

5 Phenomenology and Ontology

1. Phenomenology and the Human Sciences

[89] The attention that Merleau-Ponty pays to the human sciences seems truly decisive for the formation of his thought. The human sciences are able to reveal a dimension of brute experience in contrast to the idealist temptation of reflective philosophy. Thus, they have a double relationship with phenomenology. On the one hand, phenomenology informs the human sciences by clarifying the transcendental dimension at work in them while denouncing, consequently, the naturalism or the positivism on which they are still dependent. On the other hand, psychology and linguistics correct the meaning of phenomenology insofar as the perceiving subject and the speaking subject to which psychology and linguistics lead cannot be identified with constituting consciousness but must be characterized, on the contrary, in terms of their factual rootedness. Nevertheless, this double movement, which leads from scientific positivity to the philosophical attitude and from phenomenological idealism to contact with experience, is not Merleau-Ponty's alone; this convergence asserts itself, in Merleau-Ponty's eyes, first and foremost at the very heart of Husserl's phenomenology. The harmony between phenomenological reflection and certain results of the human sciences allows us to describe the path of Husserl himself. In other words, Merleau-Ponty is not content with taking advantage of psychology and linguistics by freeing them of their naturalistic implications. Throughout his work, he brings himself into a confrontation with Husserl's phenomenology in order to show how it testifies to the same harmony that the human sciences attest to on their side. His way of proceeding, therefore, in a sense amounts to locating himself in this still uninhabited place on which the human sciences, in their recent developments, and [90] phenomenology, at least in its later formulation, unknowingly converge. Thus, for Merleau-Ponty the conquest of his own thought passes through a permanent confrontation with Husserl, to the point that an interpretation can claim to be faithful only if it clarifies, for each question, the area of the Husserlian edifice where Merleau-Ponty's reflection is inscribed. It is clear, however, as every commentator has noted, that

Merleau-Ponty does not read Husserl as if he were a historian of philosophy; what is at issue for him is not the faithful restoration of Husserl's path of reflection but rather finding there a guarantor and a stimulus for his own thought. Merleau-Ponty explains himself on this point several times, in particular at the beginning of "The Philosopher and His Shadow." His approach to the history of philosophy is the heir of his philosophy of perception and intersubjectivity: just as the thing is not frontally and objectively possessed but rather grasped in transcendence in a lateral way, the thought of an author is not such that one can make a precise list of what belongs to it and what it has ignored. The relation of commentary is a modality of the intersubjective relation, of linguistics in particular. In dialogical experience, I do not communicate to another a thought possessed elsewhere. I think with him and make myself in his image; moreover, his thought comes to itself only by formulating itself and offering itself to me, so that there is no clear-cut distinction between what would belong strictly to an author and what the interpretation projects into the author. What defines a thought is what it was still seeking to say, its "unthought," which can be revealed only in a reflection which, on the basis of its difference, turns itself into the echo of the thought. Therefore, the rejection of the idea that one must subject a reading to objectivity in favor of the idea that one must attempt to explicate an unthought can be a higher form of fidelity. In short,

> between an "objective" history of philosophy, which would rob the great philosophers of what they have given others to think about, and a meditation disguised as a dialogue, in which we would ask the questions and give the answers, there must be a middle ground on which the philosopher we are speaking about and the philosopher who is speaking are present together, although it is not possible even in principle to decide at any given moment just what belongs to each. (S 201–202/159)

In the confrontation with Husserl that Merleau-Ponty pursues, it is impossible to extract what belongs to one and what belongs to the other, to draw a dividing line. Nevertheless, this does not mean [91] that we can speak of resemblance, of a single philosophy that would be repeated in two thinkers. We cannot speak of a projection of Merleau-Ponty's thought onto that of Husserl, and yet there is no preexistence in the one of what the other discovers in him. It is indeed in the contact going from one to the other that both become themselves. What follows from this—and this has not really been noticed—is that we cannot clearly situate Merleau-Ponty's thought on the side of Husserl's unthought, even though Merleau-Ponty claims to have brought it to light. In principle, it is impossible to circumscribe this unthought, to distinguish it from the explicit results. Rather, co-present tendencies are at issue here such that the one can prevail over the other by means of the moment of reflection. In other words, Husserl's unthought is also that of Merleau-Ponty, in that at the very moment when the latter claims to overcome Husserl's "idealism" precisely in favor of this unthought, he remains dependent on the categories which feed this idealism. The distance that Merleau-Ponty puts between himself and Husserl expresses a tendency never fully realized, at least before *The Visible and the Invisible,* and Husserl continues to envelop Merleau-Ponty at the moment when the latter claims to envelop him. The result is that Merleau-Ponty reveals himself to be in contact with Husserl from a double viewpoint: within his unthought, Merleau-Ponty conquers his own thought, but also in Husserl's explicit philosophy he discovers his own limits. Therefore, Merleau-Ponty himself is also traversed by this tension that he brings to light in Husserl; his reflection follows as well the evolution that he reveals there. By stressing the theses of the "later" Husserl in a certain fashion, he opens the way to his ontology; but by criticizing the limitations within which Husserl is still imprisoned, he surmounts what had blocked the ontological perspective in his own works. The path that leads to the *Lebenswelt* must be followed once more: ontology cannot be explicated in a single stroke. Merleau-Ponty must begin by adopting, at least for a while, the ambitions of a philosophy that is sure of itself, so that he can discover the necessity of an ontology, that is, of a philosophy which feeds and limits the classical pretensions of philosophy—a philosophy of non-philosophy.

Merleau-Ponty's reading is constructed around the clarification of a tension cutting across Husserl's enterprise, the tension between a growing recognition of the "instructing spontaneity" and the maintenance to the end of the constitutive perspective [92] of absolute transcendental subjectivity. As early as the preface to *Phenomenology of Perception,* Merleau-Ponty insists on the difference between Husserl's explicit philosophy and what, in his eyes, constitutes its truth, on "all the misunderstandings with his interpreters, with the existentialist 'dissidents' and finally with himself" (PHP viii/xiv). Because Merleau-Ponty is first concerned with opening up the phenomenological truth of Gestalt psychology, these misunderstandings are clarified on the plane of the relation between psychology and phenomenology. It is true that the discovery of the eidetic reduction allows

Husserl to draw an insurmountable dividing line between eidetic psychology, on the one hand, whose role is to open up the essence of consciousness and its lived experiences, and positive psychology, on the other, whose ambition must be limited to a summary of the contents of consciousness and their actual genesis. Scientific psychology therefore finds itself discredited insofar as it is a science of facts, dependent on the presupposition of the naturalization of consciousness. By overcoming atomism, Gestalt psychology itself does not give up naturalism, for it continues to locate the form in the geographical world, failing to note that atomism is only an aspect of a more general prejudice. In Husserl the relation of philosophy to psychology, Merleau-Ponty says, is a bit like that of form to content. However, can such a clear distinction be maintained between philosophical knowledge, which proceeds from eidetic variation, and factual knowledge, which is based on induction? Or rather, can psychology's approach be assimilated to an induction, that is, to a generality brought about on the basis of a finite number of events? In reality,

> if in Husserl's view the knowledge of facts is impossible without some
> insight into essence and is always helped by this, it follows that all
> sound knowledge of facts must include, at least implicitly, some insight
> into essences, and that Husserl must admit, as he does in effect, that
> those psychologists who have been preoccupied with facts have nevertheless been able to find out something concerning essences. (SHP 35/66)

In any case, Husserl recognizes—in a domain that is certainly not that of psychology—that science has been able to gain access to an eidetic dimension. This is [93] Galileo's situation. The discovery of the law of gravity implies an eidetic of the physical thing. Therefore, the inductive concept must be conceived not as an abstraction occurring within experience but as a construction whose validity comes not from the number of facts invoked but from the clarity with which it illuminates certain phenomena. Apprehended from the side of induction, the division between eidetic and empirical sciences cannot be strictly preserved. But Merleau-Ponty stresses as well the fact that, in reality, for Husserl the intuition of the *eidos* necessarily supports itself on an intuition of the individual. Even if perception is not the source of validity for essences, it is "fecund," which means that in principle the essence cannot be detached from the experience, fictive or real, across which the essence is brought to light. Eidetic intuition therefore aims not at reducing the world to its possibility but at making its possibility appear as the possibility *of this world*. The radical distinction between the eidetic and the inductive method cannot be established.[1] This is why Husserl's insistence on the eidetic reduction and the autonomy of the essence is in Merleau-Ponty's eyes, at least during this period, only a matter of emphasis:

> To tell the truth, we do not have to wait until Husserl recognizes that the *Lebenswelt* is phenomenology's principal theme to note the repudiation of formal reflection in his thought. The reader of *Ideen I* will have already noticed that eidetic intuition has always been a "confirmation," and phenomenology an "experience." . . . It is just that the ascending movement was not stressed. Thought barely supported itself on its actually existing structures in order to sift out its possible ones: a wholly imaginary variation extracted a treasure of eidetic assertions from the lowest-grade experience. (S 132/105)

In the end, eidetic intuition and induction correspond to one form of knowledge that functions at two levels, that of explication and naiveté (SNS 95/134–35; PRI 132/24; SHP 43/75). Science, psychology in particular, truly has a transcendental significance, and eidetics does not reject experience in favor of an autonomous sense that would be accessible only to pure thought, but rather frees the sense from experience itself. The only difference, Merleau-Ponty concludes, is the following: while induction works on perceived facts, variation supports itself with imaginary facts. And yet, Merleau-Ponty has to make this conclusion more nuanced [94] insofar as interpolation actually represents the way in which the imaginary intervenes into the very heart of the inductive method. Husserl certainly never went that far, and he always pushed psychology outside the boundaries of philosophy on the pretext that psychology ignores the essence of consciousness by locating it within an objective nature. He did, however, take an important step in this direction by recognizing a psycho-phenomenological parallelism, by asserting therefore that every phenomenological proposition shelters a truth of empirical psychology and that every statement of positive psychology anticipates a phenomenological truth. And Merleau-Ponty reports this formulation from the afterword to *Ideas I:* "every empirical discovery as well as every eidetic discovery made on the one side must correspond to a parallel discovery on the other" (SHP 42/72). On the basis of Husserl's actual evolution, or at least with the restrictions bear-

1. On this point, see part II.

ing on the purity of the division between experience and the seeing of essences, Merleau-Ponty indeed locates Husserl's unthought in the very place where his own investigations take place. Thus,

> I believe that to give weight to his eidetic intuition and to distinguish it sharply from verbal concepts, Husserl was really seeking, largely unknown to himself, a notion like that of the Gestaltists—the notion of an order of meaning which does not result from the application of spiritual activity to an external matter. It is, rather, a spontaneous organization between the distinction between activity and passivity, of which the visible patterns of experience are the symbol. (SHP 51/77)

However, it is especially in relation to language that Merleau-Ponty illuminates the mutation in Husserl's reflection. This is the case undoubtedly because Husserl, recognizing that the question of language does not traditionally belong to the domain of first philosophy, considers it more freely. But Merleau-Ponty especially turns to the question of language, because by means of it the plane of ideality and, consequently, the sense of the entire constitutive enterprise are examined. As Derrida notes, the question of the ultimate validity of an approach, which consists in exhibiting the conditions of validity, is posed by means of the question of the *fact* of language: "Attentiveness to the 'fact' of language in which a juridical thought lets itself be transcribed, in which juridicality would like to be completely transparent, is a return to factuality as the *de jure* character of the *de jure*. It is a reduction of the reduction and opens the way for an infinite [95] discursivity."[2] Merleau-Ponty distinguishes three periods of Husserl's reflections on language. First, what is at issue for Husserl is to open up, according to the eidetic method, the forms to which every possible language must be subjected, forms of which any particular language is only the exemplification. This dogmatic conception of the *Wesenschau* conceals the implicit assertion of the possibility for the thinker to detach himself from the language in which he thinks by carrying it up to the transparency of a pure object, to grasp the universal of language on the basis of an imaginative variation on his own language without passing through a confrontation with other languages. Here we can clearly see the

---

2. E. Husserl, *L'origine de la géométrie,* trans. and intro. J. Derrida (Paris: Presses Universitaires de France, 1962), 60n; trans. J. P. Leavey, Jr., as *Edmund Husserl's Origin of Geometry: An Introduction* (1978; reprint, Lincoln: University of Nebraska Press, 1989), 69n66.

problem that the eidetic reduction raises. Insofar as language is the element of his reflection, can the thinker detach himself from the experience that he has of it? Can he grasp in it an essence that owes nothing to this actual contact? Is language the empirical location or the transcendental element of thought? On the basis of an article by H. J. Pos, Merleau-Ponty opens up a second period which is characterized by the fact that Husserl defines phenomenology's primary task no longer as the apprehension of a pure possible to which every actual language would be subject, but as the contact with the experience of the speaking subject:

> Philosophy's first task in respect to language now appears to be to reveal to us anew our inherence in a certain system of speech of which we make fully efficacious use precisely because it is present to us just as immediately as our body. Philosophy of language is no longer contrasted to empirical linguistics as an attempt at total objectification of language to a science that is threatened by the preconceptions of the native language. On the contrary, it has become the rediscovery of the subject in the act of speaking, as contrasted to a science of language which inevitable treats this subject as a thing. (S 130/104)

And just as the assertion of the psycho-phenomenological parallelism converged with Gestalt psychology, so the phenomenology of language intersects with the linguistics of speech that, as we have seen, leads to a consistent linguistics of language. As soon as phenomenology wants first to return to the experience of speech, it can no longer be understood as an attempt to determine pure possibles for a "pre-empirical" subject, deprived of inscription in a language. In this desire [96] to return to speech itself, the immediate opposition between fact and essence, in Merleau-Ponty's eyes, is implicitly overcome; in fact, the phenomenologist is concerned with an object whose constitutive forms he cannot in principle summarize in a list, with an object that surpasses him just as much as he possesses it, and which he can objectify only because he is first situated in it. Therefore, the return to the *Lebenswelt* imposes itself first in the form of a return to speech. This movement completely fulfills itself in the fragment on "The Origin of Geometry," a text on which Merleau-Ponty never stopped meditating. The turn to it is quite important: instead of language being located, as it was at the beginning, on the side of natural realities susceptible to being reduced to essences, in this text language appears to be the very place of ideality. It is no longer a matter of starting from ideality considered as an autonomous reality, but rather of grasping its genesis in the element of speech. The seed of this approach was already planted in the "middle" period; the return to the *Lebenswelt* could only lead to the inverse attempt to ground within it, namely, on the plane of actual speech, the specific mode of being of cultural and ideal entities. Ideality must be understood no longer as language's other, as that in which language would come into its pure essence, but as what exists only in language, consequently as production rather than as being. And the perpetuity of meaning must be understood, in turn, as an omnitemporality whose own possibility is based on writing, rather than as eternity. Therefore,

> Husserl will only be bringing the movement of all his previous thought to completion when he writes in a posthumous fragment that transitory inner phenomena are brought to ideal existences by becoming incarnate in language. Ideal existence, which at the beginning of Husserl's thought was to have been the foundation for the possibility of language, is now the most basic characteristic possibility of language. (S 132/105)

2. The Authentic Sense of Phenomenology

This is the meaning of phenomenology, reconceived from the point of view of the movement by which it gains access to its truth: no longer the elaboration of certain knowledge, but "the vigilance which does not let us forget the source of all knowledge"; no longer the passage to an order of essences, reabsorbing the order of [97] actual things, but "a more acute awareness of the way in which we are rooted in them" (S 138/110, 131/105). The study of Husserl's evolution reveals that phenomenology is fulfilled in a way that conforms to its initial project to escape from positivism, with psychologism being its most complete form, as well as from "Platonism." It is indeed a question of leading all knowledge back to the experience in which it is rooted, but without reconceiving that experience as immediate contact with a pure fact—that is, without renouncing the possibility of the universal to which the experience of knowledge attests. One has to take account of the fact of reason without ignoring the brute world within which reason is born; this amounts to understanding reason as an "entelechy" rather than as what is given once and for all. This is Husserl's explicit purpose in his last great work when he invokes the necessity of a first reduction that leads back to the "life-world" which is given in advance; the "life-world" constitutes the implicit soil of transcendental philosophies, Kantian in particular. Regarding this ultimate decision, which to Merleau-

Ponty appears to be the very fulfillment of Husserl's reflection, it turns out to be necessary to relativize the oppositions that helped phenomenology first find its own way. Thus the point is not to reconceive the transcendental attitude as the suspension of the natural attitude, which would re-create genuine being as being that is constituted in transcendental subjectivity; in other words, the point is not to oppose the two attitudes as if they are the illusory and the true. That we can, in fact, suppress nature without suppressing spirit does not mean that the being of nature resides in spirit, that nature is a production of spirit, in short, that transcendental subjectivity reveals the ultimate sense of Being. Insofar as the reduction *begins* in the natural attitude, it cannot claim to surmount it; the natural attitude overcomes itself in the transcendental attitude, which means that the natural attitude remains itself in this overcoming, that it is not completely overcome. Conversely, just as the autonomy of the transcendental attitude is put into question, so is the positivity of the natural attitude. Insofar as the transcendental attitude remains caught in the natural attitude and is only its fulfillment, the natural attitude cannot be opposed to the transcendental attitude as the apparent to the true. Because the transcendental is always still on the side of nature, the [98] natural world is always already on the side of spirit. These two attitudes must finally be understood as two abstract determinations of a more profound situation that eludes both of them: "There is undeniably something between transcendent Nature, naturalism's being-in-itself, and the immanence of spirit, its acts, and its noemata" (S 209/166). Nevertheless, the movement so sketched is opposed by an inverse tendency which is dominant in the "first" Husserl and which he never manages to surmount completely. There is in Husserl, just as in Merleau-Ponty at the time of *Phenomenology of Perception,* a tension between this project of a return to the originary soil and the categories by means of which it is accomplished. This explains the heightened attention Merleau-Ponty pays to Husserl in this transitional period, attention which culminates in "The Philosopher and His Shadow," the genuine introduction to his ontology. What is really at issue for Merleau-Ponty is to bring to clarity, by means of an interaction with Husserl, the discordance between what he is seeking to think after *Phenomenology of Perception* and the idealist and dualist vocabulary that belongs to this book. In effect, if Husserl recognizes, on the one hand, the necessity of a contact with the instructive spontaneity, of a return to a pregiven *Lebenswelt,* this requirement is, on the other hand, concealed by the assertion of the necessity of a second reduction that leads all the structures brought to light back to transcendental subjectivity. Now, as Merleau-Ponty notes already in *Phenomenology of Perception*, "It is clear, however, that we are faced with a dilemma: either the constitution makes the world transparent, in which case it is not obvious why reflection needs to pass through the world of experience, or else it retains something of the world, and never rids itself of its opacity" (PHP 419n1/365n11; see also S 116/92, 139/110–11). Conceived as a return to the *Lebenswelt,* phenomenology can no longer be considered preparatory for the philosophy in the strict sense that would provide us with the truth of phenomenology; phenomenology coincides with philosophy itself. If the reduction to the "life-world" really consists in taking note of a constitutive opacity of sense, whether this be at the level of perception or of language, necessarily there can be no turning back from this decision; it cannot be followed by the restoration of an absolute subjectivity: "How will that infrastructure, that secret of secrets this side of our theses and our theory, be able in turn to rest upon [99] *acts* of absolute consciousness? Does the descent into the realm of our 'archaeology' leave our analytical tools intact? Does it make no change at all in our conception of noesis, noema, and intentionality—in our ontology?" (S 208/165). The task that Merleau-Ponty then assigns to himself is precisely to take note of the implications of this return to the *Lebenswelt,* namely, to overcome the transcendental formulation of the reduction that veils the world of experience just as much as it unveils it, to forge the concepts that suit this brute or wild world, to think adequately "this back side of things that we have not constituted" (S 227/180). Nevertheless, we must not see Merleau-Ponty's ontology as opposed to the phenomenological enterprise; on the contrary, it is its fulfillment. What is at issue is only to take up the task that Husserl was proposing for himself there where he left it, that is, to think thoroughly this "life-world" to which a consistent phenomenology is necessarily led. Merleau-Ponty notes this unequivocally in *The Visible and the Invisible:* "Disclosure of the wild or brute Being by way of Husserl and the *Lebenswelt* upon which one opens" (VI 237/183). Insofar as it is the attempt to bring the still mute experience to the pure expression of its own sense, the truth of phenomenology consists in the fact that it unveils a share of non-philosophy, an order that resists constituting consciousness. The truth of phenomenology resides *at the very place of its limit,* in what motivates and stops simultaneously its enterprise of understanding: "the ultimate task of phenomenology as philosophy of consciousness is to understand its relation to non-phenomenology. What resists phenomenology within us—natural being, the 'barbarous' source Schelling spoke of—cannot remain outside phenomenology and should have its place within it. The philosopher must bear his shadow, which is not simply the factual absence of future light" (S 225/178). Merleau-Ponty's ontology merges with phenomenology understood in this way. A philosophy of sense is pertinent only insofar as it is capable of integrating what precedes and feeds the capacity to give sense; it must be capable of enlarging itself to point where it comprehends what is not the same as itself, instead of closing itself off on the assertion of a pure constituting subject and of the immanence of nature to reason. This does not mean that ontology aims [100] to coincide with a brute fact foreign to sense or the affirmation of an irrational; this would be the restoration in a negative form of the order of essence. There is a fact of sense and a teleology of reason, but these exist because they proceed from a ground that they never completely reabsorb. The ontology comes about in order to fulfill phenomenology, which is still imperfectly presented in Husserl, just as it is in the "first" Merleau-Ponty. It is not the negation of sense, but the attempt of thought to situate itself at the articulation of sense and non-sense, to somehow catch sense in the act, at its very birthplace, the attempt of philosophy to measure up to its share of non-philosophy. This calls for a reflection on the status of philosophical interrogation and, beyond the acknowledgment of its validity, a more radical critique of Husserl's way of proceeding.

Part Two.
Philosophical Interrogation

6 The "Diplopia" of Cartesian Ontology

[103] We have said that the analysis of expression, and more generally of culture, leads according to a regressive movement to an interrogation of the meaning of the nature in which the world of culture is rooted. Now, in the course on nature given at the Collège de France in 1956, Merleau-Ponty describes his project for the first time in ontological terms: "The study of nature is here an introduction to the definition of Being" (RC 125/156). Merleau-Ponty considers a certain number of philosophies of nature, but he particularly dwells on the classic modern conceptions. Moreover, as the outlines for *The Visible and the Invisible* as well as some of the working notes indicate (VI 230/176, 231/177), the establishment of the ontology could be fulfilled only from the angle of a confrontation with classic modern philosophy, that of Descartes and Leibniz in particular. At issue is not so much to found a new meaning of ontology as to take up the ontological project at work in this philosophy. Therefore, Merleau-Ponty's own inspiration proceeds from a meditation on Cartesianism as well as a confrontation with Husserl's phenomenology. Cartesian philosophy is characterized by a fundamental duality of viewpoints. In Cartesianism, the world is essentially grasped by means of the alternative of Being and Nothingness, that is, as a pure *naturata* that thus refers to God, pure *naturans*. It is precisely what it must be; what it is, it is necessarily, and it appears therefore "without faults or fissures," that is, also without depth. Nature is "pure product, composed of absolutely external parts, [104] completely existent and clearly combined—an 'empty shell,' as Hegel would say" (RC 99/137). Understood as mechanism, this Nature corresponds to the viewpoint of the pure understanding; it is the nature of the natural light. The substantial duality of thought and extension, which is inherent to the requirement of clarity and distinctness, corresponds to this viewpoint. The world is then the object of intellectual knowledge, substance mixed with its essential attribute. However, this is not the sole perspective developed by Descartes:

By maintaining the contingency of the act of creation, Descartes upheld the facticity of nature and thus legitimated another perspective on this existent Nature than that of pure understanding. To this nature we have an access, not only through it, but through the vital relation that we have with a privileged part of Nature: namely, our body, through the "natural inclination" whose lessons cannot coincide with those of the pure understanding. (RC 100/138)

With the discovery of the union, which can be known only in terms of itself, the definition of Being as pure object finds itself put in question, for "how can we leave the definition of being and truth to pure understanding if it is not grounded so as to know the existent world?" (RC 100/138). The First and Sixth Meditations then really appear to be irreconcilable. If the union of the soul and body is a confused thought, how was the discovery of the *cogito* possible? And conversely, how does this discovery agree with the natured subject of the Sixth Meditation? Let us note that the solution that Merleau-Ponty proposes is situated in the tradition of Malebranche rather than that of Spinoza, these being two symmetrical modes of "re-aligning" Cartesianism; in fact, "Malebranche will obscure the *cogito*— which, henceforth, will no longer 'detach'—so that neither the 'I think' nor the proof of the existence of God will allow us to transcend our inherent nature as unreflective subjects" (UAC 16/35). Cartesianism therefore is traversed by a duality between Nature as Object and Nature as Event, between the viewpoint of essence that consists in the distinction of substances and the viewpoint of existence that the union teaches to us. In Merleau-Ponty's eyes, this duality defines the fundamental situation of Western ontology: "Do we [105] not find everywhere the double certitude that being is, that appearances are only a manifestation and a restriction of being—and that these appearances are the canon of everything that we can understand by 'being,' that in this respect it is being in-itself which appears as an ungraspable phantom, an *Unding*?" (RC 127/157–58). It is not philosophy's task to reduce this duality; it can neither opt for *one* of the terms, since each calls for the other, nor try to open up a terrain in which this duality would be null and void, precisely because the duality is irreducible. Its task can consist only in taking stock of this historical situation. History is the revelation of an ontological situation which it is only a matter of bringing to light, since the ontological situation would remain blind to itself if it stayed locked within the systems where it manifests itself. Merleau-Ponty's ontology intends to be the completion of what is expressed and simultaneously overlooked within the classic modern philosophies. It is therefore formulated at first as the comprehension of this duality:

> Could we not find what has been called an "ontological diplopia" (Blondel), which after so much philosophical effort we cannot expect to bring to a rational reduction and which leaves us with the sole alternative of wholly embracing it, just as our gaze takes over monocular images to make a single vision of them. Viewed in this way, the continual shifting of philosophies from one perspective to the other would not involve any contradiction, in the sense of inadvertence or incoherence, but would be justified and founded upon being. All one could do is to ask the philosopher to admit this phenomenon and reflect upon it, rather than merely suffering it and occupying alternatively two ontological positions, each of which excludes and invites the other. (RC 127/158)

There is a "Cartesian equilibrium" between science and philosophy, an equilibrium which must not be broken but which rather must be rediscovered. If Cartesianism, as the philosophy of the natural light, disqualifies every reflection that would not take account of the understanding, it leads just as much to an objection to a scientific approach—the very approach that Merleau-Ponty denounces in "Eye and Mind." Such a scientific approach would not take the detour through metaphysics that Descartes made at least once; it would not open the depth of the "there is" [*il y a*]. Simply put, it is true that Descartes immediately closed back up the composite dimension of soul and body, of the existent world, of abyssal Being that he had opened. He thus did not take possession of this "diplopia" that runs through him. It is this Cartesian equilibrium that [106] Merleau-Ponty aims at first to rediscover and complete. For him, it is a matter of clarifying the presence of the world in such a way that it does not exclude but instead integrates the possibility of objectification, that is, correlatively, of giving back to science a genuine foundation opposite from the scientistic perversion. It is a question of thinking *together* the dimensions of fact and essence, without either sacrificing essence to an ineffable depth or absorbing existence back into the knowledge provided by the understanding.

Taking stock of this ontological "diplopia" cannot consist only in taking note of it; one has to conceive it. Each position, that of experience or of fact, as well as that of the "in-itself" or of essence, calls the other forth in the very moment when it excludes it. There is a deep-seated instability in the philosophies of essence as well as in those of existence. Neither of the two perspectives expresses the total situation, and this is why each of them is led to pass into its other. But if there is a truth of this "to-and-fro," of this duality, this truth does not reside *in* the duality itself. It is precisely the unilateral form according to which each position expresses itself that determines its reversal into its contrary, so that if there is really a truth to the duality of fact and essence, it is not expressed in the very notions of fact and essence. The to-and-fro corresponds to a more profound situation, to an original mode of the presence of Being in which the duality is rooted, which almost inevitably calls forth a rigid oppositional formulation, but whose true meaning does not reside in this duality. In order to understand the ontological "diplopia," therefore, one must return to a relation to Being that stops short of the opposition between essence and existence, a relation of which the to-and-fro is like the distorting trace. What is at issue is to rediscover the soil in which the necessity of this philosophical alternation is grounded, a soil that can only be located deeper than each of the terms, whose "unilaterality" alone determines the alternation. One must therefore overcome the relation of fact and essence as an oppositional relation in favor of a plane where it will turn out to be a unity. By overcoming the fixity of the terms in which the opposition is expressed, we shall overcome the relation as oppositional relation. The notions of fact and essence lead us to conceive their very relation as an external oppositional relation rather than as movement; the point, therefore, is to overcome the antagonistic dimension of the to-and-fro in order to grasp the passage to essence as proceeding from existence itself, and the passage to existence [107] as proceeding from essence itself. We must understand each term as its own passage into the other—that is, we must locate essence short of its opposition to existence and existence short of its opposition to essence.

However, if the truth of the to-and-fro is not found in the terms in which it is explicated, it is still the case that there is a truth *of* the duality. That the opposition must be overcome does not mean that it must be reduced to a pure and simple unity. The duality truly remains insurpassable, and we cannot expect a "rational reduction" of it. One must not conclude that existence or essence will give us the ultimate key to the situation, or that philosophy will come to an end in one alternative. Rather, the soil where the to-and-fro is grounded must be the soil *for* this duality; that is, it must be able to give an account of the fact that the philosophies developed in our history are confronted, despite everything, with the choice between fact and essence. This means that there is a truth of objectification that does not consist in a pure and simple affirmation of the object, of the possibility of a reduction of the world to its essence; moreover, there is a truth of existence that does not amount to rediscovering an order of brute fact that would be incommensurate with the order of the object. If it is true that existence passes into essence, it is still the case that *existence* performs this movement, that it remains as well withdrawn into itself, and that it does not therefore pass into essence completely. In this sense a duality remains. And, conversely, if essence remains rooted in existence, this is not in order to mingle with the brute fact. This rootedness means only that essence can be itself only if it is withdrawn into that of which it is the essence. Thus, the truth of the movement is no more located in the opposition of the terms than in their immediate identity. If it is truly a matter of overcoming the opposition, then this overcoming cannot be accomplished in favor of an identity taken possession of in the opposition itself. To take stock of this ontological "diplopia" amounts then to opening up a truth of the unity over against the opposition, but in such a way that within this unity, the truth of the opposition remains. The difference between fact and essence will then have to be conceived as an imminent difference, always already accomplished but also always on the way to being accomplished. This means that it never surpasses itself as a duality, that it is not forgotten in favor of the terms *whose* difference it would be. The task of philosophy will be "to elaborate a concept of being such that its contradictions, *neither accepted nor 'overcome,'* still have their place" (RC 128/159).

[108] This perspective places Merleau-Ponty at an equal distance from a philosophy that, while reducing the world to its essence, remains prisoner of the duality and is confronted with the problem of the fact just when it thinks it has resolved this problem, and from a dialectical philosophy—at least in the sense of a "bad dialectic"—that absorbs the duality back into an identity by thematizing the to-and-fro as an identity of opposites. Thus, the two principal axes of the long introductory part of *The Visible and the Invisible* are justified. In the chapter called "Interrogation and Intuition," Merleau-Ponty criticizes the eidetic perspective on which Husserl's phenomenology is grounded and on which it remains dependent up to the very end. In the chapter called "Interrogation and Dialectic," Merleau-Ponty denounces Sartre's philosophy at length insofar as it attempts to take possession of the identity by emphasizing what is opposed, through the radicalization of their opposition. Husserl's phenomenology, however, will emerge as the victor in this double confrontation. As we have seen, it is incontestable in Merleau-Ponty's eyes that Husserl attempts to overcome

the duality of fact and essence, to overcome objectivism by going toward the originary soil in which its relative rights are grounded. With Husserl, the tension which, in Descartes, was not conceived as such becomes conscious of itself. Nevertheless, just like Descartes, Husserl turns out to be prisoner of a primacy of objectivism and consequently of a dualism which keeps the movement of the return to the *Lebenswelt* from accomplishing itself fully. The duality of essence and existence finally prevails over their originary unity. This is why, for Merleau-Ponty, Husserl represents simultaneously an endeavor that still needs to be accomplished, since it is dependent on Cartesian objectivism, and the very horizon of philosophy— that is, the first evidence of a reflection which attempts to overcome the aporias of objectivism without, however, turning into dialectic.

7 Fact and Essence: Phenomenology

1. Doubt and Reduction

[109] It is necessary therefore to clarify how the antagonism between the philosophy of fact and that of essence is determined, to clarify what holds them in this duality. In this way we can see how each of them lacks the relation to Being whose truth each claims to be. This critique cannot consist in valorizing one notion over the other, in opting for a realism or for an idealism; that would amount to being taken into the movement rather than understanding it. It must reveal, stopping short of their opposition, a commonality of ontological attitude, a commonality that is in some sense negative. A "to-and-fro" movement unfolds from one to the other because the same ontology—which Merleau-Ponty calls "positivism"—is expressed in each of these notions. Each calls forth and excludes the other because both attest to the same implicit determination of the relation to Being. In the philosophies of fact, as in those of essence, philosophical interrogation is subordinated to a predetermined meaning of Being. Instead of being exercised as genuine interrogation, interrogation is given as a provisional absence of a positivity. In contrast, the way of access to Being in Merleau-Ponty passes through a realization of the genuine meaning of philosophical interrogation. Although previously the relation to Being was considered on the basis of a domain of positivity or of practice in which the relation was supposed to be transparent, so that the results taken possession of in this domain were what informed the status of the reflection, now what is at issue is to open a way to Being starting from a reflection on reflection itself. The response to the question "What is thinking?" determines the orientation of the ontology. Now,

> the philosophical interrogation [110] is . . . not the simple expectation
> of a meaning that would come to fill it. "What is the world?" or "What
> is Being?"—these questions become philosophical only if, by a sort of
> diplopia, at the same time that they aim at a state of things, they aim at
> themselves as questions—at the same time that they aim at the meaning
> "being," they aim at the being of meaning and the place of meaning

within Being. It is characteristic of the philosophical interrogation that it return upon itself, that it ask itself what to question is and what to respond is. (VI 160/119–20)

To think Being therefore is to reach Being again on the basis of what is implied in thought itself. The point is to understand it as *the very same thing* that we are interrogating instead of attempting to possess it immediately. The interrogation of Being takes place first in the form of an interrogation of a being, namely, the very being who interrogates. On this condition, the ontological sense of Being will be determined authentically, beyond every prior assignation to a positivity. From this consciousness of interrogation, it will be possible to take stock of the philosophies that exhaust themselves in the question of fact or essence. Their ontological positivism will indeed appear as correlative with the misunderstanding in which they find themselves with regard to the being of interrogation.

In the first chapter of the completed part of *The Visible and the Invisible*, Merleau-Ponty grasps reflection as a single gesture common to Descartes, Kant, and Husserl.[1] At this stage of the work, reflection is described in opposition to the scientific attitude. For the scientific attitude, the world is given as a "great Object"; it passes over in silence the moment of phenomenality on which the being of the world is based. It reconceives phenomenality according to the naturalistic mode, as a real moment of the world. The reflective attitude, by contrast, acknowledges the appearance of the world and determines it as thought. At this stage, the scientific attitude and reflective philosophy are opposed as two unilateral interpretations of the perceptual faith, which is in fact characterized by ambiguity. The one tabulates on the basis of the certitude that the perceptual faith gives to us of having access to the world itself; the other thematizes the corporeal and subjective areas pertinent to this world. Because it is reconceived within this opposition, the reflective attitude could be described as a unitary gesture. And it is true that at the end [111] of the chapter on intuition, the reflective attitude will appear truly as such, but for profound reasons. Nevertheless, one must indeed draw a distinction between reflection in the Cartesian sense and phenomenological reflection, the distinction with which the chapter called "Interrogation and Intuition" begins.

Merleau-Ponty's position in relation to Cartesian doubt is the very one

---

1. Despite a reservation already expressed in relation to Husserl in the note at VI 74n/49n.

that Husserl develops throughout his work. As *negation* of the existence of the world, doubt presupposes a certain ontological sense of the world as natural or absolute existence. Its apparent radicality conceals therefore an absence of radicality, since the negation is only the reverse of an affirmation and thus does not allow one to interrogate the ontological sense of what is negated. Cartesian questioning is not in fact ontological but epistemological. Once the dubitable character of sensible experience is discovered, what is at issue is to know *if* the world exists. The issue does not lie in assuring oneself with certainty of the sense of existence, but rather in assuring oneself of an existence that is certain. Therefore, always already situated within natural Being, the negation of existence is overcome in the deferred affirmation *of a being*. The authentic transcendental perspective that, according to Husserl, is announced in Descartes is obliterated through the continuation of the natural thesis, so that thought is finally understood as *res cogitans,* as substance. The conversion to the *cogito* is only a conversion to transcendental realism. Then, instead of it being conceived as the ultimate ontological sense of the world, consciousness is defined as the place of representations and is discovered again confronted with the natural position of the problem of knowledge understood in terms of adequation. Because the *cogito* is situated within Being, that is, because it possesses the ontological sense of Nature, the recourse to divine truthfulness is necessary in order to guarantee the objective validity of representations. Finally, in Merleau-Ponty's eyes, Descartes "revives the equivocations of skepticism" (VI 144/106). Since doubt always already refers to Being, it can take refuge in it only by selecting a being, that of representation. Like the question of fact, like the question of the "*an sit,*" doubt turns out to be inadequate to the sense of philosophical interrogation. Doubt comes about in the form of a rupture within the very heart of Being, a rupture that is only the provisional reverse side of a real relation between substances. The question of fact refers to a relation of fact which cannot give an account of interrogation insofar as an *aim* of Being [112] is included in interrogation. In fact, if the question were truly only a real rupture, a "lived nothingness," a "pure gaping toward a transcendent Being" (VI 161/120), we would not have enough leeway even to raise a question. The determination of Being as natural being opens onto a positivity of consciousness. The result is that the distance of doubt turns into an absolute proximity and that the moment of phenomenality finds no place between consciousness and Being. The very being of the question excludes the possibility that the question remains without a response, gaping toward a transcendence. Insofar as it is intended by the question, Being cannot mingle with natural positivity but must be conceived as sense. Although he inaugurates the movement of reflection, in the end Descartes remains a prisoner of naturalism. The moment of appearing is absorbed into the being that appears, which is itself determined as reality in itself.

In order to fulfill the wish of Cartesian radicality, philosophy must take note of its original relation to Being, recognize this relation as the horizon of its interrogation, and turn back toward the presence of the world in order to understand its sense. It must

> take as its theme the umbilical bond that binds it always to Being, the inalienable horizon with which it is already and henceforth circumvented, the primary initiation which it tries in vain to go back on. It would have to no longer deny, no longer even doubt; it would have to step back only in order to see the world and Being, or simply put them between quotation marks as one does with the remarks of another, to let them speak, to listen in. (VI 144/107)

Therefore, Cartesian radicality can be accomplished in a lesser radicality. Instead of breaking with the world, it is necessary to grasp the "how" of its givenness, to interrogate the ontological sense of what is. This is done not to ask whether the world is but to ask *what* the world is. The form of the question calls forth the form of the response. The being of the world must be determined as what is intended in the question, the "what" to which it relates itself insofar as it is a question. As the interrogation of the "*quid sit*," the question defines the sense of Being as *being thought;* in fact, "at the same time that the doubt is renounced, one renounces the affirmation of an absolute exterior, of a world or a Being that would be a massive individual; one turns toward that Being that doubles our thoughts along their whole extension, since they are nothing—a Being therefore that is [113] sense and sense of sense" (VI 144/107). The phenomenological reduction really leads us to determine the sense of sense as *essence,* and the most important part of the chapter is devoted to a discussion of Husserl's eidetic. One can see a difficulty there: since everywhere else Merleau-Ponty is interested in the transcendental "period" of Husserl's philosophy, why does he develop his analysis here on the level of the eidetic reduction? Must we conclude from this that he has steered his interest back to the first stage of the construction of phenomenology? First, we must note that Merleau-Ponty never entangled himself in the difficult problem of the relation of the eidetic phase and the transcendental phase. He grasps Husserl's thought according to its unity of inspiration and consequently understands the transcendental reduction as the fulfillment of the eidetic reduction. The eidetic reduction is the first formulation of a movement of thought that gives way to its genuine meaning only at the transcendental level. Certainly Husserl proposes for himself first the task of an inventory of essences, but, Merleau-Ponty notes, "even at this time, he dealt with essences as they are lived by us, as they emerge from our intentional life" (RC 149/173). It seems to us, from this point of view, that Merleau-Ponty is appropriating the interpretation provided by Trân Duc Thao. The latter describes the constitutive perspective as alone having the capacity to ground the ontological meaning of the essence against the risk of Platonic hypostasis:

> The discovery of that fundamental philosophical truth, that the existent presupposes the sense of its being, is inevitably interpreted at the outset by positing this sense as an existent of a special category. . . . The first thematization could take place only on the level of the object. It met with difficulties that motivated its displacement. That the essence determines the *being of the existent* can find its true meaning only in a return to the *subject.* . . . The task of a universal ontology can be realized solely through the explication of the *intentions of the constituting consciousness.*[2]

If it is true that the eidetic perspective discovers its authentic meaning only on the transcendental level, one must wonder whether the transcendental phase is not itself dependent on the eidetic. Does the mode in which the transcendental is described allow it to overcome the difficulty raised by Trân Duc Thao at the level of essences? Once it is [114] constituted as the unity of sense in absolute subjectivity, does not the being of the existent preserve a positivity and an autonomy by which it is split off from the existent whose being it is, so that the intuitive dimension of subjectivity prevails over its "creative" dimension? This is certainly the sense of the reading given by Merleau-Ponty, which is why, in *The Visible and the Invisible,* he examines Husserl starting from the problem of essence. The continuation of the eidetic perspective truly keeps constitution from being accomplished as the constitution *of the world itself* and holds it back within

2. Trân Duc Thao, *Phénoménologie et matérialisme dialectique* (Paris: Editions Minh-Tan, 1951), 36, 37; trans. D. J. Herman and D. V. Morano as *Phenomenology and Dialectical Materialism,* ed. R. L. Armstrong (Dordrecht: Reidel, 1986), 10, 11.

a transcendental idealism. Merleau-Ponty's orientation is certainly justified by the fact that the eidetic corresponds to the properly ontological moment of Husserl's interrogation. But above all, the eidetic allows Merleau-Ponty to circumscribe, beyond Husserl's different "periods," the negative unity of his thought. Because the sense of sense is characterized as essence, because it is understood from one end to the other in an intuitive manner, phenomenology cannot accomplish its wish to be radical. For Merleau-Ponty, on the contrary, the issue lies in developing a phenomenology freed from the eidetic presupposition, in developing a philosophy of sense which would not be a philosophy of essence. Finally, it is because the ontology remains an ontology of essence that it remains devoted to transcendental idealism and fails as genuine ontology.

The essence, as the object of reflection, content to put at a distance its "umbilical" bond with the world in order to see it, truly seems to be the answer to the philosophical question. The object mingles with what is *thought* in the question "*quid sit*"; but, on the other hand, it is precisely *what* is thought, so that it does not flow back into empirical subjectivity. Essence is only what it appears to be, and thus every positing of the external world finds itself abolished. But this appearing possesses the solidarity of a being: the essence is objective; it possesses a "resistant and stable" (VI 147/109) structure. While realism lacks the phenomenon because it grounds it on a reality in itself which does not appear, the philosophy of essence understands that a thing appears only if it *itself* appears in this appearing. As essence, the thing presents itself in all of what presents it. For the essence, to be given and to be given itself mean the same thing. While the realist perspective stops us from understanding how the phenomenon can bear the [115] relation to the object, that is, how the phenomenon can make something appear, the thought of essence concludes that the phenomenon merges with the presentation of the thing itself.

2. Essence and Experience

However, essence does not constitute the response to the philosophical question any more than does fact; no more than fact is it adequate to the being of interrogation:

> The essence is certainly dependent. The inventory of the essential necessities is always made under a supposition (the same as that which recurs so often in Kant): if this world is to exist for us, or if there is to be a

world, or if there is to be something, then it is necessary that they observe such and such a structural law. But whence do we get the hypothesis, whence do we know that there is something, that there is a world? This knowing is beneath the essence, it is the experience of which the essence is a part and which it does not envelop. (VI 147/109)

In fact, the claim that we reduce the world to its essence rests on the possibility of being given an individual by which the essence is grasped, without positing the individual as existing, in order to make the individual appear as an exemplar of this essence. The individuality of the individual is inseparable from its existence; its givenness proceeds from an experience, and the essence is extracted from this experience, with the result that the essence does not provide the being of the individual but, on the contrary, presupposes it. The grasping of the essence rests on a ground of experience which motivates it, and it cannot absorb this ground back into itself precisely insofar as the ground precedes it. The positive and transparent being of essence turns out to be incommensurable with the presence that, insofar as it is actual presence, cannot be the full exhibition of what is presented in it. If the experience could be truly reduced to its essence, then the essence would lose all consistency, since its determination and its "solidity" come to it from the experiential ground that nourishes it and that it determines. The essence of essence is to be the essence of something, to relate to a being that it qualifies without absorbing. Insofar as it is a determination, essence emerges from a being that stops just short of it, that is always given as something *to* determine. If the entire experience flows back toward its determination, the latter would vanish as a determination—that is, it would vanish as an essence, since it would lack this tension which carries it toward experience. [116] Undoubtedly, presence cannot be interpreted as obscure in itself, and this is why there really are essential necessities. Appearing requires a determination and cannot be thought *without* what appears. Nevertheless, that does not mean that these laws exhaust the being of the experience; that is, these laws do not exhibit themselves as positive entities. If experience is based on essential laws, it is a matter of laws *for* this experience, laws whose being comes only from what they structure, laws which, consequently, are effective only insofar as they are not positive. Therefore, instead of facticity being based on possibility, possibility on the contrary makes sense only within this facticity, as the unfolding of its mode of being. Essences give only the manner or style of the experience, "the *Sosein* and not the *Sein*" (VI 148/109). In reality, the condition under which a thing can appear is that, in its appearing, the thing *itself* does not appear; the unity which grounds the appearing cannot give *itself* in principle. Because this unity of the thing is grasped in and as an experience, it is just as much dissimulated there. And, conversely, by conceiving experience as presentation of this very unity, we would keep ourselves from understanding the facticity that defines it as experience. As Granel aptly puts it, "Husserl's reflection does not advance . . . toward the curious status of this 'itself' found in the perceived-thing-*itself*; this 'itself' which is present as what all the rest presents is also nothing other than this 'the rest' and thus, taken precisely in itself, recoils toward a sort of absence or 'nothing.'"[3] Already therefore we can see the necessity of overcoming the opposition of fact and essence. Indeed, there is no question of renouncing essence in favor of fact—the object must really be conceived as presence—but rather it is a question of understanding that the sense of the essence is to be unable to be distinguished from the experience of which it is the essence. It is a question of the essence presenting itself only as veiled in the experience whose determination it is. Consequently, presence would not be able to merge with the presentation of *what* is present.

Essence proceeds from an act, from a variation on the experience. This is the reason why it cannot claim to provide the being of the experience. As is well known, this variation consists in imagining the object otherwise until a determination appears without which the object would no longer be what it is, a determination then that represents the invariant of the variation. But that *without* [117] this determination the object stops being what it is does not mean in any case that this determination constitutes its being. It is no longer precisely *what* it is, but nevertheless it does not stop existing. The variation indeed makes appear a "*Sosein*," the condition under which the object is thus, but this condition does not exhaust its very being. Thus, insofar as the essence is the invariant *of* a variation, it refers to an invariable term in a deeper sense on which the act of variation rests. This invariable term is the very experience which, as an experience, cannot be made to vary but constitutes, on the contrary, the variation's universal horizon. This is why "the solidity, the essentiality of the essence is exactly measured by the power we have to vary the thing. A pure essence which would not be at all contaminated and confused with the facts could result only from an attempt at total variation" (VI 149/111). We must understand

---

3. G. Granel, *Le sens du temps et de la perception chez Husserl* (Paris: Gallimard, 1968), 145.

here that Merleau-Ponty does not intend to reduce essence to an abstraction, the variation to an induction. The freed essence is not above the facts, as if it were their abstract unity; it is really a determination of the very being that is grasped in it. In fact, the possibility of variation presupposes that the "itself" of which the variants are the exemplars is already in some way intended. The variation takes place according to an axis of identity, an implicit rule of kinship, which would be impossible if it dealt only with factual individuals, with individuals who, as such, are susceptible neither to unification nor to differentiation. This is why, as we have seen, Merleau-Ponty denounces the opposition between induction and *Wesenschau*. Induction makes sense only insofar as it is already a variation, only if the unity that it produces precedes itself in the individuals on which it works. This does not mean, however, that this unity can be posited apart from the individuals that incarnate it, and this is why the solidity of essence is dependent on the scope of the variation. In other words, this "itself" that animates the variation does not transcend it and does not distinguish itself from the act that makes it appear. In the very act of variation, the "itself" will be grasped as what grounds the variation. Although the variation is distinguished from an abstraction, although it gives way to a determination of the things themselves, the determination does not transcend the movement which makes it appear right in the things, as the invariant *of* this movement.

Merleau-Ponty notes that a pure essence could result only from an attempt at total variation. We can in [118] fact imagine that in an infinite variation the thing itself would transparently exhibit itself. But this would amount to ignoring the experiential ground to which the variation refers, and consequently it would be to miss the genuine meaning of the infinite. This infinite to which Merleau-Ponty alludes cannot be traversed; it admits of no form of closure and must therefore be distinguished from an objective infinity. His infinity actually qualifies *the excess of experience over essence*. Instead of the experience being attainable in its essence through an infinite variation, the very being of the experience makes a traversal of such an infinity impossible and consequently makes an essential apprehension impossible. The infinite is synonymous with experience itself, as what in principle exceeds every traversal, every closure. The solidity of the essence is measured by our power to vary the thing. Then we must add that essence is never pure, since this power is a finite power, inscribed in an experience. Such is the situation that has to be understood. There is a power of variation, which supposes a form of unity, a structure of the thing itself. The variation brings us closer to the being of this object, which is not *of a different order* than that of the essence. And yet, it does not go beyond itself toward a pure invariant; it does not exhaust the experience. The form of unity that it presupposes exists only as what is produced within the variation, that whose purity is measured by this same variation. The result is that the object too *is not exhausted* in its essence; it remains in withdrawal in relation to its essence. Nevertheless, that experience can be susceptible to an essential determination rules out the possibility that this determination is distinguished from the experience and that this experience would be reabsorbed into the positivity of the essence. In short,

> In order to really reduce an experience to its essence, we should have to achieve a distance from it that would put it entirely under our gaze, with all the implications of sensoriality or thought that come into play in it, bring it and bring ourselves wholly to the transparency of the imaginary, think it without the support of any ground, in short, withdraw to the bottom of nothingness. Only then could we know what moments positively make up the being of this experience. But would this still be an experience, since I would be soaring over it? (VI 149–50/111)

It is true that Husserl finds himself confronted with a difficulty when he considers the material domain. This is why he acknowledges that the essences given in perception are [119] inexact essences; he describes them as morphological (S 132/105; SHP 37/67). These inexact essences are characterized by the fact that they tend toward an exact essence, one that remains asymptotic to the particular essences without merging with them. All the nuances of red can be described as the degrees of an ideal red toward which they converge but which none exhibit. This decision truly reveals, in Merleau-Ponty's eyes, the presupposition that orders Husserl's whole philosophy. From the start, the essence is understood as a positive being, with the result that even though Husserl finds himself confronted with inexact essences, he maintains the pure essence under the form of the Kantian Idea instead of questioning the positivity of the essence.

> This double thinking that opposes the principle and the fact saves with the term "principle" only a presumption of the essence, although this is the moment to decide if it is justified, and to save the presumption it entrenches us in relativism, although by renouncing the essence that is intemporal and without locality we would perhaps obtain a true thought with regard to essence. It is on account of having begun with

the antithesis of the fact and the essence, of what is individuated in a point of space and time and what is forever and nowhere, that one is finally led to treat the essence as a limit idea, that is, to make it inaccessible. (VI 151/112)

Instead of noting the inexactitude of essence and challenging its autonomy in favor of its inscription in experience—in short, instead of renouncing the purity of the opposition between fact and essence—Husserl maintains the prejudice of the essence and reconciles this with the contradictory facts by recourse to the limit idea. That Husserl appeals to the Idea really reveals the tension that runs across his philosophy, a tension between the concern for the proximity to the phenomena and the continuation of the objectivistic prejudice. Instead of recognizing inexactitude as ultimate, he apprehends it as the negation of an exact essence, situated at infinity. For Merleau-Ponty, the intervention of the Idea in the course of Husserl's reflection, which has the function of saving the closure of the essence, is always an invitation to seek a depth of phenomenon that exceeds all closure.

Our experience cannot be described as contact, fusion with a positive reality. We must reintegrate Being to the dimension of appearing; we must understand the world as phenomenon. But on the other hand, the characterization of this appearing as [120] essence is also not satisfying. Instead of restoring our relation to the world, essence still dissimulates it. Because essence is thought as a positive reality, it distances us from the world just when it would claim to give it to us. This happens not because essence gives itself the world instead of understanding the mode of its givenness, as Descartes had thought, but because it thinks the very *presence* of the world *as a world*, because it determines the thought that must open the very world to us as a positive entity. Phenomenology does not satisfy its need for radicalism, that is, its need for a return to the "how" of the givenness, since for phenomenology, to go beyond the world toward its presence always means to go beyond this presence toward essence. Doubt is a "clandestine positivism," since what it denies—and, insofar as it denies it—it still affirms: "But conversely if we wished to go beyond it unto a sphere of absolute certitude that would be a sphere of meanings or essences, this absolute positivism would mean that he who questions had distanced Being and the world from himself so much that he was of them no longer" (VI 160/120). Thus the positivism of essences in its turn dissimulates a negativism. Doubt appears as a negation interior to Being, which is why it was not adequate to the being of questioning. But conversely, the positing of the essence conceals a negation *of Being* itself; it refers to a subject who is no longer *of* the world, who has withdrawn into the bottom of nothingness and who is able to have in relation to the world the absolutely frontal gaze of one who no longer has any inscription there. From this point of view, in fact, the thing no longer allows anything "implicit," any opacity; what had corresponded to the belonging to the world, namely, the thickness of the thing, is reduced to an essential law. The positing of the essence really presupposes a passage to infinity, a traversing of the infinite that is a traversing of the world itself. If finite variation can claim to give the essence, it does so insofar as it is performed from a viewpoint situated at infinity. A finite variation can give us the essence, Husserl says, since the arbitrary form in which it is actualized replaces infinity. But in reality this arbitrariness would not be able to be sufficient if infinity were not already posited in it. In fact, one of two things must be true: either a variation is actually necessary but, despite its arbitrary modality, it will never make us equal to essence, will always reveal only a *Sosein;* or pure essences will turn out to be accessible [121] but the one who intuits them is situated outside of the world at infinity, and we are left wondering then why a variation would be necessary. There is indeed a contradiction between the necessity of variation, which derives from our inscription in the world, and the essence that it claims to exhibit.

The philosophy of essence therefore is based on the presupposition of an absolute position, of a questioning which comes from beyond Being. This means that while the philosophy of essence claims to return to experience, it submits experience to "an abstract dilemma which experience ignores" (VI 215/162). There is something, something appears: in other words, "there is not nothing." That there is not nothing means that the hypothesis of nothing is senseless; it means that what there is exists in such a way that it cannot be denied. This formulation conceals "the impossibility of the ontological void" (VI 156/117). What it is impossible to have there is nothing. Negation appears, then, not as the negation of what there is but as designating its character of indetermination. Presence formulates itself in negative terms, when it cannot convert itself into a position. The philosophy of essence proceeds from a radicalization of this formula: it consists in thinking what there is *as the very negation of nothingness;* it consists in setting presence off against the backdrop of the hypothesis of nothing. The viewpoint of essence responds thus to the implementation of the principle of sufficient reason: "The problematic is of the type: why is there a perception of the world and *not no perception*" (VI 285/231). Therefore, against the backdrop of this abstract hypothesis of nothingness, which is correlative to the absolute disengagement of the subject in relation to the world, what is not nothing will be able to appear only as something determinate, as a thing, as an essence. The positivity of the essence exists in proportion to the absolute negativity of nothingness from which it is supposed to emerge. Confronted with nothingness, what is can only be exactly what it is, self-identical; it must admit of the fullness of determination which allows it somehow to resist the nothingness which is sucking it in. *What* the thing is makes its being; the thing is that being necessarily and fully because if it were other, the thing would not be at all. In short, Being would be nothing if it were not absolutely qualified. The positing of the essence—the reduction of the thing to a being that involves no fault, no opacity—indeed proceeds from its abstract opposition to a backdrop of nothingness, against which it can [122] only emerge perfectly defined.[4] The negation of experience, on which its apprehension as essence depends, contravenes the originary meaning of this experience, which is rightly *what cannot be denied*. Far from experience emerging from the backdrop of nothingness, experience is "the backdrop that we need in order to think nothingness in any way whatsoever" (VI 215/162). The philosophy of essence is simultaneously unfaithful, therefore, both to nothingness and to the thing. It is unfaithful to nothingness because it thinks nothingness as originary even though it can make sense only within Being. No longer understood as absolute negation, nothingness must be thought as absence of the thing in relation to pure determination, as the thing's self-absence. And this absence, this character of indetermination that is proper to ex-

4. Merleau-Ponty's debt to Bergson is obvious here. Bergson has shown in a definitive way that the metaphysics which draws Being from Nothingness, and asserts therefore that there is more in Being than in Nothingness, is the prisoner of a false problem. There is more in Nothingness than there is in Being since it expresses, *within Being,* the absence of what we were expecting. Bergson here allows Merleau-Ponty to ground his critique of the eidetic on the rejection of the principle of sufficient reason. This direct line of descent can also be demonstrated at the level of the phenomenology of history. Bergson's conception of a "retrograde movement of truth" feeds Merleau-Ponty's meditations on institution. In a general way—he explains this at least twice, in *In Praise of Philosophy* and in "Bergson in the Making" in *Signs*—Merleau-Ponty sees in Bergson's method a prefiguration of the intuition which animates his own procedure, the way of "an absolute knowledge which is not surveying but inherence" (S 231–32/184). For a more detailed analysis of the connection between Bergson and Merleau-Ponty, see my *Le tournant de l'expérience* (Paris: Vrin, 1998).

perience, does not conceal a negation of presence but mingles with presence. This indetermination means presence as negation. The phenomenon is the negation of the object insofar as it is determinate; that is, it is the affirmation of the experiential ground from which the object emerges and within which it remains withdrawn. The phenomenon is negation, not in the sense that it could not be at all, but in the sense that being, for the phenomenon, amounts to denying all full determination; it amounts to being irreducible to essence. The philosophy of essence is then unfaithful to the thing, and for the same reason: because it sets the thing off against the backdrop of nothingness and conceives the thing as fully determinate—instead of understanding that there is only nothingness as *the thing's* nothingness, instead of understanding that this nothingness grants to it its thingly being insofar as it is an experiential thing. The formula "there is not nothing" therefore must not be understood as the implementation of a first negation which, being based on a pure nothingness, would transform itself then into pure positivity, as the reversal [123] of a Nothingness into Being, a Nothingness that would already possess Being's fullness negatively. "There is not nothing" must be understood as an abstract image of a more fundamental situation which stops short of negation and affirmation. Thus, Merleau-Ponty notes, "what is not nothing is *something*, but: this something is not hard as a diamond, not unconditioned, *Erfahrung*" (VI 146n/109n). Actually, this formula describes a presence that cannot be realized in positivity; it describes a presence that is still withdrawn into the absence that it denies. And because this presence cannot transcend absence by transforming itself into positive being, this absence is also not pure absence, not nothingness. Because negation does not go beyond itself toward a positivity, the nothingness on which it is based cannot correspond to a pure negativity. This means that the negation is symmetrical: it is just as much a negation of nothingness as a negation of the determinate object. "There is not nothing" also means, then, "there is something." In short, the negation of the negation does not carry itself off into a position which would cancel its movement: "negation of negation and position: one does not have to choose between them" (VI 275/222; see also 318/264).

In the end, the question of essence seems inadequate to the being of interrogation, as was the question of fact. In fact, "no question goes toward Being: if only by virtue of its being as a question, it has already frequented Being, it is returning to it" (VI 161/120). While Descartes passed over in silence what is intended with the question, which itself was allowing him to think doubt as real rupture and knowledge as contact, the philosophy of essence misunderstood the belonging of the question to Being: from this non-place, the claim that we have reached an adamantine purity of essence can then be given free rein. Now it is really the belonging of the question to Being which grounds the possibility of its intention, so that its intention cannot in principle restore its object in a transparent way. In short, just as it is impossible that the question remain without an answer, it is impossible that the answer be immanent to the question; the interrogative is not an inverse mode of the indicative. Just as it is impossible that the question be a "pure gaping toward a transcendent Being," it is impossible that it be at an infinite distance, since then "we would not even have enough of the positive to raise a question" (VI 161/120). Under the pretext that the sense [124] cannot proceed from a consciousness belonging objectively to Being, the philosophy of essence denies to consciousness all being and pushes its relation to being to an infinite distance. While the question, insofar as it intends a sense, excludes any real belonging, nevertheless it does not presuppose the absence of any rootedness. The world is reducible to its phenomenon only insofar as the phenomenon, as phenomenon of the world, still proceeds from the world itself.

We can now bring to light the profound unity of the philosophy of essence and the philosophy of fact, of idealism and realism—beyond their apparent opposition. The extent to which *The Visible and the Invisible* distances itself from the earlier works is incontestably marked in this new realization. Then Merleau-Ponty had oscillated between empiricism and intellectualism. Because he had not yet opened up their common terrain, he himself remained dependent on this terrain at the very moment when his analysis of perception had invited him to go beyond it. But a more penetrating analysis of essence and existence was necessary for this overcoming to take place, an analysis that brings to light, in essence and existence, the same ontological orientation. Whereas Merleau-Ponty before could characterize the way he was seeking only by situating it *between* empiricism and intellectualism, now the discovery of their common root allows him to situate himself *elsewhere;* this "elsewhere" circumscribes the space of ontology. In fact:

> Whether we orient ourselves upon the essences, which are the more
> pure in the measure that he who sees them has no part in the world, in
> the measure, consequently, that we look out from the depths of nothing-

ness, or whether we seek to merge with the existing things, at the very point and at the very instant that they are, this infinite distance and this absolute proximity express in two ways, as a surveying or a fusion, the same relationship with the thing itself. These are the two positivisms. (VI 169/127)

What these two philosophies have in common is the conception of knowledge as adequation, as intuition. Something must come to stop up the look, and presence must be described in terms of a present being that is fully determinate. Real coincidence, which phenomenological idealism opposes, can then be overcome only in favor of an intellectual coincidence. Whereas this philosophy is established against the conception of knowledge as real contact, it does not manage to integrate distance into its definition of the phenomenon. In the two cases, the presence [125] of the world is therefore missed. On the side of the philosophy of fact, it is missed as *presence* of the world; factual coincidence necessarily excludes the distancing that the phenomenon requires, its constitutive remoteness. The dissimulation of the same in the alterity of aspects is understood as resting on a presence that is elsewhere, preserving the possibility of a fusion. Phenomenality is defined as the failure of a real contact, as appearance. But the philosophy of essence misses presence insofar as it is presence *of the world*. Once thought takes note of the distance of the phenomenon, of the impossibility of reaching the thing again as such, it takes this distance to the absolute; it transforms the reality of the thing into the nothingness of reality under the pretext that the thing does not rest in itself and then makes the "for-itself" appear as what alone resists this nothingness. Thus coincidence in the form of intellectual adequation finds itself restored. The distance of the thing flows back toward the proximity of the noema, and the phenomenon is lost insofar as it is the phenomenon of the world. The multiplicity, the alterity of aspects is dissolved in the "itself" [*même*] of the thing itself. The other is absorbed into the unity of the same [*même*], just as before the same recoiled behind the diversity of the other. The philosophy of essence no more succeeds in integrating the distance of the world with the proximity of sense than realist philosophy succeeds in integrating the proximity of appearing to the real distance of the world. On both sides, intuitionism is correlative with a positivism. Because presence is confused with the present being, with what is perfectly determinate, presence is conceived as fusion or adequation. The being is submitted to the simple alternation of presence or absence; it is entirely under the control of the look or it is not there at all, depending on whether what is at issue is the look of the eyes or the look of the mind.

3. The Transcendental Realism of Phenomenology

By means of the unity of the viewpoint that is at work in the concepts of fact and essence, it is possible to bring to light the limitation that the eidetic approach establishes within the transcendental perspective. Insofar as it remains an intuitionism, Husserl's transcendental idealism can be characterized as a *transcendental psychologism* in a higher sense. In other words, while, in a sense, Husserl overcomes the Cartesian viewpoint [126] by bringing to light the dimension proper to the phenomenon, he nevertheless remains imprisoned in this viewpoint as soon as he determines phenomenality as essentiality. In the form of essence, the positivity of facticity turns out to be restored. The determination of phenomenality as the presence of the thing itself in all of what presents it is still dependent on a mundane viewpoint, not in the restricted sense of sensible experience but in the sense of being a *being*. The philosophy of essence does not go beyond the philosophy of fact, since it thinks the very openness to the world in a way that is still mundane. Merleau-Ponty asserts this unambiguously at least once in a working note: "The same critique applies to these physiological reconstructions and to the intentional analysis: neither sees that never will one construct perception and the perceived world with these *positive* terms and relations. The endeavor is *positivist*: with something *innerweltlich,* with traits of the world, to *fabricate* the architectonics of the *Welt*" (VI 285/231). Granel's reflection echoes that of Merleau-Ponty here and helps us clarify it:

> We see what "psychologism" essentially consists in; it is situated at a
> depth still greater than that at which phenomenology combats it. There
> is a psychologism as soon as the being itself is taken as the figure of
> being, that is, as the type of openness (of "truth") in which the being
> appears. Thus, when the thing—a thing of perception, gathered in the
> evidence at the middle of the perceived, that is, as a *given* unity—must
> serve as the figure of the *primitive Gift* of diversity, the original openness in which the diversity is diversified first and foremost, in which it
> becomes itself as the diversity of a thing, this unity as openness cannot
> be a unity at all like that of the given thing, not at all like the style of
> the being; it must be only being itself as World. I cannot gather together

a manner of things within intra-mundaneity in order to make them play the role of openness that only the *weltende Welt* knows how to play and plays constantly.[5]

Thus, somehow by virtue of its radicality the transcendental reduction opens out onto a psychologism. Of course, Husserl says that transcendental subjectivity could not have the same ontological sense as that of the world, because if it did, it would fall back into a form of naturalism. But insofar as it is thought under the presupposition of a presencing [127] of essence and consequently of its positivity, subjectivity is situated beyond the world. Instead of grasping transcendental subjectivity as the place of the Absolute, as he claims, Husserl determines the Absolute as a non-place. Therefore, he remains prisoner of the mundane level, since this non-place is still a place, since this beyond of the world can only be in some way a positive locality. The exteriority of consciousness in regard to the world requires its full positivity, that is, the restoration of a mundane being in the middle of this exteriority. Husserl indeed preserves the transcendental realism that he criticizes in Descartes at a higher level. As soon as phenomenality flows back into positive essence, transcendental openness is reenclosed within the monad as the place of this non-place. Regardless of whether the difference of consciousness from the world is determined as a mundane difference or as an absolute difference, this differentiation always amounts to being given a pole which supports this difference and which, since it is established in relation to the world, remains mundane. Because of its very absoluteness, absolute difference degrades into a mundane difference, of which it is finally only a negative form. In his well-known article "The Phenomenological Philosophy of Edmund Husserl and Contemporary Criticism," Fink conceives the meaning of the transcendental reduction in this way:

> The transcending of the world which takes place in performing the phenomenological reduction does not lead outside of or away from the world to an origin which is separate from the world (and to which the world is connected only by some relation) as if leading us to some other world; the phenomenological transcending of the world, as the disclosure of transcendental subjectivity, is at the same time the *reten-*

5. Granel, *Le sens du temps et de la perception chez Husserl*, 112.

tion (Einbehaltung)[6] of the world within the universe of absolute "being" that has been exposed. The world remains *immanent* to the absolute and is discovered as lying within it.

And Fink concludes: "Just as the world is what it is only in terms of its 'origin,' so is this origin itself what it is only with reference to the world."[7] The genuine meaning of phenomenology and Husserl's limitation in relation to his own project seem to us to be exposed in these formulas, which Merleau-Ponty knew well. Because the transcendental reduction remains dependent on the eidetic, the origin of the world that it unveils tends to become an origin *outside* of the world, with the result that a mundane relation tends to be substituted for the constitutive relation. [128] As soon as it is situated radically outside of the world, consciousness sees its relation to the world degraded into a substantial relation; it is indeed through its very radicality that the transcendental perspective sinks into psychologism. And Merleau-Ponty asserts, after the evocative note we just cited, that "physiological reconstructions" and intentional analysis have in common this "postulate that the sole *Weltlichkeit* of the mind is of the type of the *Weltlichkeit* by end-to-end causality, the kind that reigns between the Cartesian *Blosse Sachen*" (VI 285/232). In Merleau-Ponty's eyes, the fact that Husserl finds himself confronting the impossibility of reaching the genuine *Weltlichkeit* of the mind, that is, of grasping the *Lebenswelt* as an originary dimension, goes hand in hand with the determination of subjectivity as being outside of the world and consequently as substantial. The terrain on which this double implication is grounded is that of the eidetic. To borrow Fink's terms, consciousness can be absolute only insofar as it is absolute *for* the world, only if consequently the retention of the world in the absolute is also *retention of the absolute in the world*. The origin is certainly an origin only if it is of an order other than that of which it is the origin, making it impossible for it to be situated as a reality in the world. But that equally forbids the origin from being exterior, since this alterity is still a figure of the same [*même*]. Thus, the origin is really what it is by means of the world. Its non-proximity to the world cannot be synonymous

6. Understood of course not in the sense that this term has in the context of the phenomenology of temporality, but as "held within," "inscription."
7. E. Fink, "The Phenomenological Philosophy of Edmund Husserl and Contemporary Criticism," in *The Phenomenology of Husserl,* ed. R. O. Elveton (Chicago: Quadrangle Press, 1970), 99–100.

with absolute distance. The origin must be on the side of the world, *of* the world, in order to unfold it *as* world. Such is the situation that Merleau-Ponty will seek to understand with the notion of the flesh: "The mind is neither here, nor here, nor here . . . and yet it is 'attached,' 'bound,' it is *not without bonds*" (VI 275/222). As the non-worldly condition of the world, the absolute must not simply be radically distinguished from the world, it must be held and understood within the openness it unfolds. This is why ontology must be understood as "intra-ontology": "What replaces causal thought is the idea of transcendence, that is, of a world seen within inherence in this world, by virtue of it, of an Intraontology" (VI 280/227). This really means that one must renounce the idea of consciousness, since in Merleau-Ponty's eyes, everything happens [129] as if this notion led inevitably to Cartesian substantialism, as if there were a higher and unnoticed truth of Cartesianism, which is that Cartesianism still envelops the philosophies that claim to complete Cartesianism and overcome it. Every reflective philosophy, he notes, "develops under the domination of concepts such as 'subject,' 'consciousness,' 'self-consciousness,' 'mind,' all of which, even if in a refined form, involve the idea of a *res cogitans*, of a positive being of thought—whence there results the immanence in the unreflected of the results of reflection" (VI 104/74). As soon as Husserl's transcendental consciousness, which is explicated within the presupposition of the eidetic, that is, within the presupposition of an intuitionism, restores the limitations of Cartesianism on another level—that is, as soon as it is led to determine the openness to the world in a mundane fashion—transcendental psychologism appears as the truth of consciousness itself. The concern for fidelity to the very experience of the world then calls for an entirely different perspective.

We can now see more clearly the nature and foundation of this to-and-fro movement between the primacy of fact and the primacy of essence that we evoked at the beginning of this chapter. This movement is determined by the implicit positivism at work in each of the positions. Each of them makes a claim to exclusivity and, to that extent, leads back to the antagonistic position. Reflective philosophy is characterized by its instability, by its incapacity to take up one direction without being led to adopt the opposite viewpoint. Reflective philosophy takes as its starting point the determination of presence as fact, as mundane positivity, and the determination of knowledge as real contact. However, it discovers the phenomenal field and unfolds the space of a negation, whether we are dealing with doubt or reduction; the latter is then interpreted in a way that conforms to the initial positivism, that is, not as revealing an ontological mode proper to the phenomenon but as reference to a positive being, as the path to essence. As soon as we make pure spatio-temporal individuals our starting point, the comprehension of their unity, which variation reveals, can consist only in the recourse to a transcendent individual which runs across the multiplicity of factual individuals. Because reflection first grasps the world implicitly *stopping short of* its phenomenality, it is led by its very movement to situate the world *beyond* its phenomenality. Because presence is first missed [130] by a lack, in the end it is missed by excess. The determination of the world as natural reality corresponds to a *lack of presence* for which one can compensate only by its reduction to essence, that is, by an *excess of presence.* Of course, this first movement calls for its reversal. Just as the tacit reduction of the phenomenon to its factual positivity led, in a second moment, to the liberation of the specific determination of its phenomenality, the explication of its phenomenality in terms of essence, its concentration in the *eidos,* leaves the space of facticity unoccupied and thus once more provides the means for the fact to be reclaimed in a realist fashion. Just as the reduction of the world to facticity forced us to recognize the field of the phenomenon as such, the reduction of the phenomenon to the insular for itself—that is, again, to the in-itself—forces us to clarify the field of the in-itself once more. Thus: "there is a thought (reflective thought) that, precisely because it would like to grasp the thing in itself immediately, falls back on the subjectivity——And which, conversely, because it is haunted by the being for us, does not grasp it and grasps only the thing 'in itself,' in signification" (VI 252/199). This constitutive disequilibrium that, for Merleau-Ponty, characterizes reflective philosophy is at the very heart of Husserl's way of proceeding. Because of this disequilibrium, the profound identity of Husserl's procedure with the Cartesian movement prevails over the claim that they differ from one another. Concerning the reduction, Merleau-Ponty notes:

> Wrongly presented—in particular in *The Cartesian Meditations*—as a suspending of the *existence of the world*——If that is what it is, it lapses into the Cartesian default of being a *hypothesis of the* Nichtigkeit *of the world,* which immediately has as its consequence the maintenance of the *mens sive anima* (a fragment of the world) as indubitable——Every negation of the world, *but also* every neutrality with regard to the essence of the world, has as its immediate consequence that one misses the transcendental. (VI 225/171–72)

The terms that Merleau-Ponty emphasizes here are not insignificant. The determination of the world as existence, that is, the flowing of phenomenality back into natural being, amounts to a degradation of the reduction into doubt. If the phenomenal world is grasped as natural existence, then every attempt to distance oneself from it will take the shape of a negation. The fabric of phenomenality is disrupted by this initial identification so that no procedure can preserve its thickness. Then, the reduction can liberate [131] only what doubt reveals. The transcendental is understood in a mundane fashion and then it turns out to be incapable of accomplishing its constitutive function. Because Husserl begins by dissolving the phenomenon into the in-itself, the in-itself is preserved within the transcendental sphere, which is then confused with a "fragment of the world." Merleau-Ponty shows this a number of times: by describing the natural attitude in the form of naturalism, Husserl is led to give a theoretical or objectivistic meaning to the transcendental. Because the world is grasped first at the level of facticity, its condition will be the world grasped on the level of essentiality, since "to acknowledge naturalism and the envelopment of consciousness in the universe of *blosse Sachen* as an event is precisely to posit the theoretical world to which they belong as primary, which is an extreme form of idealism" (RC 112/148; see also S 206/162–63; VI 280/226–27). This reversal of realism into idealism is based on their ontological complicity; the positivity of a nature reconceived in terms of naturalism prefigures the positivity of essence. As soon as the immediate relation to the world is characterized as natural *attitude,* positivism is at work, and natural being is called forth in order to be maintained at the level of the *eidos* that must, however, reabsorb natural being.

For Merleau-Ponty, by contrast, the point is to situate oneself above pure nature while stopping short of essence, at the level of existence such as it gives itself. It is by returning to the things themselves, by understanding the phenomenon without any positivistic prejudice, that the being of the phenomenon can be explicated otherwise than in terms of essence. For an ontological way of proceeding, what is at issue is to reconceive phenomenality beyond the opposition between the natural attitude and the transcendental attitude; this is an opposition that conceals within itself an approach to Being in terms of the being.

Reflective philosophy is a way of thinking which, as Merleau-Ponty says in a working note already cited, lapses into subjectivity because it wants to grasp the thing in itself *immediately;* it is a way of thinking that lapses into essence, which is the same as saying that it lapses into the thing in itself, because it wants to possess subjectivity *immediately*. What misunderstanding is at the root of this positivism of reflective philosophy? Of what mediation does this attempt at immediate grasp remain ignorant? The response to these questions leads us back to the problem of language: "Whether one installs oneself at the level of statements, which are the proper order of the essences, or in the silence of the things, whether one trusts in speech absolutely, [132] or whether one distrusts it absolutely—the ignorance of the problem of speech is here the ignoring of all mediation" (VI 169/127). For the philosophy of fact, the world is given as an absolutely mute presence, a silence that cannot be broken: it reaches the world below all utterability; it forgets that lived experience is of the "spoken-lived." The unawareness of the phenomenon of speech, of the possibility for the world of being said, leads to its definition as factual positivity. This is why a reduction turns out to be necessary, a reduction that allows us to understand the world on the basis of this possibility, that is, to understand the world as sense. By characterizing sense in terms of positive meaning, however, the philosophy of essence testifies just as much to its misunderstanding of speech. It considers the expressive operation as something completed; it forgets operative speech in favor of constituted speech. Instead of interrogating the emergence of language in the world, it naively gives itself language in the form of a world. While the philosophy of fact apprehended the world below speech, the philosophy of essence remains somehow caught in the phenomenon of expression and moves along with it rather than understanding it. The philosophy of essence thinks the world as that which is always already said or rather as that which can be said in an exhaustive way, as that whose being is ideality, an ideality of which linguistic signs are only the contingent mark. While the first considers the world as an impenetrable silence, the second considers it as an already made language. This is why the philosophy of essence too requires a reduction, which is the reverse of that of the philosophy of fact, a reduction which allows us to reach sense again at its very birthplace, which allows us to make it appear as proceeding from the world, or at least from a dimension of the world—namely, the dimension of actual speech. Therefore, by returning to speech as fundamental mediation, Merleau-Ponty can claim to overcome the opposition between fact and essence. While the world is utterable, and this allows it to escape from pure facticity, it is never completely utterable; it remains withdrawn from what expresses it, and this allows it to escape from pure essentiality. Presence must be reconceived as *logos;* its transcendence corresponds to what, in expression, remains in principle unexpressed. And this transcendence is not the contrary of sense but its most profound dimension, since in the act of expression sense is its own imminence. Thus the critiques that are aimed at the eidetic reduction [133] can be clarified. They amount to the affirmation that the eidetic reduction passes over in silence the fact that it proceeds necessarily from speech (VI 290/236); by ignoring speech, the variation misunderstands its own inscription in the world and can claim then to fulfill itself in exhibiting the essence. But that the variation proceeds from speech equally excludes the pure and simple rejection of essence in favor of fact. The possibility of saying the world presupposes that there are determinations present in the world which, although they cannot be posited for themselves, sustain the claim to ground a rational universe:

> Each vector of the perceived spectacle posits, beyond its aspect at the moment, the principle of certain equivalences in the possible variations of the spectacle. It inaugurates on its own account a *style* of the explication of objects and a *style* of our movements with respect to them. This mute or operational language of perception begins a process of knowledge which it cannot accomplish. (PM 175/124)

Ultimately, for Merleau-Ponty, the issue lies in thinking the possibility of the variation as such, insofar as it merges with the possibility of language. However, if we rediscover the problem of language in that of variation, the recourse to the latter still clarifies the former. By considering language on the basis of variation, we will be able to reconceive language at its root, that is, at the place of its articulation with the world. It will be a matter then of understanding the world as the unity that exists only as the many within which it is sealed, as the reality whose diversity sustains itself only by being situated on an axis of unity.

8   Being and Nothingness: Dialectic

1. The Sartrean Dialectic and Its Ambivalence

[135] In Merleau-Ponty's eyes, Cartesian philosophy is character-ized by an alternation between the recognition of the unreflective—the viewpoint of "life"—and the recognition of reflection, which corresponds to the viewpoint of the understanding. This ontological "diplopia" cannot be surmounted in favor of one of its terms, since it is true, simultaneously, that we have access to a brute world and that nevertheless the possibility of a reflection is rooted in it. The result is that the world withdraws from us like an abyss. Since it is the world of experience, the world is not re-ducible to being the object of science. And yet, this experience is not the negation of all science; it harbors the possibility of objectification. Al-though the "diplopia" cannot be surmounted, nevertheless the issue does not lie in accepting it, in maintaining these two orientations as reflective philosophy has done, because they are indeed irreconcilable. One must take possession of them; that is, one must define the openness to the world in such a way that instead of making it into a blind contact with the in-itself, it appears as the beginning of reflection. One must grasp the unreflective not as the immediate negation of reflection but as "reference-negation." Conversely, this means that reflection must be defined not as proceeding from an autonomous and positive sphere, from whose viewpoint the un-reflective would be definitively incomprehensible, but as what draws its ownmost possibility from the unreflective itself. In short, what is at issue is to show how the "retiring into oneself" is identical with the "leaving of oneself." It looks as though Husserl's way of proceeding will not allow us to truly surmount the Cartesian duality. While Husserl's wish was to re-turn to the things themselves, when it is a matter of grasping the "how" of their givenness, the openness to the world [136] is still characterized in an intuitionist and positive way by means of the *eidos*. The result is that the openness comes to conceal the world instead of liberating its thick-ness. Then, the alternation reemerges between a natural attitude, in which the world is cut off from its appearing, and a transcendental attitude, in which the natural attitude is restored on another level and in which, con-

sequently, appearing itself is conceived as a positivity where the actual moment of appearing is dissolved.

It is necessary to take another path. Since reflection and the unreflective are reconciled in our life, there must be a way to conceive their unity without compromising one of the terms, to overcome this abstract duality in favor of the soil where the unreflective will be able to appear as a moment of reflection and where reflection will be able to appear as a moment of the unreflective. It seems that this is precisely what we find in dialectical philosophy. For dialectical philosophy, in fact, each of the two terms has its truth outside of itself; each is itself only by proceeding toward its other. Negation must be conceived no longer as the reverse of the two positions, but as the very movement of the content. Then there will no longer be an alternation between the in-itself and the for-itself. The in-itself will be itself truly only through its other, only through the mediation of the for-itself; and the for-itself will be itself in turn only insofar as it has become, that is, only insofar as it also has been withdrawn into its other, the in-itself, by the mediation from which it becomes what it is. The identity of each of the terms is no longer irreconcilable with their opposition. Insofar as each of them merges with its own becoming, its identity is completed only as its difference from itself. Dialectical philosophy really rejects surveying thought, that frontal thought which begins by putting itself outside of Being, which fixes the terms in order to reconstruct their relation abstractly. Dialectical philosophy, by contrast, is the thought that makes contact with experience; it is implicated in the movement and does not dominate it. Instead of imposing its own categories on the movement and thereby disfiguring it, dialectical thought is content with accompanying it. To say that each term merges with its own becoming is to say that thought is inseparable from this very becoming; it is to say that it coincides with the actual movement by which each term becomes what it is. There is no other way to conceive the movement in its truth than to carry it out. Merleau-Ponty summarizes this in the following way:

> whether in the relations within being or in the relations of being with me, dialectical thought is that which admits that each term is itself only by proceeding toward the opposed term, becomes what it is through the movement, that it is one and [137] the same thing for each to pass into the other or to become itself, to leave itself or to retire into itself, that the centripetal movement and the centrifugal movement are one sole movement, because each term is its own mediation, the exigency for a

becoming, and even for an auto-destruction which gives the other.
(VI 124/90–91)

And, Merleau-Ponty adds, "this is what we are looking for." One has to wonder, however, if the truth of dialectical thought is contained in the dialectical philosophies themselves. Does not dialectical philosophy, by thematizing itself, radically miss the movement that it wants to unveil? Does not its fidelity to experience transform itself into infidelity as soon as it is taken up as dialectical *philosophy*? Merleau-Ponty's purpose in the chapter of *The Visible and the Invisible* titled "Interrogation and Dialectic" lies precisely in the clarification of this ambiguity and consequently in determining his proximity to and his distance from this philosophy. This clarification takes place then essentially in the form of a confrontation with Sartre's philosophy: "Sartre's is a philosophy which manifests, more than any other has done, the crisis, the essential difficulty, and the task of dialectic" (RC 84/128).

Sartre is first concerned with rediscovering the world as it is given in unreflective life. What defines the world is that it is incommensurable with our thought; what defines the thing is that it remains in itself, that it is *in-itself*. Instead of reconceiving the world as its phenomenality, Sartre rejoins the world in its transcendence. The world is that which, of itself, is foreign to its phenomenality and in no way needs to appear in order to be. That does not mean, however, a return to immediate realism, nor does it raise again the question of transcendental consciousness. As Francis Jeanson has shown, for Sartre, unlike Heidegger, it is not a matter of returning to a position prior to Husserl, of engaging in a radical critique of subjectivity in order to find a way toward the plenitude of Being. On the contrary, in Sartre's eyes it is because Husserl does not think subjectivity with sufficient radicality that he finally misses transcendence.[1] From this point of view, Sartre meets up with the critique developed by Merleau-Ponty: it is the positivity of essence, and correlatively the reality of subjectivity, which keeps intentionality from being fulfilled as the givenness of a transcendence. [138] But this is true only from this viewpoint, because for Merleau-Ponty the solution will be the "decompression" of the positivity of the *eidos* in order to stop short of subjectivity, at its point of insertion

1. F. Jeanson, *Le problème moral et la pensée de Sartre* (Paris: Myrte, 1947); trans. R. V. Stone as *Sartre and the Problem of Morality* (Bloomington: Indiana University Press, 1980).

in Being, while for Sartre the solution will be to start from Husserlian consciousness by radicalizing the opposition between consciousness and the world. Thus, in *The Transcendence of the Ego,* which already contains the seed for all of *Being and Nothingness,* Sartre shows that the determination of transcendental consciousness in terms of the ego introduces an opacity, a positivity, and finally a transcendence into consciousness which, by dividing it from itself, separates it from the world of which it is conscious, the result being that it loses the status of being a non-substantial absolute and falls to the rank of being a monad. Therefore, one has to think the transcendental subject as an impersonal field: "In a sense it is a *nothing,* since all physical, psycho-physical, and psychic objects, all truths, all values are outside it; since my *me* has itself ceased to be part of it. But this nothing is *all* since it is *consciousness of* all these objects."[2] Thus to understand consciousness in a way that conforms to the truth of intentionality is to conceive it as *nothingness.* And the limitation of Husserl's philosophy lies not in the fact that he refers the transcendental field to a consciousness and in the end to ideality, but in the fact that by conceiving this ideality as a positivity, he still situates consciousness on the side of Being. Therefore it does not possess the translucence that would allow it to gain access to what rests in itself before it. By defining consciousness as nothingness, we finally find ourselves with the ability to overcome the duality of the in-itself and the for-itself. Insofar as it is nothing, nothingness is sustained only by its openness to Being, by its completion as Being. Its futility is preserved by the plenitude of Being. In fact, that nothingness might somehow be distinguished from Being in order to be posited alongside of Being would mean that we have introduced into it a positivity which, no matter how restricted it is, would contravene its nihilation. Nothingness therefore is a "fissure that deepens in the exact measure that it is filled" (VI 79/53). Its opposition to Being is synonymous with its identity with Being. The alternation between the idealist and the realist position was due to the failure to think the duality of consciousness and the world with sufficient radicality. Because the two terms were still grasped from the viewpoint of Being, because they preserved the fact of being in common, no matter how distinct they might be, they were [139] doomed to exclude one another. Conversely, the duality no longer implies a contradiction when it is no

2. J. P. Sartre, *La transcendance de l'ego* (Paris: Vrin, 1965), 74; trans. F. Williams and R. Kirkpatrick as *The Transcendence of the Ego: An Existentialist Theory of Consciousness* (New York: Noonday, 1957), 93.

longer understood as a duality *between beings* but as a duality between Being itself and what is not in any way, namely, nothingness. In a sense, for Sartre the point is to take Husserl's intuition as far as it will go, the intuition that consciousness, insofar as it must be the bearer of intentionality, cannot exist in the same sense as the object of which it is conscious, cannot be endowed with reality. Consciousness is an absolute only if it has nothing in common with that upon which it bears, only if consequently it is absolute spontaneity. Because they are radically opposed, Being and nothingness no longer play against each other and are at the same time indiscernible. In this way, the alternation that continuously confronted reflective philosophy is surmounted—that is, the alternation between the irreducible duality of the in-itself and the for-itself, on the one hand, and the necessity of overcoming this duality toward a unity, on the other. One need only reconceive the duality at such a level of radicality that the two terms, no longer being of the same order, can coexist by sustaining each other.

> Thus disappears the antinomy of idealism and realism: it is true that "knowledge" as nihilation is sustained only by the things themselves in which it is founded, that it could not affect being, that it "adds nothing" to it and "takes nothing" from it, that it is a "shimmering of nothingness" at its surface—and at the same time it is true that, again as nihilation, and inasmuch as nothingness is absolutely unknown to being, "knowledge" gives it this negative but original determination of being "Being *such as it is*," the recognized or acknowledged, the sole being that *would have a sense*. (VI 82/55–56)

Therefore there is no choice between the unreflective and reflection, between transcendence and immanence. Because consciousness is nothingness, nothing separates it from itself; it is an immediate self-relation. But because of this, nothing points it to itself any longer; nothing interposes itself between consciousness and the world, and consequently its interiority is synonymous with the openness to transcendence.

Now, Merleau-Ponty notes that this philosophy of the negative leaves an uneasy impression:

> It describes our factual situation with more penetration than had ever before been done—and yet one retains the impression that this situation is one that is being surveyed from above, and indeed it is: the more one describes experience as a compound of being and nothingness, the more

their absolute distinction is confirmed; [140] the more the thought adheres to experience, the more it keeps it at a distance. (VI 120/87)

On the one hand, the openness to the world is clarified as a unity of Being and nothingness, beyond the duality of the in-itself and the for-itself. But, on the other hand, we are able to reach this identity only by means of a radical opposition that is renewed exactly insofar as it is surmounted. The paradox is therefore based on the fact that instead of drawing the consequences of experience at the level of the categories utilized by reflective philosophy, instead of understanding its own description of experience as an invitation to transform these categories, the philosophy of the negative maintains these categories by defining them in such a way that the unity of experience can finally be reconstituted. The philosophy of the negative reflects into the categories of reflection the requirement of unity that experience embodies; consequently, it thinks the in-itself and the for-itself in such a way that their opposition no longer dismembers their relation. Their distinction is not put back into question; the distinction is radicalized to the point of making the unity comprehensible. However, can this unity, namely, the openness to Being which advents in experience, be grasped as it actually is even while the categories of reflective philosophy are maintained? Must we not finally put this alternative of duality and unity into question? In reality, this philosophy provides only "the abstract portrait of an experience" (VI 105/75). It incorporates into the in-itself and the for-itself the passage between them attested by experience, but it does not restore the very movement of this experience. The passage would become impossible as soon as, under the terms *Being* and *nothingness*, the fixity of reflective categories is maintained. The passage then would be accomplished only at the expense of renewing their opposition. The unity of experience is reconstituted or "mimed" on a logical plane; it is not actually put back together. Sartre's solution consists finally in conceiving consciousness in such a way that it leads to Being without really transforming its conscious being; it consists in conceiving Being so that it is offered to consciousness without its positivity and its density being penetrated. By defining consciousness as nothingness, Sartre does not show how it is actually open to Being; he is content to determine consciousness in such a way that it cannot be *thought* without recourse to Being. He brings to light a necessity for thought, an abstract necessity, but he does not accompany the actual movement. It is a matter of [141] conferring on each term a determination through which its identity can be sustained only by the positing of the other term. If one thinks according to the pure negative, identity or positivity is already given. If one thinks according to the pure density of Being, one has already posited the pure negativity of nothingness:

> but if they are absolute opposites they are not defined by anything that would be proper to them. As soon as the one is negated the other is there, each of them is only the exclusion of the other, and nothing prevents them, in the end, from exchanging their roles: there subsists only the split between them. Reciprocally alternative as they may be, they together compose one sole universe of thought, since each of them is only its retreat before the other. (VI 104/74)

As an immediate negation, nothingness is just as much an immediate affirmation of Being. Made explicit at the strictly logical level, the openness to the world is reduced to the abstract necessity, for an absolute opposition, of being produced as an absolute identity. As Merleau-Ponty notes, Being and nothingness are not truly united: "they only more quickly succeed one another before thought" (VI 98/ 68–69).

Since each term is itself only by being identified with the other, every actual *difference* between them turns out to be eliminated. Insofar as the movement is lacking, the reality of each of the poles between which the movement takes place is also lacking. This dialectic deforms both the relation and the terms. In fact, because the passage is immediately led back to identity, the opposites, whose opposition nourishes this identity, have no content of their own. Nothingness is already absorbed into the plenitude of Being; Being is already posited "as such" by the futility of nothingness. If each of the terms could be defined in its own terms, then a difference would reappear which, since it would no longer be an absolute opposition, could not thereby fulfill itself as an identity. In Sartre's eyes, we would then fall back into the aporias of Husserlian idealism. As soon as the movement that bears each term toward its other is not grasped in its actuality, as soon as it is always already actualized by thought under the form of an abstract identification, the poles that bear it lose their own consistency. Conversely, it is by thinking an *actual* passage, beyond pure and simple identity, that we will be able to make the moments of the passage explicit as difference or actuality while stopping short of an absolute opposition. The openness to the world in fact will be able to remain withdrawn from the world, precisely insofar as [142] it unfolds the world, only if the for-itself is not characterized as nihilation. It is only to the extent that the for-itself is endowed with a certain consistency that the openness, which requires a certain distance from the object, can be actualized. The entire difficulty will then lie in trying to conceive this consistency without reconnecting it to positivity, that is, without either transforming this distance into intellectual adequation or reabsorbing the in-itself into the for-itself. In short, Sartre does not genuinely rejoin experience; he proposes only a logical "scale model" of experience. For its own thickness, which is the identity of a proximity and a distance—a proximity which, distinct from identity, maintains distance and a distance which, not going outside of itself toward opposition, maintains proximity—he substitutes the abstract identity of an opposition and an identity. The openness to the world is schematized in the form of a necessity of the understanding, a necessity that proceeds from the prior definition of the terms through their opposition. The philosophy of the negative only apparently manages to overcome the initial duality. Since reflective philosophy based this duality on two positions, that of the subject and that of the object, the distance between them seemed impossible to overcome. Sartrean dialectic conceives each term as subsisting only by bearing itself toward the other, so that it too does not overcome the duality in favor of a deeper relation that would ground its possibility. It schematizes the to-and-fro to which reflective philosophy was led; it takes up the tension by showing that the duality of the in-itself and the for-itself, which was formerly lived as an antagonism, in reality founds a reconciliation, on the sole condition that it be thought as an absolute duality. The alternation of proximity and distance—a proximity that experience reveals and a distance that is inherent to the concepts of subject and object—the alternation which presents a problem for reflective philosophy because it accentuated the positivity of the world and of the subject, is grasped through the philosophy of the negative as characteristic of the terms in question. While formerly the positivity of the terms entailed an alternation that was antagonistic, the terms are now defined through their very alternation. The only thing to be done is to disconnect thought enough in order for it to accompany the alternation, in order for it to measure up to the vivacity of its movement. This does not amount to surmounting the antagonism, since if "philosophy is not a rupture with the world, nor a coinciding with it," it is not "the alternation of rupture and coincidence either" (VI 135/98). Thus the ambivalence [143] of this philosophy is based on the fact that at the moment when it rejoins experience, as the *mixture* of Being and nothingness, it disfigures it precisely by conceiving this mixture as proceeding from *Being* and *nothingness*. It manages to approach experience only by situating itself farther away from it.

2. Dialectic and Reflective Philosophy

This means that Sartrean philosophy does not go beyond reflective philosophy. And if this dialectic remains unrealized, that is because it remains in the end "bound by a pre-dialectical ontology" (RC 128/159). Sartre's philosophy only seems to be an alternative to reflective thought. In a certain way, it represents the most radical form of reflective thought, since, in order to reach the movement of experience again, it is forced to carry the duality of consciousness and object to its most extreme position —that is, to give the duality a definition that is fed, less than ever, on a contact with experience. In order to found the unity, the "mixture" of experience, the openness of consciousness to the world must be reconceived on the plane of pure meaning: "The thought of the pure negative or of the pure positive is therefore a high-altitude thought [*une pensée de survol*], which operates on the essence or on the pure negation of the essence, on terms whose meaning has been fixed and which it holds in its possession" (VI 99/69). Earlier we said that the philosophy of essence proceeded from an infinite distance taken in regard to the world, that this philosophy gave itself a subject that is not of the world and that could therefore dominate all the corporeal implications of the object in order to grasp it transparently. However, insofar as the appearing was precisely determined as essence, that is, as endowed with positivity, something of the subject's belonging to the world somehow remains. The mistake of the philosophy of essence was not so much that it ignored our contact with the world as that it wanted to reach the contact *itself* in an immediate way. The result was that it was led to present the contact as an entity and to miss it as an initiation *to the world*. We could say that Sartre's philosophy takes the distance of the subject to the world to the second power: this distance is not even retained in the positivity of representations. As nothingness, the subject is no longer, in [144] any way, *of* the world. This is why nothingness can be open to the world in an absolutely frontal way, even without the mediation of essence. The world is seized exactly as it is, as a transcendent reality; even the modalities of its appearance, the "how" of its appearing, do not maintain it at a distance. This absolute distance can then be produced as absolute proximity; to a subject who is in no way implicated in the world, the world will appear as a pure flatness, deprived of determination and of relief, that is, as an in-itself. The Sartrean subject is a divine subject who, from its absolute distance, can carry before it Being itself, can pierce its darkness without even going through representations. Sartre's philosophy is a phenomenology *without phenomenality* that rediscovers in the finitude of the phenomenon the sovereignty of a consciousness that is equal to God (see, for example, PHP 411/358; UAC 28/146). This is the reason why inter-subjectivity will pose such a crucial problem: it will reveal to consciousness a finitude that it will not be able to possess insofar as it is nothingness.

Thus, even though it claims to reach experience again, in the end Sartre's philosophy looks like a radical idealism. And this means that the presupposition that governed the idealism of essence eminently determines the thought of the negative. Earlier we said that just as the negativism of doubt refers to a clandestine positivism, the positivism of essence still refers to a negativism. Now we must add that the negativism of nothingness conceals in turn a positivism. It is precisely this positivistic presupposition that, in a higher form, creates a distance from experience that the philosophy of nothingness claims to reach again in an immanent way. Sartre and Merleau-Ponty are in agreement in denouncing Husserlian intuitionism; both recognize that by conceiving phenomenality in terms of essence, Husserl contravenes the requirements of intentionality. Nevertheless, Merleau-Ponty denounces the ontological presupposition of the philosophy of essence, which means that he criticizes not so much *essence itself as its positivity.* Therefore, he does not renounce the dimension of meaning. In contrast, Sartre does not bring to light the ontological attitude that is at work in the essence, namely, the determination of Being on the basis of the being. His negation of essence in terms of nothingness *is the heir,* in a negative way, *of its positivity.* Because the positivity of essence is led back to the very level of its [145] negation, negation is understood as an abstract negation. It closes off the world to us, the world that it should have been unfolding. Therefore, because the moment of phenomenality is reconceived *in opposition to essence rather than in opposition to its positivity,* it is dissolved into the nihilation of consciousness. In other words, Sartrean consciousness is as negative as Husserl's essence was positive, which means that it is negative through and through. This is where the root of Sartrean ambivalence resides: it comes as close as possible to the openness to the world, but its description remains dependent on a "positivist" presupposition. This openness then is dissolved into the abstraction of a pure nothingness. The philosophy of nothingness is still a form of immediate thought. Although it makes us see the characteristics of intentionality for the first time, the necessity of not considering intentionality on the plane of the being, this negative requirement is itself reconceived in an immediate mode. Nothingness becomes fixed in the entity and thought stops accompanying the intentional production. In fact,

> If we maintain strictly that [nothingness] is not, we still elevate it to a sort of positivity, we confer upon it a sort of being, since through and through and absolutely it is *nothing*. The negative becomes a sort of quality precisely because one fixes it in its power of refusal and evasion. A negativist thought is identical to a positivist thought, and in this reversal remains the same in that, whether considering the void of nothingness or the absolute fullness of being, it in every case ignores thickness, depth, the plurality of planes, the background worlds.
> (VI 96/67–68; Merleau-Ponty's emphasis)

The positivity of nothingness therefore is based somehow on its homogeneity, its univocity. Sartre does not see that the negation of essence makes sense only if it is exercised also *in opposition to itself as fixed negation,* that is, as nothingness. He does not see that the nihilation of nothingness also implies the dissolution of its own homogeneity. A philosophy of nothingness is still not realized as long as it defines nothingness as *pure* nothingness. Nothingness is genuinely nothingness only if it is not nothingness through and through. Such a philosophy must consist in overcoming the opposition of Being and nothingness that, as an immediate opposition, restores within nothingness the positivity of essences: "It is still saying too much of nothingness to say that it *is not,* that it is pure negation: that is to fix it in its negativity, to treat it as a sort of essence, to introduce the positivity of words into it, whereas it can count only as what has neither name, nor repose, [146] nor nature" (VI 121/88; Merleau-Ponty's emphasis). Thus, the philosophy of intuition and the philosophy of nothingness are synonymous; they are both forms of immediate thought, that is, positive thought.

We noted in Husserl that the positivity of essence was in the end a response to the maintenance of consciousness as *mens sive anima.* Likewise, we can say here that insofar as his whole analysis still takes place within the presupposition of a reality of consciousness, Sartre fixes nothingness in its negative purity, that is, in its positive purity. While, on the one hand, Sartre sees in the notion of nothingness the means of avoiding the aporias of the Husserlian conception of consciousness—that is, the means of thinking the openness to Being in such a way that no opacity holds consciousness back in itself—on the other hand, he characterizes this nothingness itself as consciousness. Thus he situates it in an absolute distance from Being and then determines intentionality in an abstract way, as proceeding from a reality which, being nothing through and through, is open to a transcendence which is entirely in-itself. Instead of the authentic discovery of phenomenality as nothingness leading him to reject consciousness—which would suppose in the same movement that one conceive nothingness as what has "neither name, nor repose, nor nature"—Sartre somehow props nothingness up against consciousness and then reconceives intentionality only as a relation between two poles. Even though his project lies in purifying consciousness of every substantial qualification, he is still dependent on these qualifications as long as he continues to conceive of nothingness as the determination of consciousness, rather than as the nothingness of consciousness. The double relation, of rupture and coincidence, which characterizes the openness to Being "remains . . . incomprehensible . . . because it is still a consciousness—a being that is wholly appearing—that is charged with bearing it" (VI 135/99). And Merleau-Ponty adds, in terms that are exactly parallel to those with which he denounced Husserl's Cartesianism:

> Therefore sense is not nihilation, nor a sacrifice of the For Itself to the In Itself——To envisage such a sacrifice, such a *creation* of the truth, is still to think according to the model of the In Itself, on the basis of the In Itself, and, since it escapes, to confide in the For Itself the heroic mission of making it be——To envisage that is still to think the *Weltlichkeit* of minds according to the model of Cartesian space. (VI 269/216)

[147] Through a circular movement, Sartre's philosophy leads us back to that of Descartes, and even, in a sense, back farther than Descartes. Sartre's positivism, in the sense we have explicated it, leads back to a realism. Through its very "massiveness," nothingness can open out only onto the flat positivity of the in-itself. By questioning the natural position of a reality in itself, Descartes brings the problem of phenomenality to the first level. Phenomenology fulfills this movement by attempting to think phenomenality in itself instead of subordinating it immediately to the in-itself, which was still the case with Descartes, who, from the moment of doubt, remained dependent on the natural thesis. Husserl, however, tends to determine the moment of the phenomenon as a positivity and thus restores the Cartesian equivocation. Since it is the intellectual possession of the essence, the openness to Being is understood as the position of a being; a certain sense of Being is still presupposed instead of being thought. It is really this of which Sartre becomes aware. However, in proceeding, by means of the notion of nothingness, to an immediate negation of essence,

he brutally leads us back to the in-itself and makes us lose in a single stroke the dimension of the phenomenon in which Descartes was already entrenched. Thus, "The long evolution that had moved the positive from the world over to the side of the consciousness, which had become the correlative of the world and its connecting principle—but at the same time prepared philosophy to install non-being as the pivot of being—would abruptly be concluded at the extremity of idealism by the rehabilitation and the primacy of the In Itself" (VI 134/99). And we have to add that this outcome, at the extremity of idealism, is an extreme idealism, since in the end it is the determination of the openness to the world in mundane terms which characterizes it: nothingness is only a "little part of the world," a negative part.

Earlier, we raised the issue that the intuitionism of the philosophy of essence supported itself with the abstract hypothesis of a negation of Being, against the background of which presence could only be full determination. However, one must not draw the conclusion, under the pretext that it is not offset against the background of absence, that the irreducible presence of the world coincides with the fullness of the in-itself, that it is pure position and consequently the reverse of a consciousness that is fully negative. Insofar as it appears, Being is at a distance and truly involves a certain nihilation, even if that does not mean that this nihilation [148] can be pushed so far that it turns into the hypothesis of non-existence. This nihilation, which is within Being, is precisely the determination of it, the *Sosein* inherent to *Sein*. It is this determination that Sartre is unaware of since he defines consciousness as nothingness and Being as absolute density; thus, he misunderstands "the thickness, the depth, the plurality of planes, the background worlds." Under the pretext that there is not nothing and that presence cannot consequently be offset as essence against the background of nothingness, he concludes that the "there is" coincides with the "something" understood as a block of in-itself. Insofar as there is not nothing, presence cannot coincide with the determination of what is thought, nor can it abolish itself in the indetermination of a being which is exclusively positive, laid out before the nothingness of consciousness. Phenomenality is just as much negation of determination as it is negation of the in-itself. One has to say instead that phenomenality stops short of both affirmation and negation. It is a negation that not only does not dissolve into the positivity of essence but still negates *every form of positivity,* so that it also cannot affirm itself as pure, univocal negation nor abolish itself in favor of fully positive being. Against the viewpoint of the in-itself, one must say that negation is determination, but it is necessary to add, against the viewpoint of essence, that determination remains negation. They cannot be thought in exteriority: the very sense of determination is to exist as negation, that is, to be not fully determinate; the very sense of negation is to be based on a determination which it is and in which it nevertheless does not dissolve. The determinate is only insofar as it is determinable. It is precisely in this sense that Merleau-Ponty characterizes the openness to the world as a "qualified nothingness," as a "structure of void."

The situation of the philosophy of nothingness is indeed symmetrical with that of the philosophy of essence. Because it wants to set itself up as the negation of the philosophy of essence, the philosophy of nothingness leads back to its difficulties and restores "positivism," though certainly in a more covert manner. It thereby makes us lose the dimension of the phenomenon. While with Husserl thought was too closed in on itself to be able to bear the actuality of the world, nothingness is too outside of itself to be able to support the *openness* to Being. Both cases missed the unity of distance and proximity, either through the reduction of transcendence to immanence or through the absorption of immanence into transcendence. The philosophy of nothingness deforms the experience that it claims to restore and thereby truly looks to be a form of abstract thought. [149] Taken literally, the philosophy of nothingness in the end turns out to be incomprehensible, since "if being is wholly in itself, it is itself only in the night of identity, and my look, which draws it therefrom, destroys it as being; and if the For Itself is pure negation, it is not even For Itself, it is unaware of itself for want of *there being* something in it to be known" (VI 106/75; Merleau-Ponty's emphasis).

Nevertheless, Sartre's philosophy is founded not so much on a misunderstanding of experience as on the exclusive theorization of *one* experience. In fact, after having described the dialectic of Being and nothingness, Merleau-Ponty adds that these definitions

> assuredly express the experience of vision: the vision is a panorama; through the holes of the eyes and from the bottom of my invisible retreat, I survey the world and rejoin it where it is. There is a sort of madness in vision such that with it I go unto the world itself, and yet at the same time the parts of the world evidently do not coexist without me (the table in itself has nothing to do with the bed a yard away); the world is the vision of the world and could not be anything else. Being is

bordered along its whole extension with a vision of being that is not a being, that is a non-being. (VI 105/75)

The philosophy of essences conceals a naiveté in regard to language such that, by virtue of the work of speech, it was led to forget speech in favor of the meanings that it institutes. The philosophy of nothingness proceeds just as much from a naiveté in regard to vision, a naiveté that is rooted in the very act of seeing. What defines seeing is a forgetfulness of oneself as incarnate experience in favor of the spectacle in itself that vision unfolds. The subject of vision goes right to the world before him and conceives himself inevitably as non-situated, as nothingness. Sartre's philosophy therefore testifies not to a pure and simple rupture with the sensible order, but rather to an immediate submission to a dimension of the sensible order. In vision, sensation forgets itself as situated and incarnate, that is, as an openness to a depth; it appears then according to the duality of the in-itself and the for-itself. Vision is a theoretic relation, face-to-face. This means that the critique of reflection cannot consist in an immediate return to the sensible. Before the work of language, the sensible itself tends already to lay itself out in the form of a positivity which, even if it is not yet that of meaning, dissimulates the genuine being of the phenomenon in such a way that the sensible looks to be not of the world. Therefore, just [150] as it is necessary to reduce language, it is necessary to reduce vision, that is, to see, in the absolute distance, a proximity, to learn "to know, within the vision itself, a sort of palpation of the things, within the over-head survey itself, an inherence" (VI 115/83). This is where the importance of touch in the explication of the flesh comes from. What is certainly at issue, against the idealism of essence, is to rediscover the sensible under language, in order to make the way that language is rooted in the world appear. But this sensible does not have a univocal status, and the task of ontology consists also, obviously in contrast with the philosophy of Being and nothingness, in rediscovering the tactile under the visible. While it is necessary to grasp language as a modality of perception, it is just as necessary to understand vision as a modality of touch. In fact, the identity of proximity and distance to Being appears most clearly in touch. This justi-fies the emphasis on the visible in Merleau-Ponty's last work. It is indeed a matter of reconceiving the visible in its unity with the other senses, that is, in contrast to how it seems, as a mode of carnal inscription in the world. It is only to the extent that a thickness and a depth will be brought to light in the spectacle and that an invisible will be brought to light in the visible—only insofar as the visible will appear as irreducible to the pure in-itself which it seems to be—that the invisible, that is, sense, then will be reconceived short of all positivity as the very being *of* the visible. If speech is rooted in the sensible, the sensible cannot be defined in a univocal and uncritical way as *visible*. That would be to restore, on the plane of perception, the positivism that the work of speech feeds from its side. Thus, "Every relation between me and Being, even vision, even speech, is . . . a carnal relation, with the flesh of the world. In this case, 'pure' being only shows through at the horizon, at a distance which is not nothing, which is not spread out by me, which is something, which therefore itself belongs to being, which, between the 'pure' being and myself, is the thickness of its being for me" (VI 116/83–84). Beyond the opposition between speech as expression of essence and vision as immediate contact with the in-itself, the openness will have to be rigorously reconceived as *flesh*.

Sartre's philosophy is really the farthest removed from experience since it ignores the moment of phenomenality [151] and dismembers it into the duality of Being and nothingness. No one can ignore that Being, insofar as it appears, is not entirely in-itself; Being hollows itself out with a nihilation. Correlatively, "consciousness" is not nothing but the being who, through its belonging to Being, bears this nihilation. And it is this nihilation which, through its own thickness, determines the distance inherent to what appears. In short, we have to start from the fact that there is phenomenon. Insofar as Husserl's approach is inaugurated in this consciousness, we must admit that the truth we find in Husserl holds against Sartre. This is why, in *The Visible and the Invisible,* the examination of phenomenology follows the critique of the dialectic. However, it is just as true that Sartre is situated closer to experience. The truth is not that he starts from a dualist presupposition in order to reconstitute experience after the fact; it is rather his wish to coincide with this experience that leads back to a dualist thought. Sartre "describes our factual situation with more acuity than anyone has ever done before"; opposing the idealist reduction of the world to its phenomenality, he attempts to reach again our presence *to the world itself.* But by fixing this presence as nothingness, in a way he goes too far and loses the precise moment of appearing. There is therefore an ambiguity to the philosophy of nothingness: in a sense, this notion truly designates what has to be understood, but precisely insofar as it designates it, it misses it. What is in question is not so much nothingness as the possibility of restoring experience with the help of a univocal concept: perhaps it is characteristic of the openness to the world to contest the pretension to say it *immediately*. From this viewpoint, in *The Visible and the Invisible*, it is only a matter of reaching again what is aimed at yet ignored by the dialectic of Being and nothingness, only a matter of constructing an authentic philosophy of nothingness.[3] Nevertheless, the shortcoming of this dialectic forces us to take up the description of the openness of the world. The starting point is not "being is, nothingness is not"—a formula which is still based on surveying thought—but "there is being, there is world, there is *something*" (VI 121/88); and, in all strictness, "it is through the openness that we will be able to understand being and nothingness, not through being and nothingness that we will be able to understand the openness" (VI 135/99).

3. The Abstraction Involved in the Problematic of the Look

[152] The chapter that Merleau-Ponty devotes to Sartre in *The Visible and the Invisible* involves a long analysis that is critical of the Sartrean conception of intersubjectivity. There are at least two reasons for this. First, the theory of the look plays a decisive role in the economy of *Being and Nothingness*, since it is only at the heart of the relation to the other that the nothingness of consciousness leads to the facticity of an ego and can therefore be constituted as a human reality. A penetrating critique of Sartre would have to make the ambivalence of his dialectic appear as well at the level of intersubjectivity. But, on the other hand, the importance granted to this question is explained by the decisive role, as we have mentioned, that the reflection on the other plays in the development of Merleau-Ponty's thought. Since Merleau-Ponty exposes the fact that Husserl's approach— which is imprisoned in an egological framework—cannot account for the transcendence which is constitutive of the other, Merleau-Ponty can only situate himself in the vicinity of a philosophy, that of Sartre, which makes us see this transcendence and which attempts, in opposition to intuitionism, to reconceive the originality of the experience in which this transcendence is given. Nevertheless, there is only an apparent kinship between Merleau-Ponty and Sartre in regard to intersubjectivity: Sartre's theory of the look denies the transcendence of the other rather than respecting it,

---

3. See, for example, VI 311/258.

because it does not recognize a phenomenon of this transcendence. Just as at the level of the experience of the world, Merleau-Ponty is really attempting to map out an original path between Husserl and Sartre.

The experience of the other is that of an encounter. It is not to be asked, then, how knowledge of the other is possible, as one need only clarify the meaning of this encounter. Sartre says that it is necessary to acknowledge a *cogito* concerned with the other, a consciousness which gives to me immediately the existence of the other, just as the Cartesian *cogito* immediately reveals the existence of my consciousness. There is certainly no question of abandoning the viewpoint of consciousness: the other will never be given to me such as he is present to himself. If we could prove that it could, we would prove too much, since the fusion of its ego with mine would cause its alterity to disappear. The separation between the other and me remains genuinely insurmountable. There is no higher viewpoint that would allow a totalization of our relation. But that the other refers to my consciousness does not mean that my relation to the other is of the order of knowledge. The choice is not between a coincidence of our consciousnesses that would [153] abolish the other's alterity and an intuitive appresentation that would make the other fall to the level of an object. Only insofar as we identify consciousness and knowledge are we led to investigate the other on the level of an object. If the other refers to my consciousness, the other concerns my consciousness in *its very being;* my consciousness must discover the other in itself as a dimension of its being prior to knowledge. Just as the idea of the infinite allowed Descartes to bring to light the divine transcendence at the heart of the immanence of the *cogito,* it is necessary to discover, in the heart of consciousness as it is lived, a dimension which throws it back out toward the exteriority of the other. Because the relation of consciousness to the other is a relation of being rather than of knowledge, its lived immanence does not entail the negation of all transcendence. Thus, at the bottom of itself, consciousness must find not reasons to believe in the other but the other itself as what is not me: "each must be able, by starting out from his own interiority, to rediscover the other's being as a transcendence which conditions the very being of that interiority."[4] Understanding the existence of the other therefore requires that we distinguish an internal negation from an external negation. The

---

4. J. P. Sartre, *L'être et le néant: essai d'ontologie phénoménologique* (Paris: Gallimard, 1943), 283; trans. H. Barnes as *Being and Nothingness* (1956; reprint, New York: Washington Square Press, 1966), 329.

other is not me; but that does not mean that it remains in itself like a substance, separated from me by an uncrossable distance, by a nothingness subsisting in itself. This negation that defines the other is not the reverse of a position within Being; it is a negation of mine, which belongs to me even while I suffer it, a dimension of consciousness. The other is not therefore the negation of my experience, but my experience of a negation. The conditions of the experience of the other are then given by what the notion of consciousness implies. The other is another subject, and what defines the subject is that it is situated before the world, that it possesses objects. This is why the other cannot appear before me. Insofar as my experience of the other is the experience of another subject, it can be produced only in the form of my object-being for him: the experience of the other is that of a look, which makes sense only as the feeling of being-looked-at. Sartre's approach consists, finally, not in stopping short of the opposition between the other and me but, on the contrary, in radicalizing it in order to provide a passage from one to the other. The movement here is the same as on the level of the relation of consciousness to the world. The dialectic of Being and nothingness allows us to account for [154] this passage. The description of nothingness in the form of a "reality" whose nihilation sustains itself only by absorbing itself into a being, by identifying itself with the in-itself, is still abstract. In fact, if I really knew, before the appearance of the other, that Being owes nothing to my conscious states, "the nothing I am and the being I see all the same formed a closed sphere" (VI 86/59). The absorption of nothingness into Being can in no way mean a belonging of Being to consciousness; what it really means is an inscription of consciousness in Being. Nothingness can truly forget itself in favor of Being only if it is not coextensive with the totality of Being, only if, consequently, it supports itself with a situation. Nothingness subsists as such only on the condition of realizing itself as passivity within Being. Insofar as it sustains itself only by turning itself into a passivity within Being, this originary negation which defines nothingness goes in some way before the other; it exposes itself to another negation. The appearance of the other is correlative with the sinking of nothingness into Being. It is the active reverse side of its fundamental passivity:

> If I am nothing and if in order to come to the world I support myself particularly on one part of being, then, since that part does not thereby cease to be *outside* and to be subject to the actions that traverse the world, and since I am not informed about all those actions, there are

some whose consequences I will have to assume as brute facts; my situation is opaque to my eyes, it presents aspects that escape me and upon which an exterior look, if such were possible, would have more light. What I am altogether overflows what I am for myself, my universality as nothingness is only presumption on my part. (VI 87–88/60)

The possibility of this escape is confirmed by the experience of shame. In fact, shame is structurally shame-of-myself-before-the-other. There I am revealed to myself, but as what I am in the eyes of the other. I appear to myself as escaping myself toward the other. Shame is characterized by the upsurge, within unreflective consciousness, of a self which I am, in which I can only recognize myself, and from which I am nevertheless separated by the uncrossable nothingness of the other's subjectivity: this self is a limit that I cannot reach and that, however, I am. In short, shame confirms the identity of my consciousness and its being-as-object, that is, its being-other. It is "an experience of my total being as compromised in the visible part of myself" (VI 88/61). [155] In the end, Sartre's solution consists in taking note of one of the dimensions of the experience of the other revealed by Husserl. To perceive the other is not only to experience a subject within the world, but it is also to be an object for him, to participate in the objective transcendence correlative to the plurality of consciousnesses. Instead of subordinating this objectification to the actual apprehension of an alter ego, Sartre defines the relation to the other *by* the experience of this objectification. According to Sartre, one cannot go any farther. Only the experience of my being-looked-at establishes a relation to the other which does not compromise its transcendence, that is, which preserves its identity as subjectivity. The other never appears in person, but this negation becomes the object of a specific experience; the other is inaccessible, but the affirmation of this absence does not lead to solipsism since it responds to the other's for-itself and therefore has the ordeal of my objectification as its correlate. Thus the relation to the other mingles with the experience of my being for-the-other. Consciousness never has any dealings with the other in person but only with itself; this is in conformity with the transcendence of the subject-other. And yet, consciousness experiences itself as a non-revealed self who throws it back toward an other. This aptitude of consciousness to be open to an other without compromising the other's transcendence proceeds from its characterization as nothingness: it is itself only by being capable of passivity.

So we can say, once again, that Sartre is simultaneously the closest to and the farthest from what must be understood. He is the closest because he makes us see the absence of the other to which my experience of the other attests; he is the farthest because he fixes this absence in a dogmatic way and consequently misses its true status. Insofar as I have the experience of the other, this absence cannot be radical, that is, it cannot be strictly identical with the experience of my objectification. Once again, the experience is reconstructed on the basis of a logical relation, while it appears in reality as something that questions every essentialist perspective. In fact, the failure of intellectualism in regard to the other was ultimately based on the fact that the other was apprehended on the level of essence. Because the other was defined by its identity with me, because both the other and I were grasped as exemplars of a unique egological essence, its experience, which is an experience of transcendence, became incomprehensible. The other is not only an other me, an exemplar of the essence "ego" [156]; it is a me which *is* other. The actual alterity of the other is therefore ineluctably missed as soon as the other is understood as a unity of sense constituted in me, as an *analogon* of the ego. Although it becomes the object of an experience, although it presents a meaning and does not therefore reveal pure facticity, the other is never located in the neutral. The experience of the other is always a relation to a Thou; the alter ego is other only on the condition of never being entirely an ego, of preserving an irreducible singularity. What defines the ego and consequently the other is that its essence subsists only as its own differences, its own "variants"; its essence does not gather itself up beyond the actually lived consciousnesses. The question is whether it is mine or the other's, which is why the other cannot be constituted as a unity of sense within a transcendental ego. Sartre makes us see all of this by freeing the other from every essence, from every meaning, by not allowing it to appear, that is, by characterizing it as negation or absence. However, this absence is grasped in a univocal way, conceived dogmatically. It refers to a surveying position vis-à-vis experience, so that the transcendence of the other is denied just when it is recognized. By fixing the other in the form of a radical absence, we are still considering it from the viewpoint of its essence. By *positing* the other as inaccessible, by taking as a starting point the *concept* of the transcendence of the other, which by definition would be correlative with pure immanence, Sartre abolishes the transcendence which he claims to grant to the other instead of interrogating the experience of this transcendence:

This agnosticism in regard to the other's being for himself, which appeared to guarantee his alterity, suddenly appears as the worst of infringements upon it. For he who states it implies that it is applicable to all those who hear him. He does not only speak of himself, of his own perspective, and for himself; he speaks for all. He says: *the For Itself* (in general) is alone . . . , or: *the being for another* is the death of the For Itself, or things of this kind—without specifying whether this concerns the being for itself such as he lives it or the being for itself such as those who hear him live it, the being for another such as he experiences it or the being for another such as the others experience it. This singular that he permits himself—the For Itself, the For the Other—indicates that he means to speak in the name of all, that in his description he implies the power to speak for all, whereas the description contests this power. (VI 111/79)

Intellectualist philosophy [157] attempts in a paradoxical way to remove itself from its lived belonging to a community of consciousnesses, to overhang the intersubjective universe in which it participates and on which it feeds. It attempts to render the other transparent like an essence. But by characterizing the other as negation, as what would never be able to appear, Sartre really reenacts this idealism. Instead of expressing the recognition of its lived transcendence, the unequivocal affirmation of its absence amounts to positing an absolute immanence of for-itselves to the thinker; it amounts to reabsorbing them into essence and consequently to establishing a radical solipsism. In order to constitute the other, intellectualism "withdrew to the bottom of nothingness," passed over in silence the belonging of the thinker to a human world. But by thinking this belonging as the objectified-being of consciousness, correlated with the negation brought about by the consciousness of the other, Sartre merely takes up and radicalizes the intellectualist perspective. As soon as it is made absolute, negation is transformed into position. Defined in a univocal way, the invisibility of the other refers to the absence of a visibility, that is, to an essential characterization of all consciousnesses as pure for-itselves. Instead of being reconceived within the relation that I maintain with it, the other is secretly posited as a positive for-itself, in order to then be described as pure negation: the truth of the "internal negation" really rests in an external negation, that is, in a negation which is only the opposite of a position. The radical absence of the other in experience is contradicted by the essentialist character of this affirmation of absence. The ontological relation by which the other advents as its own absence is finally subordinated to an epistemological relation.

If, by determining the invisibility of the other as absolute, we encroach on its alterity, we must still conclude that this invisibility makes sense only insofar as it is not fully realized, only insofar consequently as the other can be the object of an experience which is no longer simply that of my destruction. The other is truly transcendent only if it is not so absolutely. The experience of the other challenges the transcendental immanence of the intellectualist philosophies, but it forbids just as much a univocal and radical transcendence, which is a dissimulated and aggravated form of immanence. In truth,

> I cannot even go the length of this absolute in negation; the negation
> here is a dogmatism, it secretly contains the absolute affirmation of the
> opposites. It is necessary that there be transition from the other to me
> and from [158] me to the other precisely in order that I and the others
> not be posed dogmatically as universes equivalent by principle, and
> in order that the privilege of the For Itself for itself be recognized.
> (VI 112/80)

It is true that the other cannot arise from knowledge, from an intuitive givenness, but its very absence must correspond to an experience, at the price of which the absence is preserved. Therefore the issue lies in starting neither from an insular for-itself nor—this amounts to the same thing—from its negation in shame. Instead, one has to start from the interrogation of the phenomenon of this absence or, rather, from the forging of an idea of the phenomenon that suits the experience to which the transcendence of another consciousness attests. Therefore, the existence of the other is no more attributable to an ontological relation than an epistemological one; or rather, it is only insofar as it is given, that is, only insofar as it arises out of a knowing in this sense, that the other can affect me in my being. Starting from a relation of knowledge would amount to denying its alterity, but keeping to a relation of being would amount to misunderstanding the specific experience by which this alterity is supported.

Sartre reconstructs the experience of the other with the help of a logical "scale model" which, when it is tested by experience, turns out to be incomprehensible. He notes that "every look directed toward me is manifested in connection with the appearance of a sensible form in our perceptive field, but contrary to what might be expected, it is not connected with any determined form."[5] What we really must do is interrogate the relation between this sensible form and the experience of the other as such. We must ask *how* the other appears, if the ordeal of being-looked-at is really the appearance of the *other*. Insofar as it is subject and not object, the other is not given as a determinate form; it is not identical with the appearance of its face. It is not therefore because I perceive such and such a form that I gain access to the existence of the other. On the contrary, it is insofar as I feel shame that this form can be posited as a manifestation of the other in the world, and that this body can be understood as a living body. But must we conclude, as Sartre does, that "the fact of being-looked-at cannot therefore *depend* on the object which manifests the look," that "the convergence of the other's eyes in my direction" is only "a pure *monition,* as the pure occasion of realizing my *being-looked-at*"?[6] That the experience of the other does not [159] depend, in the mechanical sense of the term, on any form—which means simply that it does not coincide with a thing— does not mean that it has no relation with something perceived, that no form manifests the other in a privileged way. In fact, if the experience of the other were really independent of the perception of a worldly object, what would we still be able to say of the *other,* that is, of a specific experience? If the access to the other is identical with the ordeal of my being-looked-at, it stops being an experience since it does not reveal something *of which* it would be the experience. It amounts to the discovery of my being-for-others, that is, it amounts to the discovery of a structure of *my* consciousness. Understood as shame, the experience of the other is no longer an experience of an other, but the revelation of my finitude, of my belonging to a humanity: "the relationship remains one between me as nothingness and me as a man, and I do not deal with others, at most I deal with a neutral non-me, with a diffused negation of my nothingness" (VI 100/71). Moreover, this is where Sartre explicitly ends up:

> Being-for-others is a constant fact of my human reality, and I grasp it with its factual necessity in every thought, however slight, which I form concerning myself. . . . To withdraw, to approach, to discover this particular other-as-object is only to effect empirical variations on the

5. Sartre, *L'être et le néant,* 297; *Being and Nothingness,* 346.
6. Sartre, *L'être et le néant,* 316; *Being and Nothingness,* 369 (slightly modified).

fundamental theme of my being-for-others. The other is present to me everywhere as the one through whom I become an object.[7]

In reality we have to make a choice: either the experience of the other coincides with the lived experience of shame, but then nothing qualifies it as experience of the *other;* or there is a genuine experience of others, but then it cannot be exhausted in the lived experience of my objectification. In fact, if it is true that another consciousness can never appear in the world, it is still the case that I am not always in shame, that shame is an event that, as such, must correspond to the appearance of certain sensible forms in my field. In order that I feel shame, it is necessary that the other be described in some way. In order that this negation be actually lived, it is necessary that the absence of the other be qualified in itself and not by the transformations that it entails. The look therefore cannot ground the experience of the other. On the contrary, it is because I see that *someone* looks at me, because something from the world indicates to me my alienation, that I can gain access to shame. In short, "far from the sense of the other's look being exhausted in the burning it leaves at the point of my body he looks at, it is necessary that there be something [160] in the other's look that designates it to me as a look of the other," so that "instead of my shame constituting the whole sense of the other's existence, the other's existence is the truth of my shame" (VI 102/72, 103/73).

The faithfulness to experience of which Sartre proves himself capable turns back on itself eventually because it is faithfulness to only *one* experience, that of the look. The philosophy of vision, the thought of nothingness is realized, insofar as it concerns the experience of the other, as a philosophy of the look. Sartre reconceives the perception of the other on the basis of one modality, which is the most radical, of the relation that we maintain with others. The dimension of negation, of conflict, inherent in the lived experience of shame represents only one extreme variant of one relation to the other, a relation which can also be harmonious, and which is in the end neutral in regard to the alternative of conflict and harmony. Certainly the other would not be able to appear as an object, but must we conclude that it is accessible only as the look, as the judge or the God who smashes me to smithereens? In Sartre, the phenomenology of the other in fact conceals a phenomenological psychology, and even an empirical psy-

7. Sartre, *L'être et le néant,* 319; *Being and Nothingness,* 373 (slightly modified).

chology. An extremely specific experience is presented as the very structure of the relation to the other. In reality, the experience of the other does not exhaust itself in the ordeal of a look that annihilates me. On the contrary, the other can come to represent the negation of my freedom only because there is first a current of communication, an adjustment of our looks to each other. Vision itself "produces what reflection will never understand— a combat which at times has no victor, and a thought for which there is from now on no titular incumbent" (S 24/17). This does not mean that I can perceive the other frontally, and therein lies the truth of Sartre's position. But precisely because the other never appears in front of me, I can also never be in front of it and thereby reduced to an object. The other is given to me only laterally; it envelops me rather than looks at me. And the face-to-face from which a victor must emerge represents only the most radical modality, which is never completely realized, of this primary "laterality."

For Sartre, there is no relation to the other that is not conflictual, no communication that not does proceed from an antagonism. For Merleau-Ponty, in contrast, contradiction is always a modality [161] of communication, of an originary harmony that no conflict can break up absolutely. While in Sartre's eyes every agreement is in the end suspect and necessarily dissimulates an intention of mastery, for Merleau-Ponty there is no discord from which one cannot return, no tension which eliminates the possibility of negotiation. For Merleau-Ponty, the relation to others is profoundly mediated by the relation to the world. Because the subject is first a calm relation to the plenitude of a world, its openness to others is animated by the intention of a reconciliation in the unity of Reason, of which the presence of the world is the promise.

4. The Hyperdialectic

What then is dialectic? The examination of Sartre's philosophy really aims to bring to light its instability, its deep-seated ambiguity. On the one hand, the dialectic is the closest to our inscription in Being; it uncovers each term as its own mediation and coincides with the actual movement of manifestation. It understands that meaning cannot make itself autonomous beyond the becoming which produces it; it possesses reality only by withdrawing into its other. However, as soon as this dialectical "consciousness," as we could call it, sets itself up as *philosophy,* it already contravenes its own requirement. It betrays itself as soon as it is formulated. In fact what does this mean, this notion of *self-mediation* by means of which the dialectic is thematized? It is not possible that the mediator and the mediated be the same in the sense of identity, "for then, in the absence of all difference, there would be no mediation, movement, transformation; one would remain in full positivity" (VI 126/92). But, on the other hand, the actuality of the movement forbids that this difference be stated in terms of opposition, that the mediator be conceived as the simple or absolute negation of the mediated, since then "the absolute negation would simply annihilate the mediated and, turning against itself, would annihilate itself also, so that there would still be no mediation, but a pure and simple retreat toward positivity" (VI 126/92). Then, as soon as it is formulated, dialectical philosophy fixes the movement in the terms of a pure negation and abolishes it by exceeding it toward positivity. It simultaneously stops short of and goes beyond mediation: stopping short of it as identity and going beyond it as simple negation, [162] that is, still as identity. Movement as such is missed as soon as it is thematized, since in reality it is unassignable. The overcoming of immediate identity is not so much a passage to the opposite as it is still belonging to this identity. It is identical, in its difference, to this very identity. There is really, if you like, identity of identity and difference, but this first identity is not itself identifiable; it is not immediate, thematizable identity. This identity, in which the movement is thematized, is nevertheless still fragmented by the identity and the difference it gathers. Negation is actual negation only insofar as it remains unrealized. Its truth lies in not being able to split itself from that of which it is the negation. It is actual, therefore, only if it is unassignable; it determines a becoming only if it remains quasi-identity. And because negation is not yet opposition, movement is not already closed off at its end point. Concerning Sartre, Merleau-Ponty notes, "For an ontology from within, transcendence does not have to be constructed, from the first it is, as Being doubled with nothingness, and what is to be explained is its doubling (*which, moreover, is never finished*)" (VI 290/237; my emphasis). The actuality of movement indeed resides in this doubling which never reaches its completion in a duality, which is accomplished only insofar as it remains unaccomplished. Also, the truth of the dialectic lies in the notion of *difference* rather than negation. This difference is *non*-identity rather than opposition; the negative term means that identity remains, closed in upon itself, even while negation opens and splits it. Identity closes back on the "non" that divides it. Difference, stopping short of opposition, is "difference between the identicals" (VI 316/263). The movement by which Being yields to itself on the basis of negation is synonymous with the movement by which negation is born within Being. Being is the possibility of negation only because negation is the possibility of Being. By describing the movement with the help of a thematization of negation, dialectical philosophy exceeds actual becoming and reabsorbs the movement into a final position, while what defines movement is that it contests every final position, that it realizes itself as identity of position and its having become. While the truth of movement is escape from totalization, dialectical philosophy "extrapolates" [163] or imposes a law on the content instead of grasping the movement of the content as its own law. In short, thought stops accompanying the movement; instead, thought precedes it. Thus, as soon as it sets itself up as philosophy, as soon as it thematizes movement, dialectical philosophy regresses toward a "pre-dialectical" ontology, that is, toward the ontology of reflective philosophy.[8] This is why the truth and the fulfillment of the dialectic reside, in Merleau-Ponty's eyes, in the refusal to thematize it. The dialectic is itself only insofar as it is practiced rather than formulated into a thesis. If thought is truly movement, thought will be adequate to it only by abandoning the attempt to totalize it. Dialectic characterizes the situation of thought rather than being an "object" of thought, and this is why it makes sense only as "consciousness," not as philosophy. The dialectic cannot be mastered in a statement but designates instead the excess of Being over the statement and the consciousness of this excess. Therefore, dialectic is lucid in regard to the fact that no thought, and consequently not even dialectical thought itself, can complete thought. It must be understood instead as the "vigilance" which will not let us forget the rootedness, the source of all knowledge. Thus,

8. The critique is addressed principally to Sartre. If his philosophy valorizes "more than any other" the task of the dialectic, it also reveals dialectic's "crisis," its "essential difficulty." Merleau-Ponty's position in relation to Hegel is less clear. It seems to us that even in Merleau-Ponty's own eyes, this relation is still in the process of being clarified. However, Hegel's dialectic could not escape from the general frame of the critique, as the summary of the course devoted to dialectic shows: "In Hegel, we examined the transition of the dialectic to speculation, of the 'negatively rational' to the 'positively rational,' which finally transforms the dialectic into a system. And in the definition of the absolute we saw the balance swing in favor of the subject which thus gives an ontological priority to 'interiority' and in particular dispossesses nature of its own concept, making exteriority a 'feebleness of nature'" (RC 82/126).

the bad dialectic begins almost with the dialectic, and there is no good dialectic but that which criticizes itself and surpasses itself as a separate statement; the only good dialectic is the hyperdialectic. The bad dialectic is that which does not wish to lose its soul in order to save it, which wishes to be dialectical immediately, becomes autonomous, and ends up at cynicism, at formalism, for having eluded its own double meaning. What we call hyperdialectic is a thought that on the contrary is capable of reaching truth because it envisages without restriction the plurality of the relationships and what has been called ambiguity. (VI 129/94)

This hyperdialectic, this "dialectic without synthesis," does not dissimulate [164] a return to skepticism, and it does not take up "the rule of the ineffable": "What we reject or deny is not the idea of a surpassing that reassembles, it is the idea that it results in a new positive, a new position" (VI 129/95). The acknowledgment of the genuine meaning of the dialectic passes through the critique of what Merleau-Ponty calls positivism, that is, the pretension of reflection to enclose Being in the fixity of ideality, a pretension which is also that of a philosophy of pure negation. The true dialectic, however, is the consciousness that thought gains of itself as unfinished thought, as a thought that cannot total itself up and is included in Being just as much as it includes Being. The true dialectic is this reflection in contact with Being, which attempts to hold together the access that it manages to gain toward Being and the withdrawal of Being in front of this openness. Is it not the case, then, that Merleau-Ponty reconciles the idea of dialectic with the idea of transcendence, that is, "of a being which is in principle at a distance, in regard to which distance is a bond but with which there can be no question of coincidence" (RC 79/123)?

9 Philosophical Interrogation

[165] Whether it leads to the exhibition of an essence or to the affirmation of the in-itself by the mediation of a negation, reflective philosophy appears to be a form of immediate thought. It thinks presence in a frontal way, as coincidence or proximity: either it empties consciousness of all consistency in order to make it equal to Being itself or, by making us see the distance from Being, it restores proximity in the form of the intuition of essence. In other words, we always reach Being in the figure of the being, and this is why it is not grasped radically. The requirement of coincidence or adequation always forces us to think presence as exactly what comes to fill up the look, as what cannot have indetermination. This limitation of reflection proceeds from a naiveté, which is a naiveté with respect to itself. In each case, reflection is never considered as a *problem;* it seems to be already completed, to be possible in principle. The moment of reflection is always passed over in silence in favor of the being that it expends itself trying to rediscover. Because reflection does not gain access to a genuine self-consciousness, because it does not make a return to itself, it describes presence in the figure of the being, remaining then imprisoned in Being and prohibited from returning to the question of its sense. The philosophy of the in-itself is diverted from its own possibility as philosophy, which is an enterprise of meaning, and consequently is diverted from the phenomenality of Being. It understands itself in such a way that it dissolves itself in favor of the existing thing; it misunderstands the fact that being-as-posited is a being-as-thought. But the philosophy of essence, conscious of what is implied by reflection, forgets that reflection is given only as a fact, that it cannot be considered as possible in principle; this philosophy then defines essence as the necessity to which Being is submitted. It ignores the belonging of phenomenality to Being; it ignores the incapacity of thought to [166] exhaust the object that it thinks. Thus, because it lacks an interrogation of its own possibility, reflective philosophy cannot give rise to a genuine ontology. In contrast, by determining the status of reflective philosophy, Merleau-Ponty opens the way to ontology. Instead of consisting

in rediscovering in Being a positivity which reflects its image back to it, the work of philosophy is the interrogation of its own possibility, and philosophy in the end coincides with this interrogation. It is "astonishment before oneself" (RC 147/172). By coming to terms with itself as such, philosophy will be able to clarify its astonishment before the world, beyond the ontic prejudice. To interrogate oneself on the possibility of philosophy amounts to defining philosophy by this possibility of self-interrogation, to characterizing it as "pure interrogation." Such are indeed the stakes of this long critique of reflective philosophies: to discover "interrogation as the ultimate relation to Being and as an ontological organ" (VI 162/121), to discover consequently that "the existing world *exists in the interrogative mode*" (VI 139/103; my emphasis).

As an object of interrogation, Being is not a stranger to the order of sense. What really defines a question is that it involves the possibility of an answer, at least as a horizon. Herein lies the truth of idealism: to acknowledge meaning, the being-as-intended, as the genuine sense of Being in such a way that there is no question of rejecting the order of essence. But, on the other hand, as questioned, Being turns out to be equally irreducible to the presence of a pure meaning. If interrogation refers to a horizon of sense, it is nevertheless the case that it could not be conceived as the simple absence of a positivity. What defines interrogation, as pure interrogation, is that the question accepts no answer that would conclude it. If Being is not in-itself and does not allow a knowledge by coincidence, if it is therefore susceptible to being signified, it is still the case that this meaning exists only as its own veiling: it is never given in person. Sense is precisely interrogative sense, present as something *to* interrogate, withdrawing itself behind the question that gains access to it. This interrogative sense is given at one and the same time as response and reenactment of the question within the response; it is present only at a distance. The sense is a solicitation, a call rather than a positivity. Interrogation proceeds therefore from a double polarity: Being is what [167] I interrogate, what, in the questioning, is intended. But it is just as much what interrogates *me;* it maintains a sort of blindness, a sort of astonishment within the very heart of the gesture which appropriates it. Instead of supporting itself with a subject—it would then be resolved into a representation—interrogation defines the ultimate reality of an openness to Being in relation to which subject and object are already abstract moments. In fact, as soon as philosophy is acknowledged to be interrogation, it is necessary to say that it is also Being that interrogates itself in philosophy, produces itself as a question about itself, and then remains veiled in its very givenness. To define philosophy as interrogation is to take what reflective philosophy had put in the column under subjectivity and put it under Being: it is to reconceive interrogation as the ontological mode of Being. As soon as it is subordinated to a subject, interrogation finds itself reabsorbed into ideality. Conversely, to understand ideality as the very being of the subject is to reintegrate the subject into Being as its very teleology. There is a depth of Being which is not based on its distance from a subject—relying on that would be to restore the horizon of a coincidence—but which is instead constitutive of Being. It is not a subject that holds Being at a distance, but it is Being that holds itself in its own distance. Reflective philosophy, Merleau-Ponty notes, maintains the principle of coincidence *as opposed* to the authentic fact of non-coincidence. In fact, experience imposes non-coincidence as a matter of principle. At the moment when perception is on the verge of being pure contact with the thing, it is "extinguished." As soon as it is "ignited," it stops coinciding with the object. Reflective philosophy translates this situation into the form of a *duality* of subject and object, and it does so as soon as it takes the definition of knowledge to be adequation.

> If the coincidence is never but partial, we must not define the truth by total or effective coincidence. And if we have the idea of the thing itself and of the past itself, there must be something in the factual order that answers to it. It is therefore necessary that the divergence, without which the experience of the thing or of the past would fall to zero, be also an openness onto the thing itself, to the past itself, that it enter into their definition. (VI 166/124)

For Merleau-Ponty, then, what is at issue is only to take stock of what experience implies, and that experience proceeds from a distance cannot mean that Being is absent from it. "There is something": something is given which, insofar as it is given, is not indeterminate. But it is [168] itself which is given, and thus it conceals its own determination, is absent. The "there is" [*il y a*] subsists as something only insofar as the something remains what *there is* [*ce qu'il y a*], that is, captive of the Being of which it is the presentation. This is the very situation of experience. In Merleau-Ponty's eyes, the difficulty in accounting for this situation really lies in the projection of categories that are foreign to it. Presence contradicts absence only if it is understood straightaway as the presence of a present thing, of a being. Conversely, under the condition of abandoning this objectivistic presupposition, it becomes possible to reach presence again as what is also the absence of every determinate being.

To think Being on the basis of interrogation implies as well the renunciation of the distinction of "layers" or "levels." It does not make sense to oppose, as Merleau-Ponty still does in *Phenomenology of Perception,* the order of the perceived in the literal sense to the order of thought. Perception and vision are interrogation;[1] they do not open onto an in-itself but instead deliver a sense; they are really a thought but a thought in the brute or wild state. Sense shows through there only as the very thickness of the world; thought lives there only as solicitation or call. This is why the pure visible is already response, why it bears within its thickness every response to come. But, correlatively, speech is equally interrogation, "inspired exegesis," since this *silent logos* which is vision does not shed its thickness in favor of pure ideality in speech; it is renewed in speech rather than finding an answer there. Speech is the question continued and, from this viewpoint, speech is not distinguished from vision itself. While realism, banking on vision, forgets it in favor of the visible spectacle for which vision sacrifices itself, idealism, banking on language, neglects speech in favor of the sense that speech institutes and then absorbs sensible vision into intellectual vision. There is only a single vision, neither sensible nor intellectual, which is a question, and a single silence that is already speech, but speech that remains mute:

> The facts and the essences are abstractions: what there is are worlds and a world and a Being, not a sum of facts or a system of ideas, but the impossibility of meaninglessness or ontological void, since space and time are not the sum of local and temporal individuals, but the presence and latency behind each of all the others, and behind those of still others [169]—and what they are we do not know, but we do know at least that they are determinable in principle. (VI 156/117)

Also, the response to philosophical interrogation is situated "higher than facts, lower than essences" (VI 162/121). Insofar as it is susceptible of being interrogated, Being is on the side of essence, at least in that it is not of another order and experience is not already thought. But insofar as interrogation proper proceeds from an act of ideation, that is, an act of expression, which, as such, requires a soil which "precedes" it, Being cannot be reduced to pure ideality, and experience cannot be reduced to pure thought.

1. See, for example, OE 59/138.

The ultimate reality resides in what Merleau-Ponty calls "wild essence," an essence which is not a possibility above facticity but the possibility *of* facticity itself:

> The possibilities by essence can indeed envelop and dominate *the facts;* they themselves derive from another, and more fundamental, possibility: that which works over my experience, opens it to the world and to Being, and which, to be sure, does not find them before itself as *facts* but animates and organizes *their facticity.* When philosophy ceases to be doubt in order to make itself disclosure, explication, the field it opens to itself is indeed made up of meanings or of essences—since it has detached itself from the facts and the beings—but these meanings or essences do not suffice to themselves, they overtly refer to our acts of ideation which have lifted them from a brute being, wherein we must find again in their wild state what answers to our essences and our meanings. (VI 148–49/110; Merleau-Ponty's emphasis)

In *The Visible and the Invisible,* the only question is that of exploring the obscure domain of this wild essence.

In the end, what is at issue is "to return to this idea of proximity through distance, of intuition as *auscultation* or *palpation* in thickness" (VI 170/128; my emphasis). The choice of terms here is significant. We have noted that in order to restore the signifying and ultimately the interrogative dimension of vision, as opposed to Sartrean abstraction, Merleau-Ponty appealed to the experience of touch. Ultimately interrogation itself, at all levels including linguistic, turns out to be defined by this reference to touch. This is not a metaphor. It is not a matter of describing interrogation by comparing it to a specific layer of experience, that of tactile sensation; that would be to [170] preserve the autonomy of the intellectual order as what is properly interrogative. Merleau-Ponty's formula is situated beyond the opposition between a tactile world and an intellectual world. Thought is touch; touch is thought. Or rather, insofar as it is originary interrogation, "auscultation or palpitation in thickness," our relation to Being proceeds from an originary Touching. The notion of the *flesh* corresponds to this originary Touching; strictly speaking, it is the body of interrogation, the body as interrogation.

We can finally take stock more clearly of the meaning of this project that we evoked at the beginning, the project of taking possession of the ontological "diplopia" proper to Western thought. While this "diplopia" is characterized by the to-and-fro movement between complicitous and antagonistic positions, Merleau-Ponty lays out the terrain in which this alternative is rooted, that is, he attempts to grasp each term according to the movement of its passage into the other. The notion of wild essence describes this ultimate level where the fact exists only as the possibility that articulates it, where the essence makes sense only insofar as it remains caught facticity. The Being of interrogation therefore designates Mediation as the last reality, and, in a sense, there is only mediation. However, the issue is not to return, by means of this notion of wild essence, to an originary place which would be susceptible to an immediate apprehension, in which duality would dissolve purely and simply. Realism and idealism are not so much overcome as restored in their truth, namely, as poles of a singular teleology. Instead of expending itself in the affirmation of a reality in-itself, the truth of realism is that there is transcendence only as ground or soil of a becoming of sense. And yet, insofar as this becoming is infinite, we can say as well that we are in transcendence through and through. Correlatively, instead of returning to the establishment of a universe of essences, the truth of idealism is that there is meaning only as experience, as ordeal of a world, whether it is a question of the perceived world or the cultural world. And yet, in virtue of its very infinity, this teleology is without beginning and always already accomplished because it is never fully accomplished. So, we can say that we inhabit the order of sense through and through. Ultimately, as Merleau-Ponty put it well, "if sense figures everywhere, then sense is at issue everywhere" (S 228/181). [171] The genuine unity of idealism and realism is grounded in this teleological life of wild being. This unity is not a confusion—in favor of what could this distinction be overcome?—but an overhang [*porte-à-faux*] where, although actual, the difference of terms remains unattributable, where each term, stopping short of its difference from the other, nonetheless remains beyond its identity with it. This is why this mediation is ungraspable and why thought is almost inevitably devoted to being able to grasp it only as the terms that it mediates, to fixing it from one side to the other as simple fact or pure essence, to restoring an abstract duality within which it indefatigably runs. In fact, because Being does not exist as anything other than as its own sense, because it coincides with the teleology of meaning, idealist philosophy feels entitled to think it as essence. Idealist philosophy is correct in what it denies, even though sense cannot coincide with the positivity of the *eidos*. Likewise, since sense never arises on its own but only as what *there is* [*il y a*], since it withdraws itself under the look which comes to appropriate it, realist philosophy feels entitled to think Being as an in-itself; here too, realist philosophy is correct in what it denies, even though the in-itself does not in any way constitute the truth of transcendence.[2]

2. Marc Richir thematizes this double decentering inherent to the apprehension of the phenomenon by bringing to light within the phenomenon an *illusion* that is necessary to it: "the pure vision in coincidence, which it brings to bear on the pure fact, on the pure phenomenal individual, or on the pure essence or idea, is only an *illusion of the phenomenon which participates integrally in the phenomenon* and which is equally necessary to the phenomenality of the phenomenon." It is illusory because it fixes the movement of phenomenalization between two poles; this illusion is also truth because this double polarity is inherent to phenomenalization, raised up by the life of the phenomenon. That is why "this illusion becomes truly illusory only if it becomes in itself autonomous, if it detaches itself from the phenomenon in order to erase it." But, conversely, that the phenomenon cannot be reabsorbed into the factual or eidetic coincidence does not mean that it escapes entirely from this tension (it is then that the vision in coincidence would be fully and solely illusory), so that "a phenomenon stripped of its illusion, and of the two poles of its illusion, would be entirely as *illusory* as the illusion of the phenomenon which would be abstracted from the phenomenon" (Richir, *Phénomènes, temps et êtres: ontologie et phénoménologie* [Grenoble: Jerome Millon, 1987], 78–79).

Part Three.
The Visible

[175] The core of the completed part of *The Visible and the Invisible* is an introduction to the exposition of the ontology as such, even if, of course, this confrontation with reflective philosophies allows us to anticipate extensively the exposition itself. But we must press beyond this preliminary moment where Merleau-Ponty continues to base his reflection on a symmetrical rejection of the philosophy of essence and realism, even if he does so in a much more radical manner than before. The essential text at our disposal is the fragment titled "The Intertwining—The Chiasm," which follows the chapter on intuition. It is difficult to situate this fragment in the general economy of the projected work. Claude Lefort notes that one could treat it either as the last chapter of the long introduction concerning philosophical interrogation or as the first chapter of the first section, devoted to the visible (see VI 12/xvii). In fact, neither of these solutions seems satisfactory. The critical dimension is resolutely abandoned here; according to Merleau-Ponty, what is at issue is rather to "seek to form our first concepts in such a way as to avoid the classical impasses" (VI 180/137). This should exclude the possibility of treating the fragment as part of the introduction. Even so, we cannot relate it to the explication of the visible. As a matter of fact, every level of constitution, from the "solipsist" world of the sensible impression to speech and ideality, is treated there. This text thus presents itself instead as a sort of abridged version of what *The Visible and the Invisible* in its entirety should have been; Merleau-Ponty indicates, moreover, that this is no more than a "preliminary outline" (VI 185/140). Do we finally have to admit then that this chapter concludes the introduction, by serving as the transition to the explication of the visible? If so, Merleau-Ponty would be trying to demonstrate for the first time, at all levels, the new domain opened by interrogation. [176] It is not certain, in our

view, that this chapter was intended as a part of the definitive work: Lefort even points out that it is not mentioned in the last outline we have available, which dates from November 1960 (VI 11/xxxvi–xxxvii). It seems to be a general rough draft where Merleau-Ponty puts to the test the concepts he is forging, a rough draft that called for a systematic reworking into a whole what was still in gestation at this point in time, as the working notes attest.

Two nearly contemporaneous texts must be considered alongside this difficult fragment. The first is the lecture devoted to Husserl titled "The Philosopher and His Shadow," which constitutes a sort of rehearsal of "The Intertwining—The Chiasm" in the context of a reading of *Ideas II*. Showing through here more than in any other text is the movement by which Merleau-Ponty conquers his own philosophical terrain in a confrontation with Husserl, by bending his own way of proceeding in a direction which was sensed by Husserl but which was never fully taken up by him. Thus the initially Husserlian notion of *flesh* is here liberated from the constitutive perspective, from recourse to "acts of absolute consciousness," and acquires such an extension and radicality that one is finally dealing with a new concept. The second text to be considered is "Eye and Mind," which confirms, from another point of view, *The Visible and the Invisible* in its entirety. The study of painting allows Merleau-Ponty to open up a point of access to the pretheoretical terrain to which Husserl could only point. It therefore serves as a genuine phenomenological reduction, one freed of its idealistic implications; that is, it allows for the restoration of the originary perceptual soil. Most of the concepts at work in the ontology of the visible are elaborated in this text. However, we find our essential support in the remaining working notes, those magnificent traces of an intuition in its pure state. Often brilliant in their freedom and succinctness, the notes allow us to confirm and deepen what remains ultimately allusive in "The Intertwining—The Chiasm." Must it be added that a reconstitution undertaken essentially on the basis of fragments is inherently uncertain?

As the title of the work indicates, the question of the sensible is completely inseparable from that of the visible. What significance should be attached to this primacy of vision? Certainly "our world is principally and essentially visual; one would not [177] make a world out of scents or sounds" (VI 115/83); but this preeminence does not boil down to noting this fact. It refers primarily to the fact that vision alone gives us access to the world as world. Merleau-Ponty indicates as much in "Eye and Mind": "The 'visual quale' gives me, and is alone in doing so, the presence of what is not me, of what *is* simply and fully" (OE 84/147). In hearing or touch, the object does not have access to this exteriority and autonomy: in touch, occurring through physical contact, the thing is experienced "at the tips of the fingers" rather than outside of the one sensing, and I hear the sound "in the ear" rather than situating it in space. In the two cases, the perceiving body is referred back to itself; it fails to forget itself in favor of a pure exteriority. Only with difficulty does the sensed then distinguish itself from the experience that the one sensing always has of itself. In contrast, there is "more world" in vision, since the sensed is given in vision only as split off from sensibility, as resting in itself. It is precisely this specificity of vision that founds the traditional misinterpretations of perception. By its very exercise, vision ignores itself qua sensible experience; the self-forgetfulness inherent to the natural attitude is achieved in vision. By a kind of inversion, the for-itself is captivated and captured by the phenomenon that it brings to presence; it forgets its phenomenal dimension and grasps itself on the basis of the visible, which is conceived as a thing in itself. The experience of vision feeds the realist illusion. Because vision is seen as the illumination of a latent presence which awaits the look to draw it from the darkness, realism concludes that the object was actually there and that its being consists in resting in itself. We have seen that the Sartrean perspective remains eminently dependent on this illusion. It is true that Sartre tries to restore, in opposition to intellectualism, the opening to the thing itself that is incontestable in visual experience. But at the same time he remains farther from this experience because, in defining its correlate as a pure in-itself that is only itself, he subordinates vision to the visible to which it gives birth and hence remains in naiveté. By conceiving Being as full self-identity, Sartre splits Being off from its visibility and does not integrate into its mode of being the aptitude Being has for giving itself to be seen. And in the end he prevents himself from understanding vision itself, which vanishes in its turn because it lacks any substantiality [178] that might separate it from that on which it opens, because it lacks a distance into which the visibility of the object might be inscribed. Symmetrically, Cartesian philosophy is unaware of vision in its actuality, that is, as an opening to "what *is* simply and fully," because it wishes to account for the dimension of vision as such without subordinating it immediately to the being-seen. Under the pretext that there is no vision without thought,

Descartes concludes that it is sufficient to think in order to see. Vision is reconceived not as a certain relation to the things themselves but as a thought brought into action by signs given in the body. In place of factual vision, an "institution of nature" is substituted which creates a regulated correspondence between bodily indications and representation. Vision is not described on its own terms, but is reconstituted from the initial duality between extended substance—whose plenitude, falling short of the visible, therefore excludes visibility—and thinking substance, which is always beyond vision. Now, insofar as it is fed by a negation of actual visual experience, intellectualism remains captive of this negation. Rejecting the visible as a subsistent reality, intellectualism transposes its density onto the intellectual level, and then reduces visual experience to *intuitus mentis*. Thought fails to equal actual vision, because thought is finally defined as intellectual vision and, by virtue of the naive sense of sensible vision, as an opening to a subsistent reality—in this case, to the concept. Merleau-Ponty explains this in one of the last notes:

> The definition of the *intuitus mentis*, founded on analogy with vision, itself understood as thought of a visual indivisible (the *details* that the artisans see) . . .
> This analysis of vision is to be completely reconsidered (it presupposes what is in question: the thing itself)——It does not see that the vision is tele-vision, transcendence, crystallization of the impossible.
> Consequently, the analysis of the *intuitus mentis* also has to be done over: there is no indivisible by thought, no simple nature——the simple nature, the "natural" knowledge (the evidence of the I think, as clearer than anything one can add to it), which is apprehended totally or not at all, all these are "figures" of thought and the "ground" or "horizon" has not been taken into account——the "ground" or "horizon" is accessible only if one begins by an analysis of the *Sehen*. . . . (VI 327/273)

To the ontological positivism mentioned above corresponds a certain idea of vision inherent in its very exercise. Whether one thinks in terms of essence or of fact, one determines knowledge as vision, and one determines it such that it is spontaneously lived, that is, as actual coincidence with a definite object. This is why the critique of intuitionism in all of its forms must proceed by way of a return to active vision, by way of a reduction of naive vision. This visual experience more than any other crystallizes the paradox that is constitutive of perception. Even though the presence of a visible depends on this experience, the visible gives itself as owing nothing to it. What, one must then ask, is "this talisman of color, this singular virtue of the visible that makes it, held at the end of the gaze, nonetheless much more than a correlative of my vision, such that it imposes my vision upon me as a continuation of its own sovereign existence?" (VI 173/131).

10 The Flesh: The Visible and the Invisible

1. The Chiasm

[181] Merleau-Ponty's meditation takes its point of departure from paragraph 36 of *Ideas II*, titled "Constitution of the Body as bearer of localized sensations (sensings)." When I touch my left hand with my right hand, I am able to feel it first as a physical thing through definite tactile appearances (soft, smooth, etc.). However, Husserl adds,

> when I touch the left hand I also find in it, too, series of touch-sensations, which are "*localized*" in it, though these are not constitutive of properties (such as roughness or smoothness of the hand, of this physical thing). If I speak of the *physical* thing, "left hand," then I am abstracting from these sensations (a ball of lead has nothing like them and likewise for every "merely" physical thing, every thing that is not my Body). If I do include them, then it is not that the physical thing is now richer, but instead *it becomes flesh, it senses.*[1]

Even though the left hand is touched, it is the site of local sensations. It makes itself sentient, so that the right hand sinks in its turn to the rank of touched object at the very moment when it experiences the left hand. Hence a "kind of reflection"[2] is produced by which the roles are continually exchanged: each hand is successively, or rather quasi-simultaneously, touching and touched. As Husserl notes, the only thing one can say is that

1. E. Husserl, *Ideen zu einer reinen Phänomenologie und phänomenologischen Philosophie: Zweites Buch,* ed. M. Biemel, Husserliana 4 (The Hague: Martinus Nijhoff, 1952), 145; *Ideas Pertaining to a Pure Phenomenology and to a Phenomenological Philosophy, Second Book: Studies in the Phenomenology of Constitution,* trans. R. Rojcewicz and A. Schuwer (Dordrecht: Kluwer Academic Publishers, 1989), 152.
2. E. Husserl, *Méditations cartésiennes,* trans. G. Peiffer and E. Levinas (Paris: Armand Collin, 1931), 81; trans. D. Cairns as *Cartesian Mediations* (The Hague: Martinus Nijhoff, 1960), 97 ("reflexively related to itself").

the localized sensations come to be *added* as new properties to the left hand, first perceived as a physical thing. The hand is originarily [182] touching and touched, "sensing thing," "subject-object" (S 210/166). As Merleau-Ponty says elsewhere, it is a subject that exists "as collapsing into space, a large piece of extension intimate with itself" (HN 261/164). The distinction between the hand as a physical thing and the sensibility that awakens within it is clearly an abstraction carried out on a deeper reality. This hand is sentient only insofar as it is susceptible to being sensed; its sensibility settles on its own surface and becomes incarnate. And, conversely, the hand is sensed (i.e., object) only to the extent that it is always already subject (i.e., sentient). The body reflects itself, comes together with itself; there is no point of itself where it fails to grasp itself already as perceiving. This body is not, therefore, a reality extended in exteriority, *partes extra partes*— it sketches an interiority. However, precisely because the left hand's sensibility is apprehended on the hand itself, because the sensing is immersed in it, the reflection is not carried to completion but remains imminent:

> My left hand is always on the verge of touching my right hand touching the things, but I never reach coincidence; the coincidence eclipses at the moment of realization, and one of two things always occurs: either my right hand really passes over to the rank of touched, but then its hold on the world is interrupted; or it retains its hold on the world, but then I do not really touch *it*—my right hand touching, I palpate with my left hand only its outer covering. (VI 194/147–48)

In fact, the completion of reflexivity would correspond to a splitting of one's own body. If an actual coincidence, a pure subjectivity, could advent in it, this subject would not *have* a body. The body would not be *its own* body, but would emigrate to the side of the objective world. The experience of one's own body, the apprehension of a touching right up against this body, of a touching-touched, prohibits this apprehension from being carried away beyond its incarnation and completing itself as a pure consciousness. Because the body is a sentient thing rather than a pure object, it is not a pure subject any longer but rather an incarnate sensibility. Subjectivity is present in the body only as its own absence. And the specific dimension of incarnation—the hand as touched—corresponds to this lack as if it were its trace. At the level of the hand, the being-as-touching and the being-as-touched are not exterior to one another, as this would restore the positivity [183] of a consciousness and, consequently, its frontal relation with the pure object. Instead, each is the inverse of the other. Sensibility, in this case touch, is achieved as body, as tangible hand, and the dimension of incarnation is simply the other name for this exteriority from oneself proper to sensing. But accordingly, the body is never grasped as pure exteriority, because the self-absence of sensing constitutes its own mode of immanence—a sensation is always already sketched in it. Thus, one's own body reveals a self-relation that is neither identity nor difference. It is "higher" than the exteriority of the physical object in that it is sentient. And it is "lower" than the pure interiority of consciousness, since sensibility is incarnate, or rather is its own incarnation.

We shall need to return to this analysis of one's own body, but we must follow its implications here. Henceforth, "we may literally say that space itself is known through my body" (S 210/167). Incarnation is not contingent, and it does not conceal some type of external relation between sensibility and the body. If such were the case, sensibility would not *have* a body. In the end, it would be the work of a pure consciousness, and we would be confronted with the insoluble problem of a correspondence between a part of extension and a "psychic lived experience." The experience of the "touching-touched" reveals the quasi-identity of sensibility and its body, or rather that the objective body and the phenomenal body are like two sides of a deeper reality. But then to say that sensibility is nothing other than its body, that it *is* incarnate, is to admit that it is produced as the very presence of the sensed. The incarnation of perception signifies that it cannot be distinguished from the world that it brings to appearance. By giving itself a body, sensibility descends into the world and makes itself world, and only on this condition can the world as world be reached. The becoming-world of sensibility is synonymous with the advent of a sensed world, and that sensibility consents to being sensation cannot be distinguished from the fact of its being world. In other words, the thickness of the body does not impose a distance between sensibility and the world. On the contrary, the very possibility of a sensible experience requires this thickness. It is by virtue of this ontological kinship with the world, a kinship conferred on it by the body, that "consciousness" can open itself to the world itself. A consciousness that would not be *of* the world would be consciousness of nothing, since it would fail to have this ontological complicity. Deeper, therefore, than the opposition of consciousness and object or consciousness and its body there is [184] the irreducible advent of the world—and, strictly speaking, there is only the world. Because sensibility is synonymous with its incarnation, its being-world, it finds fulfillment as the world's presence.

What holds true for touch also holds true for vision, thanks to the unity of one's own body. Despite the pronouncements of the natural attitude, vision could never be described as the unfolding of a completely objective world before a ubiquitous consciousness. Vision also is incarnated, *is* visible, with a visibility which is consubstantial to it; vision occurs in the milieu of the world. This amounts to saying that vision advents *as* the actual presence of a visible world. I see the world: it "stops up my view," surrounds me, surpasses me. It is not *before* me, reduced to what it is, but *around* me as an envelopment irreducible in principle to a frontal grasp. Although I am situated "within" it, the designation of a limit between the world and me, between what would belong to it and what I would hold as my own, loses all meaning. I am immersed in it, made of the same texture, and hence it is immersed in me, invades me, fills me. In fact,

> We have to reject the age-old assumptions that put the body in the world and the seer in the body, or, conversely, the world and the body in the seer as in a box. . . . Where in the body are we to put the seer, since evidently there is in the body only "shadows stuffed with organs," that is, more of the visible? The world seen is not "in" my body, and my body is not "in" the visible world ultimately: as flesh applied to a flesh, the world neither surrounds it nor is surrounded by it. (VI 182/138)

Vision is the world's opaque evidence, an invasion that cannot be dominated, a presence that cannot be held at a distance. Vision is inscribed into the plenitude to which it gives consistency. Merleau-Ponty can also revive for his own purposes Bergson's reflection: "We must take literally what vision teaches us: namely, that through it we touch the sun and the stars, that we are everywhere at once, as close to the distances as to nearby things" (OE 83/146). Vision would never be able to distinguish itself from the advent of the visible; it does not occur "in me" but over there, right up next to the thing. The exteriority of the world is accessible only to an experience absolutely outside itself, to an absence of self, and in the end this experience is [185] mingled with the world's thickness. It follows from this that vision is inhabited by an irreducible non-vision. The world achieves visibility only to the extent that it fills me up, circumscribes me in such a way that I cannot traverse its thickness, bring it to transparency, and transform this vision into a possession without remainder. The ontological affinity of vision and the visible means that the world transcends vision with all of its opacity, that vision cannot pierce the ontological texture out of which it is made—and this very transcendence is the condition of visibility. The openness to the world conceals a relation of being that cannot be converted into having. No vision can break, in order to recompose it, the fabric that connects it back to the world, and then pass beyond itself to appropriate its own rootedness; if it did this, vision would no longer be what it is. Vision reaches the world only as that which exceeds it, an "atmospheric" and lateral presence. Vision makes itself world in order to present a world, but this sacrifice is without return: there is no vision that is not encompassed by what it encompasses, and that would not then be struck blind at the moment when it functions.

However, the belonging of vision to the world, which prevents us from understanding vision as intellectual possession, must not be interpreted in an objective mode. In fact, understanding the incarnation of vision as the objective presence of the body within the world would amount to restoring the positivity of vision itself, that is, to referring it to a pure consciousness: "I must no longer think myself *in the world* in the sense of the ob-jective spatiality, which amounts to autopositing myself and installing myself in the *Ego uninteressiert*" (VI 280/227). Vision's passage into the world is not a passage into its other: this would be precisely to maintain vision's alterity vis-à-vis the world. The world in which vision fulfills itself, insofar as vision is incarnate, cannot be conceived as the negation of vision except by conceiving vision as a positive pole. If vision made itself other, it would remain just as much identical to itself, the position over and against which this negation would function. Therefore vision can deny itself for the sake of the world only if this negation is not radical—only if in so doing vision is itself preserved and if, consequently, the world is the *very site* of vision rather than its negation. Paradoxically, the radicality of incarnation is missed when vision's becoming-world [186] is conceived radically as a passage of vision into its other. Also, the movement by which sensibility becomes world makes sense only to the extent that it is the identical movement by which the world advents to sensibility. Vision actually unfolds itself as world only if it too remains in this dehiscence—only if, consequently, the world makes itself vision. The absence of exteriority between vision and the world should therefore be grasped according to all of its implications: since vision cannot be distinguished from the world, neither can the world be distinguished from vision. Incarnation, which grounds the identity of vision with the world, means as well the identity of the world with flesh. Just as there is no vision that would not be recaptured, encompassed within what it claims to cover over, there is no part of the world which would not be already inhabited, haunted by a vision. And to the same extent that the world is not in-itself but already carnal—that is, visible—vision does not proceed from the for-itself but unfolds an actual world. In fact, to say that the world surrounds me is certainly to challenge the autonomy of sense and to refuse to reduce sense to the "how" of its appearance, to *what* it is. But equally, to say that the world surrounds me makes it impossible for the world to subsist as a pure fact, as an atom of being; this would be to conceive knowledge still as a kind of frontal gaze. The world's laterality with respect to intellectual possession is equally laterality in relation to a factual contact, in such a manner that the world's transcendence is not reducible to the position of a transcendent. Possessing the world intellectually and reaching a pure fact where it lies are two ways of not being *of* the world. The world surrounds me and escapes me with all of its thickness, but, by the same token, it does not exhaust itself in the flatness and punctuality of the simple fact: this thickness is already *my* thickness, which means that it is also transparency. The immersion of perception into the world makes sense only as the immersion of the world into perception; the becoming-body of the one who perceives is the becoming-flesh of the perceived. The subject can truly abdicate in favor of the world only if he rediscovers himself in this renunciation, only if, consequently, the world returns to its visibility in this ekstasis. The world "stops up my view": "that is, time and space extend beyond the visible present, and at the same time they are *behind* it, in depth, in hiding" (VI 152/113). On the one hand, the world never presents itself transparently as a pure signification; it "stops up my view" would be understood as an intellectual act. But if, on the other hand, it were then treated as facticity, pure transcendence, it [187] would be immediately reached again in coincidence without offering any resistance—and in the end there would be no world. Hence the thickness that obliterates the intellectual gaze is equally opacity for factual vision: the depth of the world is not that of an atom of being but is a depth of a sense. The world "stops up my view" only on the condition that the screen presented by it allows a depth to show through, retains a transparency. The thickness of the world that makes its escape from intellectual possession possible is truly preserved in its distance only if it stops short of facticity. Such is the meaning, then, of the intertwining and of the chiasm: the duality of subject and object, which merges at the level of the one perceiving because the one perceiving makes himself world, merges thereby at the level of the perceived; the perceived is "on my side," it is set into my flesh, in agreement with visibility rather than the negation of vision. Ultimately, it is a matter of taking literally Husserl's formula according to which the thing is grasped "in person," "in the flesh (*Leibhaft*)": "the flesh of the sensible, this close grain which stops exploration, and this optimum which terminates it all reflect my own incarnation and are its counterpart" (S 211/167). In order for the thing to be reached in person, with the density proper for a thing, it must consent to this grasp and its being must consist in offering itself to a perception, the call or requirement of a sense. The thing is characterized by this immersion of the sense in its own distance, by its identity with its own imminence, to which the experience of one's own body attests in a privileged way. The "close grain" of the thing is not the negation of sense but the sole manner of being suitable for it, because this sense is sustained only by remaining on this side of itself, only by not dissolving into transparency. Sense *is* incarnate, the world *is* sensible: there is a being of the sense only to the extent that the sense exists as being and as world.

The analysis of the sensible-sentient has revealed that reflexivity, as imminent, does not engender a subject in opposition to the world but is synonymous with the advent of the world itself. To touch is to touch oneself; to see is to see oneself, and conversely. Thus, "in going into the details of the analysis, one would see that the essential is the *reflected in offset [refléchi en bougé],* where the touching is always *on the verge* of apprehending itself as tangible, misses its grasp, and completes it only in a *there is*" (VI 313/260). The "there is" of the world is not [188] the other of carnal reflexivity. Since this reflexivity advents only by falling short of itself, it realizes itself only as the upsurge of a world. The world is like the site or the being of this lack, the trace of this imminence. In other words, there is an "insertion of the world between the two leaves of my body" (VI 317/264). The objective body does not join up with the phenomenal body, although it cannot be distinguished from it like a pure thing, which is why they are separated by all the thickness of the world. But that implies that the self rediscovers itself in the world, that the moment of lack is not something other than that of which it is the lack, and that the trace is not based outside of that whose imminence it is. The world is just as much a self that is inchoative, sense in the state of being born. So that, conversely, there is an "insertion of my body between the 2 leaves of each thing and of the world"

(VI 317/264). In effect, the world comes to appear, to make itself into a thing, only because it is woven from the signifying power of the body. The dimensions of appearance are the modalities of carnal life. Thus, the incarnation of perception means that the withdrawal of the world into its sense is just as much the identity of the world with sense, the coming to itself of sense as world. Merleau-Ponty says that flesh is a "mirror phenomenon" (VI 309/255), from which we must understand that perception achieves a unity of proximity and distance, a unity proper to reflection. To the extent that the world reflects the self, it remains withdrawn and transcendent. In fact, there could be no "recognition" of a pure transcendence, but a pure immanence would also be unrecognizable since it would lack the distance between reflecting and reflected by which the reflected precisely recognizes *itself*. The self must make itself other in order to rediscover itself—that is, in order to be *for* itself. The being of the world is nothing other than this distance into which the self is thrown outside itself in order to conquer itself as what it is; there is coincidence with the self only as divergence [*écart*] from the self, self-presence only as self-absence (VI 246/192). The condition of all possession is the dispossession by the world, in which perception is summed up: perception gives sense and succeeds in sketching out a self only because it rebounds onto its own thickness. Perception possesses the world only because it is "possessed" by it. Also, perhaps by having recourse to the concept of *forgetting* [189] we would be able to reach more closely what Merleau-Ponty is trying to name with the notion of *chiasm*. Forgetting can be characterized by a double dimension. Unlike ignorance, it must be conceived not as a negation or an absence, but as a certain mode of presence of what is forgotten. Insofar as it is connected to what is still veiled and incarnate in it, the world is very much a place of forgetting. However, in contrast to remembrance, forgetting remains truly the absence of what is forgotten: what is forgotten is defined by the fact that it is not unknown to me but nevertheless it is not present to me. In fact, if forgetting were only the inverse of an always actualizable remembrance, the very possibility of forgetting, the dimension of remoteness, would become incomprehensible. Merleau-Ponty tirelessly addresses precisely this objection against Husserl's presentation of the transcendental reduction. If the natural attitude truly is *only* an illusion of positivity, a forgetting of the transcendental attitude, and if the being-in-itself of the world is *only* ignorance of its being-constituted, then how is the natural attitude possible? Merleau-Ponty asks, "how could the working of my own thought be concealed from me, since by definition my thought is for itself?" (PHP 247/213). Forgetting therefore makes sense only if, as forgetting, it involves a certain positivity that is interposed between itself and presencing, only if remembrance is not involved. Insofar as it is impossible for what remains concealed in it to reach unconcealment, the world is really a place of forgetfulness. Thus the perceived, reconceived by means of the notion of chiasm, can be described as the domain or the being of a forgetfulness. It refers to a sense that is *only* forgotten and is therefore announced in its very absence, but which, as *forgotten,* remains truly immemorial. The world offers itself as a call for a restoration and clarification which is forever impossible.[3]

3. By determining knowledge to be recollection, Plato tries to reconceive experience on the basis of the idea of forgetfulness. However, in representing the process of knowledge through the opposition between two places in the myth of the cave—a place of shadow and a place of light—he misses what is specific to forgetting. Enclosed in the cave, the prisoners are unaware of the whole exterior world (which is why liberation can come only from a third party). Because there is first a division between the cave and the exterior, the prisoners are not even in forgetfulness, since they lack the relation with what is forgotten, which is their own; they are not even in misunderstanding, since they lack any relation with the knowable. If the cave is truly only the domain of shadow, one cannot understand how an ascension is possible, since nothing orients it: the shadow absorbs the light. But if the ascension is progress toward a full light, a passage to another world, the cave is no longer *only* the other of this world, and the shadow is no longer *only* the forgetting of the light. How a state of obscurity was able to precede the ascension can no longer be understood. If the soul is merely deprived of a relation to the intelligible with which it is consubstantial, forgetting becomes unthinkable once again, because it lacks a genuine amnesia or separation, a withdrawal of the known. The cave can no longer subsist as a specific place, and the light absorbs the shadow (which is why shackles are required in order to interrupt contemplation and violently turn the prisoners away from the light). Here forgetting becomes incomprehensible, no longer through excess but through lack. These two moments are correlative: because sensible experience is understood as an obscurity within which nothing is shown, knowledge is understood as an evidence so clear that no forgetting could obscure it. The *process* of knowledge is therefore impossible, being either never or always already accomplished. Thus to rigorously grasp experience starting from forgetting requires thinking the shadow and the light in such a way that they pass into one another. The ascension is possible, and the prisoners are always already making progress: the shadow is already light. And yet, insofar as forgetfulness was and remains possible, there is indeed a reality to the shadow that invades the light and, in a sense, always gets the better of it. The access to full clarity is forever impossible, and the light is always shadow for another

2. The Visible and the Invisible

[190] We are now ready to specify the meaning of the invisibility belonging to the visible. The visible does not give itself as meaning, as "the what," but remains at a distance and transcendent; sense remains invisible in the visible. However,

> the invisible is not the contradictory of the visible: the visible itself
> has an invisible inner framework (*membrure*), and the in-visible is
> the secret counterpart of the visible, it appears only within it, it is
> *Nichturpräsentierbar* which is presented to me as such within the
> world—one cannot see it there and every effort to *see it there* makes
> it disappear, but it is *in the line* of the visible, it is its virtual focus, it is
> inscribed within it (in filigree)—— (VI 269/215)

Thus, Merleau-Ponty adds, there is

> [a] certain relation between the visible and the invisible, where the
> invisible is not only non-visible (what has been or will be seen and is
> not seen, or what is seen by an other than me, not by me), but where its
> absence counts in the world (it is "behind" the visible, immanent or
> eminent visibility, it is *Urpräsentiert* precisely as *Nichturpräsentierbar,* as
> another dimension) where the lacuna that marks its place is one of the
> points of passage of the "world." (VI 281/227–28; cf. 282/229, 300/247)

[191] The recourse to the notions of the visible and the invisible aims at defining the being of the world on this side of the opposition between sense and fact. It aims at showing that what defines sense is to dissimulate itself under the form of the visible, and that what defines the visible, correlatively, is to be a mode of presentation of sense. Sense is invisible, and the sensible *is* this negation, this invisibility of the sense. However, if the sensible were thought as the immediate negation of the sense and, correlatively, the sense as other than the visible, then the meaning of this invisibility would be missed. By explaining the invisibility of the sense through the dissimulation of the sense into its other, one restores the positivity of the sense and one turns it into a being that is visible elsewhere or other-

---

light. Such is the meaning of the chiasm: the shadow is always luminous, and the ascension always begun; there is no bottom to the cave. But, correlatively, the light remains always veiled, and the ascension has no end point.

wise. The invisibility of sense, then, does not mean that the sensible, by which invisibility realizes itself, would be of another order than that of the sense: the sensible presents sense as "a certain absence." The sensible must be characterized as "negation-reference," not as immediate negation of sense. Invisible in the form of a pure sense, sense is retained nevertheless in visibility, as the meaning that invisibility conceals: the sense is the "zero" or the "power" of visibility (VI 311/257, 190n/145n5). Sense truly makes itself invisible in the sensible world only insofar as the sensible world carries the invisible within it as its own signifying power. This is why the visible is truly the "presentation of a certain absence" and the "*Urpräsentierbarkeit* of *Nichturpräsentierbar*" (see VI 257/203, 272/218–19, 292/239). Not that the visible, insofar as it is sensible, is distinguished from a sense by being its *sign,* but insofar as the visible *is* this presentation. Therefore the visible remains itself—on this side of a pure, distant, transcendent sense—only if it is not *other* than sense, only if it already carries sense in filigree and makes itself into the absence needed by sense in order for sense in its turn to be itself. In short, the notion of the visible gathers together the double sense of invisibility, which is *qualitative* and *being.* The visible is *invisible,* or sense is invisible in it, only if the visible is *the* invisible; the visible remains irreducible to sense only to the extent that it is already sense. By the same movement, therefore, the sensible diverges from the in-itself and is distinguished from sense. By positing the sensible as in-itself, one restores opposite it the positivity of sense, thus initiating the reflexive reversal; inversely, by situating the visible "above" the in-itself, sense is prohibited from splitting off from that of which it is the sense, thereby preserving its intentional status. Because the sensible is folded back into the sense, sense is [192] at the same time retained in the sensible. Because it is always already sense, the sensible is never entirely sense, that is, the sensible remains itself. Sense preserves its identity by being always still sensible. Thus the opposition of sense and sensible, and of invisible and visible, vanishes, since it is always based on the decision to think the two as beings. The being of the sensible precisely consists in not being based in itself like a being, but instead in being woven from the invisible, in exhibiting the invisible as its secret counterpart. Correlatively, the being of the sense consists in its incapacity for gathering itself together beyond the sensible whose sense it is; it consists in its incapacity thus to subsist as its own concealing. Each term is itself only by passing into its other, or, rather, there are not two terms but a place where they are destined for each other, where the surpassing of the world toward its sense is equally the inscription of the sense in or as a world. Consequently the sensible, in particular, must not be conceived as a being as it would be in the natural attitude. Instead it must really be conceived as a certain mode of sense's being, or rather, as *this* mode of being which suits sense: "The sensible is precisely that medium in which there can be *being* without it having to be posited; the sensible appearance of the sensible, the silent persuasion of the sensible is Being's unique way of manifesting itself without becoming positivity, without ceasing to be ambiguous and transcendent. . . . The sensible is that: this possibility to be evident in silence, to be understood implicitly . . ." (VI 267/214). Elsewhere Merleau-Ponty adds more pointedly, "seeing is this sort of thought that has no need to think in order to possess the *Wesen*" (VI 301/247). The being of the sensible is truly the being of what is hinted at, or rather what is hinted at as being: not the indication of an *other* presence, the trace of a text that would be written *elsewhere,* but presence as its own allusion—comparable to a text that, by its own strangeness and ellipses, would deliver to us the key to its translation. Symmetrically, there is sense only to the extent that it cannot be posited apart from what it is the sense of, apart from its own incarnation or figuration: there is sense only inasmuch as it is invisible, that is, sensible. To think a being *proper* to sense, which would not be the being *of which* it is the sense, is the same as recoiling into nothingness, such that sense has reality only insofar as it is not *itself* a being. It is truly because sense is made sensible, that is, invisible, that its identity is preserved.

[193] It must be concluded from this that sense's identity with the sensible is synonymous with its difference. It is a question of grasping phenomenality, Merleau-Ponty says, as "identity without superposition," "difference without contradiction," "identity within difference" (VI 179/135, 279/225)—namely, as this unassignable place where the sensible remains itself only by opening beyond itself, by opening a beyond of itself which, however, it still is. Phenomenality is this pure difference, or differentiation rather than difference, into which Being splits itself by phenomenalizing itself only in order to fill itself up with itself. Phenomenality is this distance that is immediately recaptured by what it puts at a distance, the distance that is encompassed by what it encompasses. The being of the phenomenon consists in being its own imminence, which is also to say its own absence. This is why it would be necessary to speak, in all strictness, of *phenomenalization without phenomena.* What defines the phenomenon is in fact to be always before or beyond the point where one seeks to arrest it. And this is the case not because the look would find itself decentered in

relation to a fixed point, but because the phenomenon is its own decentering. It cannot be grasped as sense because it is held on this side of itself; it remains held in the depth of the world because it *is* in truth this depth. But it would be just as futile to try to assign a place to this withdrawal and arrest this hither-side of sense, because at the very moment when the phenomenon withdraws into itself, it is transported beyond its opacity and already exceeds the point where one seeks to apprehend it as a sensible in its pure state.

The relation of proximity and distance that Merleau-Ponty, by his own admission, maintains with Sartre's philosophy can be evaluated more clearly here. Sartre indeed tries to conceive an invisibility of sense, sense as invisible, and by doing so, he tries to distance himself from the philosophies of essence that reabsorb the world into meaning rather than grasping meaning as an openness to the world. However, by determining this invisibility as nothingness, he restores the opposition that he is trying to overcome. The invisibility that in fact characterizes sense finds itself radicalized in the form of a nihilation that maintains a relation of opposition or immediate negation with Being: as *pure* nothingness, the invisible becomes the absolute other of the visible, which behaves like a positive essence confronting it. It matters little whether visibility is understood as essence or as nothingness: in both cases, the inscription of the invisible in the visible is finally missed, [194] and in this regard there is no difference between Sartre's philosophy and Husserl's eidetics (VI 249/196, 324/270). From this point on, the simple opposition of Being and nothingness is achieved as immediate identity: the negative homogeneity or "positivity" of nothingness call for the full positivity of the in-itself. However, to the extent that visibility is held fast beyond the Being that it makes appear, the visible itself is missed in its visibility. In other words, the visible is grasped, as a pure in-itself, on this side of visibility: the absolute negation that the visible represents is just as much the absolute positing of the visible as being. Because he separates visibility from Being and fails to reach the invisible as invisible *of* the visible, Sartre equally ignores the very being of the visible as presentation of the invisible, bearer of its own visibility. To determine the being of sense as nothingness is still to conceive it as a being, which leads one to distinguish it from that of which it is the sense. The being of the sensible then is in turn missed, because positing sense in exteriority in relation to Being is just as much to situate Being on this side of sense, that is, to understand it as an opaque in-itself. In short, in a single movement Sartre misses phenomenality by an excess, when he grasps it as nothingness, and by a lack, when he posits a full density of Being. He is closest to the phenomenon when he conceives sense as invisible. But he is farthest when he holds the invisible under the form of a pure negation of the visible, rather than understanding that this invisible makes sense only if the negation remains unfinished, held back within what it negates. Likewise, Merleau-Ponty can assert that

> I take my starting point where Sartre ends, in the Being taken up by the for Itself——It is for him the finishing point because he starts with being and negentity and *constructs* their union. For me it is structure or transcendence that explains, and being and nothingness (in Sartre's sense) are its two abstract properties. For an ontology from within, transcendence does not have to be constructed, from the first it is, as Being doubled with nothingness, and what is to be explained is its doubling (which, moreover, is never finished). (VI 290/237)

To conceive the invisible as nothingness is ultimately to miss the nihilation in it; it is precisely because the alterity of nothingness is without mixture that it degrades into positivity. Conversely, its nihilation is preserved by conceiving it as invisible. Truthfully, "nothingness is nothing more [195] (nor less) than the invisible" (VI 311/258). The nihilation of the doubling is maintained to the extent that the doubling is "never a completed thing," to the extent that nothingness does not split itself from the Being toward which it carries itself in gathering itself beyond it, and to the extent, then, that the invisible remains concealed within the visible. The negation of nothingness makes sense only if its difference in relation to what it negates remains unassignable and does not exceed itself in duality; the impurity of nothingness is indispensable to its intentional status. Being has access to presence by a negation that is just as much a position. Visibility must be grounded on an invisibility which, in order to bring the visible to presence, must be on the side of what it nonetheless negates. It is a question then of describing not a negation which from the exterior would project Being in its plenitude but Being *as* its own negation, and consequently the negation as being.[4] There is an identity of the visible and the invisible that is not

4. As Garelli puts it, "Nothingness, according to Merleau-Ponty, is not a 'non-Being,' a Non-Esse, but a *Non-ens*, a Non-entity, and in this sense a dimension of Being— its zone of emptiness and of invisibility into which every visible manifestation is inserted. It is not, then, the frontal negation of a full and massive Being, but the condition of possibility for the upsurge of the being and, therefore, the revealer

constructed on the basis of their opposition, but is based on a negation that is sustained only by remaining intermingled with what it negates; it is based on a transcendence which is sustained only as the presentation of an unpresentable, that is, finally, on the basis of being its own negation. To conceive the invisible requires that one conceive negation authentically, as becoming rather than being; it requires that one understand invisibility as the "power" of the visible and the phenomenon as its own imminence. This is why the nihilation of nothingness must be exercised against itself qua *pure* nothingness. The invisible provides the genuine meaning of nothingness because the invisible never exceeds the visible that it nevertheless negates. Correlatively, the visible provides the genuine meaning of Being, since its positivity does not consist in being gathered up on this side of all negation, since it is pregnancy or latency of the invisible: "*there is Being, not Being in itself, identical to itself, in the night, but Being that also contains its negation, its percipi*" (VI 304/250–51). The notion of the invisible represents the truth of a philosophy of nothingness, just as it constituted the truth of a [196] philosophy of essence. On the condition of conceiving it as "the difference of identicals," the notion of Nothingness allows us to reconceive the movement of phenomenalization, in which the phenomenon is constituted while remaining unassignable. As pure difference, the ungraspable life of phenomenalization, "nothingness . . . is hollow and not hole" (VI 249/196), or better, a *fold* in the thickness of being: "The only 'place' where the negative would really be is the fold, the application of the inside and the outside to one another, the turning point——" (VI 317/264).

3. The Flesh as Visibility

This analysis of phenomenality in terms of the visible and the invisible, in terms of the chiasm or intertwining, amounts to a profound renewal of Fink's formula, quoted above, that "Just as the world is what it is only in terms of its 'origin,' so is this origin itself what it is only with reference to the world." The origin is genuinely itself only if it is retained in what it is the origin of, only if it is made from what it constitutes. The origin is genuinely absolute only insofar as it does not posit itself outside

---

of Being which, for Merleau-Ponty, is always 'Being of the being,' and not pure ideality" (J. Garelli, "Le lieu d'un questionnement," *Les cahiers de philosophie*, no. 7 [1989]: 133).

of what it "origins." There is then an apparition of the world only if it is the world *itself* that unfolds *itself*, that is its own unfolding: the appearance is truly a fold in Being, a dehiscence that, in order to bring to presence, must remain coincidence at the same time, included in the distance that it institutes. The world is this being that is its own sense and that draws from its facticity the possibles according to which it is incarnated. Whereas by conceiving the origin of the world as a being distinct from the world, we continue to be situated on a mundane level, we definitively transcend this level only by reconceiving the origin as the world itself, that is, the world as its own origin. What is needed is a "relation to Being," Merleau-Ponty says, "that would form itself *within Being*" (VI 268/215); ontology must be conceived as an *intra-ontology* (VI 280/227; cf. 290/237, 298/244). Then the immediate opposition of empirical and transcendental, of fact and essence, is surpassed. The facticity of the world is just as much the transcendental power, the unfolding of the possibility [197] according to which it advents. And insofar as this unfolding is achieved on the basis of the world itself or as the very world, the transcendental remains held back within the empirical, and the moment of essence is never posited for itself. In the world, actuality and possibility, individuality and universality are no longer opposed. The world is the absolute Fact, and to this extent it contains everything, *including its own possibility:* its universality is neither that of an essence nor a law; it merges with the depth of its facticity. The Fact of the world is identically Right: the conditions of the world can proceed only from what they condition. In the end, the uniqueness of the world does not mean that it subsists in itself as a pure individual, a member of a virtual multiplicity, but that

> it is at the root of every thought of possibles, that it even is surrounded with a halo of possibilities which are its attributes, which are *Möglichkeit an Wirklichkeit* or *Weltmöglichkeit,* that, taking on the form of the world of itself, this singular and perceived being has a sort of natural destination to be and to embrace every possible one can conceive of, to be *Weltall.* Universality of our world, not according to its "content" (we are far from knowing it entirely), not as recorded fact (the "perceived") but according to its configuration, its ontological structure which envelops every possible and which every possible leads back to. (VI 282/228-29)

How can we comprehend this notion of flesh that directs all of Merleau-Ponty's reflection? The analysis of incarnation shows that sensation, adventing in the body or as body, is immersed in the world that it senses, and it makes the world appear somehow from the middle of itself, with the result that sensation preserves the thickness, the transcendence of the world. But precisely to the extent that this openness to the world does not proceed from a positive consciousness, it cannot be distinguished from the world that it brings to presence; the world itself cannot be circumscribed as a being that is based in itself beyond the openness in which it advents. At the same time as perception makes itself world, the world "rises" to visibility, so that in all strictness there is neither consciousness nor world but a unique visibility. The world is always already visible; but precisely insofar as it is always already visible, it could never be referred to a positive vision—which would be again to conceive it as that in itself that the look comes to draw out of obscurity. The world does not gather itself as a pure sense beyond the moment of its visibility. The notion of flesh thus corresponds [198] to the decision to conceive *visibility as being* or Being as visibility. The flesh is "of the Being-seen, i.e. is a Being that is *eminently percipi,* and it is by it that we can understand the *percipere*" (VI 304/250). It is necessary to understand the sensible consistently with the ambiguity of the sense of this word, to reconceive it before the distinction of sentient and sensed, namely, as "sensible in itself" (VI 182/138), "visibility in principle" (VI 184/140). The flesh is the sensible "in the double sense of what one senses [*ce qu'on sent*] and of what senses [*ce qui sent*]" (VI 313/259); there is no sensed that is not already sensibility [*sentir*], that does not adumbrate a sensibility [*sensibilité*], that is not given as the concretion of a sense. Accordingly, "I cannot posit one sole sensible without positing it as torn from my flesh, lifted off my flesh" (VI 313/259). Correlatively, there is no sensibility [*sentir*] that can subsist in a pure state, that would not itself be sensitive to the sense of what is sensed, that would not be immersed in what it unveils: sensibility exists only as this sensible which is one's own body. The flesh is truly synonymous with visibility, which is the being of every being. There is no being that pulls itself back to this side of its manifestation, no being that cannot offer itself to a vision. But this presence to vision conceals an ultimate ontological mode and not the *relation* of a presence to vision. Instead of being based on a vision that would be distinct from it, the visible contains vision as a moment of its visibility. Vision is "anonymous," "scattered," and the moment of vision designates only this very visibility insofar as it is "gathered up" (VI 181/138). The flesh qualifies the being of sense as errant, figured sense, the call of a vision that it awakens, that in a sense it already contains, but in which it is never completely concentrated. The flesh, then, "is not matter, is not mind, is not substance. To designate it we should need the old term 'element,' in the sense it was used to speak of water, air, earth, and fire, that is, in the sense of a *general thing*, midway between the spatio-temporal individual and the idea, a sort of incarnate principle that brings a style of being wherever there is a fragment of being" (VI 184/139). Elsewhere, Merleau-Ponty says, "it is the concrete emblem of a general manner of being" (VI 194/147), that is, the concretion of every vision, the precession or latency of all sense.

[199] The duality of matter and form according to which Husserl tries to comprehend (that is, to reconstitute) intentionality is finally surmounted with the flesh, thus understood. Merleau-Ponty's ontology proceeds entirely from the decision to reconceive intentionality as an originary "reality," to recognize the irreducible and in some way unrendable character of the intentional fabric. Thought through to the end, intentionality rejects a type of analysis that tries to undo it in order to reconstruct it, to rediscover in it a unity starting from a prior duality. In other words, for Merleau-Ponty the issue is one of understanding *intentionality as being* through the notion of flesh. In *Ideas I*, Husserl describes intentionality as the apprehension or the animation of a hyletic layer—constituted by the pure *data* of sensation—which confers on it a figurative function, that is, constitutes it as appearance or adumbration of something.[5] The whole difficulty then consists in reconciling the moment of transcendence—the thing is *only* adumbrated in the *hylē*—with the moment of presentation or immanence: *in* every adumbration, the thing appears. It is a question of understanding how matter can remain itself while at the same time making an object appear, how it is not exhausted in the "what" which its function is to make appear. It is a question of conceiving the unity of what appears in such a way that it continues to be an *appearing unity;* that is, the unity does not absorb that in which and as which it appears. Now, formulated in this way, the difficulty seems insurmountable. Because the *hylē* is from the first posited just short of all manifestation, the moment of the manifestation is inevitably grasped as apprehension. That is, this moment is grasped as proceeding from an act whose dynamism comes to compensate in some way

5. E. Husserl, *Ideen zu einer reinen Phänomenologie und phänomenologischen Philosophie: Erstes Buch*, ed. K. Schuhmann, Husserliana 3-1 (The Hague: Martinus Nijhoff, 1976), §97, 203; trans. F. Kersten as *Ideas Pertaining to a Pure Phenomenology and to a Phenomenological Philosophy, First Book: General Introduction to a Pure Phenomenology* (The Hague: Martinus Nijhoff, 1982), §97, 238.

for the passivity of the matter, so that in the end the manifestation is exhausted in the presence of the manifested. Because the *hylē* is not reconceived as adumbrating the object *by itself*, because it is split off from what it makes appear, the specific moment of the adumbration is overshot, that is, missed, in favor of a noema conceived as a unity of sense. Only on the condition that the appearing proceeds from the very depth of the *hylē*, in fact, can it arise *as* this depth, that is, continue to be transcendent in its manifestation. The moment of appearing is then decomposed, immediately situated short of itself and beyond itself: appearing too little in the *hylē*, the thing for the same reason appears too much in the *morphē*. At first cut off from the sense that it must adumbrate, the matter is consecrated to being absorbed by the sense aimed at in the apprehension. [200] Thus, "the whole Husserlian analysis is blocked by the framework of *acts* which imposes upon it the philosophy of *consciousness*" (VI 297/244). It is true that Husserl tries to resolve the problem by recourse to the Idea in the Kantian sense. The perfect givenness of the thing is *only prescribed* insofar as it is an Idea. As soon as it is grasped as the pole of an infinite process, the unity inherent to the appearance can reconcile itself with the indetermination of adumbrations, that is, with the transcendence of the thing. The recourse to the regulative Idea as closure of the infinite aims to found the presence of the thing itself in an adumbration that, as such, nonetheless moves it again to an infinite distance. In fact, "The idea of an infinity motivated in conformity with its essence is not itself an infinity; seeing intellectually that this infinity of necessity cannot be given does not exclude, but rather requires, the intellectually seen givenness of the *idea* of this infinity."[6] It seems then that the Idea allows for the reconciliation of the duality between matter and form—since this Idea contains the infinite —and their unity, since this infinity advents only on the basis of its own closure in the Idea. But in reality, the infinity or the depth of the thing is missed even in this case. In fact, by a single movement the *hylē* is posited as what is not in any case the thing, and the infinite is determined, beside the finite, as an ultimately positive being. The "exteriority" of the infinite with regard to the finite proceeds from the fact that the determination of the *hylē* is *first* a negation. Because each adumbration is grasped directly from the perspective of its being split off from the thing, the infinite gathers itself beyond every adumbration and encloses itself in the Idea. As soon as matter is understood as indetermination rather than as positive *deter-*

6. Husserl, *Ideen I*, §143, 343; *Ideas I*, §143, 298.

minability, the object is synonymous with a full determination, a determination that the infinite growth of the object does not succeed in breaking apart. The genuine meaning of the infinite is therefore missed to the extent that it is split off from the finite: thought as immediate negation of the finite, or as that of which the finite is the immediate negation, the infinite is displaced into a position where its infinity is seen as compromised. In other words, the infinity cannot be understood as *in-finity,* that is, as the absence of the thing itself in *each* profile. In fact, to say that *no* adumbration is the thing is the same as saying that it is *not at all* the thing, and consequently it amounts to fixing the thing itself as exterior to what manifests it; that is, it is the same as betraying its infinity by considering it as [201] traversed. As Merleau-Ponty notes laconically, "*Unendlichkeit* is at bottom the *in itself,* the *ob-ject*" (VI 305/251), and he then adds that "the genuine infinite cannot be that: it must be what exceeds us: the infinity of *Offenheit* and not *Unendlichkeit*——Infinity of the *Lebenswelt* and not infinity of idealization——Negative infinity, therefore——Sense or reason which are contingency" (VI 223/169). Infinity makes sense only if it is conceived in its unity with—rather than as the negation of—the finite; or rather, there is infinity, insofar as it is the negation of the finite, only to the extent that this negation does not get carried away with itself, to the extent that it continues to be retained in what it negates. The infinite can be preserved as what never presents itself only if it is conceived not as what infinitely exceeds all presentation, but rather as what always already presents itself. As is well known, there is genuine negation only insofar as it is not absolute; otherwise it becomes the inverse of a position. For Merleau-Ponty, the infinite must therefore remain "negative infinite," the being which is its own promise. The infinite is synonymous with the "openness of the *Umwelt,*" synonymous, that is, with a matter where the infinity of what it makes appear—its own thickness, in other words—is preserved to the very extent that this matter is not cut off from what it makes appear. The infinite is not other than the finite but is its signifying power, which is synonymous with its opacity. Appealing to the notion of flesh amounts in the end to surpassing the immediate opposition of finite and infinite, to understanding that the truth of the infinite is situated just short of this opposition. The infinite is itself only if it is retained in the finite or as the finite, because posited as infinitely beyond the finite, absolutely exterior to it, the infinite immediately degrades itself into finitude. Appealing to the notion of flesh amounts to conceiving the infinite as the openness itself instead of recomposing it on the basis of a duality of the infinite and finite in which both are disfigured. Infinity is the *Offenheit* as relation to a being that cannot be posited, to a being that is its own negation.

This is why finally the flesh must be conceived as a horizon: it designates precisely *the horizon as being*.

> When Husserl spoke of the horizon of things . . . it is necessary to take the term seriously. No more than are the sky or the earth is the horizon a collection of things held together, or a class name, or a logical possibility of conception, or a system of "potentiality of consciousness": it is a new type of being, a being [202] by porosity, pregnancy, or generality, and he before whom the horizon opens is caught up, included within it. (VI 195/148–49)

When Husserl characterizes the horizon as what "belongs to"[7] *each state of consciousness*, as what is co-present to the *present lived experience*, he makes it recoil into absence, reduces it to an *other* presence, and compromises the indissoluble unity of determination and indetermination by which he had begun to characterize it. The present lived experience genuinely *has* a horizon only if it passes into it, only if it *is* then this horizon and consequently stops being a *present lived experience*. The horizon continues to be a horizon, rather than referring to a full determination of which it would be nothing but the negation, only on the condition of being determined in its very indetermination, only if its indetermination is not indetermination of a being but *is* insofar as it is indetermination. So the actual lived experience is in its turn traversed by this indetermination; the horizon stops "belonging to the lived experience," and the "lived experience" is the lived experience of something only by slipping into it. To speak of flesh is to conceive presence as a horizon rather than the horizon as the horizon of a presence.

---

7. Husserl, *Méditations cartésiennes,* §19; *Cartesian Meditations,* §19.

Dimensionality: The Thing
and the World

1. The Dimension

[203] We must penetrate more deeply into this horizon and try to understand better the invisibility proper to the visible. How can the perceived be characterized insofar as it escapes the opposition of fact and essence, insofar as it is set into a flesh? In a working note concerning the world, Merleau-Ponty proposes to "Replace the notions of concept, idea, mind, representation with the notions of *dimensions,* articulation, level, hinges, pivots, configuration" (VI 277/224). As we have said, perception is not the positing of a content nor contact with a thing in itself. But that the thing is not to be confused with the pure individual does not mean that it exhausts itself in meaning, that its determination is possessed in a frontal manner. The perceived thing possesses me as much as I possess it: I perceive *according to* or *with* it rather than perceiving it itself. Perception is then perception of something only if the perceived continues to be the "according to" of this perception—the measurement, level, dimension of this perception: "With the first vision, the first contact, the first pleasure, there is initiation, that is, not the positing of a content, but the opening of a dimension that can never again be closed, the establishment of a level in terms of which every other experience will henceforth be situated" (VI 198/151). In other words, it is necessary to conceive the thing perceived itself as an *organ.* What defines vision, for example, is that it functions and institutes a visual world only to the extent that it forgets itself as vision. [204] Strictly speaking, things are grasped as belonging to the visual order only during the transition from one sense to another, as when, absorbed in listening to music, we suddenly open our eyes and see the world. But once instituted, vision forgets itself in the things that it gives to be seen. The things are presented only if vision is unaware of itself in them, and they manifest vision only as a secret ontological community. Vision is actual and opens onto something only if no proper determination interposes itself between vision and its object, only if for itself vision is made non-

vision, blindness. Thus, Merleau-Ponty remarks, "for example, a color, yellow; it surpasses itself of itself: as soon as it becomes the color of the illumination, the dominant color of the field, it ceases to be such or such a color" (VI 271/217; see also 301/247). Because they make us see, vision and color become neutral. Insofar as they are that according to which I perceive, vision and color make themselves invisible in what they present, they efface themselves in order to make it appear, and therefore they give themselves in what they present as a certain absence. In the same way, to understand the thing as organ is to acknowledge that it shows itself only to the extent that it does not show *itself* but is merely indicated as this secret axis along which its visibility gathers. It gives seeing rather than is seen, shows rather than shows itself. The thing is the articulation between the perceiving and the world, the modality, the "according to" of a perception; and in this measure the thing is not itself seen but continues to be retained, like a line of flight, in the world that gives itself in the thing. Also, there is no reason to distinguish the perceiving from the perceived thing. This was the problem for every philosophy of consciousness. Because the philosophy of consciousness distinguished the subject of vision from the thing it perceives, it was led to think the latter as pure ideality and to miss its worldly texture. Now, to see something is not to see it itself but to see *in* or *by* it, in such a way that vision advents as a moment of the thing, a moment which cannot be detached from it. The perceiving is *in the very place* [*au lieu*] of the thing. The perceiving grasps the thing only insofar as it is surrounded by it, immersed in it; it makes the thing appear only because it is adorned with the thing's texture. One must not even say that perception is perception of a dimension: it *is* dimension or dimensionalization, the exercise or inscription of an organ as world. The world proposes dimensions just as much as it is posited by them. The dynamism of the flesh must be [205] grasped as institution rather than as constitution: the flesh is made of these levels, of these axes around which "subject" and "object" turn. From this it follows that no thing *itself* can be perceived. "The thing is not really *observable:* there is always a skipping over [*enjambement*] in every observation, one is never at the thing itself. What we call the *sensible* is only the fact that the indefinite [succession] of *Abschattungen precipitates*" (VI 245/192). To see is to grasp "something," an "*etwas,*" Merleau-Ponty says, which is not a thing in the strict sense. Perception's inherent incapacity to apprehend the thing itself does not stem from an excess of distance but rather from an excess of proximity. Perception cannot distance itself from itself in order to reveal the level at which it unfolds the world, for then the world would vanish. In fact, returning to the comparison with sense organs, it is clear that to the extent that I see or touch, I do not *know* what it is to see or to touch. To say there is a world is to say there is vision or touch, and one cannot go beyond this. Vision and touch give themselves only as absent from the visible and tangible world to which they give birth. In the same way, the thing is perceived only if it is ignored as *thing* perceived. The appearance of the world certainly means that there is something, that there are "some things," but also that no thing breaks away from the world, that this world is not made of things. No thing "remains at hand" because it is not a noema but the very texture of the intentional fabric: "the things are structures, frameworks, the stars of our life: not before us, laid out as perspective spectacles, but gravitating about us" (VI 273/220). In other words, they are "the nuclei of meaning about which the transcendental life pivots, specified voids" (VI 292/239) or even "structures of the void" (VI 289/235). These are not at all pure voids sacrificing themselves to the thickness of the in-itself, nor determinations by which positivity absorbs negativity. Rather, they are beings that, while preserving their own emptiness by accomplishing it as world, confer on the world the structure by which this emptiness is sustained in order to make the world appear. The structure of the void retains in the void of appearance the fullness of the thing that this void nevertheless sustains. There is therefore genuinely neither "void" nor "fullness" but a structure, a dimension which remains itself only because it makes itself world.

[206] The dimension must then be understood as the "principle of equivalence," as the kinship to which the moments of the spectacle bear witness, as the allusion of each part of the spectacle to all the others. It is necessary, Merleau-Ponty says, to define "each perceived being by a structure or a system of equivalencies about which it is disposed, and of which the painter's strokes—the flexuous line—or the sweep of the brush is the peremptory evocation" (VI 261/207–208). In fact, the pictorial sense comes to germinate on the canvas, not as an assignable entity present for itself but under the form of a "coherent deformation," under the form of a secret web that unites the aspects of this deformation and is situated between the aspects as a principle of transposition. In the same way, insofar as it brings to appearance, the dimension is given not by itself but solely in, or rather as, the differences in which it advents. This does not mean that one is returning to pure multiplicity. In their turn, the aspects or differences are themselves only to the extent that they are disposed around the dimension, around a fabric that, by joining them together, allows them to be dif-

ferentiated. On the one hand, the thing appears and, to this extent, it cannot be a pure multiplicity; it adumbrates a unity. But, on the other hand, insofar as it is the thing itself that is appearing, this unity is given only as crystallized in each part as the difference between them. In fact, just as a unity posited alongside diversity would vanish as a unity, a pure multiplicity deprived of a principle of unification would not even be a multiplicity; it would disappear into the night of the in-itself. There is, then, no distinction between the proper unity of the thing and its internal diversity. The notion of dimension aims precisely to reconceive the reality of the thing just short of this opposition. As a pure unity, the thing would lose its transcendence; as pure multiplicity, it could not appear but would lapse back into the in-itself. It follows that there is a genuine unity only as the differences into which the unity dissolves itself in order to gain itself, just as there are genuine differences only insofar as they are disposed on an axis of identity, on a dimension on the basis of which they can spring up again. The principle of equivalence that sustains the appearance of the thing makes sense only if it cannot be posited for itself or gathered up into a unity distinct from what it unifies. There is a principle of equivalence only as merging with what it brings to equivalence, that is, only as difference. Realized as an entity, this principle would be dissolved [207] as such because it lacks distinct terms on which it can function. The unity of the dimension means therefore that the dimension is just as open, disjointed by what it unifies. The dimension withdraws into each of the differences that it reconciles and does so precisely because it reconciles them. Conversely, differences in the pure state would not even be differences, because they lack a principle of unity on the basis of which they can appear. There is genuine difference therefore only if it is not absolute, only if it does not go up as far as the pure multiple. Difference subsists only by means of the dimension according to which it is disposed, only in relation to a level from which the divergences can be measured. Dimension is really synonymous with difference on the condition that the latter is understood rigorously, not as an abyss between different things but as a tear that is still a fabric, a disjunction that is also a conjunction. The dimension is the point of articulation where the thing maintains its unity only by recoiling into its differences and gains its identity only by making itself multiple.

The unity of the thing must be reconceived as the openness of each part to all the others, the openness which, as such, is at the same time distance: the thing announces itself in each aspect as their presumptive or imminent unity. Correlatively, each part becomes itself only in and by this unity that, however, is nothing *other* than it. In other words, there is, strictly speaking, neither thing nor aspects, neither unity nor diversity, but one sole fabric which is unifying-differentiating, which conquers its cohesion within its differences and diversifies itself by means of this unity. The thing is born *between* its parts, but the parts themselves are born of this interstice. There is then no precession between the "whole" and the "parts": the latter become themselves only by the whole they nevertheless compose, while the former becomes itself only by the parts that it nevertheless totalizes. The parts of the thing appear only thanks to what they make appear: each difference is like a variant that is understood [*s'entend*] only because a theme is heard [*s'entend*] in it. The unity gives life to the differences so that the differences in return instill their life into the unity. To speak of dimension is to say that the thing is unified only insofar as it remains open, destined *to* itself—that is, just as much open *in* itself. As dimension, the thing is truly this equivalence without content, this principle of transposition which makes us say that the thing is *there,* but without the place of this appearance able to be circumscribed. Just as the sense of the painting emerges in it as an atmosphere, at once omnipresent and unlocalizable, [208] the sense of the thing is self-agreement, "cohesion without concept," a unity which has no need to be posited for itself. To understand sense as dimension is to recognize that it offers itself only as the solidity of a "there": "Perception as imperception, evidence in non-possession: it is precisely because one knows too well what one is dealing with that one has no need to posit it as an object" (VI 254/201). Finally, therefore, the dimension can be described as something "partly expressed" [*entre-expression*] or a relation of *pars totalis:* each part expresses all the others, articulates itself in them without this expression referring to a plan [*géométral*] and without their relation being mediated by a third. Each part expresses *by means of itself.* Consequently, it manifests an agreement with the others, enters into kinship with them, without however this unity proceeding from the relation of each to something expressed. The expression lacks the expressed that nonetheless confers its expressivity on it; it precedes in some manner the expressed toward which it tends. In the end, it is from the secret articulation, from the implicit equivalence, that the expressivity of parts and the plan [*géométral*] are born together. Thus the intentional link of the "parts" to the "whole," of the "adumbration" to the "noema," turns out to be deeper than what it connects. The intentional fabric is truly the horizon, the being of "pregnancy" and "porosity" that leads to unity—that is, accomplishes its function as openness—only by being lacerated and obscured by what it joins together and makes appear. The thing is flesh, "contact in thickness of self with self" (VI 321/268), agreement with self which is also separation, thickness which is also transparency.

It is clear that the dimension delivers the genuine sense of the notion of Gestalt from which Merleau-Ponty had begun in *The Structure of Behavior*. It is the "process of *Gestaltung*," of unity by segregation: "It is a principle of distribution, the pivot of a system of equivalencies, it is the *Etwas* of which the fragmentary phenomena will be the manifestation" (VI 258/205). The figure-ground relation, "the simplest *Etwas*," is the model of every *Etwas;* it is the "key to the problem of the mind [*l'esprit*]" (VI 246/192). A figure exists only as held back in a ground, only as this structuration or configuration whose unity is achieved only by the moments that they structure. And the ground appears in the figure as that from which the thickness is constituted, starting from the hollows that break up the figure. Figure and ground [209] turn around one another: the void of the structure is filled by the fullness that the figure brings about in configuring the ground.

It can be determined here to what degree Merleau-Ponty's analysis is accomplished entirely in the element of language. His study was centered on the discovery of the diacritical structure of the sign. Against the intellectualist conception which posits the material sign and the signification side by side as positive entities, linguistics discovers that sign and signification become positive beings and are then ordered to each other only by a process of active differentiation carried out first on the signifiers themselves. It is truly by this process that the signifiers become signifiers in the strict sense, that is, carriers of significations. The signification is not attached in a univocal manner to a sign but is situated between the signs as the invisible place where the signifying acts intersect. The sense intended in speech is a "qualified nothingness" whose unity is designed by means of the incessant differentiation of spoken words. Consequently, the sign is never truly isolable and the sense never strictly present in any spoken word; it is sketched in them as their secret web and remains therefore allusive, by principle disappointing every attempt to possess it in person. The sense is reached only in a lateral fashion, beside itself, across the figures in which it is incarnated. Now, this analysis is not merely a model for the description of the perceived, as if the perceived were of a completely different order than that of language. To say that the sense is never present in person, that it is strictly speaking invisible, is on the contrary to recognize that it merges with the thing itself, that speech does nothing other than give the world to be seen and extract the sense from it, and that to this extent, speech is perception. The invisibility of sense is synonymous with the transcendence it signifies. In fact, we have to make a choice. One can claim to distinguish the linguistic sense from the perceived sense, but then there is no problem of language, and the very fact of language becomes truly incomprehensible, since this linguistic sense can refer only to already acquired significations. Or else one can acknowledge the imminence of sense in speech, but then language must be considered as a relation to the thing itself and finally as a modality of perceiving. But then, if language is perception, perception can be understood as a language, as a *logos*, Merleau-Ponty says, and the perceptual sense could be described in the very terms by which linguistic sense was clarified. This is precisely what Merleau-Ponty does throughout the working notes. [210] The perceived signification, the thing, is only the presumption of an incarnation in the aspects where it will remain the same, the unity that gains itself within the very heart of its differences. There is certainly a distinction to be made between language and perception—the distinction that produces the illusion of a positivity of signification—which depends on the fact that speech works with already signifying entities, that it engenders new significations on the basis of established significations, while perception is the givenness of an originary sense. But this difference is, in part, illusory. In fact, the established signification, to the very extent that it is established, loses its signifying power and flows back into the night of insignificance. It lives only by the signifying life that it engenders; the established signification preserves its signifying power only if it stops being instituted. Only the act of appropriation can instill in it a new sense as a dimension of "speaking" speech. The established signification continues to signify, then, only through the new unity to which it gives way in its confrontation with other significations within a new speech. In short, in view of the sense to which it *is going* to give birth, the established signification is no longer signifying. In relation to the established significations, the new signification is given as *originary*. On the occasion of each expressive act, we try out and test a sense that is about to be born. In view of their identity, therefore, the difference between language and perception amounts to little. In language, one is truly present at this engenderment of sense, to which, in other respects, perception attests. The consciousness of this identity supports all of Merleau-Ponty's descriptions. In fact, the dimension is nothing other than the "*logos* that pronounces itself silently in each sensible thing" (VI 261/208), than the "message" around which the sensible thing varies and that it frees up only because it retains it in its depth. One must grasp the law of language as the very law of the perceived and speak literally of a *diacritical* structure of the thing. There are only "differences of significations" (VI 277/227, also 265/211), and the Gestalt is indeed "a diacritical, oppositional, relative system whose pivot is the *Etwas*, the thing, the world, and not the idea" (VI 259/206). This is to say in the end that perception is, strictly speaking, *pure expression*. Far from naively understanding expression on the basis of an already signifying ground, one must grasp the perceived itself on the basis of [211] the expression, as primordial expression, neither more nor less signifying than linguistic expression—or rather less "explicitly" signifying, since it is source of all signification, signification in a "wild" state. The perceived is the dimension for other acts of expression. It opens a future, suggests a principle of unity that nonetheless truly will become itself only within the acts of appropriation to which it gives rise. The sensible is not the other of sense because it includes the fate of expression in its entirety; it is absolutely unified, but by a unity that is absolutely presumptive. It is a sense at its maximum degree of errancy, nowhere gathered together, pure allusion, horizon. The whole difficulty then lies in not referring the incontestable thickness of the sensible, the resistance it always offers, to any positivity whatsoever, in not attaining what nonetheless gives itself as real. This "relative positivity of the perceived," Merleau-Ponty says, is only "non-negation," it "does not resist observation," "every crystallization is illusory in some respect" (VI 267/214). The thickness of the sensible is just as much translucidity of sense. The sensible offers a resistance because it is source of all sense. Its relative positivity proceeds not from the absence in it of any signification but on the contrary from the excess of sense that it comes to crystallize. Because the absolute unity of the Universal is announced in the sensible, the sensible is given equally as absolute opacity or Fact. Thus, even by virtue of their unity, things cannot close up on themselves so that their transcendence still encompasses their appearance, so that they are collapsed into their own differences. The thing has genuine unity only insofar as it remains in the process of unification.

2. Individuality and Generality

As dimension, the thing must be characterized by its *generality*: it is "a field being" (VI 273/220). Even so, it is not a matter of situating it in an indeterminate manner *between* the universal and the singular; generality is rather an ultimate ontological mode. There is individuality only as generality or as "pre-individuality" (VI 315/262). Thus the notion of dimension corresponds to a [212] radically new approach to the question of individuation. Consider the problem as it is posed by Aristotle. The entire structure of the *Metaphysics* follows from the decision to put the substantial individual, the *sunolon,* in the forefront, in opposition to Platonism that, ultimately determining the Idea as a substance, divides it from concrete reality. But the *sunolon* is put in the forefront also against skepticism that approaches the real in such a way that the identity of the Idea, and consequently the very possibility of thought, turns out to be incomprehensible. Substance is characterized as a composite of matter and form, terms whose unity is ensured by recourse to the decisive notions of actuality and potentiality. Matter is potential form or the potential of the form, the collapsing of the essence into or as concrete individual. Therefore, matter cannot subsist in a pure state; it is always already "clothed." Form, in its turn, is the actuality of a potentiality, an actuality that, at least at the level of the sublunary world, cannot completely reabsorb the potentiality of which it is the actualization, and consequently involves indetermination. How then can the individual substance be individuated? If Aristotle did not raise this question explicitly, which is perhaps significant,[1] the com-

1. From the superlunary perspective, it is true that substances are entirely polarized by the unity of the pure divine act such that materiality has an essentially negative signification. This is an argument in favor of individuation by form: God, absolutely singular, is endowed with an absolute formal purity. However, one could emphasize Aristotle's awareness of the world's irreducible contingency: from the sublunary point of view, the quiddity appears rather as the inaccessible pole of a movement of actualization. In other words, what defines substance would be in principle to be in withdrawal from an actuality that it nonetheless sketches and which determines it as substance, while substantial determination would be characterized by its withdrawal into indetermination. The unfulfillment of substance would not express a defect with respect to the quiddity but indeed its deepest reality: the quiddity would then be defined as being always unassignable. As, moreover, the theory of categories shows, Being can be conceived not as a supreme genus, nor as an impenetrable abyss, but as that whose unity is synonymous with a division into a multiplicity of dimensions of sense or discourse. Far from closing itself on the identity of the *eidos,* Being preserves its depth only by breaking up into a plurality of dimensions that signify it without ever exhausting it (see P. Aubenque, *Le problème de l'être chez Aristote* [Paris: Presses Universitaires de France, 1962]). To the extent that Aristotle had the intuition of this irreducible contingency, the pure divine act tends to be deprived of its ontological function in favor of a regulative function within the moral domain.

mentators have certainly struggled with it. Actually, the search for such a principle turns out to be doomed to failure. The quiddity being by itself universal, this principle could [213] reside only in the matter; the latter realizes the passage from the *species infinita* to the individual and confers to the essence the existence of the sensible "this." However, how could that which is itself indeterminate individuate anything? Only the form seems able to correspond to the principle of individuation, since it grounds the possibility of distinguishing a being as *such and such* a thing rather than some other. But then, by means of its purity, the formal determination exceeds the concreteness of the individual. How can what is universal in itself possess an individuating power? Thus as soon as one *isolates* a principle of individuation, one finds oneself led back immediately to the opposite pole. Taken at the level of matter, individuality disappears into indetermination; but assigned to a form, it dissolves into the universality of the *quid*. The individual, then, is always missed—by excess or by lack—by the principle that is supposed to account for it. This is why certain commentators[2] draw the conclusion, paradoxically, that recourse to *two* principles of individuation is necessary. The first, matter, would account for numerical individuality, while the second, form, would found the individuality of the determination. But this avoids the problem, or rather transposes the problem into the solution by making matter and form coexist, rather than questioning the relevance of the search for such a principle. Undoubtedly Merleau-Ponty did not explicitly put the question to himself in these terms, but nonetheless his reflection on the thing fully addresses the difficulty and draws out the consequences of it. An investigation that aims at subordinating the individuality of the concrete existent to a principle of individuation is doomed to aporias revealed by Merleau-Ponty's theory of dimensionality. His theory shows that it is a question not of starting from the constituted individual at the end of an individuation for which it would be necessary to seek the principles, but rather of grasping the individual on the basis of and as its individuation. The theory contains the idea that the individuation does not designate an incomprehensible phase *preceding* the individual whose clarification then necessitates recourse to a principle; individuation is instead a positive and ultimate moment. For what is really in question is whether individuation requires a *principle*. There is something paradoxical in the attempt to find such a principle. At the moment when one wants to meet up with the individual itself, one re-

2. Notably Léon Robin.

fers it to something other than itself or makes it go beyond itself toward a matter or a form. The *principle* of individuation cannot be the principle [214] of *individuation*. As soon as one adopts the perspective of seeking such a principle, as soon as one opts for matter (or form), for quantity (or quality), the individual is dismembered and made to go beyond itself toward indetermination or universality. The result is that it becomes necessary in the end to "compensate" for this distance by recourse to a second principle. Just when one principle is fixed, it becomes two. In short, the individual is understood in a strictly negative manner, as the *meeting* of a matter and a form; what is positive and irreducible in it is ignored. Conversely, to recognize individuals is to admit that individuality belongs to them, that nothing other than themselves precedes them or constitutes them. Only in the name of abstraction can matter and form or a specific dimension and a numerical dimension be distinguished in them. Thus, in understanding the thing as dimension, Merleau-Ponty recognizes that individuality makes sense only insofar as it does not proceed from a principle, and that the individual has individuality only insofar as individuality cannot be assigned. The individuality of the thing can be maintained only by remaining unfulfilled, just short of the point where it could be fixed as a principle. The thing is itself—that is, individual—only if it is not posited for itself, only if it does not possess a form proper to it. A perfectly fulfilled thing, an essentially individuated thing, would stop being a thing; it would be dissolved into the universality of the concept. Therefore, the thing has a unity only insofar as this unity cannot be closed or confused with a form playing the role of a principle and distinguished from the individual whose individuality it ensures. This does not mean that the thing has merely numerical individuality, or that its identity derives from pure matter. Certainly it cannot be characterized by formal closure, but this does not mean that it is based in itself. Neither can the thing's incontestable facticity be pushed all the way to the extreme and grounded on an autonomous material order. This is why a thing that would not be on the way to unification, that would be reduced to a pure multiple, could not be an individual thing. In the end, then, the individuality of the thing makes sense only to the extent that it is situated just short of or beyond every principle that would gather it together. The sensible thing is between quantity and quality or, rather, beyond this distinction (VI 289/236); its individuality is actual only if it does not go all the way to the numerical, nor [215] all the way to the specific. The individual exists, then, only as pre-individual, general, in the course of or on the way to individualization. Individuality is essentially next to the point where one seeks to fix it: always already beyond the atom, yet never essence; it sustains itself only by escaping identification.[3] The individual thing is flesh, that is, according to the example of one's own body, a multiplicity that agrees with itself and sketches an interiority, but just as much an identity which is determined only because it remains open, is sustained by remaining presumptive and on the way toward completion. Individuality must also be conceived out-

3. This perspective is developed by G. Simondon in his remarkable work, *L'individu et sa genèse physico-biologique* (Paris: Presses Universitaires de France, 1964). Dedicated to Merleau-Ponty, it probably owes much to him. Simondon asserts immediately that "What is a postulate in the search for a principle of individuation is that individuation has a principle" (1). The hylo-morphic perspective takes the *constituted* individual as its starting point; this individual is cut off from the operation of individuation, which must then be *explained* by recourse to a principle. Thus, "the principle of individuation is therefore grasped not in this very individuation as an operation, but in what this operation has need of in order to exist, namely, a matter and a form. It is supposed that the principle is contained in the matter or the form, since the operation of individuation is not thought capable of *carrying* the principle itself but only of *putting it to use.* . . . This operation is thought of as something to explain and not as something in which the explanation should be found" (3). For Simondon, one does not approach individuation starting from the individual. It is a matter of grasping the individuated being starting from individuation, and individuation starting from the *pre-individual* being. This perspective, then, calls for a radical ontological reversal. Being can be characterized as substance and subjected to the principle of identity no longer. It must be thought on the basis of the possibility of the individuating processes, that is, as "not consisting solely in itself," "more than a unity," capable of "being out of phase with itself, to overflow itself here and there from *its center*" (6, 16). The notion of *transduction,* by which Simondon characterizes Being as a process of individuation, is inherited from the Merleau-Pontian conception of dimensionality. It designates the process of unification of beings insofar as this process proceeds from their very difference. It is by their depth, their difference, that beings join themselves together, for this depth is not the other of sense but truly the sole mode of being—invisibility, withdrawal—suitable for its richness and its infinite potentiality. The negative is not substantial; it is the other face of signifying positivity. Also, transduction is not to be confused with deduction, because it draws out the resolving structure, the dimension of unification, of the very tensions of the real. Nor is it to be confused with induction, since the structuring is done without loss: "the resolving transduction *performs an inversion from negative into positive.* That by which the terms are not identical with each other, that by which they are *disparate* (in the sense given this term in the theory of vision), is integrated with the system of resolution and becomes the condition of signification" (21).

side any reference to a positive principle, that is, as "process," "vector": [216] "understand that the Gestalt is already transcendence: it makes me understand that a line is a vector, that a point is a center of forces——There are neither absolute lines nor points nor colors in the things" (VI 248/195). Since the attempt to fix individuality by a principle leads to its dismemberment into the duality of numeric and specific, one must conclude that individuality is characterized by its ability to foil every search for a principle of individuation; to be attentive to the individual is to understand that the search for such a principle is meaningless. One must instead say that the individual produces its own "principles" as asymptotic poles of its pre-individual life, poles on which thought is almost inevitably destined to fixate.

This remark leads us to deepen our prior analysis; that is, we are led to interrogate the relation of the thing to the world, to reconceive the thing in the perspective of the world. In fact, our first description of the dimension was still abstract. We defined it as a unity that is realized only as its differences, and, according to Merleau-Ponty's formula, as a "principle of equivalence." But what carries this equivalence? If the unity of the thing is realized only *as* its differences, then it could not be as *its* differences that it is achieved. Rigorously understood, dimensionality puts into question the principle of a distinction between what would be attributable to the thing itself and what is exterior to it. In other words, there is a choice: if the thing's unity exists only through *its* differences, if the differences are *its,* then the differences flow back toward identity and what defines the dimension is missed. But, on the other hand, if the thing is truly the principle of equivalence, pivot, hinge, then one cannot rigorously speak of differences that would belong to it, and the distinction between what belongs to the thing and what is foreign to it is groundless. If the thing refers to forms of appearance that define it, if the appearance is given as appearance *of* the thing, the distinction between the moment of the appearance and what is constituted in it is no longer meaningful. To the extent, then, that the thing appears—that is, that it is not present itself in what presents it—one must admit that the moment of its appearance *is not proper to it.* It is also necessary to conceive at the most profound level the unity of dimension and difference: the ground from which the thing proceeds, in which it manifests itself [217], comes to belong to the thing only in the movement by which it manifests the thing. The belonging of the aspects to the thing is achieved at the same time that the thing appears. To the extent that the thing does not appear *itself*, that it is never completely constituted, these aspects are not rigorously attributable to it. The thing would not be able to be located then *in* the aspects or differences which would belong to it, *in which* it would come to presence; to speak in these terms amounts to maintaining an abstract viewpoint, to situating oneself a priori within the thing's frame. The terms between which the principle of equivalence is unfolded, precisely insofar as it wins its identity only in them, cannot be circumscribed. Thus, to recognize that the dimensional unity of the thing advents only in its differences amounts to saying that these differences plunge into the thickness of the world. Consequently, this amounts to thinking the thing *in the very place* of its articulation with the world, *as* its own inscription in the world. This is precisely the signification of the individuality of the thing: it exists only as retained in a generality, in the depth of the world, from which, however, it breaks off.

Merleau-Ponty shows this in an important working note which is a continuation of the reflection referred to earlier on dimensionality—that is, the neutrality of color:

> With one sole movement it imposes itself as particular and ceases to be visible as particular. The "World" is this whole where each "part," when one takes it for itself, suddenly opens unlimited dimensions—becomes a *total part*.
>
> Now this particularity of the color, of the yellow, and this universality are not a *contradiction,* are *together* sensoriality itself: it is by the same virtue that the color, the yellow, at the same time gives itself as a *certain* being and as a *dimension,* the expression of *every possible being*——
> What is proper to the sensible (as to language) is to be representative of the whole, not by a sign–signification relation, or by the immanence of the parts in one another and in the whole, but because each part is *torn up* from the whole, comes with its roots, encroaches upon the whole, transgresses the frontiers of the others. It is thus that the parts overlap (transparency), that the present does not stop at the limits of the visible (behind my back). Perception opens the world to me as the surgeon opens a body, catching sight, through the window he has contrived, of the organs in full functioning, taken *in their activity,* seen sideways. It is thus that the sensible initiates me to the world, as language to the other: by encroachment [218] *Ueberschreiten.* Perception is not first a perception of *things,* but a perception of *elements* (water, air . . .) of *rays of the*

world, of things which are dimensions, which are worlds, I slip on these "elements" and here I am in the *world,* I slip from the "subjective" to Being. (VI 271/217–18)

The thing comes into the world that it makes seen, with the result that no principle of distinction can be drawn between the two. However, this cannot mean that the thing is lost in an obscure ground, since the world would immediately cease to be for lack of individuals in which it can appear. There is therefore a relation of coextensivity between thing and world such that the dimension which characterizes the thing is equally the dimension of the world itself, such that the thing encroaches on the totality of the world and plunges its roots into the world's depth. Every thing is a ray of the world, and every dimension is a dimension for the world itself: "In the very measure that I see, I do not know *what* I see . . . , which does not mean that there would be *nothing* there, but that the *Wesen* in question is that of a ray of the world tacitly touched. . . . The invisible of the visible. It is its belongingness to a ray of the world" (VI 300/247). One must take literally the proposal that the thing is an organ; the thing is an organ exactly in the same sense that are sense organs, in the same sense as well that speech is an organ. Just as the world can be transposed entirely onto the visual plane, in the same way nothing escapes speech; every thing is suited to express the world. It follows that the thing's ultimate ontological mode consists not in being situated in the world but in radiating as "active *Wesen,*" in irradiating the world; its ontological mode consists in its becoming-world. The thing is somehow situated between itself and the world, in that place where it is made world so that the world passes into it. The thing is the "world's point of passage," "hinge." Consequently, that there are things, that is, individuals, engenders rather than excludes the possibility of universality. Because it is pre-individual, the thing is itself only in expressing the universality of the world into which it plunges. Universality and individuality are born together. As purely individual, the thing would destroy itself as individual, that is, as an individual *being,* because the world by which its solidity is sustained would be reabsorbed into the thing. But a world whose universality would not be fragmented into individuals that arise there would lose its universality, since it would fail to *appear* as world. This is why there is [219] no contradiction between the yellow as particular and the yellow as world. It is a total part: it is a part only by not closing up on itself, only in agreeing with the totality, with the added condition that there is a totality only as distributed in its parts.

There is no contradiction between the yellow as particular and the yellow as a world, "for it is precisely within its particularity as yellow and through it that the yellow becomes a universe or an *element*. . . . The universal is not above, it is beneath (Claudel), it is not before, but *behind* us" (VI 271–72/218). It is indeed by remaining immersed in the universality of the world that the thing acquires its individuality, or rather, there is only the generality of "hinges" around which the individual and the universal gravitate as asymptotic limits. The thing is itself, namely, particular, only to the extent that it sets up a system of equivalences for the world itself. Its unity to itself, a determinate thing, is an open unity, exceeded by what it gathers, a unity not so much unified as unifying, that mingles with the world whose equivalence it establishes. The thing rises to identity only in the measure that the world holds it back in its plenitude. As Jacques Garelli says, "the pre-individual is always co-present to beings without, nevertheless, being reabsorbed into them."[4] Establishing a limit between the thing and the world really amounts to destroying the unity of the thing by closing it on itself, to losing its individuality by losing the omnipresence of the world. The thing acquires its identity only within the fabric that joins it to the world; it is then at the same time this tissue itself, this framework, armature, dimension of the world. Although it is not nowhere, since it is indeed in the world, one cannot say that it is here or there. To survey it, to exhaust its "essence," would require exhausting the totality of the world. Such is the meaning, finally, of the pre-individuality of the thing. It draws its difference only from its identity with the world; it is the identity of its identity with, and of its difference from, the world.

Hence, the relation of the thing to the world must be characterized as a *chiasm*. The thing is a thing of the world—it is entirely in the world, but the world is entirely in it. It makes the world appear, and the world exhibits itself in it, in such a way [220] that it makes itself world and is nothing other than world. But this is the case on the condition that the world is not an abyss of the in-itself, that it flows back entirely into each thing, that in its turn it is nothing other than the thing. It is no more the case that the world is other than the thing than that the thing is other than the world. Inevitably, this separation would amount to subordinating the world to the things or, alternatively, the things to the world. The thing, to appropriate Marc Richir's formula, is then "the place of the world," in the double

4. J. Garelli, "Temps et phénoménologie: temporalité originaire, *ereignis* et jeu du monde," in *Ed. de l'Université de Bruxelles* (1989), 161.

sense of the word: "The phenomenon appears, therefore, in its two transcendental and ontological dimensions, as a sort of 'place of the world' (in two senses) *with* all the concreteness that can be recognized there and all the phenomena that can, in their turn, be schematized there."[5] The thing takes place in the world, but as that place where the world takes place. It can be characterized as "openness-opened":[6] it is opened up, it is arranged, and it appears as a thing only if it is an opening, that is, on the condition that it leaves room for the world itself. It is opened up, then, only if it is itself the openness in which it appears. It is unified only in the measure that it is unifying; its unity overflows the limit that it nonetheless circumscribes; its unity is made generality, world. The ultimate ground of the real consists in these "rays of the world" which do not lead to the rank of principles, which become qualifiable only in the measure that the equivalence they establish extends to the borders of the world. The *quid* needs the infinite extension of the world in order to return to its comprehension. The recourse to the notion of *element* proves valuable here. Merleau-Ponty defines it as "concrete emblem of a general manner of being" (VI 194/147), as that which "brings a style of being wherever there is a fragment of being" (VI 184/139). It is what is perceived only insofar as I am caught in it, what I dominate only insofar as it encompasses me. The element is given only in tacitly invading the landscape; it becomes itself only in dressing everything in its particularity. Every element is like the sea (VI 327/237). It surrounds me, indeed before I could have become aware of it, in the form of a littoral landscape; it is like these disheveled and quivering trees, like a certain flatness of the earth, like the whiteness of the light, quasi-liquid. The sea mixes equally with the sand, [221] the nearby rocks, to the point that one doesn't know which borrows its being from the other: is it the foam which is born from the rock, or the latter which emerges from the foam like an extension that it is given and that it shapes in its own image in order to complete its whirling existence? If I try to approach it, it will slip away, I will overstep again the point in which it gathers itself. Again, it will invade me like this sky, the grayness of which seems to reflect the murky depth of the water. Insofar as it is an element, the sea is truly just short of and beyond the place where I seek to grasp it; it is present only in surrounding me, only in being generalized to all aspects of a world the

5. M. Richir, *Phénomènes, temps et êtres: ontologie et phénoménologie* (Grenoble: Jérôme Millon, 1987), 291.
6. This is Jacques Garelli's expression.

unassignable limits of which it nevertheless traces. Like the sea, things are elements, extending to the borders of a world, being made universe in order to be themselves, in such a way that "any entity can be *accentuated* as an emblem of Being" (VI 323/270). Or rather, through its originary complicity with a Being, from which finally it is not substantially distinguished, a being is made existent.

Here Merleau-Ponty is simply coming to terms with the difficulties resulting from Husserl's distinction between interior and exterior horizons. The interior horizon refers to the exterior horizon: the thing is surrounded by the world and emerges in it such that the clarification of its aspects includes its articulation with its environment. But, inversely, the exterior horizon refers to the interior horizon: the world, to which all things refer, is itself constituted of things. It is just as much out of the question, then, to maintain the closure of things within their interior horizon, that is, to refuse them a relation to exteriority, as to give them a pure exterior horizon which would not come to converge toward things. It is a matter then of taking stock of what is implied by this notion of horizon. It leads to the fact that there can be no principle of a univocal distinction between interior and exterior. In fact, if the horizons of the thing were genuinely interior to it, there would no longer be any sense in speaking of horizon. Referring by itself to the thing, attesting by itself to its interiority, this horizon would stop indicating the thing as a latent reality. For the horizon to be truly interior, it would be necessary that the thing confirm this interiority by appearing itself, that it consequently stop being presented at the horizon. There is then, conversely, an interior *horizon*, only in the measure that this interiority is not yet qualified, attested, in the measure that the thing itself [222] is not strictly delimited. In other words, the horizon's ontological mode concerns not only the aspects but the *interiority* of these aspects. The interior horizon drifts, slips beyond its limits toward exteriority, the thing opens out toward the world, and the criterion of the distinction between the interior and the exterior is itself only at the horizon. That does not mean, however, that it confines itself to exterior horizons alone. Strictly exterior, these would be destroyed as horizons, and for the opposite reasons. In fact, the horizon would then fall to the rank of a pure non-signifying content; it would be the horizon of nothing, or for nothing, because it would lack a distinction between interior and exterior. There is exteriority, then, only on the condition that it is not pure, that it ebbs toward interiority. Thus it is indeed necessary to distinguish these two horizons, even though this distinction proves incomprehensible if strictly determined: whether it is interior or exterior, the horizon makes sense only on the condition that this interiority or exteriority is not assigned. There are things, there is a world, and yet each of the two passes into the other in such a fashion that their limit is as indeterminate as it is incontestable. One cannot go beyond this co-belonging of things and the world, which is itself constituted out of things. There resides the chiasm evoked earlier: ultimately, there are not things and a world but a world which is made of things only because each thing is made of world, which is co-present to each of the things of which it is nonetheless constituted. The things stand out against the world only if the world invades each of them. The visible is not a chunk of hard being, offered to a vision that could be only total or null,

> but rather a sort of straits between exterior horizons and interior horizons ever gaping open, something that comes to touch lightly and makes diverse regions of the colored or visible world resound at the distances, a certain differentiation, an ephemeral modulation of this world—less a color or a thing, therefore, than a difference between things and colors, a momentary crystallization of colored being or of visibility. (VI 175/132)

The thing is this unassignable point of contact, in which the interior horizon drifts toward the exterior horizon entirely while remaining itself, in which the interior horizon is closed onto itself entirely while unfolding beyond itself. The thing is a "thin pellicule" (VI 182/138), a thin difference or passageway. Both the interiority of the thing and its exteriority, [223] both its identity of being a thing and its mundaneity, are circumscribed together, while remaining open to the other on the basis of their difference.[7] In sum, it is necessary to conceive the world itself as a diacritical

---

7. It goes without saying, therefore, that for Merleau-Ponty, "thing" does not designate what one usually means with this term, namely, a being of delimited and determinate reality based in itself—an object, in short. By "thing" one must understand the "something" (what "there is" [*il y a*]), the *etwas*, *Sache* rather than *Ding*: Merleau-Ponty sometimes uses the term *Wesen*. He does not then begin from the framework of the thing in order to interrogate it afterward about its mode of givenness. The point of departure would determine the response, since to be given "things" is to be prohibited from grasping their articulation with the world. He calls "thing" the phenomenal reality as it is given originarily and, in precise terms, the goal of his analysis is to show that it is never given in the form of a completed, circumscribed, fully determinate thing. Because Merleau-Ponty rejects the pure

system, as a process of universal differentiation, which means equally a process of universal allusion: things are "like *differentiations* of one sole and *massive* adhesion to Being which is the flesh" (VI 324/270). The world is this universal sense which expresses itself only through the individuality of "things" in which it is at once both formulated and missed, doing so consistently with what it is, namely, universal, and escaping therefore from all definitive closure. One must characterize it by this aptitude of every thing to set itself up as an *emblem* of all the others, to constitute itself into a level for them:

> There is no emplacement of space and time that would not be a variant
> of the others, as they are of it; there is no individual that would not be
> representative of a species or of a family of beings, would not have,
> would not be a certain style, a certain manner of managing the domain
> of space and time over which it has competency, of pronouncing, of
> articulating that domain, of radiating about a wholly virtual center.
> (VI 154/114–15)

The world is a place "that exists by piling up, by proliferation, by encroachment, by promiscuity—a perpetual pregnancy, perpetual parturition" (VI 155/115), where each thing makes allusion to all the others and is constituted as a thing by this very allusion. There are no determinate things but kinships, and therefore differences, kinships which are differences, differences which are kinships, and according to all [224] possible degrees, no being which does not form an alliance with the others, echoing them, but no unity which would not remain allusive, unassignable. The sense, in each thing, remains figurative because it figures all the others at the same time: the individuality of the thing is indeed synonymous with its universality. This is why, finally, "This world, this Being, facticity and ideality undividedly, is not one in the sense that being one applies to the individuals it contains, and still less is it two or several in that sense" (VI 157/117). The world does not go all the way up to the plurality of the things that take root there, although it does not subsist in the form of a unique Individual that would contain them. The originary layer is situated "higher"

---

sensible given, in the sense of empiricism, because every content already sketches a sense, it is unnecessary to resort to the thing to unify these contents: the sense remains always set into the depth of the world and is never "thingified." There are [*Il y a*] not things but divergences [*écarts*], accents, "ephemeral modulations" of the world.

than uniqueness since it makes room for the infinite diversity of beings, and yet "lower" than the multiplicity of things since this diversity is diversified only by remaining set into this sole world that it figures.

3. The Metaphoric of the World

Merleau-Ponty's reflection is animated in its entirety by the question of metaphor. It seems to us that in this regard, even though he is mentioned rarely and only in *Phenomenology of Perception,* the influence of Binswanger[8] is decisive. Ultimately, it is a question of considering the world on the basis of the possibility of metaphor and, therefore, of grasping in metaphor the attestation of a signifying depth that its classical descriptions do not restore. It is a question of conceiving ontology as the making explicit of a transcendental of the metaphor, as the response to a question (that Merleau-Ponty does not explicitly ask but which clearly drives him): under what conditions, from the side of the world, is metaphor possible? In fact, it is necessary to reverse the order in which it is usually described. We are first given beings circumscribed in the objective world to then relate them on the basis of properties or aspects that they have in common: metaphor, then, is "transfer." Now, rather than posit beings carrying these properties and consequently defining the latter as attributes, we must reconceive them on the basis of the possibility of establishing a relation between them, of figuring each one by the other. The possibility of metaphor attests to an ontological mode that is irreducible [225] to that of the determinate individual, the subject of predicates; it is based on the dimension, proceeds from this axis around which things are constituted as variants. It is true that in the working note which bears on this question, Merleau-Ponty appears to reject the concept of metaphor: "A 'direction' of thought——This is not a *metaphor*——There is no *metaphor* between the visible and the invisible . . . : *metaphor* is too much or too little: too much if the invisible is really invisible, too little if it lends itself to transposition" (VI 275/221–22). But when considered closely, it seems that Merleau-Ponty rejects not so much the metaphorical relation itself, here the articulation between visible and invisible, as a certain conception of metaphor as "transfer." As soon as the terms of the relation (the visible and the invisible, spatial direction and intellectual direction) are

8. Notably in L. Binswanger, *Analyse existentielle et psychanalyse freudienne: discours, parcours et Freud,* trans. R. Lewinter (Paris: Gallimard, 1981).

understood as circumscribed beings—such is the presupposition of the classical conception of metaphor—the idea of transfer indeed expresses too much or too little. Too much, because if it is truly the case that the two terms are radically separated, one cannot even see how a relation could be established; if the invisible is conceived as negation of the visible, nothing in it would ever be signified by the visible. Too little, because if the terms consent to the transposition, *one could no longer speak solely of transposition.* The visible and invisible can signify each other only because it is not a question of two radically separate worlds, because a deeper unity, an ontological complicity, crosses them. The notion of metaphor as transposition is thus inadequate due to the lack of distinct terms. In short, either the relation does not enter into the definition of the terms, but then one cannot even speak of transposition; or else the transposition is proved possible, but, in that case, the word is too weak because it supposes an axis of identity between the terms—their adherence to the same dimension— which contests the existence of distinct entities and then, because it lacks a divergence, the possibility of a transfer. Thus, Merleau-Ponty's approach consists here not in rejecting the metaphorical relation but on the contrary in making it present, in its strangeness, in order to draw from it the consequences for the ontological plane: these are brought together in the concept of dimension. To speak of a "direction" of thought is not, in fact, to appeal to a strictly spatial term in order to represent figuratively a strictly mental event; it is first to reveal—and to support oneself with—a dimension common to spatiality and [226] meaning, "prior" to their distinction. Certainly one can speak of transfer in a sense, with regard to the constituted world, but it nonetheless remains the case that the metaphor is meaningful only to the extent that it is rooted in a milieu where the two orders are not yet differentiated. There is a dimension, deeper than the distinction between spatial and spiritual, of which both are crystallizations, both are modes of differentiation. The immediate ambiguity of the notion of "direction" is adequate to the status of what it designates originarily and consequently precedes the distinctions which are supposed to remove this ambiguity. Far from the metaphor bearing on objects already circumscribed, things proceed from a general "metaphoricity," from a universal *participation* that they concentrate or crystallize in order to be constituted into things. The dimension of sense, at once figurative and figured, is the truth of sense itself. "Claudel has a phrase saying that a certain blue of the sea is so blue that only blood would be more red" (VI 174/132). It is not an issue here of seeking what in the blue of the sea or the red of blood, conceived as distinct entities, justifies their being put into relation, what justifies the expression of each by the other. One must recognize, on the contrary, that the blue and the red, clearly defined colors, advent on the basis of a unique "behavior"—which is not *common* to them, since they are not yet distinguished in it—a dimension "prior" to their difference, the very one that Claudel tried to indicate. Blue and red are variants in the dimension of color; they are so also in the dimension of a muted "thick" depth that is *at the same time* that of blood red and sea blue. These two terms, in their sensible reality, harbor a depth, crystallize this dimension, render visible this invisible, or rather are the visibility of this invisible. The depth of the sea is a ray of the world from which the blue emerges and which it concentrates as a sensible quale, but which it does not exhaust. This element of depth radiates beyond the blue, comes to "touch at a distance" the red of blood, is given another figure in it. Thus the metaphorical expression should be conceived not as a relation between terms whose meaning is given elsewhere, but as the attestation of an ultimate reality, of a "pregnancy" of which the expressing and the expressed are, within the metaphor, provisional and never completely circumscribed poles. The world is the place of the metaphor or the metaphor as place. [227] The figuration of every thing by every thing reveals the ultimate ontological texture. Things are merged with this figuration, this encroachment; they become themselves only at the crossroads of the rays of the world. It follows from this that in Merleau-Ponty's eyes, poetry, as the work of metaphor, has an ontological meaning comparable to that of painting; it leads back to the originary experience in opposition to the objective cutting up of the world issuing from instituted language. The poetic work tries to attain, within language, that which exceeds and precedes its objectifying power and tries to grasp its point of insertion into the silent universe. Just as painting, by means of the picture, restores the "cohesion without concept," the "principle of equivalence" which governs the phenomenal world, poetry breaks, by means of the metaphor, the structuration of the world instituted by common language, and leads back to the wild world and thereby takes the place of the phenomenological reduction.[9]

9. This does not mean that Merleau-Ponty falls, with respect to metaphor, into what Ricoeur terms ontological vehemence, which, taking metaphor literally, leads to emphasizing unilaterally the ecstatic moment of language and thereby to reintroducing philosophy of nature into philosophy of spirit. Metaphor does not refer to a beyond

We have seen that the way to the discovery of brute Being is by way of a critique of the essence such as Husserl conceives it. It appears more clearly now that it was not so much a question of rejecting essence as of rediscovering its actual meaning, that is, of reconceiving it from [228] the eidetic variation from which it proceeds. Whereas eidetic variation remains in Husserl a means of freeing the essence as an autonomous entity on the basis of exemplary individuals, for Merleau-Ponty it is the very place where the genuine meaning of the world can reveal itself. In fact, it is not so much a matter of understanding variation as a mode of access to essence as it is seizing the world as that place from which being responds to the possibility of variation as such. As we have said, the fact that essence proceeds from a variation cannot be deducted from its definition; the result is that it is first of all necessary to reject the possibility of exhibiting an essence in the pure state. If such an essence truly could be provided, a variation would not be necessary, would not even be possible, since it would lack the sensible individuals in which the essence could announce itself. But it is still the case that the possibility of variation is incontestable: "I have," Merleau-Ponty says, "leeway enough to replace such and such moments of my experience with others, to observe that this does not sup-

---

of language where indistinction would finally rule. While it is true that all things crystallize a dimension, remain on the way to individuation, it is no less true that the dimension is nothing other than what gathers it together and that nothing precedes this process of individuation. Every being could be accentuated as an emblem of Being, and metaphor reveals well the co-belonging of every thing at the world; but, just as much, Being is always already emblematized. And it is because metaphor establishes *identity in the heart of difference* that in metaphor the chiasm of the thing and the world shows through. Every spoken word is still perception, enrooted in a mute world and its merely presumptive objectifying power: as such, there is a truth of the metaphor over against instituted language. But, conversely, lived experience is always spoken-lived experience, the world already meaningful. Therefore, there is a truth of instituted language over against metaphor, and the specificity of metaphor as *rupture* vis-à-vis ordinary denotation is preserved. Thus, it seems to us that Merleau-Ponty's ontology allows the notion of "metaphorical truth" that Ricoeur thematizes essentially at the linguistic level to be ballasted on the side of Being; it allows the founding of this "being-as" which, in metaphorical expression, should be understood as a modality of the copula itself rather than the addition of a term of comparison (cf. P. Ricoeur, *The Rule of Metaphor: Multi-disciplinary Studies of the Creation of Meaning in Language,* trans. R. Czerny with K. McLaughlin and J. Costello [Toronto: University of Toronto Press, 1977], in particular the chapter "Metaphor and Reference").

press it—therefore to determine the inessential" (VI 150/112). It is, therefore, just as though one could always intend the thing as an example even while lacking the paradigm of which it is the image. Thus, insofar as they are susceptible to being made the object of a variation, the things are on an axis of unity; but insofar as this variation is actual, as it bears on sensible individuals and is confirmed then to be infinite by principle, this axis of unity subsists only as the exemplars in which it attests itself. Of course, the exemplars are not definitively circumscribed as pure sensible individuals any more than the essence is defined; they remain held on the axis of variation, illuminated by its determination. Things are truly variants in the strict sense, concretions of a theme that, as soon as the variation is in principle unfulfilled, cannot be posited for itself. Sticking to the fact of variation is not to posit the paradigm and the exemplar in exteriority, which would be the same as misconstruing each of them: it is to define the theme in terms of its own variants. The facticity of the variant responds to the infinity of theme which it conceals; it does not deny the identity of the theme, but on the contrary confirms it as that which is irreducible to any variants and cannot *consequently* subsist outside of them, as this thickness of which they each hold a fragment. Each individual must be strictly understood as that which belongs, by its concreteness, to the infinity [229] of the theme; it is not other than the theme, but exactly what is needed to preserve its meaningful plenitude, its infinity. True essence, wild essence, indeed consists in this fabric of variation, in this theme which, as such, articulates the variants and just as much distinguishes them, because its very essentiality does not allow it to be able to make itself autonomous; its very essentiality demands therefore an infinite diversity. The essence "is neither above nor beneath the appearances, but at their joints; it is the tie that secretly connects an experience to its variants" (VI 155/116). The essence that founds the possibility of variation is nothing other than dimension, of which the determination sustains itself only by crystallizing itself in the individuality of variants. It is invariant *of* the variation, point of passage from one experience to another, which cannot be posited for itself and flows back into the thickness of each experience, but which nonetheless retains in itself each one of them as a variant of itself. The variation makes sense, finally, only insofar as it is based on a *complicity* of experiences rather than on their *knowledge*. From then on, before language, perception can be conceived as a variation on the theme of the world: each entity is in fact, in its ultimate depth, variant of the world-dimension, universal dimension.

4. The Flesh

We must finally return, in light of this analysis of dimension, to consider the status of one's own body whose description inaugurated our analysis. As the touching-touched experience shows, the touch is produced only insofar as it is immersed in a body; it advents only as this very corporeality. The touch is itself, that is, sentient, only to the degree that it is unaware of itself in or as the world that it reaches. The incarnation of touch corresponds to the fact that its object is not clearly laid out in front of it but is given only as the obscure presence of a tactile world, the presentation *as* tactile world of a dimension that is non-presentable by itself. The absence of this dimension to the world responds to the absence of touch to itself, that is, to its carnal being. Insofar as it unfolds the dimension common to a group of experiences, a dimension which remains veiled in them, [230] touch can proceed only from a subject which is its own absence, which is outside of itself. Thus the tangibility of the touching body corresponds to the invisibility of the dimension that it unfolds. There is touch only as the secret dimension of tangibles; one's own body does not escape this law. Insofar as a touch is produced in it, and in order that it is produced there, one's own body must itself remain tangible, must itself be a mode of crystallization of a dimension which offers itself elsewhere and otherwise. In this way, the body is of the world, it is held in the dimension that it unfolds, it makes itself tangible in order that through it a tactile world can advent. In brief, the senses can make things appear only if they are already a mode of crystallization of the dimension according to which they make things appear. What is true for touch is also true for the relation between touch and vision, and generally for the relation of the senses among themselves. If the senses were all of a piece, they would lose their sensibility; if only sight existed, for example, the world, all of what it can be, would be exhaustively expressed in sight, which would be the same as saying that this vision would in reality be thought. To recognize that an exhaustive and frontal presentation of the world is impossible is to understand that the plurality of the senses is consubstantial with them. Just as each sense exists only as the difference of the sensibles that are its domain, sensibility itself advents only as the difference between senses. Moreover, this difference is already at work, Merleau-Ponty notes, at the heart of each sensible organ: "Consider the *two*, the *pair*, this is not *two acts, two syntheses*, it is a fragmentation of being, it is a possibility for divergence [*écart*] (two eyes, two ears: the possibility of *discrimination*, for the use of the diacritical), it is the advent of difference" (VI 270/217). Nevertheless, one must not understand this divergence, which is a synonym of incarnation, as pure difference. Insofar as the senses make things appear, they also exhibit a common dimension; they are open to one another: the visible and tangible are "mounted" on a common axis, to which the possibility of expressing, for example, the tangible with the visible, of transposing one universe in terms of another, responds. Each sense truly sketches out a unity of the sensible *itself*, beyond the diverse regions; it is not a rival with the other senses but communicates with them by its very singularity: the visible is the "zero" of the tangible, and vice versa. To grasp the point where the tangible and visible are articulated is to progress toward the depth of the thing. In fact, [231] this is not a synthesis of tactile and visible properties but the dimension by which these properties communicate, the dimension which, insofar as it corresponds to a superior degree of universality, is closest to the being of the thing. Thus, each sense is a total part, freeing a universe that is complete in itself and yet open onto that of the other senses: "Each 'sense' is a 'world,' i.e. absolutely incommunicable for the other senses, and yet constructing a *something* which, through its structure, is from the first *open* upon the world of the other senses, and with them forms one sole Being" (VI 271/217). Just as the corporeity of touch is at first only the inverse of the secret dimension exhibited at the heart of tangibles, so it corresponds in its obscurity to the articulation of the tangible and the visible. Because the tangible and the visible communicate, the body cannot be pure exteriority; but because this communication remains dimensional, comes to pass only as a divergence [*écart*] between the "worlds," the body cannot be pure reflexivity. The self-relation that characterizes flesh must consequently be described as an axis of equivalence, as place of a possibility of conversion of experiences whose principle is never given, such that this relation is identically distance from self, belonging to the world. It is the same thing to say that the self is incarnate and that it is sentient, that is, that it possesses several senses: the self is the place of their communication, its incarnation corresponds to their distinction. Because dimension has reality only as incarnated, the perceiving body makes itself world also; its tangibility or its visibility are also themselves the modalities of this dimension that the perceiving unfolds. Sensibility is spread throughout the world as a universal possibility of transposition or reversion in which one's own body itself participates. Such is the true meaning of the flesh: vision must be understood as a scattered visibility, a universal axis hidden in each of its variants, variants *of which the body it-self is a part.* That is why one can speak of the "mirror phenomenon." Body and world are variants of a single dimension of visibility and, consequently, variants of each other, as are all the things of the world: "in which sense it is *the same* who is seer and visible: the same not in the sense of ideality nor of real identity. The same in the structural sense: same inner framework, same *Gestalthafte*" (VI 315/261). This point of view justifies the usage of [232] the concept of flesh beyond the distinction of perceiving body and world.

Must one, however, eliminate every distinction and purely and simply mix together the body and the things of the world on the pretext that both escape ideality as they do facticity? Are my body and the things made of the same flesh, or rather can one rigorously say that they are flesh in the same sense? Does not fidelity to experience impose recognition of a difference beyond this ontological complicity of the body and the world? In fact, "The flesh of the world is not *self-sensing* [*se sentir*] as is my flesh——It is sensible and not sentient [*sentante*]" (VI 304/250). How then to reconcile the fact of sensibility, as the advent of a sensible world, with the originary unity of sensibility, of visibility, that is, of the flesh? Let us note, first of all, that the "self" of one's own body must be thought following the example of the perceived object: "The self-perception is still a perception, i.e. it gives me a *Nicht Urpräsentierbar* (a non-visible, myself), but this it gives me through an *Urpräsentierbar* (my tactile or visual appearance) in transparency (i.e. as a latency)" (VI 303/249–50). One must then wonder what this presentation and what is presented in it consist of. The self itself must be understood as a dimension since it comes "in transparency" in or as a body. Thus, "my flesh itself is one of the sensibles in which an inscription of all the others is made . . . the dimensional sensible. My body is to the greatest extent what everything is: *a dimensional this.* It is the universal thing" (VI 313/259–60). And Merleau-Ponty elsewhere specifies that it is not simply one perceived among others but "measurant [*mesurant*] of all, *Nullpunkt* of all the dimensions of the world" (VI 302/249). The self of the body and its interiority are nothing other than the principle of universal equivalence, the dimension of all dimensions. Whereas all the other dimensions, in their particularity, are concretized in the form of a world *in front of* me, the universal dimensionality draws a self which is in some way at the limit of the world. The fact that the body is "on my side" does not mean that it is situated outside the world, but corresponds to the universality of the dimension that it crystallizes. "Consciousness" is only the ultimate dimensionality, principle of all equivalence, and consequently it is only as world. Therefore, how [233] does this "consciousness" incarnate itself? How does it present itself? That the body is a universal thing means not that it is far away from the world in a position overlooking it, but on the contrary that it is inscribed in its deepest part. To say that the body is "on my side" is in reality to mean that it is farthest from me, farthest from an "ego" [un moi]. To the very extent that this dimension is universal, it can present or crystallize itself only in an absolute depth, that is, as pure Fact. Thus, the body is *more than any other thing* on the side of the world, "thicker" than each of them because it is the dimensionalization of each of them. Insofar as it can be reached only at infinity, this dimension of all dimensions gives itself only as the infinite depth of the world. It is because the body is at the bottom of this depth that it can unfold this dimension. That is why sensibility is "at the same time the culmination of subjectivity and the culmination of materiality" (VI 302/248). One's own body is more "thing" than any thing because it is more dimension than any dimension, because it crystallizes the universal. On the other hand, the thing in front of me and the sensed are that much less factual than they are dimensional, which is precisely why they can appear in front of me; they rise from the depth of the world because they are content to intersect a ray of the world. With the perceived thing, I am at the point of arriving at dimension itself to the extent that it stays particular and consequently detaches itself from the night of the world. As for my body, it is eminently a thing to the extent that it hides their general equivalence; it is therefore very much on the side of the world and, one must say, on the other side. It is filled up with subjectivity and filled up with materiality, on one side of the world and on the other, in the middle of which it is born. Or rather, it is the same thing for it to be situated on my side, as *Nullpunkt of all the dimensions of the world*," and on the side of the world, inscribed in its depth. In it, the unfolding of the very world mingles with the advent of a sensibility "facing" the world. There is really a chiasm in that it is by being the world itself, not yet as thing but as its ontological texture, that it makes the world appear—which means not that it "becomes conscious" of it but that it unfolds the dimensions in which things can constitute themselves. In short, it is ultimately because the body is more "world" than things that it is more "self" than the world. It offers the things in front of it to be seen [234] because it comes from behind the spectacle, so that perception is truly phenomenalization of the world in both senses of the genitive. Thought all the way through, flesh appears as the dehiscent unity of the Fact and the Universal.

Because the world is made of this flesh, of these dimensions, of these axes of which my body is the pivot, it is an incarnate—that is, transcendent—world. One's own body is truly the middle [*milieu*] of the world: at once surrounded by it and the very element in and according to which the world is born. It is this originary scission, which is just as much originary identity, that one can characterize at the same time as depth of Being and the advent of sense, scission, and identity, in which world and self, subject and object, are born. The body is the point of origin of phenomenology; it makes the world appear and, in a sense, overlooks it because it proceeds from its most extreme depth.

12 Originary Spatio-Temporality

[235] Up to this point, we have tried to clarify the notion of flesh by way of the notion of dimension, which we have first reconceived from the viewpoint of the originary relation between thing and world. We must now take an additional step and attempt to characterize dimensionality itself, that is, we must attempt to reach the very heart of the flesh, the very heart of phenomenalization. The concepts of space and time come to the forefront: the originary unity of the perceived, the co-presence of the world to what manifests it, must be reconceived as spatiality and temporality, but at a level of originarity such that it is finally the very opposition of space and time that is put into question there. The flesh is ultimately this point where space and time cross each other, where the difference of the simultaneous and the successive is nevertheless an identity.

1. Philosophy and Space

Merleau-Ponty's reflection on space, which several paragraphs of "Eye and Mind" provide, is implied by his interrogation of vision. Vision alone gives me access to what is not me, to what is "fully and simply." To see is not to coincide blindly with the object, but it is to unfold an exteriority. Insofar as they are seen, the things do not rest in themselves at an absolute distance, but they nonetheless remain far away, thick. They recede into a distance which, measured from me, is nevertheless proximity. Spatiality is then synonymous with the "being-there" [*l'être-là*] of the thing, with its appearance as thing. The attempt to conceive spatiality is an attempt to draw a little nearer to the heart of the experience, a little nearer to the carnal chiasm.

Descartes appears here again as a privileged interlocutor. He has the merit of surpassing the empiricist approach [236] that consists of treating space as an abstraction carried out on the basis of the sensible contents; he makes extension appear as the very being of objects, if indeed an object must be given to us. The thing is *res extensa*, an object transparent to our understanding; it is without secret, entirely unfolded, contained within definite limits. Or rather, things are only modes of a unique extension to which the being-there of the world is reduced. Extension itself is an entirely positive being, measured according to three absolutely equivalent and reversible dimensions. It is a milieu of pure exteriority, deprived of envelopment, of encroachment; each thing occupies a determinate place there and articulates itself in relation to others only by means of its radical exteriority: "space is in itself; rather it is the in-itself par excellence; its definition is *to be* in-itself. Each point of space is, and is thought as being, right where it is—one here, another there; space is the self-evidence of the 'where'" (OE 47/134). Now, according to a movement of thought familiar to him, Merleau-Ponty acknowledges only a negative value in the Cartesian approach. It is true in what it denies but false in what it affirms: "It was necessary first to idealize space, to conceive of that being—perfect of its kind, clear, manageable, and homogeneous—which an unsituated thinking glides over without a vantage point of its own: a being which thought transcribes in its entirety onto three right-angled axes—so that subsequent thinkers could one day experience the limitations of that construction" (OE 48/134). If its merit is really to recognize a spatiality irreducible to sensible qualities, what is wrong with the Cartesian conception is to erect one property of beings into a structure of Being, that is, to project on the plane of the in-itself the experience of exteriority. Nevertheless, one must immediately specify that the Cartesian approach consists not so much in affirming an essence of extension as in exhibiting the conditions under which it can be clearly thought. According to Merleau-Ponty, Descartes never intended to eliminate the enigma of vision and the space to which it initiates us: there is an experience of vision that, although obscure, is nonetheless irreducible. Even if there is no vision without thought, thinking does not suffice for seeing. The experience of vision and space refers to the dimension of the composite of body and soul: next to vision as thought or formulated—which opens out necessarily onto a theory of the "completely naked" extension—"there is the vision that actually occurs, an honorary or established thought, collapsed into a body—its own body, of which we can have [237] no idea except in the exercise of it and which introduces, between space and thought, the autonomous order of the composite of soul and body" (OE 54/136). Nevertheless, it is still the case that Descartes pushes this dimension of "abyssal Being," this "depth of the visible," to the side the instant he recognizes them. Because the philosophical character of a spoken word is measured by its submission to the requirements of geometrical understanding, because clarity and distinctness remain the criterion of a discourse of truth, the only way to conceive vision is to make it a thought of seeing; the only way to conceive space is to reduce it to pure extension. In Descartes's eyes, to think vision is to think it as thought. Such is the situation from which Merleau-Ponty seeks to escape. The possibility of reaching that point depends on transforming Cartesian space, of *thinking* an originary spatiality.

Does a thought of space necessarily lead us to confer on it this transparency that characterizes it? Is a philosophy of vision constrained to detach itself from its actual practice, to turn it into an intellection? That would be to reduce thought to its intellectual version. Now, "We *are* the compound of soul and body, and so there must be a thought of it" (OE 58/138), but in an entirely different sense. Thus, all throughout "Eye and Mind," the question of spatiality is doubled by another interlocutory question: is a *philosophy* of space possible, and under what conditions? That is: must one choose between a silent vision and a thought whose clarity requires that one surpass actual vision toward intellection, lived depth toward geometric expanse? Insisting on this alternative would be the same as setting up the evidence of the understanding as the criterion for all meaningful discourse, the same as identifying meaning with intellectual possession. The intuition that precisely underlies Merleau-Ponty's final philosophy is that no alternative exists between clarity and obscurity, distance and proximity, the coincidence of experience and its appropriation in a spoken word. Merleau-Ponty's purpose, particularly in "Eye and Mind," is really to show that a *thought* of space is possible, to develop not a *philosophy* of vision that reabsorbs vision into the kind of thought defined by the understanding, but rather a philosophy of vision that lets vision itself think, which is therefore vision making itself philosophy. How can vision say itself in the very moment when it functions? How can it make itself a spoken word [238] without ending its silence? How can it think without making itself thought? The solution can be found in pictorial activity. In pictorial activity, the two interconnected terms of the alternative—a vision that would be without distance, incapable of signifying itself, and a thought that would overhang without being rooted in spatiality—are superseded. Through painting, vision makes itself philosophy. And the role of the philosopher, then, is not to submit the silent word of the painter to the reign of the understanding, but to extend the silence at the heart of his own word to the painter. The word of the philosopher does not cover over what he attempts to appropriate, because, as we know, in making itself verbal, the word does not stop being inhabited by silence—because the

Cartesian ideal of transparency is based on the forgetting of the corporeal and spatial rootedness of thought. In short, there is a genuine thought of space only as thought *in* space. It is this very thought in space that "animates the painter—not when he expresses opinions about the world but in that instant when his vision becomes gesture, when, in Cézanne's words, he 'thinks in painting'" (OE 60/138–39).

2. Depth

The center of Merleau-Ponty's reflection on space is entirely a meditation on depth. In this meditation one can read, in a privileged way, a primordial experience of spatiality. In fact, while the other dimensions are unfolded in front of the subject and seem to belong to the things themselves, depth is measured on the basis of the subject. It expresses his perspective on the world and corresponds to the very unfolding of exteriority. As Merleau-Ponty notes in *Phenomenology of Perception*, "it is not impressed upon the object itself, it quite clearly belongs to the perspective and not to things. Therefore it cannot either be extracted from, or even put into that perspective by consciousness; it announces a certain indissoluble link between things and myself by which I am placed in front of them, whereas width can, at first sight, pass for a relationship between things themselves, in which the perceiving subject is not implied" (PHP 296/256). Depth can be characterized only in a paradoxical manner; recognizing a depth of space is saying the object is given at a distance, without [239] this distance itself being given: "I see objects that hide each other and that consequently I do not see; each one stands behind the other. I see depth and yet it is not visible, since it is reckoned from our bodies to things, and we are confined to our bodies" (OE 45/133). From the Cartesian point of view, this paradox does not pose a problem; this mystery is a false mystery. There would never be a specific, irreducible experience of depth—this is only another width, that is, the distance actually unfolded between my body and things for a *conveniently situated* spectator. The objects never *are* graduated, one *behind* another; they can only be side by side, but only for a look that is laterally situated. The impossibility in which I find myself perceiving it as width is due to the punctuality of my situation within an objective space. I cannot be here and there at the same time such that what is width for me would be depth for another and vice versa. Because space is in-itself, and because I can occupy in it only a determinate place, what makes depth invisible for me renders it visible for others. Thus, instead of opening a positive and irreducible dimension of the world, the experience of depth expresses only a deficiency of perception—inherent in its situation in space —vis-à-vis a position of overhang, vis-à-vis a position of a look coming from the understanding in front of which space would be entirely unfolded, without any latency. In the Cartesian perspective, we are always situated just short of or beyond depth. From my point of view, depth is nothing; it corresponds only to my incapacity to dominate the distance that unfolds itself from my body to things, to a kind of incapacity inherent in my objective situation. But insofar as it is a dimension of space, it is always already exceeded as depth, already another width for a look that would adopt the true viewpoint on the object. In short, either depth is nothing, or it is already unfolded right on the things. Simply put, I have the capacity to transcend my corporeal situation by picking out the signs of this distance traced between myself and the object, to which depth is reduced. Thus can I deduce from the apparent size of the object, or from the degree of convergence of the ocular globes, the real distance separating this object from my body. For Descartes, space is a reality in itself, entirely unfolded, each part exterior to itself. Thus defined, it corresponds to a viewpoint of absolute overhang, [240] that of a divine look traversing it entirely without resistance. Space is not first of all this unfolding of exteriority whose openness cannot itself be situated within exteriority; it is pure extension, co-presence of all to all by exteriority, and therefore it is finally dominated, surmounted exteriority, false exteriority. But then, the *experience* of space can refer only to the objective, punctual situation of a consciousness, consequently incapable of dominating it according to all its dimensions. The spatiality of consciousness means only its assignment to an objective body, to a fragment of extension, whose finitude must be overcome by the decoding of signs. It is thus in a single movement that the world is reconceived as this pure extension to which only an inspection of the mind can have access and that belonging to the world is understood in a strictly objective sense. The realistic inscription of the body in space and the idealistic determination of the world as pure extension, the affirmation of the finitude of incarnated life and the affirmation of the ubiquity of intellectual knowledge, are truly the inverse of one another. In other words, because depth, as originary experience of space, is missed by excess, always already unfolded in the form of an objective distance, it is missed by a lack—that is, it is conceived as inaccessible to an incarnated consciousness. It is clear that the intellectualist conception of space cannot take into account the specific experience of depth; it is content to *explain* it, by giving itself already this objective space to which depth was supposed to initiate us. In fact, because the subject of experience occupies a determinate place within extension, the experience of depth can consist only of decoding facts (convergence of eyes, apparent size of the image) by placing them back into the context of objective relations which explain them, that is, by suddenly adopting the viewpoint of an absolute spectator. If I can re-ascend from the apparent size to its meaning, it is on the condition of situating myself in a world of "inalterable" objects and of conceiving my body as this fragment of extension that, like a mirror, receives an image of the object situated outside of the body, at a certain distance. In the same way, if I can understand convergence as a sign of distance, it is on the condition of representing the looks to myself as lines and, consequently, of inserting eyes, the body, and the exterior world in a single objective space. In short, "the 'signs' which, *ex hypothesi*, ought to acquaint us with the experience [241] of space can, therefore, convey the idea of space only if they are already involved in it, and if it is already known" (PHP 297/257).

Space can be given only to one who is there. What defines space is that it really includes everything, encompasses what encompasses it; it really disappoints every attempt to dominate it totally. Nevertheless, in no case does the belonging of the experience to space have an objective, specifically local meaning. To the extent that space cannot be understood as pure objective extension, the experience that initiates us to it can never be conceived as strictly included in it. Instead of corresponding to an objective placement, the belonging to space is synonymous with its very unfolding. Space surpasses me, the things "flee into a remoteness out of reach of all thought" (OE 50/135), but this surpassing is not itself carried away in the form of a pure extension, of an "empty envelope"—so that it is equally proximity, and, as proximity, space belongs to me. Because perception is inscribed in space, it can unfold it, since, space not being based in itself, this inscription cannot mean a determinate localization: the belonging of perception to space is just as much the belonging of space to perception. The experience of depth is the ordeal of this surpassing, of this flight of things, insofar as this flight could never be dominated in the heart of an objective extension; that is, it could never be reduced to a measurable distance between my body and the things. Depth, the remoteness that cannot be carried forward in the form of an outline within things, is the first dimension. Whereas height and width seem to belong to the things themselves and to owe nothing to the subject, depth corresponds to the originary unfolding of spatiality. The priority of depth does not therefore mean a privilege that would be granted to it, within objective space, vis-à-vis height and width; in this space, all of the dimensions are equivalent. Depth is of another order than actual distance; it is situated just short of metrical space and reveals thereby a new sense of dimension. What does it mean, in fact, to say that a thing is in space, to say that it is *there*? Must this be understood to mean that it occupies a place in a point of an unfolded and homogeneous extension, that the exteriority of this thing in relation to my body is capable of being measured, both belonging to the same milieu where all places [242] are comparable? This would be to deny space, the originary remoteness of the thing, while ignoring the irreducible rootedness of my body in it. As soon as the objects that space separates are defined by their placement, as soon as they are grasped against a backdrop of homogeneity, their exteriority—which can refer only to a ubiquitous point of view for which all places are equivalent—thereby finds itself denied as exteriority. Thus, precisely because the thing is "over there," "in space," it cannot be *in* space, as in a container; that is, it cannot occupy a determinate place within a *medium* that is homogeneous and without thickness. That the thing is over there means that its "there" cannot be shown for itself, distinguished from its appearance as such a thing. Its transcendence is not itself carried away in the form of a milieu of transcendence within which all things would be ordered. Thus, space would be based in itself and my body within it, so that no experience of remoteness would be possible. On the contrary, there is transcendence only as transcendence *of* this thing; its remoteness appears only as veiled in it, which is why there can be an experience of it. Transcendence makes sense only if it is nothing other than the appearing thing itself: it is a "pure transcendence, without an ontic mask" (VI 282/229). In other words, that the thing is over there signifies that it is not at a distance measured *between* it and me, that its "over there" is not the reverse of a "here," that our situations are not interchangeable. My body is not in space: it is an absolute "here"; correlatively, the distance of the thing refers to a place that is not comparable to my "here": the "over there" is also absolute. In other words, it is not because the thing is at a distance that it is over there, but because it is over there that it is at a distance. This distance is not unfolded from it to me but is somehow interior to it, and in this way the thing is synonymous with its own distance. The remoteness in which it gives itself cannot be distinguished from its manner of being a thing. One must understand here the word *distance* according to the ambiguity of its psychological sense and its spatial sense. The thing is in space, at a certain distance, only because it is "distant," opposing an insurmountable resistance, an insurmountable refusal, to my approach. The experience of space is the experience of an ontological thickness rather than a quantity capable of being traversed. Conceived in a geometrical manner, distance [243] can in principle be annulled, remoteness can be converted into coincidence. Genuine distance remains therefore infra-geometrical, and this divergence is not a relation between two terms posited beforehand, because the spatial object and the subject which experiences it advent together. Thus, the thing is in space only to the degree that this space remains or makes itself invisible in it. The thing makes itself remote only on the condition that this remoteness not be the inverse of a proximity, only on the condition that it not be its own remoteness. There is space, that is, things always farther away beyond the spectacle, precisely only if this distance cannot itself be crossed. Invisible in this sense, depth cannot be understood as a dimension in the Cartesian sense; it frees up a more originary sense of spatiality: "The openness upon the world implies that the world be and remain a horizon, not because my vision would push the world back beyond itself, but because somehow he who sees is of it and is in it" (VI 136/100). The experience of depth reveals space as a reality that does not "extend itself," which remains hidden in the thing itself, or rather, coincides with the thing itself insofar as it is dissimulated, invisible, existing [étante]. The thing recoils before the look, slips under the frontal grasp, precisely in order to show itself: it gives itself to seeing, and this gift makes sense only insofar as it is nourished by an insurmountable divergence.

Space is the order of coexistence; in it, things are given "together." How can one characterize this "being-together?" Must one say that things join themselves together by virtue of the extension in which they are situated and within which their distance is measured? That is not the originary experience of coexistence. In fact, what is given first of things is precisely their very coexistence: "whereas, by virtue of depth, they coexist in degrees of proximity, they slip into one another and integrate themselves" (VI 272/219). In short, they *are* together. The thing is not situated here rather than elsewhere: it is elsewhere while remaining itself, while being situated here, or rather while being its "here." In fact, unfolded on its own, distinct from the thing, spatiality would be closed and would become a thing in its turn: it could not then "contain" all that coexists there. This spatiality, belonging to a single space where all things can coexist, gives itself [244] therefore only as presence of the thing itself. By remaining itself, the thing can join itself to all other things. It gathers space into itself, and space diffuses itself around the thing, because its plenitude and its infinity demand that it not distinguish itself from what it nevertheless contains. The thing concentrates in its "there" all locality, or rather its "there" appears as the crystallization of a pre-spatial locality. Precisely because it is of infinite dimension, space cannot be fully unfolded; it cannot accomplish itself in pure extension. In order to not close itself off, space must remain just short of itself, not unfolded, a measureless divergence. Because by definition space is always "beyond," it is itself only in remaining in retreat from itself as pure extension. Space turns itself into things in order to remain what it is, that is, to contain them all. That is why things "oppose to my inspection obstacles, a resistance which is precisely their reality, their openness, their *totum simul*" (VI 273/219). But as much as the thing would be alone and visible, this does not mean that it would be fully determinate and localizable. It is, in its turn, held back in this depth that elsewhere it preserves; it is not itself properly visible but emerges from a ground that it cannot entirely concentrate. In order to be spatial, it must certainly remain gathered in itself; but in order to be itself, it must not become localizable. In fact, perfectly defined, pure quale, the thing would once again demand a completed space in which its link with all the others can weave itself: "there would not be a world or Being, there would only be a mobile zone of distinctness which could not be brought here without quitting all the rest—'synthesis' of these 'views'" (VI 272/219). Thus, by depth, the thing grounds itself in its own surroundings; it still leaves room for others and is haunted by them, as its own atmosphere, even while the look is fixed on it. As Merleau-Ponty notes again, "Depth is the means the things have to remain distinct, to remain things, while not being what I look at at present" (VI 272/219). In this space, all things appear exhaled by "the thickness of a medium devoid of any thing" (PHP 308/266) within which the presence of all the others remains outlined. Things *are* around me: this determination makes their being. They are accessible together, not [245] because each one of them would be situated at a certain distance from me, but because all of them polarize a "being-around," a diffuse and nonetheless impenetrable proximity, which is the fabric from which they are made and which they cannot manage to tear entirely. Held back in this depth, each thing is therefore somehow around itself, between itself and the others, at the jointure. On the one hand, it gathers together space, which merges with the thing's own opacity, in order to articulate itself with all the others, so that space seems to be born from the things themselves; it cannot in any case be distinguished from them nor be posited itself as a thing. But, on the other hand, all things appear held back in the invisible ground that it unfolds, so that they are never completely differentiated, never manage to coincide with themselves, and finally seem to be exhaled by this ground. If space polarizes itself in the opacity of each thing, this happens in order that space continue to be the depth upon whose ground all things outline themselves. The thickness of the thing is equally the plenitude of the world from which it detaches itself, so that its own consistency is at the same time transparency. The thing borrows from space, in order to make itself thing, only to liberate the illumination of space and to dissolve itself in its depth.

The enigma of depth, Merleau-Ponty notes, is that there is a *between* of things. The things must distinguish themselves and be graduated; they must diverge from one other, or the notion of space would make no sense. And yet this divergence is not an interval, not a place homogeneous with the place that things occupy elsewhere. Depth is this divergence that hollows out distance only because it is not other than the things that it nevertheless makes remote. In fact, to the extent that it remains unassignable, non-objectifiable in the form of measurable distance, the divergence remains uncrossable. The invisibility of the divergence, difference always being born and always fulfilled—that is, the reflux of space in the thickness of each thing—ensures precisely its remoteness. In short, depth is "their exteriority, known through their envelopment, and their mutual dependence in their autonomy" (OE 65/140). Thus, the things do not *occupy* a space [*un lieu*]—we must say a place [*une place*]—they are beyond every identical space. They *are* the space, their own space; they spatialize themselves rather than being situated in space. While maintaining the ambiguity of the formula, we must say that depth is what "makes room" [*donne lieu*] for things, that by which they "take place" [*ont lieu*]. For things, taking (a) place [*avoir (une) lieu*] cannot [246] mean occupying room [*une place*] but only adventing. Primordial space [*lieu*] is indistinctly place [*place*] and event: beyond the qualitative punctuality of the event, but just short of the quantitative monotony of the extension, or rather beyond this opposition. The space [*le lieu*] cannot therefore be qualified as extension, by opposition to the order of quality. It resides just as much in color, texture, or form. What the experience of painters reveals is pre-spatial space which is itself and which distributes places [*places*] only because it is itself placeless [*sans place*]—pre-spatial space whose extension is without quality, or rather stops short of the opposition of quantity and quality. Color and space cannot be treated separately. The work of painting, modern painting in any case, consists on the contrary in breaking this opposition; it consists in finding again space in color and color in the modes of spatiality. It consists in grasping in the picture the very space of things before space is unfolded by the objectifying look at the moment when it exhales color or texture. Painting reveals that "we must seek space and its content *together*" (OE 66/140–41). From then on, insofar as they have a space [*un lieu*], things do not have definite limits; they are spatialized on the level of their quality. In depth, each thing lets itself be haunted by the ground that it concentrates in such a way that no circumscribed place [*place*] can be attributed to it; its contours are blurred by the indetermination of the depth from which it draws. As painting again has shown, contours "are always on the near or the far side of the point we look at. They are always between or behind whatever we fix our eyes upon; they are indicated, implicated, and even very imperiously demanded by things, but they themselves are not things" (OE 73/143).

Depth is truly the first dimension. This does not result from the fact that there are definite forms and planes only if one stipulates at what distance they are located in relation to me, but rather because depth frees a sense entirely other than dimension, an originary *dimensionality* which is irreducible to the dimensions of metric space. Space does not possess therefore "precisely three dimensions (as an animal has either four or two legs)"; the dimensions are "taken by different systems of measurement from a single dimensionality, a polymorphous Being, which justifies all of them without being fully expressed by any" (OE 48/134). Depth [247] is therefore in no case another width for a correctly situated spectator. Rather, because the object is there in front of me, because it opposes an absolute resistance to my look and is in this way deep, I can extract from it a metrical height and width. Instead of my depth being reduced to a width for another, depth for me is only the presentiment of the depth of the object. The aspects, the parts of the thing in front of me, *are* not side by side in width, but merge with the blossoming of the thing; they are spatialized only by remaining held back in each other. They do not manage to extend themselves completely but are just short of all measurable width. The width of the thing remains an abstraction extracted from its thickness, from this envelopment that we can never manage to convert into surface. Thus, the hypothesis of the deduction of depth on the basis of the apparent size of the object is senseless. An object that makes itself remote is neither smaller nor identical; it is the same object seen from farther away, according to another depth. In short, the dimensions of objective space "explain" a depth that is not itself unfurled, that is measureless or rather is not of the order of measurement. Objective spatiality proceeds from an originary spatialization, a spatialization that is pre-spatial, deeper than the distinction of dimensions: "Depth thus understood is, rather, the experience of the reversibility of dimensions, of a global 'locality' in which everything is in the same place at the same time, a locality from which height, width, and depth are abstracted, a voluminosity we express in a word when we say that a thing is *there*" (OE 65/140).

3. Space Is Time

Such is the originary sense of spatiality. Originary spatiality is collected as the "there" of the thing; it is itself only by continuing to be just short of itself as pure extension; it extends itself only in gathering itself up. Originary spatiality is just short of quality; it is what quality needs in order to appear there in front; it is this stability that allows quality to remain under my look. And yet, originary spatiality is not other than quality, "lower" than quality but "higher" than quantity. Rather, quality and quantity are born as interconnected abstractions from originary spatiality. [248] With depth thus conceived, we meet up with the genuine meaning of the invisible; in fact, instead of being of a purely spatial order, depth is nothing other than the "deflagration of Being" (OE 65/140). Thus, depth comes to qualify dimensionality itself, and we must note here that the choice of the term *dimension* indicates that all original dimensionality proceeds from this originary dimension.[1] Dimensionality is this co-presence of all things in which they remain, that is, appear—the co-presence that, in order to gather all things together, is not other than what it joins together. Thus phenomenalization must ultimately be understood as spatialization; all phenomena should be considered "the concretion of a universal visibility, of one sole Space that separates and reunites, that sustains every cohesion" (OE 84/147). One must define the articulation of each phenomenon and the world as spatialization; the world maintains itself in itself only by passing into the phenomenon, and the phenomenon ascends to itself only by making itself co-present to the world and consequently to all the others. Spatiality is Presence without content, that is, the presence

1. Of course, Merleau-Ponty was not ignorant of Heidegger's use of this notion (*Unter-schied*). See, for example, *Poetry, Language, Thought*, trans. A. Hofstadter (New York: Harper and Row, 1971), 131, 203.

of Being. Depth is thus itself—that is, "spatial"—only by remaining ontological depth, only by remaining enclosed in what it unifies, only therefore by being as well the depth of sense. It follows from this that coexistence must be understood in a new sense; it cannot be confused with strict contemporaneity, which supposes precisely a space entirely unfolded. As soon as the being-together of phenomena is determined as depth, their articulation cannot go up as far as the order of the contemporaneous; their articulation cannot coincide with the axis of the "now." The articulation slips beyond itself, it encompasses time itself. Because depth unfolds a space for the coexistents only by concealing the space in the "there" of phenomena, it does not exhaust itself in the contemporaneity that it institutes; it opens the "there" toward a past and a future. To say that it is pre-spatial is to recognize that it does not coincide with extension, that it gives itself as not being entirely unfolded, so that what depth conceals in its depth is as well always and forever. The elsewhere which it unfolds transcends the spatial plane, straddles past and future. It [249] is the depth of this space only by being depth for all coexistence, for all that can come to pass in it, that is, also for the future; it opens contemporaneity toward a trans-spatial coexistence, the allusion or participation of all in all. As we said, depth is itself only by continuing to be just short of itself as pure extension. Instead of understanding that we return thereby to singular contents, we must conclude from this that depth is just as much beyond itself as pure space. In other words, if the remoteness and depth of the thing merge with its invisibility, with the impossibility of traversing its ontological thickness, its distance is synonymous with its belonging to the past or to the future. The remoteness of the object means that I do not possess it entirely and that I am oriented toward it as what escapes me, so that its presence in depth opens the dimension of a future. As Merleau-Ponty already notes in *Phenomenology of Perception*, "when I say that I see an object at a distance, I mean that I already hold it, or that I still hold it, it is in the future or the past as well as being in space" (PHP 306/265). It is only from an objective viewpoint that space can be defined by reversibility; for an absolute spectator, all places [*toutes places*] are equivalent, the here and the there are interchangeable. But, in reality, the originary experience of space must be characterized by irreversibility. Depth designates the pole of an orientation that is in some way existential just as much as it is spatial; it designates an orientation that goes from a here toward an over there without any possible inversion, and it unfolds itself therefore at once in space and in time.

The object at a distance is not properly absent, *in* the past or the future—
that would lead to denying the temporal flow by supposing it already unfolded. But it is nevertheless not strictly contemporaneous; if it were, that
would be the same as denying the originarily situated character of all
spatial experience by positing an absolute viewpoint to which all positions would be given together. The object at a distance escapes the order of
pure succession, as it does the order of pure contemporaneity; its remoteness has a deeper sense than this distinction. Remoteness, which makes
sense only on the basis of an orientation, characterizes what I have not yet
reached, that is, what is indistinctly over there and later.[2] In short, space
[250] excludes time only if one is considering an objectified space; but understood as primordial spatiality, or even as depth, space surpasses itself
toward its other, articulates itself to temporality, or rather corresponds to
a deeper dimension than the opposition of space and time. Such is the conclusion to which Merleau-Ponty is led: all phenomena are the concretions
of this unique Space which underlies all cohesion "and even that of the
past and the future, since there would be no such cohesion if they were not
essentially parts of the same space" (OE 85/147; cf. PHP 475/415).

4. The Problem of Time

The reflection on time is, incontestably, a primordial axis of Merleau-
Ponty's philosophy. It represents also—and Merleau-Ponty is not alone,
from this point of view—a point of Husserl's philosophy on which he concentrates his attention most particularly. In fact, he never stops making the
distinction between the idealist version of constitution and that "ultimate

---

2. This idea of a depth which is indistinctly spatial and temporal is developed at
length by Erwin Straus—to whom Merleau-Ponty makes a brief and unique allusion
(PHP 306n1/265n1)—in *Vom Sinn der Sinne* (trans. J. Needleman as *The Primary
World of Senses: A Vindication of Sensory Experience* [London: Free Press of Glencoe,
1963]), particularly in the last chapter, where distance is defined as "the spatio-temporal form of sensibility." Straus could develop this essential perspective only because
he reconceived the originary unity of sensibility and "being moved" [*se mouvoir*]: it
is around the motor direction that spatial and temporal remoteness are joined together. In our view, Merleau-Ponty never treated this central question of motility in
a satisfying manner, though it is the object of a circuitous chapter in *Phenomenology
of Perception* and is mentioned in several working notes. We are considering taking
up this question elsewhere, as it seems to us essential for the understanding of flesh.

consciousness" which constitutes the temporality of lived experience. Husserl, of course, only alluded to this ultimate consciousness in *Ideas I*, even though he had already explained it at length in the [*Lectures*] *On the Phenomenology of the Consciousness of Internal Time*. In that difficult work, the analysis of temporality allows us to gain access to a more profound sense of intentionality, a sense that calls into question the predominant schema during the "middle" period: "Husserl, for example, for a long time defined consciousness or the imposition of a sense in terms of the *Aufassung-Inhalt* framework, and as a *beseelende Auffassung*. He takes a decisive step forward in recognizing, from the time of his *Lectures on Time*, that this operation presupposes another deeper one whereby the content is itself made ready for this apprehension" (PHP 178n1/152n1; cf. VI 74n/49n, S 209/165). This [251] allows Merleau-Ponty to evoke this important note from the time-consciousness lectures: "not every constitution has the schema: apprehension–content–apprehension."[3] We do not propose to evaluate to what extent the intentionality brought to light in these lectures constitutes a deepening and an anticipated reworking of the schema of *Ideas I*, or if on the contrary the two planes coexist without Husserl's being able to conceive their unity.[4] What is essential is that Merleau-Ponty deliberately situates his reading of Husserl on this terrain. The theory of the living Present truly makes the description of intentionality appear in terms of acts, that is, in terms of matter and form, stemming from Husserl's "misunderstanding" of himself evoked by Merleau-Ponty in the preface to *Phenomenology of Perception*. In his eyes, the operant intentionality that animates time is the truth of "thetic" intentionality. Thus, the entire structure of *Phenomenology of Perception* rests on a chapter devoted to temporality, in which the identity of ultimate subjectivity and time is demonstrated: "we must understand time as the subject and the subject as time" (PHP 483/422). In spite of this chapter's ambiguity, the analysis essentially consists in appropriating the theory of the living Present, especially as it is explained in Husserl's unpublished writings.[5] Now, the texts after *Phe-*

3. E. Husserl, *On the Phenomenology of the Consciousness of Internal Time*, trans. J. Brough (The Hague: Martinus Nijhoff, 1992), 7n7 (section 1).
4. On this point, we refer to the work of G. Granel, *Le sens du temps et de la perception chez E. Husserl* (Paris: Gallimard, 1968). See also E. Levinas, "Intentionnalité et sensation," *Revue internationale de philosophie* 19, nos. 1–2 (1965): 34–54.
5. See on this point Paul Ricoeur's article "Par-delà Husserl et Heidegger," *Les cahiers de philosophie*, no. 7 (1989): 17–23.

nomenology of Perception are marked by a waning interest in the theory of time and its role.[6] Of course, Merleau-Ponty does not turn his back on this question, but his relative silence indicates his awareness of the need to appropriate and deepen this question. It is essentially in the working notes of The Visible and the Invisible that we see the nature and scope of this reworking. In fact, in these notes Husserl is criticized in terms that are no longer those of Phenomenology of Perception. Finally, it is through Husserl that the elaboration to which the theory of time in [252] Phenomenology of Perception had given way is called into question. As always, it is by way of Husserl that Merleau-Ponty grasps his own thought. Obliquely, it is through this confrontation that Merleau-Ponty manages to mark his distance vis-à-vis Husserl's philosophy—a distance that nonetheless lays claim to Husserl's own "unthought." Thus, at the level of Phenomenology of Perception, Merleau-Ponty has not yet extricated himself from the difficulties that confront Husserl himself. The living Present appears at this time as the very place of his unthought, as the originary level that must be valorized against the analyses of Ideas I or Cartesian Meditations. In contrast, in The Visible and the Invisible the issue is to demonstrate the unthought of time itself, to rediscover the truth of the Husserlian approach and, from there, that of Phenomenology of Perception, as opposed to a conception of time that remains abstract and idealizing. If the about-face that characterizes the final work allows a new approach to temporality, it seems equally that the deepening of the reflection on time, the reworking of what had been considered ultimate beforehand, constitutes an essential passageway toward ontology. Far from being a question of reconceiving being-in-the-world as time, one must seize flesh as the very truth of time, and this is the reason why the reflection on time partly marks time.

The problem is posed in this way:

> The upsurge of time would be incomprehensible as the creation of a supplement of time that would push the whole preceding series back into the past. That passivity is not conceivable.
>
> On the other hand, every analysis of time that views it from above is insufficient.
>
> Time must constitute itself, be always seen from the point of view of someone who is of it. (VI 237/184)

6. See on this point J. F. Bannan, "The 'Later' Thought of Merleau-Ponty," Dialogue 5 (1966): 383–403.

Time poses therefore the very problem of the phenomenon. It gives itself as an originary transcendence that insofar as it *gives* itself, cannot proceed from a transcendent, but of which the givenness, insofar as it is givenness of a *transcendence,* cannot on the other hand refer to an imposition of sense. If, as soon as it is *lived* as such, time excludes a pure passivity of consciousness, the "activity" from which it proceeds could never in any case be distinguished from its movement of transcendence: consciousness "possesses" time only as that which de-possesses it. Consciousness is not in time—this passivity would be "incomprehensible"—and time is nevertheless not [253] in consciousness. This activity would cancel its constitutive ekstasis. Time is that being that presents itself only in the form of what exceeds all presencing; it solicits consciousness as an irreducible alterity.

The Husserlian solution is based on the notion of *retention,* demonstrated by the commonplace example of the melody. The present moments of sound flow continually, but the present moment A is retained in the following present moment B, which will itself be in the present moment C which follows, thus modifying and causing the set of the interlocking retentions to recede. The entire force of the analysis is based on the determination of retention as *originary* intentionality:

> One speaks of the dying-away, the fading, and so on, of the contents of sensation when perception proper passes over into retention. Now it is already clear, following our explanations up to this point, that the retentional "contents" are not at all contents in the original sense. When a tone dies away, it itself is sensed at first with particular fullness (intensity); and then there follows a rapid weakening in intensity. The tone is still there, still sensed, but in mere reverberation. This genuine tone-sensation must be distinguished from the tonal moment in retention. The retentional tone is not a present tone but precisely a tone "primarily remembered" in the now: it is not really on hand in the retentional consciousness. But neither can the tonal moment that belongs to this consciousness be a different tone that is really on hand; it cannot even be a very weak tone equivalent in quality (such as an echo). A present tone can indeed "remind" one of a past tone, exemplify it, pictorialize it; but that already presupposes another representation of the past. The intuition of the past cannot itself be a pictorialization. It is an original consciousness.[7]

7. Husserl, *On the Phenomenology of the Consciousness of Internal Time,* 33 (§12).

Thus, the sound that has flowed is a primary memory; it is not another sound but *another presence of sound,* namely, its presence as absence. The consciousness of the past is not a representation, because the sound is not present such as it is in the present, and yet the past presents itself to this consciousness as past. Consciousness of the past is thus rather consciousness *in* the past; it is this modality of consciousness by which it is its own past and in which nevertheless it does not lose itself but finds itself again. The possibility for each sound to appear in continuity with [254] others, that is, to give itself as manifestation of a single melody, is based on retention. Even though melody is nothing more than the set of sounds in their flowing, each sound appears as sound *of* the melody, manifests the melody that it nevertheless constitutes. As Granel says, "The melody walks on the head of sounds and maintains them underneath the level of attention, or even better: *it* makes them spring up *under its steps,* as that, however, on which it puts its feet."[8] With retention, the duality of matter and form, across which intentionality at the level of the constitution of the thing had clarified itself, is then surpassed. We are dealing with a presence without form, without apprehension, with a presence that remains the absence of what it presents, with a presentation that is a de-presentation.

5. The Dimensional Present

Merleau-Ponty's approach—such as we can reconstitute it from the working notes, in any case—consists in demonstrating a divergence between the implications of the notion of retention put forward by Husserl and the categories, on the other hand, by means of which it is clarified. It is a question of drawing out from this notion all that it can give, beyond Husserl's thematization, which retreats from what it reveals. It is the position of the present that is in question here: "Husserl's error is to have described the interlocking on the basis of the *Präsensfeld* considered as without thickness, as immanent consciousness" (VI 227/173). At the same time as the present, this "proto-intentional" consciousness that is in a sense ultimate, from which Husserl derived the axis of interlocking protentions and retentions, is called into question. Merleau-Ponty's orientation consists then in finding fault with the philosophy of consciousness on the basis of the terrain that it opens. Time makes sense only if it does not proceed from a subjectivity, even a proto-impressional one. Thus, retention repre-

8. Granel, *Le sens du temps,* 107.

sents not so much an originary intentionality as the calling into question of intentional analysis. Merleau-Ponty makes this more precise in another note: "Husserl's diagram is dependent on the convention that one can represent the series of nows by [255] points on a line" (VI 248/195). It is not the spatialization of time that is in question here, because "space does not comprise *points, lines* any more than time does" (VI 248/195). The difficulty instead consists in the fact that retention cannot in reality be supported by the present, conceived as punctuality. In fact, if the present is first of all accentuated, if it is present "before" becoming past, then this presentation of the past of which retention consists can mean only the *positing* of this present in the form of a past, which would then be disjointed from its presentation. Because the present is first of all cut off from its own past, this past is in its turn cut off from its own presence as past. The past, then, would no longer be a mode of presence, presence as absence, but presentation of what *was* present—that is, presence of an absent. From the instant when the punctuality of the present is maintained, the specific mode of the presence of the past in the retention is abolished. As soon as the present is immediately conceived as positivity, positivity transfers itself inevitably to the past that it becomes. And the irreducible presence of the past surpasses itself toward the presence of another present, of another positivity, namely, the present that it was. While retention designates a mode of pure presence and not a representation of the past, by describing it on the basis of the present, one is led to fold this original presence back onto the past which presents *itself there*. Husserlian retention indeed requires the renunciation of proto-impressional consciousness. In fact, the past can present itself as absence only to the degree that it had not *first of all* been present. This absence that characterizes it on the level of retention must first of all be the fact of the present that it was. In other words, all the difficulty lies in the fact that starting from a punctual present, Husserl reintroduces the scission between matter and form within retention, a scission that the notion of retention was supposed to contest. The limit of the intentional analytic is that it "tacitly assumes a place of absolute contemplation *from which* the intentional explication is made, and which could embrace past, present, and even openness toward the future——It is the order of the 'consciousness' of signification, and in this order there is no past-present 'simultaneity,' there is the evidence of their divergence" (VI 297/243). Even while he characterizes retention as another irreducible form of presence, Husserl continues to explicate it on the ground of this presupposition regarding presence, [256] which consists in subordinating it to a present. While retention allows us to contest the determination of phenomena as beings, Husserl reconstructs retention on the basis of a punctual present, on the basis of a present that *is* first of all, as little as it may be, "before" passing, so that its being-past is degraded into the positing of the past as being. Because the present is first of all *too* present, by passing it becomes *too little* present; it contaminates its own past with its initial positivity, which then comes back as pure negativity. Understood as a present being, presence calls for a determination of its own absence as being. There is therefore a dissymmetry in the analysis; Husserl emphasizes that the past presents itself as absent, just as it was first of all present, instead of recognizing that it absents itself *only in presenting itself*. While it is true that the past is not present, that its presence is that of an absence, it is still the case that its absence supports itself only from its self-presenting and consequently its escaping the opposition of present and past as punctual contents. As absent, it presents itself; but in presenting itself, it absents itself.

It follows from this that the moment of *passage* is ineluctably missed. Instead of being grasped the moment when it is still retained in the presence of the present, the absence of the past is finally understood as the presence *of the melody itself*. Because the present is determined as positivity, its passage is explicated in terms of a negation. The past is characterized as that which is *not* present rather than that which is *no longer* present. It becomes this positive being on which temporal negation is based. Grasped as positive, the presence of the sound degrades into a pure absence, which is then destined to be exceeded toward the presence of *what* passes. The deficit of presence that characterizes the past as soon as it, following the present, is posited as a being must be compensated for by the pure presence of the melody. Coming to be on the basis of a punctual present, the passage recedes toward the pure absence of the past, which can then sustain itself only with the positivity, in some way trans-temporal, of the melody itself. In short, because it is first of all grasped *just short* of itself, that is, as present, the passage is at the same time fixed *on the far side* of itself, in the form of what presents itself in these flowing present moments.

The problem of time, then, can be resolved only on the condition of renouncing the punctuality of the present: "The contradiction is lifted only if the new present is itself a [257] transcendent: one knows that it is not there, that it was just there, one never coincides with it" (VI 238/184).

Time makes sense as the passage of a present to the past only if the present is already past, only if this passage forms its being. There is a present only as not "presently" present, only as transcendent. This is not to say that it is something other than present or that it is an absent, which would boil down to conferring a positivity on it, but that it is its own de-presentation, that it carries itself outside of itself, beyond itself, or rather that it is this very slippage. Absence can present itself only if the present is absent to itself. Perception is imperception, and "this is at bottom what Husserl means when he considers retention to be fundamental: that means that the absolute present which I am is as if it were not" (VI 244/191). The present is not elsewhere than in itself, but it is its own absence; it oscillates around itself. Correlatively, the past is nothing other than the present; it is still present. Because the present absents itself, absence can present itself. The past can still be present, that is, retained, only if the present merges with its own negation. The past may give itself "in the present" because the present never was present. It is itself only by still presenting; it preserves its being-past only by remaining on the side of its other, just short of its own perdition. Moreover, the present does not present anything unless it comes in front of the past, unless it anticipates its own disappearance. In this sense, time is reduced to a single dimension, which we can indifferently characterize as present or as past. Everything is always past, in that there is never anything *in front of* me, punctually. Everything is always present precisely because with nothing being present in front of me, nothing can be present elsewhere or later either. The relation of the present to the past must be characterized as a *chiasm*. The present envelops the past because the past presents itself as such, because the past designates a modality of presence; but to this degree, the past envelops the present, because in order to give rise to the past, the present must slip into it and participate in its being. The truth of the chiasm truly resides in temporality. The passage of the present in no case hides the possibility it has of *being* past, because as being, it would remain subordinated to presence. The result is that the present presents itself in its turn only on condition of not *being* present but truly of passing. [258] The belonging of the past to the present is just as much the belonging of the present to the past, "past and present or *Ineinander,* each enveloping-enveloped—and that itself is the flesh" (VI 321/268). Thus, the phenomenon of flowing described by Husserl contains "something else entirely" than this interlocking of pasts with each other and with the present. Husserl's explication is a "*positivist* projection of the vortex of temporal differentiation" (VI 284/231; cf. 298/244). The phenomenon of flowing contains in reality

> "simultaneity," the *passage,* the *nunc stans,* the Proustian corporeity as
> guardian of the past, the immersion in a Being in transcendence not
> reduced to the "perspectives" of the "consciousness"—it contains an
> intentional reference which is not only from the past to the factual,
> empirical present, but also and inversely from the factual present to a
> dimensional present or *Welt* or Being, where the past is "simultaneous"
> with the present in the narrow sense. This *reciprocal* intentional refer-
> ence marks the limit of the intentional analytic: the point where it
> becomes a philosophy of transcendence. . . . And in fact here it is in-
> deed the past that adheres to the present and not the *consciousness* of
> the past that adheres to the *consciousness* of the present: the "vertical"
> past contains in itself the exigency to have been perceived, far from
> the consciousness of having perceived bearing that of the past. (VI
> 297/243–44)

The present cannot then present anything except in the degree that it is just as much required by what it presents and is consequently immersed in it, enveloped by the past that it envelops. There is therefore, strictly speaking, neither present nor past but passage itself, vertical Being, dimensionality, which remain themselves only by making themselves always other— whose plenitude is sustained only by being made new. There is only this unassignable point in which past and present pass into each other, are reconceived, catch up with each other. The present is itself only on the condition of not fully being present, of not *being* present, of being past, if you like, but in the sense of a past which is not gathered in itself but remains therefore just as much present—and does so in order to be past. Past and present are truly "simultaneous" because the present proceeds from a Being whose transcendence supports itself but only with its manifestation in the present. Through time, Being makes itself new always in order to find itself again. In fact, the presencing of Being in the present or as [259] present, its absolute newness, are only the advent of an originary, vertical past, and therefore at the same time absolute perenniality. It is a question, Merleau-Ponty says, "of finding in the present, the flesh of the world (and not in the past) an 'ever new' and 'always the same'——A sort of time of sleep (which is Bergson's nascent duration, ever new and always the same). The sensible, Nature, transcend the past present distinction, realize from within a passage from one into the other Existential eternity. The indestructible, the barbaric Principle" (VI 320–21/267). The presents that advent are each already the pasts that they will be, or rather a single Past-ing [*Passé(r)*]. They proceed from Being, emerge from an infinite depth, but this depth preserves itself only insofar as it is not other than the present, in the form of another presence, but the infinite differentiation of presents. Its thickness sustains itself only on the basis of making itself evanescence; its infinite self-alterity is at the same time quiet identity. Such is the meaning of time: the temporal present does not enjoy the stature that would allow it to be opposed to another, to differ from another thing in order to become it. It always exceeds the point where one seeks to fix it, so that its passage is just as much immobility. The present becomes nothing—or rather, its becoming involves no station in which it might remain, not even a "moment" in order to pass into its other—and to this degree, nothing becomes. Exceeding in principle all fixation of an identity, and consequently of a difference, the course of time resolves itself in pure immobility—or rather, escapes the opposition of becoming and immobility as properties of a being. The irreducible continuity of passage, such that no punctuality can be isolated, prohibits a genuine transformation, a birth that is not a rebirth, and the continuity merges then with a pure remainder. Time is truly "existential eternity," the absolute identity of the same and the other: always other in order to be the same, exceeding every station, every being, in order to complete itself as Being. This identity of the same and the other is itself an unstable identity, which cannot, for the same reasons, resolve itself into *a* same or *an* other: time is too "other" to be the same, too "same" to be other. The notion of the flesh, finally, corresponds to the decision to think through to the end what is at the same time revealed and hidden by Husserl's notion of retention. It is not a question of understanding retention on the basis of [260] subjectivity, "time as subject"—which always comes down to restoring the duality of present and past, and consequently to missing the being of the past—but of grasping time as being, as "the time-thing, the time-being" (VI 254/200). Time is the "symbolic matrix" (VI 227/173), "the system that embraces everything" (VI 244/191), the universal Dimension—that is, the flesh. In it, on its axis, the universal equivalence of the world is made; in it, every phenomenon gives itself as the phenomenon of Being, that is, as referring to a wholly other by its very difference. Time is this unassignable "place" [*lieu*] where the individual and the universal give birth to each other. Time is Dimensionality, phenomenality as openness to Being; by it, I am always in being in this instant.

6. Time Is Space

Reconceived in all its depth, temporality can no longer be simply opposed to space. We had concluded from Merleau-Ponty's indications on space that it is itself only insofar as the remainder that it institutes does not complete itself in extension, in a spatial being. Just short of itself, never unfolded, invisible as such, space is in that very way beyond itself as space. Thus understood, depth opens onto the past and the future just as much as onto the elsewhere, because in order to be depth, it must hide a pre-spatial "interiority." There is spatial presence only if this spatiality is not itself unfolded, present, but gathered in the heart of the thing which, in its invisibility, articulates itself at once temporally and spatially in relation to the others. It appears now that the self-divergence, the past of the present, institutes a remainder that transcends the axis of time as the succession of presents. There is passage only as the simultaneous birth and rebirth of what remains at rest in itself: the presence of the past in the present is thus just as much the belonging of the present to a past "being." From then on, the "contemporaneity" of the present with the other dimensions of time proceeds from a height of time itself, which, while it is not spatial, is not strictly temporal. What defines time, the passage that it is, is to surpass itself as succession, as time in the strict sense, in favor of a reality that, properly [261] speaking, does not pass. Insofar as its ekstasis has, in a sense, always already advented, time gathers beyond itself, in the form of a "dimensional" or "vertical" present in which the universal equivalence of the world institutes itself beyond the successive present of strict time. Present and past are simultaneous, that is, contemporaneous, and consequently proceed from a unique "space" in which this contemporaneity is instituted. This intuition, which is only sketched out in the working notes, is really the necessary consequence of a philosophy of flesh: "In what sense the visible landscape is not exterior to, and bound synthetically to . . . other moments of time and the past, but has them really *behind itself* in simultaneity, inside itself and not it and they side by side 'in' time" (VI 321/267). The ultimate "reality" is truly situated beyond the opposition of space and time; it is the same ontological depth that Merleau-Ponty joins together through these two fundamental dimensions:

> In fact it is a question of grasping the *nexus*—neither "historical" nor "geographic" of history and transcendental geology, this very time that

is space, this very space that is time, which I will have rediscovered by my analysis of the visible and the flesh, the simultaneous *Urstiftung* of time and space, which makes there be a historical landscape and a quasi-geographical inscription of history. (VI 312/259)

Depth is not extension, is not properly spatial; it conceals all that can advent, or rather, all that advents proceeds from it. That is why it is not itself present: it is rather the ground of all presence. But to this degree it is not purely temporal either, because everything remains in it nonetheless, because if it gathers itself into itself just short of unfolded exteriority, this is done not in order for it to crumble into the evanescence and transparency of presents. Presence must then be conceived beyond the simultaneous and the successive. There is no genuine simultaneity, because there is nothing in which it can advent, there is no Nature in itself: Being is made of *my* flesh. The very co-presence of every being to every being prohibits assigning them a place [*lieu*], and therefore Being is not strictly of the order of spatiality. However, it is precisely *in order that* there be co-presence, universal equivalence, and world that Being does not rest in a place. Being does not rest in a place in order to remain "the system that embraces everything," flesh of the world, in order that flesh remains mine. This is why Being is not temporal as Husserl understood it.

13 Merleau-Ponty's Leibnizianism

[263] As we have shown, Merleau-Ponty's ontology is rooted in the necessity of taking possession of Western philosophy's "ontological diplopia," of which Descartes is the first representative. Descartes's philosophy reveals a tension between a reality entirely subject to the requirements of scientific reason and the further recognition of an existence that is not the thought of existing, of a world that is irreducible to the law of the understanding. Since this tension is insurmountable, it cannot be taken up as such, and this is why what is at issue is to unveil the viewpoint where the two perspectives will no longer oppose one another. This is the reason why Merleau-Ponty is led to pay particular attention to post-Cartesian philosophies. They are characterized, in fact, by an attempt to reconcile these two dimensions, to conceive science and finitude together—that is, to rediscover, without ever renouncing Descartes's requirements, the order of existence that he ultimately neglects. Now, even though Merleau-Ponty's early texts testify to an interest in Malebranche, the name that reemerges in the working notes of *The Visible and the Invisible* is Leibniz. These notes tell us that the chapter that would have made up the first part of this work, a chapter on classical ontology, would have consisted of a confrontation between Descartes and Leibniz (VI 231/177). While taking account of its limitations, Merleau-Ponty recognizes an incontestable proximity between Leibniz's philosophy and his ontological vision. It is probable that as his ontology was being constructed, Merleau-Ponty came to recognize this [264] convergence and consciously situated himself in proximity to a philosophy of expression.

For Leibniz, the unity inherent to substantiality forbids one from conceiving substance as a material reality, as an atom. In fact, matter is essentially divisible. Pure multiplicity, the absolute exteriority of *partes extra partes* which characterizes Cartesian extension, would not be able to express a genuine substantiality. But insofar as it is a real being, substance cannot be characterized as an abstract reality either, such as a mathematical point; in an abstract unity, the diversity that defines the real is dissolved. Along with materialism, Leibniz rejects the Platonic idea whose pure identity, in his eyes, absorbs diversity; the Platonic idea cannot constitute a real being. This is why substance must be rigorously defined as the expression of diversity in unity, that is, as *perception*. One has to hear a new sense in this term, stripped of its psychological implications, namely, strictly as the expression of the multiple in the one; one must not conceive expression on the model of perception understood as representation. Instead of expression referring to perception, it is, on the contrary, representative consciousness that constitutes one mode, among others, of expression. Leibniz thereby manages to conceive substance beyond the opposition of interiority and exteriority. It is an interiority that, insofar as it is real, involves a diversity and is not purely identical to itself. In this way it is endowed with an exteriority, which is not, however, unfolded as such, because it is held back in a pole of unity, because it interiorizes itself. In relation to Leibniz, therefore, one has to speak of spiritualism rather than of intellectualism. All substance can be conceived on the model of the soul; the soul contains a diversity that does not compromise its simplicity. This is why substance must in the end be understood as Action rather than as Being—multiplicity is preserved within a substantial unity only if the latter is not a unity *beside* the multiple; rather, it must be a unity *in* the multiplicity, that is, a power of unfolding immanent to what it unfolds: entelechy. The events refer to a substance that exists only as their actual production, so that substance can be conceived on the model of force or on the model of the law of a mathematical series.[1] Each of them appears then [265] as a modality of expression, a "viewpoint" on the same universe. The events included in the "complete notion" of each substance regain the totality of the world in the double dimension of space and time, but according to a certain relation of obscurity and clarity that defines the viewpoint of each of them; the most profound sense of substantiality corresponds to this viewpoint. Here there is still a double envelopment between the substances and the world: each substance expresses one same universe, which is nonetheless nothing other than the set of its expressions, that is, nothing other than the unfolding of the predicates of each of them. The world can therefore be situated neither in interiority nor in exteriority in relation to substance. Its exteriority responds strictly to the zone of obscurity of substantial expression, so that it remains equally interiority. Obscu-

1. It is interesting to note that Merleau-Ponty compares the relation of sound to sense and, in the end, of appearing to what appears, to that of the differential and the integral, typical Leibnizian models (VI 190/144, 287/233).

rity is not the other of clarity but really an inferior degree of clarity. What is obscurely expressed by a substance will be clearly expressed by an other, so that if the world does not belong fully to any of them, it nonetheless does not differ from the infinity of substances that express it. The substances belong to one world by virtue of the obscurity of expression, but this world belongs in turn to substances by virtue of its clarity.

Without a doubt, there is an affinity between the Leibnizian universe, whose essential features we have just briefly recalled, and the ontology of the flesh. Leibniz's philosophy indeed represents, in Merleau-Ponty's eyes, the most successful attempt to discover a way between the viewpoint of essence and the recognition of the finite. Thus he notes, for example, that on the theological plane Leibniz's philosophy sums up the effort of Christian thought "to find a route between the necessitarian conception of Being, alone possible, and the unmotivated upsurge of brute Being" (VI 264/211). Nevertheless, Leibniz's solution is still something of a "compromise"; the concept of expression is in the end subordinated to the perspective that it serves to surmount: "The pre-established harmony (like occasionalism) always maintains the in itself and simply connects it with what we experience through a relation from substance to substance found in God—instead of making it the cause of our thoughts—but it is precisely a question of rejecting entirely the idea of the In Itself" (VI 276/223). In effect, instead of [266] understanding Being on the basis of expression, or rather than conceiving expression as the ultimate sense of Being, expression is subordinated in the end to the plane of essence, to the plane of the expressed that ontologically precedes its expression: namely, the complete notion of each substance and, therefore, of the world in God. The expressive hierarchy is entirely polarized toward God, so that the finite is reconceived by means of its opposition with the objective infinite; this is an opposition that leads one to provide infinity with only a negative meaning (VI 223/169). While expression seemed at first to give an account of the unmotivated upsurge of the world—neither fact nor essence, neither exteriority nor interiority—the irreducibility of the multiple to the one by which it is characterized appears rather as a negation, which is inherent to the finite, of the full unity of the mundane essence. As for God, he does not express the world; he conceives it. The obscurity of expression in all the monads is then not so much a condition of clarity and synonymous with it as it is an inferior degree, a degradation of clarity. Thus, the theological context keeps one from recognizing in the notion of expression the attestation of a discovery of the world as the ultimate fact, present in its very distance, manifest by its obscurity. In other words, the relation between substances is not ultimately founded in the substances, that is, on their respective modalities of expression, which nevertheless looked to constitute the genuine meaning of the "mutual expression" [*l'entre-expression*]. This relation is founded in a "plan" [*géométral*], a complete notion located in the divine understanding, in relation to which each of them is only an imperfect view. Therefore, what is at issue here is a "compromise." The notion of expression does not intend to give an account of the "upsurge of brute Being," an account which would presuppose that we situate essence within expression and recognize in it a fundamental opacity. The function of the notion of expression lies in granting a specific status to the finite, without, however, calling infinite Being into question; it aims to situate the finite within the hierarchy of essence but not to reject this opposition.[2]

Nevertheless, we do indeed have to speak of a Leibnizianism of Merleau-Ponty, not only because the two philosophies proceed from the same attitude in relation to Cartesian ontology [267] but also because Merleau-Ponty sees himself explicitly in Leibniz's development of the ontological problem:

2. We have to add that the tension subsists in God. If it is true that God chooses the best possible world, it is still the case that by means of the "mystery" of compossibiiity, he must choose between the worlds. There is a law proper to the world that prescribes the compatibility between the series of predicates, a law to which even God is subject. Even so, the choice of the best world is described, in *De rerum originatione radicali,* in terms of a "metaphysical mechanism." Essence tends toward existence in proportion to its quantity of perfection, and there is a "battle" between the possibles for existence. The movement by which God makes the world pass into existence in proportion to its essence can be equally understood as God's submitting to an existence which, as such, involves a maximum of essence. On God's plane, Leibniz's rationalism seems to coexist with the recognition of an irreducible facticity of the world, simultaneously as *world* and as *this* world. In any case, Merleau-Ponty seems to be attentive to this point, since he notes in *Sense and Non-Sense* that the Leibnizian theodicy "in the last analysis perhaps consisted— even for Leibniz himself—of evoking the existence of this world as an unsurpassable fact which from the first solicits creative actualization and therefore of rejecting the point of view of a worldless God. God then appears, not as the creator of this world—which would immediately entail the difficulty of a sovereign and benevolent power forced to incorporate evil in His works—but rather as an idea in the Kantian and restrictive sense of the word. God becomes a term of reference for a human reflection which, when it considers the world such as it is, condenses in this idea what it would like the world to be" (SNS 192/96).

The *In der Welt Sein* relation will take the place held in Leibniz of the relation of reciprocal expression of the perspectives taken on the world, and hence God as the unique author of these diverse perspectives which emanate from him as thoughts. The Being thus discovered is to be sure not the God of Leibniz, the "monadology" thus disclosed is not the system of monads—substances; but certain Leibnizian descriptions—that each of the views of the world is a world apart, that nonetheless "what is particular to one would be public to all," that the monads would be in a relation of expression between themselves and with the world, that they differ from one another and from it as perspectives—are to be maintained entirely, to be taken up again in the brute Being, to be separated from the substantialist and ontotheological elaboration Leibniz imposes upon them. The expression of the universe in us is certainly not the harmony between our monad and the others, the presence of the ideas of all things in it—but it is what we see in perception, to be taken as such instead of *explaining* it. Our soul has no windows: that means *In der Welt Sein*. (VI 276/222–23)

As we have seen, perception is the openness of a level, of a dimension of the world; each experience is a modality of the expression of the world. And the world exists, in turn, only as its expression, as these axes, these rays that preserve its depth by making it appear. Their unity supports only [268] the open multiplicity of which the rays unfold the secret equivalence. Instead of reabsorbing the world into the thing and the expression into the expressed, which would amount to positing the pure interiority and immanence of an expressor, each thing is strictly a mode, a dimension of the expression of the world; in this way, expression does not go all the way up to essence. Expression does not refer to a perspective *upon* the world, a perspective that would be distinguished from the world; expression is the world itself, *as* the world putting itself into perspective. Or rather, expression is deeper than the expressor or the expressed, deeper than "consciousness" and the world, which in the end are only moments of expression. Expression is simultaneously clarity and obscurity: it is clarity because the world does not withdraw itself into transcendence but rather is always already phenomenality; it is obscurity because expression never dissolves into the immanence of representation. Phenomenalization remains the fact of the world. The thing conquers its individuality only by remaining co-present with the world, so that there is closure of the subject only as openness to the world itself according to or as its dimensions. Thus, as Leibniz said already, each substance is a world, that is, "an organized set, which is *closed,* but which, strangely, is representative of all the rest, possesses its symbols, its equivalents for everything that is not itself" (VI 277/223). In all strictness, there is neither thing nor world nor subject nor in-itself, but expression itself, axes, articulations, inner frames from which things and world, subject and object proceed as abstract moments. In the end, what is at issue is to understand Being as "mutual expression" instead of subordinating the "mutual expression" to a "comprehensive plan" [*géométral*] and consequently referring it to localized, substantial viewpoints. The world is constituted around points of passage, axes of equivalence, through which everything communicates, gaining access simultaneously to their identity and to their difference. The "mutual expression," the allusion that everything makes to every other, therefore precedes their distinction; rather, from this "mutually expressive" tissue things surge forth, as things of the world, that is, as things still enveloped in what they envelop. The chiasm is "the truth of the pre-established harmony——Much more exact than it: for it is between local-individuated facts, and the chiasm binds as obverse and reverse sets unified in advance in process of differentiation" (VI 315/262). This is why the world is neither one nor many; it is a plurality [269] that is not a pure multiplicity but already an accord, the interiority of everything to everything—the interiority that, in turn, cannot complete itself in pure identity, which is only discordance in this accord. Thus, it is really necessary to think about the world of Merleau-Ponty in the image of the Leibnizian universe. There is no thing that would be a pure exteriority, that would not already express the world or would not sketch a dimension of sensibility in the very heart of its opacity of sensed being. And yet, there is no being that would stop being a thing of the world by definitively moving toward the pure interiority of representation, that would not remain expressive and immersed in this world that it makes appear, whose signifying clarity would not at the same time be an opacity. There is "dimensionality of every fact and facticity of every dimension" (VI 324/270). This means that intersubjectivity itself too must be understood as "mutual expression," as the extension of the relation that is set up between the things themselves, and between the perceiver and the things. It means that "consciousness" in the proper sense—the consciousness that reaches meanings "in the pure state"—must be reconceived as a moment of expression, the unfolding of the world itself according to another dimension, and not as a rupture with the world.

Part Four.
The Invisible

[273] Merleau-Ponty's thought is animated throughout by the desire to elaborate a meaningful critique of the intuitionist and positive conceptions of ideality. This critique is motivated not by the empiricist claim of facticity, a claim that proceeds from the same ontological presupposition as the philosophy of *eidos,* but indeed by the desire to reestablish the experience itself of ideality. Meaning cannot be closed on itself into an autonomous universe, and because it is not endowed with positivity, it is not cut off from what it means. Meaning is in principle open, unfinished—rooted, that is, in a Being that it means only because it appears within it, not enveloping it completely. Thus through an analysis of expression as the phenomenon of ideality, Merleau-Ponty had been led to reject the dualities of reflective philosophy still at work in *Phenomenology of Perception* and to open the way for an ontological questioning. The irreducible opacity and rootedness of meaning, the envelopment of the subject by the world that it means, call for the disclosure of an originary, pre-significative, pre-objective world. However, this wild universe does not represent the negation of all meaning. In fact, as soon as the positive conception of ideality has as its inverse an approach to the perceived as pure facticity, the discovery of a "facticity" of ideality, of its incapacity to be closed onto itself, has as its correlate the recognition of an ideality at the heart of the perceived. What Merleau-Ponty is attempting to do is present an originary articulation and, finally, a quasi-identity of the visible and the invisible. The invisible is not the other of a visible conceived as positive in itself, but rather it is what makes itself visible in order to preserve its distance, its signifying power; the visible, in turn, is not then the negation of the invisible, but the element of its manifestation and, in being so, a primitive mode of ideality. The visible is indeed the "presentation [274] of an unpresentable." Insofar as it manifests itself as a tacit unity, a "cohesion without concept," it is

already "exploration of an invisible" and, like science itself, "disclosure of a universe of ideas" (VI 196/149). Now, Merleau-Ponty notices that "once we have entered into this strange domain, one does not see how there could be any question of *leaving* it" (VI 199/154). The sensible givenness of the idea, which seems to be only "veiled in darkness," appears as the very law of every idea and, ultimately, as the very law of spirit: "what is called spirit is inseparable from what is most precarious about [humans]; for light would not illuminate a thing unless there were something to screen it" (RC 27/84). It is necessary to recognize, then, a universality of the sensible, a universality of flesh: as Merleau-Ponty says, "there is no intelligible world, *there is* the sensible world" (VI 267/214). Still, one must not mistake the sense of this "there is" ["*il y a*"], but instead we must understand that the sensible is not based in itself, that it is synonymous with phenomenalization: that is, that it is the exhibition of a universe of ideas within the darkness; it is the presentation of an invisible. The sensible is *what there is* everywhere, what bears every experience and every production of sense.

It follows that the domain of the sensible possesses an extension that exceeds the limits we have ascribed to it up to this point. It follows that the place that we have assigned to it remains abstract; in short, the sensible world cannot be confused with the visible as such, with the universe of perception as the ordeal of an actual exteriority. If it is true that there is only the world, it cannot be limited to the pure visible. If it is true that the flesh is universal, it must not be reduced to the strictly corporeal flesh. The fidelity to experience, to which the dialectic of visible and invisible bears witness, imposes the recognition of the intelligible as a specific experience; that is, the fidelity to experience imposes that we distinguish ideality in the strict sense from the "ideas" that are inscribed within the heart of the sensible. That every intelligible is given only in withdrawal, that is, as sensible in the widest sense, does not mean that the sensible in the proper sense— namely, the visible—represents the sole possible modality of this withdrawal. Merleau-Ponty's fundamental decision certainly consists in addressing the intelligible starting from its phenomenon, rather than [275] subordinating phenomenality to the intelligible. But this decision is meaningful only on the condition of being accompanied by a radical extension of the domain of phenomenality. That the visible and the invisible cannot be distinguished as positive entities equally prohibits their being merged, the invisible dissolving itself in favor of a visible that would then flow again inevitably toward full positivity. The temptation to reduce the phenomenon of the intelligible to the visible phenomenon would be not only inadequate but genuinely ruinous to experience, because it would open out onto a disguised empiricism and onto the necessity of carrying out a genesis of the intelligible within the sensible. While the idea appears only hidden in the sensible, it is still the case nevertheless that the idea could never be fully exhibited by such a mode of sensible presence, and therefore that visibility, precisely insofar as it bears ideas within it, must surpass itself toward another mode of givenness. In other words, the assertion according to which the sense *is* sensible can be maintained only if the sensible in the strict sense, that is, the visible, is no longer conceived as the sole mode of sense donation. Just as the visible, insofar as it is an exhibition of an intelligible, surpasses itself as pure fact, so it must necessarily surpass itself as strictly visible. While the visible is only the still unpolished mirror of the intelligible, it is destined to give birth to other reflections. The field of the visible cannot, then, be rigorously circumscribed. As soon as the visible attests to an invisible, the visible could never be definitively fixed as the sole mode by which the intelligible is given; it slips beyond itself as pure visible and is articulated as another "visibility" of the invisible, which is *sayability.* Because it is always already "on the side of" the invisible, the sensible is destined somehow to respond to this call that it carries within it and to surpass itself as a strict visible. The recognition of the phenomenon of the intelligible leads us therefore to eliminate not only the positivity of the sensible but also the possibility of assigning a definite extension to it. Or rather, because the sensible is not a positive being, it is not only visible. It gives rise to other modes of the presentation of the invisible; it makes itself speech. The invisible, which the visible manifests and dissimulates at the same time, absorbs in turn the element of its presentation and gives itself a mode of manifestation which is peculiar to itself. The invisible establishes a "sublimation" of the sensible.

The entire difficulty here is to take the phenomenal difference between sensation and ideality into account while preserving their absolute continuity. Speech says nothing other than what [276] perception "says," but it says it otherwise; the sensible already carries within it the entire destiny of meanings, but in it meaning remains opaque and allusive. That is why the notion of the invisible, like that of the sensible, has a meaning that is, at the same time, singular and multiple. It is multiple because it is necessary to distinguish the invisible, as invisible *of* the visible, from what is made transparent in this singular sensible that is speech. The invisible is singular because it is truly the unpresentable universe of the visible that is signified in speech, because it is the visible which itself is surpassed in order to return to itself, to signify its own depth. There are therefore not two distinct layers but a single movement that is indistinctly the growth of the visible toward a speech and the growth of its invisible toward ideality; there is, finally, the transformation of the mode of co-belonging of the "visible" and the invisible. That is why, strictly speaking, one passes, with speech, not from the visible to the invisible but from one sensible to another sensible, a linguistic sensible, and correlatively from one invisible to another intelligible invisible. In speech, the invisible remains the same because speech still belongs to the flesh and truly proceeds from the sensible world, because the sensible already unveils the universe of sense. And yet, the invisible becomes other because it does not subsist elsewhere than in the sensibles through which it gives itself; the invisible does not distinguish itself from its modes of manifestation. In short, the difficulty consists in trying to conceive the mode of articulation, ultimate this time, between ideality and perception, between the phenomenon that defines the intelligible and the strict visible. The difficulty consists in trying to understand how Merleau-Ponty manages to preserve the phenomenal specificity of the domains of experience without putting forward again what we could call an ontological monism of the sensible. Nevertheless, before we confront this difficulty, first of all we must try to carve out a path that leads from the sensible "solipsistic" flesh to the shared domain of ideality, and try to demonstrate the belonging of ideality to the flesh while preserving the specificity of ideality. In order to carve out this path, we have to present a distinction in the heart of flesh between its strictly corporeal life and a "less heavy, more transparent body" at the heart of which visibility is "freed from every condition" (VI 200/153).

14 The Inner Frame of Intersubjectivity

1. The Chiasm of the Other and the World

[277] Merleau-Ponty qualifies the experience made explicit on the level of the visible, that is, on the level of the sensible in the strict sense, as "solipsistic." This solipsism does not mean that the flesh at this level experiences itself as isolated, that it understands itself as a private experience; a private experience would already presuppose intersubjectivity. Rather the solipsism means that on this level, the identity of sensibility and therefore its solitude as separation vis-à-vis others are unknown, since there is no relationship to a genuine alterity. Solipsistic experience remains an anonymous one.[1] At the level of sensibility, the one who senses and the world still constitute a closed sphere, within which no divergence, no distance, can insert itself. If experience at this level is truly the initiation to a world, the experience is nonetheless attained only as the world that it unfolds; nothing reflects its image back to it, nothing allows it to contract an identity and to appear to itself as a part of the world it makes appear. Self-presence is at this level "self-absence." With sensibility, "there is" the world and not a transcendence recognized as such. Now, experience incontestably involves the dimension of objectivity. The world appears to me as a totality that surpasses me, which as such is accessible to others, and in which I participate as an "object" for them—in short, as an objective transcendence. On the one hand, this transcendence is itself surpassed by what is still obscure and contingent in it, by the constitution of an immutable universe where consciousnesses seem to be able to [278] overcome their separation, that is, by logical or rational objectivity. This objectivity explains and completes what remains latent in the experience of a transcendent

---

1. "The I, really, is nobody, is the anonymous; it must be so, prior to all objectification, denomination, in order to be the Operator, or the one to whom all this occurs. . . . [It] is the unknown *to whom* all is given to see or to think, to whom everything appeals, before whom . . . there is something" (VI 299/246). See also S 220/174.

world. From then on, explanation of sensibility on the level of the solipsistic layer truly appears as an abstraction. Not that the explanation of sensibility opposes itself to the explanation of the object as if sensibility were the illusory opposed to the true. The sensible has never been the other of objectivity and does not correspond to the claim of a virgin experience from which all rational horizon would be absent. Merleau-Ponty's approach inaugurates itself, on the contrary, by calling this opposition into question. The sensible contains everything, including the acts that thematize it and thereby surpass it as the pure sensible; the sensible is truly the place or the source of objectivity. But it is still necessary to develop all that is implied in it, to free the possibility of objectification on the basis of the originary chiasm—that is, to resituate it in the heart of the teleology to which it gives rise, precisely in order to avoid its reduction to sensation in the empiricist sense, which inevitably complies with the positing of an autonomous universe of sense. The passage from a solipsistic world to an objective universe is accomplished by the mediation of the experience of the other. By its inexhaustible depth, the sensible grounds the openness to an alterity that, in return, comes to confirm its transcendence. The appearance of the other breaks the closure of flesh and of its world, the anonymous co-belonging of the one who senses and what is sensed. Discovering its own mirror in the world, the flesh can return to itself and overcome its generality, and the world can then appear as what does not belong to it as its own, as objective transcendence. The experience of the other is, like that of the world, "presentation of an unpresentable" (VI 257/203). But while the invisible appears in the order of the visible in the strict sense only as hidden in the thickness of the world, with the other we witness a first initiation to the invisible as such. The passage to intersubjectivity truly constitutes, at the heart of the sensible, a first step toward the invisible; or rather, this experience takes the place of articulation between the planes of the visible and the invisible. In fact, the other is constituted at the very level of mute experience, as an extension of the carnal relationship, that is, just as much as a dimension of sensible Being itself. And yet, with intersubjectivity, the sensible world doubles itself with a new depth where the invisible as a whole exists already and acquires a consistency on which the unfolding of [279] logical objectivity is fed. Intersubjectivity is truly this "point of passage" of rational teleology, where the sublimation of the visible realizes itself in meaning at the same time as the inscription of the invisible in the visible. The relation to the other cannot, strictly speaking, be situated on one side or the other. Rather, it imposes a reformulation of the strict opposition between the sensible order and the universe of meaning. The possibility of the other and of an intersubjective experience attests to the belonging of the sensible to a rational teleology and reveals the precession of the Universal in the heart of primordial experience. But conversely, the other depends on an irreducible *experience* in which it remains other, at a distance, even on the level of linguistic communication. To the degree that it is a modality of intersubjectivity, that is, of incarnation, rationality belongs to sensible Being and cannot claim to reabsorb it.

As we have seen, by distancing himself vis-à-vis Husserl and Sartre—and for the same reasons in both cases—Merleau-Ponty sketches a path toward a rigorous positing of the problem of the other. It is true that the other cannot be the object of knowledge, that it does not present itself as ego for ego. The problem of the other should not be posed as the problem of the alter ego, because starting in this way from the identity of consciousnesses, one finds oneself immediately constrained to reject such consciousnesses in favor of a radical alterity. The relation to the other must be sought just short of this level, at the point where neither the other nor I are yet pure consciousnesses; that is, it must be sought on the plane of corporeity. But, on the other hand, it is nevertheless not a question of identifying the experience of the other with the revelation of this corporeity; instead of the other proceeding from the ordeal of my objectivation, it is because the other first appears that I can discover for myself an objective body. Precisely insofar as it is truly the vector of the openness to the other, that is, to a determinate experience, corporeity cannot be understood as pure passivity, thrown back onto the side of the object. In short, in order that the other may remain transcendent, it is necessary that its givenness not proceed from an ego that is closed in on itself. But in order that this transcendence might be preserved, as appearing transcendence, it is necessary that the passivity to which it responds be simultaneously activity, that the movement of disappropriation, by which alone the other can advent, equally be appropriation. Incarnation is not the passage from a transparent consciousness into its other but the very modality according to which it can be in relationship with itself. The other [280] is truly invisible only if it is not absolutely invisible, only if this very invisibility is susceptible to a presentation.

With the notion of flesh, we have the wherewithal to satisfy the conditions of the problem. All that is required is the development of all of its implications. It is a matter not of starting from the me–other difference but of installing oneself in the heart of flesh in order to reconceive it as the place of their articulation. The carnal "me" is itself only by making itself other, only by being filled with the thickness of the world, such that it can open itself to what is not it. In other words, instead of making the objectivity of the world rest on the experience of the other, it is necessary to make this objectivity appear as a moment of the carnal openness to the world, even if, in turn, this experience transmutes the modality of this openness. That is why the question of the order of priority between the constitution of the other and of objectivity is nonsense in Merleau-Ponty's eyes.[2] The other does not "precede" the world. On the contrary, the other appears in the world, and it is from the world's thickness that the other draws its identity, that is, its alterity. The other is not an other ego but, like me, an articulation of the world. A world that would be only the correlate of a plurality of monads would not be a world, since it would not rest in itself; correlatively, subjects subsisting "before" the world would not be subjects since they would not have a world on the basis of which they might constitute themselves by making the world appear. The originary layer of the sensible truly contains all ulterior layers; "everything rests upon the unsurpassable richness, the miraculous multiplication of the sensible" (S 23/16). This starting point alone conforms to the meaning of the other. The other is itself only on the condition that it itself does not appear, on the condition that it remains dissimulated under the figure of the world. Its alterity does not conceal the positing of a being. It is only a moment of the radical alterity of the world. Nonetheless, this does not mean that the world "precedes" the other. Strictly understood, this would mean that the world is unfolded on a plane of pure transcendence, foreign to all consciousness. As we know, such a determination secretly refers [281] to a pure subject who contemplates it, to the positing of the ego *uninteressiert,* in such a way that its objectivity is denied at the very instant when it is affirmed. Now, if it is true that the other proceeds from the world, one must not forget that the world has been characterized as flesh. The subject sees the world only because an ontological complicity is established be-

2. This was already Husserl's conclusion, according to Merleau-Ponty. The constitutive layers cannot be ordered according to anterior and posterior layers; each begins to exist completely only on the basis of the one to which it nevertheless gives rise. Therefore, it is at the same time anterior and posterior to the one that "follows" it. This is why Husserl was hardly surprised, as Merleau-Ponty notes, by the circles encountered in the constitutive approach (S 219/173, 222/176).

tween them, because the world is on its side; the subject is a moment of a world that the look does not need to draw out from the night, a moment that is already visibility. The transcendence of the world makes sense only if it is not other than what gives it to be seen, only if it makes itself flesh. The retreat of the world does not correspond to the negation of the appearing, but is its condition. *There is* in fact a world only to the degree that it does not offer itself to a pure vision in which all facticity would vanish, but remains dimension, measuring, scattered vision. From then on, insofar as it *is* visibility, the world is always already inhabited by others. What in the world transcends my momentary vision is not the negation of all vision but diffuse and dispersed sensibility, that is, the pregnancy of other visions. This description, again, is the only one conforming to the meaning of the other. The other is not a transcendent existent, a being resting in itself, but another openness to the world. What is being put in question, then, is the very idea of an anteriority, whatever the order of it may be. The search for a ground or an origin always refers to an objective viewpoint that captures the other and the world in exteriority, while both must be apprehended together, on the basis of the unity of experience—that is, as inscribed in the depth of sensible Being. In short, if the world is "lower" than the states of consciousness of insular subjects, if it "precedes" all real vision, it is nevertheless "higher" than pure transcendence, already situated on the axis of vision. Thus it announces a multiplicity of possible visions. There is therefore neither an autonomous objective layer, a first transcendence, nor a multiplicity of consciousnesses—these two positions call for each other and exclude each other at the same time—but a single vision, a single openness. Because of that single openness, the other precedes the world—which is fulfilled only by crystallizing itself in the thickness of mundane "thises," only by differentiating itself in obscurity from singular sensibilities, and thus the world "precedes" the other. Just as it is futile to seek a precession between *my* vision and the world, it is futile to constitute the other starting from the world or the world starting from the other; they are born from a universal visibility, from a Dimension of vision that is synonymous with the "there is" of the world. There is no [282] sense in carrying out a constitution of the other on the basis of the ego [*moi*]. They are inscribed in a single carnal openness; the other is given with this world whose depth my flesh unfolds in a single stroke, "the other and my body are born together in the original ecstasy" (S 220/174). It is necessary then to speak of a *chiasm* between the world and others. Consciousnesses all belong to a world, which is nevertheless only what they constitute in common; they are enveloped in the world that they envelop. And it is precisely because they are contained in it, woven of the world's flesh, that they can contain it; it is by their very difference that their unity, the possibility of a communication, is realized. The other is truly born in the world, but in a world that is not other than it, whose transcendence therefore does not compromise the other's identity as one who perceives. All vision is a variant of a unique Vision that conquers its unity only by differentiating itself from distinct and insular visions. Thus,

> The things [my body] perceives would really be being only if I learned that they are seen by others, that they are presumptively visible to any viewer who warrants the name. Thus being in-itself will appear only after the constitution of the other. But the constitutive steps which still separate us from being in-itself are of the same type as the unveiling of my body; as we shall see, they make use of a universal which my body has already made appear. (S 212/168)

Everything rests, of course, on the thickness of sensible Being, on this "culmination of subjectivity" that is also a "culmination of materiality" (VI 302/248) and is consequently open, in its very insularity, to other sensing subjects. The distance of the other

> becomes a strange proximity as soon as one comes back home to the being of the sensible, since the sensible is precisely that which can haunt more than one body without budging from its place. . . . Everything depends on the fact that this table over which my glance now sweeps, interrogating its texture, does not belong to any "space of consciousness" and inserts itself equally well into the circuit of other bodies. Everything depends, that is, upon the fact that our glances are not "acts of consciousness," each of which claims an invariable priority, but openings of our flesh which are immediately filled by the universal flesh of the world. (S 23/15–16)

2. The Reversibility of Sensibility as the Ground of Intercorporeity

[283] Let us return, then, to the description of flesh. Merleau-Ponty characterizes carnal corporeity by its aptitude for reversibility; touched as object, the left hand is at the same time reached as touching. This touch is

a localized sensation, which means that it does not pass into the rank of pure object, that it sketches a consciousness. Correlatively, my right hand is itself touching only to the degree that, by virtue of this reversibility, it is susceptible to being touched by this left hand that it nevertheless senses. We are not, then, dealing with an object-body presenting itself to a disincarnated subject, but with a body that is touching only because its touch never gathers itself beyond itself, only because it remains tangible in this very touch. It senses itself only in remaining collapsed into itself, passive in the very functioning of its sensibility. Undergoing the ordeal of a world, sensibility incarnates itself, and it must rather be understood as the advent of a Sensibility [*une Sensibilité*] that is without an assignable subject. The self-relation that characterizes sensibility is accomplished only as self-difference, an exteriority in the form of a divergence between touching and touched hands. In truth, neither of the two hands is strictly speaking sensing or sensed; nowhere can one isolate a moment of pure consciousness or a moment of pure passivity. One must instead speak of an axis of equivalence—the possibility of changing roles—which is dismembered by what it joins together. Corporeity corresponds to the moment of difference; consciousness corresponds to the moment of reversibility, which is only the other side of the preceding moment. This relationship can be generalized, as we have seen, to all the other senses, as well as to the relationship among the senses. Every sensation, vision or touch, is in accordance with every other through this possibility of reversion. Such is the sense of the flesh: a unity that is realized only as possibility of passage, equivalence without principle between singular sensibilities. Now, to the degree that this carnal unity merges with the articulation of its differences, it cannot be understood as a closed unity—*it also differs from itself*. Because it is sustained only by its differences, these differences come to contaminate it in a way; they transport the carnal unity beyond itself by opening it onto other "unities." The differences, the sensible lived experiences of this or that sense, cannot be [284] conceived as differences of a carnal unity, as *its* differences, because it is only in them that the unity is realized; they are then not assignable to *one* body, characterized as *mine*. To the degree that each sensation surpasses itself toward the other sensations of the same body, where the identity of the body subsists only in the form of this encroachment, we are unable to strictly circumscribe the scope of this encroachment. Each sensation is itself surpassed as the sensation of this body, toward the lived experiences of other bodies. Because it differs from the other sensations and is exteriorized, because the unity of sensibility is gathered in this difference, a sensation cannot be definitively distinguished from the sensations of others. Insofar as this difference is not gathered under a principle of unity that distinguishes itself from it, this difference is devoted to differing from itself. The movement of reversibility must then be reconceived somehow at the second power. The movement of reversibility sketches the unity of a flesh only by opening and surpassing the unity that it sketches. The unity of the body must be conceived as an articulation that cannot be posited separately from what it articulates; this unity would not then be itself except in sliding outside itself, except in making itself a moment of a superior articulation, a difference of another unity. There are no tiered strata, and consequently there is no ultimate layer. If there is not one point on the body that does not sketch a sensibility, not one difference which does not participate in the unification or joining together of the body and the world, neither is there a unity that might close itself on itself, that does not then remain difference, no body that would not be open to other bodies. In fact, the only way to guarantee the identity of the body would be through recourse to a pure subjectivity, which would be the same thing as compromising the specificity of sensibility. Endowed with identity, accomplished as "self," one's own body would lose its corporeity. Conversely, as soon as it is incarnated, perception no longer possesses an assignable identity and institutes a relation of reversibility with the other perceptions. Each sensation is itself only if it is not carried by a consciousness, only if it is open, in its very difference, to other sensations. It is clear, then, that the scope of this openness cannot be measured, that by the depth of the world from which it proceeds, it will be open to every possible sensation, that is, to the sensations of all others. Because every sensation is rooted in the world itself, the "subject" that carries it possesses the infinite extension correlative with the depth of this world. It is not because sensibility is mine that it makes the world appear; it is on the contrary because it is [285] geared into the flesh of the world that it is mine, which means that it is just as much not-mine, that it is articulated to every other sensibility. Of course, just as there are sensations, there is truly a body, grounding the relative unity of lived experiences. But just as on the plane of sensibility, this unifying power of one's own body does not rest on the possession of a meaning. It is instead like a sensation of a higher order, a new dimension, which itself subsists only as difference and as articulation with other bodies. At no moment can the unity of sensibility cease to be veiled, dispersed in other fleshes, because it is synonymous with openness to a generality of the world. One's own body thus appears as a "strait," a point of passage between subordinate differences, which are only relatively their own, and other carnal openings. It crystallizes an intersubjective style of vision, just as each sensation crystallizes a particular style of vision. There are no insular subjects but a universal Dimensionality of vision, of sensibility, of rays of the world which really belong to no one—but in which, rather, each one advents. Thus, just as the "place" of the thing is unassignable, so the limit of one's own body, of the "ego" ["*moi*"], is not graspable. The place is beside itself *with* the world and with others, *between* itself and the world, and consequently between itself and others. Each sensation encroaches on Being, makes itself universal by its very singularity, and encroaches then on the sensations of others:

> Being is this strange encroachment by reason of which my visible, although it is not superposable on that of the other, nonetheless opens upon it, both open upon the same sensible world——And it is the same encroachment, the same junction at a distance, that makes the messages from my organs (the monocular images) reassemble themselves into one sole vertical existence and into one sole world. (VI 269/216)

Recaptured in its carnal depth, transcendental subjectivity is truly transcendental intersubjectivity.

The relationship established between my two hands may then be generalized: "The handshake too is reversible; I can feel myself touched as well and at the same time as touching" (VI 187/142). In fact, because my touch remains imminent, it is truly realized as the tangibility of my body. On the basis of the solipsistic touch, the body is other to itself, and sensibility is present as its own absence. The body is this visible in which [286] the invisibility of vision announces and preserves itself at the same time. This imminence remaining irreducible, this invisibility without appeal, the "self" of touch is at the same time passivity, and it is open in this way to the transcendence of the other. Because sensibility presents itself only as its own absence, the absence of sensibility in another visible body no longer means the negation of its presence. Since my passivity is no longer other but is now the condition of my activity, the transcendence to which it exposes me can be a transcendence that appears. Since it is itself invisible, that is, since it is incarnated in an irreducible depth, my vision is at the same time exposition to the vision of the other and presentiment of this vision within the other's body. To say that I see is to say that I incarnate myself, but it is thereby to recognize that it is Being itself that ascends to a vision which, from then on, is no longer only mine—or rather was never mine. Thus,

> to say that the body is a seer is, curiously enough, not to say anything else than: it is visible. When I study what I mean in saying that it is the body that sees, I find nothing else than: it is "from somewhere" (from the point of view of the other—or: in the mirror for me, in the three-paneled mirror, for example) visible in the act of looking——
>
> More exactly: when I say that my body is a seer, there is, in the experience I have of it, something that grounds and announces the view that the other acquires of it or that the mirror gives of it. (VI 327/273–74)

The originary identity of my vision and my visibility grounds the experience of the other as identity of its visibility and its vision. In order to be vision, the body is transported toward a visibility on the other side of which other visions emerge without compromising its own:

> To see is not to see—to see the other is essentially to see my body as an object, so that the other's body-object could have a psychic "side." The experience of my own body and the experience of the other are themselves the two sides of one same Being: where I say that I see the other, in fact it especially happens that I objectify my body, the other is the horizon or other side of this experience. (VI 278/225)

Here we find the truth of Sartre's philosophy. The other *itself* is irremediably absent; the other is only the diffuse inverse of its visibility. But by its radicality, or rather its simplicity, this analysis distracts us from the true implications of the experience. In fact, Sartre conceives this absence that characterizes the relationship to the other as an immediate negation of vision [287] and of subjectivity, which is the same as saying that he confuses the appearance of the other with the objectification of the body. This negation is itself correlative with the position the other had before as pure for-itself. In doing this, Sartre makes visibility pass to the side of the object, and therefore restores, opposite it, a pure subjectivity, the inverse of my alienation. As the negation of consciousness, the visible body is just as much a body for a consciousness, precisely for the consciousness of the other. Just when he claims to recognize the alterity of the other, Sartre encroaches on it because he ultimately defines it as a for-itself, identical to mine, to which I can consequently relate myself only by being absolutely exposed to it. Instead of reconceiving, on the basis of the fact of the other, the indissoluble unity of vision and visibility, he hollows out between them an uncrossable abyss, an abyss that separates the subject from the object. The invisibility of the other is missed, confused with the existence of a positive consciousness, that is, with a radical absence. The visibility of my body, or rather my belonging to the visible as a body, is in its turn surpassed toward objectivity, immediately correlative with the look of the other. Now, Merleau-Ponty's entire analysis comes down to showing that the carnal subject is genuinely visible only if this visibility is not the negation of its vision but truly the sole mode of being that is suitable for it. As intrinsically visible, it need not be sustained by the vision of the other. In order to be a seer, the seer makes itself visible. Correlatively, the invisibility of the other, to which the visibility of the carnal subject corresponds, makes sense only to the degree that it does not conceal the actual presence of another vision elsewhere, only if it is synonymous with and not the other of its own visibility. The invisibility of the other is absolute—that is, invisibility *of the other*—only on condition of offering itself again to a vision, of not being the inverse of its actual vision. Such is the sense of the imminence of the other in or as its flesh. The other is not absent from a body that would then be without inhabitant, and consequently the other is not a trans-worldly presence that ensnares me in shame. Instead, the other is a presence suitable to its absence, an absence responding to its presence as other. By asserting that the seer is visible *as seer,* Merleau-Ponty shows how I can be offered to the other without being negated by it, how the other can be present to me without being negated by me—in short, that the other's transcendence does not contradict its appearance. While with Sartre the seer made itself visible only by becoming the object for another look, for Merleau-Ponty the seer makes itself visible only in order to find itself again, [288] so that the other, from the viewpoint from which it is seen, is still encompassed in its own point of view. The subject is made body and is thus exposed to others, but this de-possession is at the same time presence to self, so that the others are just as much exposed to the subject. Because we are ourselves only by remaining exposed to Being, the other and I are in the mode of being-exposed to each other. I make myself my own outside and, in this exteriority in which a "self" is constituted, which brings me back then to myself, the other is caught, its destructive power circumscribed by what it intended to objectify. The movement by which I make myself visible for another vision is not distinguished from that by which I make myself seer in order to grasp this other vision in accordance with what it is—namely, invisible. This self-negation, in favor of which the other appears, is just as much a return to self, that is, an experience of the other consistent with its absence. The other responds well, as Sartre said, to an internal negation, but to this degree, the experience I have of the other does not merge with the ordeal of my objectification. This negation is not the effect of the other's presence as a for-itself; it defines first of all *my* existence. My alienation is therefore at the same time appropriation, and the other appears to me in its turn only under the figure of negation or the absence of the for-itself. In short, it is a matter of renouncing all duality. My flesh "is fundamentally neither only thing seen nor only seer" (VI 181/137); just as my visibility is also vision, the vision exercised by the other will not exclude its visibility. Thus one must say, in opposition to intellectualism, that the other, to the degree that it must be like me, cannot itself appear, and it is therefore only the inverse of my visibility. But one must add, in opposition to Sartre, that this visibility of my flesh, not being the inverse of *the other's* own vision but the only mode of being suitable to my own, can ground an *appearance* of the other in accordance with the transcendence of the other.

3. The Inner Frame of Intersubjectivity

This analysis nevertheless still remains abstract because it starts from egologically constituted poles in order to then make the possibility of their relation appear. It is precisely because Sartre treated intersubjectivity as a relation *between* an ego and [289] another ego that he was obliged to ground their relationship on the negation of their egoicity, which compromised an actual *experience* of alterity. Now, to say that the seer is constituted as such only in making itself visible is to assert that, properly speaking, there is no circumscribed and completed seer as such, that there is no me *and* the other as positive poles. As the analysis of the carnal chiasm has shown, the subject is completed only in de-possessing itself in favor of the world; its presence to itself is absence to self, that is, the absence in itself of an insular self. The subject's vision makes sense only as a moment of a universal visibility, that is, as flesh of the world. This means that the for-itself is never fully realized as such, that the subject of sensibility remains anonymous, general, bereft of the positivity which would permit it to split off from others; it is situated just short of the opposition between the other and itself, drawn up from a general sensibility [*la sensibilité*]. If the subject of sensibility can open itself, therefore, to the other, this is because they have never been separated, because they are still merged as moments of a unique visibility that, nevertheless, they institute in a differentiated way. Because what defines carnal "egos" [*des "moi"*] is characterized by the unity of an "already" and a "not yet," intersubjectivity can enter into their definition. In fact, insofar as there is a world only for a body that makes itself world and still does not reach full self-consciousness, the relation to others in some way precedes personal identity through the mediation of the appearance belonging to the world. And yet, because the world is not the negation of subjectivity but is set into flesh, woven of visibility, sensibility is already individualized, and the intersubjective relation does not end up in pure and simple confusion. The intersubjective relation accepts differences into itself, remains *inter*subjectivity. Thus the relationship precedes the terms between which it is nonetheless established. Each "consciousness" envelops the world only by remaining enveloped in it and therefore conquers its own difference only at the heart of its identity with all the others. The originary chiasm permits the best possible restitution of intersubjectivity as the identity of identity and of the difference between the carnal poles. Thus,

> In reality there is neither me nor the other as positive, positive subjectivities. There are two caverns, two opennesses, two stages where something will take place—and which both belong to the same world, and to the stage of Being.
>
> There is not the For Itself, and the For the Other   They are the other side of the other. This is why they incorporate one another: projection-introjection——There is that line, that frontier surface [290] at some distance before me, where occurs the veering I-Other Other-I. (VI 317/263)

It is necessary, then, to speak of a chiasm between me and the other that is only an extension of the chiasm of the flesh and the world and that, in reality, is implicated in this chiasm. Just as the objective body and the phenomenal body gravitate to each other, just as they are immersed in each other, so the other and I are characterized by our reciprocal envelopment. Merleau-Ponty reconceives this situation in the notion of *Ineinander* (VI 228/174). Each of the terms is in the other, possessed by it, only if it is not reabsorbed into the other and consequently possesses it in turn. In other words, here it is a matter of drawing out all the consequences of the relationship established between the individual and the universal. The analysis of perception has shown that the "ego" is itself, individual, only if it dives into the universality of the world, only if it remains pre-individual.

Its singularity, then, is just as much generality. This is why the "ego" is at the very place of the other, or rather, situated just short of its opposition to the other, merged with a unique generality which is "syncretism," "transitivism," "pre-egology" (VI 274/221). Each one of them is itself only as an openness to a single world; it is itself only on the condition of joining up with its other. Nevertheless, this syncretism must not be understood as a pure and simple identification. Such was Merleau-Ponty's temptation in *Phenomenology of Perception* when he expounded the problem of the other in the form of an alternative between the insularity of the Husserlian ego and Schelerian non-differentiation. Because Merleau-Ponty remained tributary to a philosophy of consciousness, he could reconceive the specificity of the experience of the other only in terms of an identification that, for a second time, led back to the requirement of a duality of egological poles. At that point, Merleau-Ponty oscillated between radical alterity and pure identity, missing therefore the hinge of intersubjectivity. At first he was situated too close to consciousness, beyond intersubjectivity, so that after having recognized the actuality of the relation with others, he was led to situate himself too close to the world, just short of intersubjectivity. Now, this generality on which the relationship to the other is based is not the negation of the ego but truly its only mode of completion; it is itself only by remaining difference. If it is necessary to restitute, under insular egos, [291] a "pre-egological" layer, one must recognize that this layer exists in turn only as carnal poles. The generality of the flesh does not merge with the obscurity of the world; it sustains itself only in individuating itself, and that is why there is no alternative between me and the other, between alterity and communication. The ultimate reality truly resides in this "*Ineinander*," this "connective tissue," which is "neither object nor subject" (VI 228/174) nor "group soul," but is rather "co-functioning" (VI 268/215) of myself and the other, the conjunction which is just as much disjunction, "surface of separation between me and the other which is also the place of our union, the unique *Erfüllung* of his life and of my life" (VI 287/234). It is to this surface of separation and union "that the existentials of my personal history proceed, it is the geometrical locus of the projections and introjections, it is the invisible hinge upon which my life and the life of the others turn to rock into one another, the inner frame of intersubjectivity" (VI 287/234). Here we reach the geometrical locus, the central hinge of Merleau-Ponty's very philosophy. If the relation to the other has a meaning, the relation cannot be reconstituted on the basis of poles closed in on themselves, nor can it be reconceived on the basis of a neutral element within which every distinction would be abolished. The relation is this point of contact between subjectivities which is also a point of disjunction, this "surface" of separation where, finding themselves again, they are pushed back toward their difference, where the difference and the identity of consciousnesses and, consequently, the depth and the phenomenality of the world are constituted at the same time. It is necessary therefore to understand this *Ineinander,* this "inter" of intersubjectivity, as an ultimate, irreducible reality and finally as the fundamental Dimension of the world. There are not consciousnesses, because if the consciousnesses were truly consciousnesses, they would make one sole consciousness, and the solidity of the world would disappear in the inconsistency of a pure thought. There is no world or Being, because cut off from its phenomenalization it would not even be a world, it would disappear into nothingness. *There is intersubjectivity,* a hinge around which the world gains its unity, achieves a sense by dispersing itself in a plurality of experiences, thus preserving its depth and therefore also the depth of this sense. Intersubjectivity is this "field of fields" (VI 281/227) that is none other than [292] those it articulates, the element in which the unity of carnal poles is at once both announced and differentiated. It announces itself by differing from itself; it is in this way synonymous with fundamental Historicity. As we have said, experience can be characterized by Dimensionality. Dimension is this unity that, as unity for the world, gathers itself only by being crystallized in its differences and subsists nowhere but in them—which distinguishes it from representation. It now appears that intersubjectivity is an ultimate dimension for the world, a dimension in which its being takes refuge from the world. The world "forms its unity across incompossibilities such as that of *my* world and the world of the other" (VI 268/215), but this incompossibility is final and therefore constitutes the element in which the world and its very identity are simultaneously veiled and unveiled. Intersubjectivity is the point beyond which the world would flow back toward pure representation, the element where the strictest identity of a manifestation of the world as such and of its withdrawal would be realized. In and by its differences, the final unity of the world is accomplished. In the final unity of the world, each worldly "this," each experience of the world, is announced as a moment of a closed and unitary universe that is nevertheless nothing other than these moments, as moments of a complete determination of the world. In short, intersubjectivity merges with the very being of the world insofar as it is sustained only by remaining dispersed in the opacity of intra-worldly experiences.

If it is on the basis of an originary chiasm that one can restore the experience of intersubjectivity, if the possibility of the relation with the other is understood in the reversibility of sensibility, it is plausible, nonetheless, that it is on the basis of this fundamental given, bequeathed by experience, that Merleau-Ponty forges the guiding concepts of his philosophy. Undoubtedly, the world was reconceived on the basis of the implications of the relationship with the other, as that in which an intersubjectivity must be able to ground itself. It is the place of the agreement *and* the difference of consciousnesses—more precisely, of their difference at the very heart of the agreement and their comprehension at the very heart of the difference. It sketches a unity that remains buried and dispersed, that exists only as its own future, and is thus just as much a diversity of the "lived experiences" and of consciousnesses. An insular and empirical subjectivity would never be able to agree, even presumptively, with others, since it would lack a meaningful unity of the world; but a unique transcendental subjectivity [293] that would be the agreement of consciousnesses in the unity of Spirit would be cut off from all actual presence, would have nothing to signify, and would disappear into inconsistency since it would lack the determination that alone offers actuality. That is why the meaningful unity of the world subsists only as veiled in the multiplicity of experiences, in the multiplicity of subjectivities. The world is *between* the others and me, present to all but possessed by no one; it is the promise of a unity, the horizon of reconciliation and finally of truth, that place where each one can get along with all others. But insofar as the subjects join together only by remaining ineluctably distinct, transgress their insularity only to return to themselves, the world is also the place of discordance and conflict, the reconciliation must always be done over, and the truth is always dissimulated. If in the world each subjectivity surpasses its empirical inscription, opens itself and is in harmony with others, this is not in order to dissolve itself into the unity of a shared truth; each subjectivity remains just as much resting on its difference, open to a history, and the harmony is just as much dissonance. Because subjectivity is individual only in being universal, because its individuality is veiled universality, for the flesh the contraction of its identity will be synonymous with its openness to others and consequently will be the guarantee of a harmony. But because universality is itself only by remaining veiled, only by being dismembered by the plurality of carnal perspectives, for flesh the access to the universal means the maintenance of a distance with respect to others and is therefore also disharmony. For Merleau-Ponty, then, the relation to the other is situated beyond the congealed alternative of harmony and conflict. Merleau-Ponty thus maintains himself at an equal distance from reflective philosophy, which tends to ignore the plurality of consciousnesses in favor of the unity of spirit, and from Sartrean philosophy, which grounds the relationship with the other on a will to mastery. It is by what is most dissimilar in them that subjectivities can enter into relation, because this dissimilarity corresponds to their inscription in one same world, just as it is what is closest in them that allows them to enter into conflict, since this proximity expresses in principle a relation between distinct perspectives. Negativity, this separation of consciousnesses inherent in their worldly rootedness, is the source of positivity, just as the positivity of sense, which is never gathered beyond its differences, remains traversed by negativity. The relation with the other is indissolubly understanding and incomprehension, agreement and antagonism, the conquest of sense identical to the fortunes and risks of [294] historicity. Finally, Merleau-Ponty attacks equally the illusion of an agreement without shadows—which often survives only to hide the disagreement—and that of a radical antagonism that often hides an understanding, at least an understanding about the antagonism itself. Because we are of the same world, there is no uncrossable distance; but no convergence can advent without reserve, in both senses of the term, because in each experience the unity of the world remains reserved. There is no becoming-self except as becoming-other, no conquest of identity except as openness to others, but in such a way that the alterity always maintains itself at the heart of this openness. In short, there is no choice between empirical subject and transcendental subject. The transcendental subject completes itself only as held back in the diversity of empirical subjects. In sum, this consciousness that Merleau-Ponty takes from the Fact of intersubjectivity leads him to conceive of Being as Historicity, historicity as Being.

We then understand more clearly the relationship between the experience of the other and the "objective transcendence" of the world. As we said, we cannot posit the other and the world in exteriority in order to establish a grounding relationship between them. The other is a moment of one world that gains its unity only by giving itself to a plurality of "consciousnesses." Thus, everything proceeds from the sensible Being and from the movement by which it dimensionalizes itself. Each experience and each "subjectivity," dimensions for a set of differences within a single sense or between the senses, must themselves be situated in the "higher" dimension of intersubjectivity, which is none other than the dimension of teleology—that is, the dimension of the world in its being. In this dimension, experiences and subjectivities are articulated in their very insularity to other subjectivities, thereby mutating themselves into experiences of one *same* world, making themselves appear as lived experiences of a unique object. There is no relationship of anteriority between the other and objective transcendence; this is the same as saying that each consciousness joins together with the others, that its field belongs to an intersubjective dimension, and, on the other hand, that experience refers to the unity of one world, that is, becomes a moment of one object. Objectivity does not designate an in-itself that is based on itself and from which singular experiences, that is, appearances, would be extracted. Nor is it a construction, the correlate of a transcendental activity; objectivity is a dimension of visibility, or rather, Visibility itself as dimension. [295] Because this Visibility, around which the world is ordered, remains dimension, it merges with the givenness of an *objective* world, instead of gathering itself in the transcendence of a sense or a condition of possibility. Within every experience, by the mediation of its relationship to others, a unity of the world is drawn. But this unity is nevertheless not other than the plurality of the experiences in which it is attested. So that far from detaching itself from the world and grounding an autonomous universe of meaning, this unity gives itself first of all only as the consistency of the world, objective transcendence. The other visions "bring out the limits of our factual vision, they betray the solipsist illusion that consists in thinking that every going beyond is a surpassing accomplished by oneself" (VI 189/143). Whereas in solipsistic experience lived experience is not even singular, since it lacks a relationship to others, in the intersubjective experience, by contrast, lived experience crystallizes the ultimate Dimension of visibility; it gains its singularity on the ground of this universality and makes itself appear then as an experience or a moment of an object.

4. The Phenomenon of the Other

While it is true that the possibility of the experience of the other is rooted in the carnal existence of the world, it is still the case that the other is not a mundane thing. We must truly reach the specificity of this experience. This does not mean, as we have seen, that it is necessary to seek the other as another consciousness. On the one hand, it cannot be necessary for me to take from it what I am not myself, namely, a pure consciousness; on the other hand, the transcendence which defines the other prohibits that it be presented itself. The other is, strictly speaking, "*the originary presentation of the unpresentable*"—not in the sense of a determinate and objective presence, which would refer as a sign to a consciousness absent from our eyes because it is present to itself, but as a presence which is suitable to absence (VI 257/203; see also 292/239). Or rather, because this definition is valid as well for the perceived thing, the other is a *certain* presentation of the unpresentable; it is in and as *its body* that the other appears. Because everything proceeds from the sensible Being, including what gives the sensible Being to be seen, the problem of the other brings us back to the description of a certain visible, namely, of an [296] other flesh. Insofar as it appears, the other is not "trans-worldly," as Sartre asserted, but is on the contrary inscribed in the world; and this inscription does not contravene its identity, because by virtue of chiasm, the other makes the world appear only because it is encompassed in the world, only because it is reckoned in the visible. Nevertheless, the other is in the world only insofar as it is not elsewhere; the other cannot in fact be situated within objective space, and least of all on the same plane as perceived things.

> Where is the other in this body that I see? He is (like the meaning of the sentence) immanent in this body (one cannot detach him from it to pose him apart) and yet, more than the sum of the signs or the significations conveyed by them. He is that of which they are always the partial and non-exhaustive image—and who nonetheless is attested wholly in each of them. Always in process of an unfinished incarnation—— Beyond the objective body as the sense of the painting is beyond the canvas. (VI 263/209–10)

The other, unlike the things of the world, is animated under my eyes and unfolds a behavior. Clearly, the other manifests a unity, a cohesion, an orientation which prohibits situating it on the objective plane, which prohibits reducing it to mechanical movements. Instead of the other's presence being inferred from the similarity between its objective movements and my own movements, the presence of the other is attested to immediately in a certain modality of movement. Certain gestures are given right away and indissolubly as meaningful and as echoing my own. Thus, the body of the other presents itself as the crystallization of a living, the incarnation of a life, which is none other than its very incarnation. The body of the other is then not perceived by itself, as an object of the world, but is immediately surpassed toward the aim that it is realizing. All of the movements of the other, in their divergences, their modulations, their sudden changes of direction or orientation, which never seem haphazard, are numerous differentiations of a single dimension, or rather, of a single dimensionalization. Every singular aspect of the other's behavior is always already lived as a moment of a unique openness to the world, referred, in its very singularity, to other confirmed or possible gestures situated on an axis of cohesion or of equivalence. Just as the thing attests, in each of its "aspects," to a single principle of variation, so the other is that being whose every gesture testifies to a single style; we perceive the other as the trace of this style. One could object that the behaviors proceed [297] nevertheless from a body that, itself, must be situated on the same plane as things. But strictly speaking, this distinction does not exist. Insofar as the movements of the other are precisely behaviors, they cannot be rooted in a body that would be foreign to them, which itself would only be an object. What is valid for behavior is valid for the body itself. What is true of movement is true of immobility. Just like my own gestures, the gestures of the other cannot be situated on an objective plane, submitted to the alternative of movement and rest.[3] The movements of the other are never fully unfolded in exteriority. They do not follow one another in a jerky manner but slip into one another, hold themselves back and anticipate each other, and never unfold themselves completely; they bear witness to the unity of a power, of an "I can," and in this way are truly situated just short of the objective world. Now, because the other's movement is not unfolded in exteriority, one cannot speak, in regard to the other, of rest as coincidence with a place; one cannot speak of the other belonging to a circumscribed "here." Precisely because there are no fixed emplacements in relation to which an objective divergence would be measured, there is no movement fully exterior to itself. All "rest" is situated on the dynamic axis of a behavior—it is a "pause," an interrupted movement rather than the negation of movement; rest is a mode of crystallization of an "I can." And the body of the other itself, in its "materiality," attests to this dynamic of dimensionalization, of the unfolding of a world. As Merleau-Ponty notes elsewhere, instead of gestures being determined by the physical structure of the body, the structure, on the contrary, bears witness to a harmony, a coherence with the observed behaviors, which seem to be its crystallization or trace. There is not, then, on the one hand, an objective body and, on

3. "My body is never *in movement perspectivisch*, as are the other things—— It is not *in rest* either like some of them. It is beneath objective rest and movement" (VI 278/224–25).

the other, movements which would animate it, but truly a unique visible which, in each point of itself, is given as differentiation and concentration of a certain mode of openness to the world, as *incarnation* in the active sense.

Thus the comparison with the sentence is justified. One could say that the phenomenon of the other is characterized by its "diacritical" structure. Just as the reality of the signifier proceeds from the oppositions and the kinships in which it participates, so that of the [298] body of the other is born of the incessant differentiation of behaviors. The body unfolds coherent behaviors only because these first give rise to the body. From then on, to the degree that the other is an other flesh, the other does not distinguish itself from movements through which it is manifested; its invisibility does not carry it beyond its visibility and thus is preserved as invisibility. If the other is "more than the sum of signs" which are visible, it is nothing other than them, nothing *other* than this flesh, and it is to this degree that the flesh can surpass itself as a simple object and bear witness to a presence. If each gesture gives to the other only a "partial and non-exhaustive image," the other attests to itself nevertheless "wholly in each of them" (VI 263/209). The dimensionality that the other unfolds, or rather that the other is, subsists only as differences, that is, as the behaviors in which the other advents—just as, in the sentence, the sense preserves its richness only because it is held back in the signs that allow it to be understood. The other is not this presence that would be elsewhere, indicated by its visible gestures; the other is between them, at their jointure, immersed in this living body, possessed by the behaviors that it possesses. There is therefore no body of the other *and* the consciousness whose body it would be, but a single flesh, the indissoluble unity of a principle of cohesion and the differentiated terms between which it is developed. As Merleau-Ponty says, "the soul is the hollow of the body, the body is the distention of the soul. The soul adheres to the body as their signification adheres to the cultural things, whose reverse or other side it is" (VI 286/233). The soul is not the other of the body, this absolute non-being adhering to a being that would be plenitude; it is "hollow" and not "empty," decompression at the heart of the body, divergence and difference in its mass, transparency *of* this thickness. Soul and body are the obverse and reverse of the flesh; the body is the thickness that the soul requires in order to hollow itself out, the differentiation with which it sustains its identity.

It is clear that the other cannot be localized in the heart of the world before me, situated on the same plane as the visibles in the strict sense. As we have said, insofar as it is the crystallization of a dimension, the perceived thing itself can never be strictly circumscribed; it is never frontally observable, "never stays in the hand," remains far away and, as it were, atmospheric. What is valid for the thing will be valid a fortiori for the other, because the other is the one who makes the things appear. The dimension, [299] remaining concealed in the visible thing, gives cohesion to the presence of the other and finally appears itself in the interstices of the other's behavior. Because dimension finds in the other a more differentiated and, in some way, more fluid element, it gives itself differently than as a visible thing and gives the body of the other as seeing body. Thus, the diffuse character of perceived presence defines, all by itself, the presence of the other. Like the thing but better than it, the other opens the world and cannot be strictly situated within it. One must say of the appearance of the other what Merleau-Ponty says of my own body: "it is not *elsewhere*, but one cannot say that it is *here* or *now* in the sense that objects are" (VI 193/147). The other never presents itself frontally but surrounds and envelops me, circumvents me, its presence remaining diffuse like a haunting. I am certain that the other is there, but this "there" does not accept any determinate place, and cannot be confused with a localized object. Specifically, the other is really over there, on the side of the world, because it appears; but insofar as the other is for itself a "here," it flows back toward my here and inscribes itself in my openness to the world. The other is just as much on my side as on the side of the world, enveloping the visible that envelops it. The other is a "presence"; it inhabits the world, radiates in it, invests it everywhere, always beyond the point where I fix it, rather with me than in front of me, and nevertheless distinct, at a distance. The other is "almost" in the world, an imminent thing—because, as a seer, the other is at its closest to me, but is at the same time at its farthest away, that is, ungraspable, escaping all frontal grasping. At the margin or reverse of my field, the other never truly descends into it without nevertheless merging with me; the other is this "double errancy," at once close and far away, which comes to decenter my perspective on the world. It is, Merleau-Ponty adds, "always a *little further* than the spot I look at . . . —*Posed* on the visible, like a bird, clinging to the visible, not *in* it. And yet in chiasm with it" (VI 314/261). With the appearance of the other, I am present in some way at the advent of the carnal chiasm; around the other, the becoming-world of a flesh and the becoming-flesh of a world cross each other. The visible decenters itself, runs away, escapes itself, but in favor of an appearance in its heart, that is, in favor of another visible. The other is not integrated in the visible as are the other things, and yet the other does not go far away; it is, [300] Merleau-Ponty says, "overhanging" ["*en porte-à-faux*"].[4] "Overhanging" does not characterize an objective relationship between two visibles on the same plane, the body of the other and what it perceives. On the contrary, insofar as a certain visible testifies to this overhang, it gives itself as the body of the other. In other words, the other is born from the overhang itself; the other is not a mundane object, nor is it another thing, but a divergence and an articulation, a hold on the world and an impact of the world. The relation of the other to the world and the style of openness that it unfolds precede somehow its corporeal presence and that of the field that it inhabits. The other and its world are born together around a certain accent, around a certain dissonance at the heart of the spectacle. The other separates itself [*s'écarter*] from the world in a distance that is nevertheless not objectifiable, which is measureless because it is not sustained by any positivity. That is why the other is nothing other than this very divergence; the other gives itself only as the axis of a look, a line of flight at the heart of the sensible, as that crumbling of the world that however never goes as far as the emptiness of another consciousness. Thus, emerging suddenly into my "solipsistic" world, but overhanging in relation to it, the other produces a displacement, a decentering at the heart of my relation to the world. The other is inscribed at the heart of my flesh—too close to the world to escape me, but too close to me not to break the closure of my experience—winning over to its favor the carnal openness in which it nevertheless remains enveloped. The other's overhang proceeds from mine, because the other is born from the depth of the object and is never unfolded in front of me; but in return the other comes to emphasize it by presenting, on its behalf, the dimensions that dissimulated the object for me.

Thus, the appearance of the other is above all the ordeal of a divergence, of a dissonance at the heart of my visible. The overhang that characterizes the other is finally reconceived as the transformation of the visible itself; just as the carnal self is itself only by forgetting itself in favor of the world,

---

4. "The sensibility of the others is 'the other side' of their aesthesiological body. And I can surmise this other side, *Nichturpräsentierbar,* through the articulation of the other's body on *my sensible,* an articulation that does not empty me, that is not a hemorrhage of my 'consciousness,' but on the contrary redoubles me with an alter ego. The other is born in the body (of the other) by an overhanging of that body" (VI 286/233).

so the other will not be other than this world but truly a certain modality of its appearance. The other is, like me, dimensionalizing, the crystallization of the very element of visibility, and the dimensions that it unfolds can therefore be apprehended only right up against the [301] world that they make appear. The other is open only as something that opens and is thus seized only from the world whose openness it unfolds. The openness that the appearance of the other in the world represents is not other than the world that it articulates and toward which it transports me: "The visible-seer (for me, for the others) is moreover not a psychic something, nor a behavior of vision, but a perspective, *or better;* the world itself with a certain coherent deformation" (VI 315/262). Thus, I see, for example, other looks only insofar as "they sketch out a dis-position of the table, linking its parts together for a new compresence" (S 23/15–16). It is right down against the lawn in front of me that I apprehend the impact of green on the vision of the other, as it is on the basis of the music that I penetrate the other's musical emotion. The sensible, as we have seen, never presents itself in the form of a completed individual, but remains the crystallization of a dimension, the principle of equivalence; each sensible plunges into the thickness of the world, is a ray of the world, that is, institutes a secret equivalence. For vision, things are not unfolded *partes extra partes;* they sketch an interiority, agree among themselves, announce me to myself. From this moment on, the thing is not completely homogeneous to the world of which it is a part, since it is what opens as much as what is opened, already "overhanging"; it is next to the point where I seek to grasp it and slips toward the others, radiating instead of being strictly localized. The appearance of the other only declares this decentering. The secret equivalence of the world is doubled by another axis of deformation, and things respond to each other according to another dimension, "a little more" visible or, at least, visible otherwise than as the dimension according to which I perceive them. This possibility is included in the givenness of the sensible thing; in its depth, it tacitly contracts a unity and already sends my image back to me. Its presence is the promise of other visions; it possesses, in its heart, the wherewithal to crystallize other dimensions, to present other absents. The unity of my perceptual field, which was merged with its differentiated unfolding, shows itself even more to be a new principle of equivalence, to be a novel perceptive style which decompresses its thickness; with the other, the sensible rises toward its visibility, acquires, in its very differences, a surplus of unity, of cohesion, of transparency. With [302] the other, the thing stops being the pole where the self encounters only a pale reflection of itself; in its very alterity, it sends my image back to me, it announces a me which is other. It is no longer only sensible *by* the dimension that it incarnates, but is in some fashion sensible *for* this dimension. There is no other as "consciousness," as a principle of a synthesis, nor are there atomic sensibles, but another mode of articulation, a new axis of cohesion around which the other and the world are constituted together. That is why one must not distinguish the other and me as positive entities. Rather one must recognize as ultimate a visibility, a givenness of the world at the heart of which we give birth to one another (see VI 274/221): we are different, because the world does not gather itself beyond its thickness, because the world remains what "there is"; and yet we are identical, because the world's thickness is based on the dimensions, the subjectivities which are inscribed in it. The entire difficulty therefore lies in understanding that the world can involve degrees of unity while remaining sensible and preserving the invisibility of the invisible all the while. The world has certainly never been unfolded in full exteriority, but the appearance of the other corresponds to a surplus of interiority; the allusion of each sensible to every other is made less tacit, and the world rises up from its thickness toward a line of flight where the invisible in the strict sense is already indicated. The visibility of the visible splits itself off fugitively from the world where it was first hiding, even if it is still in order to flow back immediately toward the visible. Correlatively, thanks to the other, I appear more clearly to my own eyes. While in immediate perception, the sensible sends back to me a weakened image of myself, the appearance of the other brings with it a decentering thanks to which I can perceive myself:

> We no longer have before us only the look without a pupil, the plate
> glass of the things with that feeble reflection, the phantom of ourselves
> they evoke by designating a place among themselves whence we see
> them: henceforth through other eyes we are for ourselves fully visible;
> that lacuna where our eyes, our back, lie is filled, filled still by the visible
> of which we are not the titulars. (VI 188/143)

While on the sensible level, the world exhibits dimensions as its own rather than as mine; but with the other the world comes to open itself onto its very visibility and, consequently, makes these [303] dimensions appear as my own. In other terms, while, on the "solipsistic" plane, the visible hides the invisible as that which it needs to make itself visible, with the other the visible gives itself as that which the invisible needs in order to appear itself. The differences at the heart of which the thing was constituted as the secret principle of cohesion come to be carried out of or beyond themselves; the thing is no longer differentiated *in* itself but truly *of* itself. By this divergence, it closes itself back into a new unity, sketches the domain of a "for" which nevertheless is not based on a "self," which does not mean the closure of the thing in a meaning, because it still fulfills itself with visibility. Thus the closure of originary sensibility is broken, and the thing can reach the rank of object.

From this it follows that there is a full continuity between the thing and the other, and that finally the pertinence of a distinction between them must be called into question. Even if this distinction has a descriptive validity, it could never have an ultimate ontological meaning or cover over an originary duality between beings. The philosophy of the flesh has the consequence of making the thing and the other appear as abstract moments of a deeper presence, as abstract moments of an originary fabric of visibility that accepts within it several modes of crystallization. In fact, there is no thing that is fully unfolded in exteriority; all things exhibit a style, are already a manner of articulating the world and of making it be seen, are already a manner of "behaving." Things "speak to me of others." But, correlatively, it is not possible that the other gives itself as pure interiority; the other is still a mode of equivalence, a manner of radiating around the self, a general style of the world. There is no world that does not indicate a mode of formation and finally a self. But there is no self that does not outline a world by dissimulating itself in it. This is why Merleau-Ponty rejects the principle of a distinction between the thing and the other:

> Describe this experience of qualified non-being.
> Before *the other* is, the things are such non-beings, divergencies——
> There is an *Einfühlung* and a lateral relation with the thing no less than with the other: to be sure the things are not interlocutors, the *Einfühlung* that gives them gives them as mute—but precisely: they are variants of the successful *Einfühlung*. Like madmen or animals they are *quasi-companions*. They are lifted from my substance, thorns in my flesh.
> (VI 234/180–181)

The world is a silent *logos;* after the fashion of the other, it speaks to me already. But the other speaks to me just as the [304] world gives itself, that is, in a way that is still figurative. Here it clearly appears that the opposition between perception of the thing and the experience of the other is surpassed in favor of a unique mode of donation that Merleau-Ponty characterizes as *Einfühlung*. We have noted above that experience of the other informs that of the thing. On the level of *Phenomenology of Perception,* it is still the case that a displacement remains between perception and the relation to the other; the description there is carried out under the objectivistic framework in which the thing is reconceived in such a way that the transcendence of the other is finally missed. In *The Visible and the Invisible,* on the contrary, the notion of flesh allows the grounding of the unity of these two donations, that is, the reconceiving of the openness to the thing outside of all subjective polarity, at such a level of depth that the transcendence of the other can inscribe itself there. The philosophy of the flesh leads us to situate the world just short of interiority but beyond exteriority; this philosophy leads us to conceive the world as the concretion of a universal self who, by virtue of this universality, presents itself only as absent and is destined consequently to pluralize itself. There is nothing that is on the side of the things in the strict sense which does not already express a way of being. But there is no single existence which is subjective in the strict sense, which is not dissimulated or hidden from itself and others—that is, which does not make itself world in order to make the world appear. All presence is already "self," but all "consciousness" absents itself in the form of a worldly style. There is therefore no me, no other, no world but a single universal fabric where I and the world, things and others, are mingled, encroaching on each other in a confusion that is inextricable in principle, like so many differentiations and exhibitions of one same sensible Being.

In other words, it is the principle of an originary opposition between nature and culture which here finds itself surpassed: "everything is cultural in us (our *Lebenswelt* is 'subjective') (our perception is cultural-historical) and everything is natural in us (even the cultural rests on the polymorphism of the wild Being)" (VI 307/253). Their relationship is therefore chiasmic: the natural world always envelops the cultural world, which nevertheless always expresses and envelops the natural world. There is no object that does not announce a modality of forming the world, which does not refer to a body and finally to a history, which is not an expression; in the sensible world, the entire field of culture is deposited. But for the [305] same reasons, there is no cultural being which does not finally remain a mode of reworking of the sensible, where its transcendence and opacity are preserved, and which does not then remain "natural." The flesh designates exactly the point of articulation of nature and culture, of their passage into each other. The perception of the body of the other corresponds to a certain general deformation of the spectacle; in the body of the other, the world begins to reach expression. That is why Merleau-Ponty characterizes the body of the other as "the first cultural object" (PHP 401/348). It is this space of the natural environment where the horizon of a culture is primed. This is the point of the spectacle where allusion, the general participation of the world, begins to be gathered in order to reach itself. The other is not a consciousness but truly the birth of expression in the world; as a cultural quasi-object, the other primes what art and language will accomplish. But this means that no more than the other, art and language cannot be understood as the sign of a consciousness possessing meaning in transparency; they remain modes of articulation of the world itself, coherent cuts made into its thickness. The mode of existence of the other is that of the work of art, but the work of art does not give itself otherwise than the other.

15 Desire

1. Desire as a Work of Flesh

[307] The strength of Merleau-Ponty's approach rests in the fact that it starts with the meaning of the other. The other is alter ego; he is nothing other than me, he is not an other me than me, he is only "a me which is other" (PM 187/135), that is, the me insofar as it is still other to itself. Consciousness is in principle unique, and an actual plurality of consciousnesses strictly speaking makes no sense. Every other consciousness, insofar as it is genuinely consciousness, merges with my own; such is the truth of transcendental idealism. But, on the other hand, insofar as it is sensible and carnal, consciousness is other to itself, decentered or dispossessed of itself; it reaches itself only through its own reflection in the world or in the other. *There is* the other; such is the truth of realism. But the other is not an other subject; it is only the unique openness to the world insofar as the openness is separated from itself by the world that the openness advents. Thus the egos [*les moi*] are distinct only because they are not completely themselves. Intersubjectivity is the identity of the "me" insofar as it is synonymous with its difference, with its self-divergence. There is no me and the other, but only *the experience* of the other, the intersubjective fabric where sense is disjoined within itself, where sense multiplies itself in making itself world. In this experience, neither of these two is still "me," which is why they can be differentiated. And yet, they are not something else, which is why they can recognize each other. The relation to the other must be situated "higher" than numerical difference—me and the other are a single "me"—and yet "lower" than specific or spiritual unity. Insofar as it is flesh, the [308] "me" escapes itself and is made plural in itself. The alterity of the alter ego does not conceal a relation *between* already constituted egos, nor does it designate the property of a subsistent ego; it is the alterity of the ego to itself, an alterity that is not the negation of the ego but truly its only mode of completion as carnal ego. Thus, like the world, the other reflects my image back to me, but what it reflects back is an image that is less obscure. In this experience a commencement of appropriation advents. If the me is made other, it still does not know itself, and it is as

itself that it is not known. The "me" is then extracted from the other, recognizes itself and reaches itself in this presence which surrounds it, sees itself at the periphery of itself, is haunted by its own self.

Desire extends and completes the immediate perception of the other in the world; it is the first attempt at self-appropriation by the intermediary of the other, that is, the first attempt at the appropriation of the dimensions of visibility. Insofar as it is this appropriation, desire is truly the birthplace of expression:

> For the first time also, my movements no longer proceed unto the things
> to be seen, to be touched, or unto my own body occupied in seeing and
> touching them, but they address themselves to the body in general and
> for itself (whether it be my own or that of another), because for the first
> time, through the other body, I see that, in its coupling with the flesh
> of the world, the body contributes more than it receives, adding to the
> world that I see the treasure necessary for what the other body sees. For
> the first time, the body no longer coupling itself up with the world, it
> clasps another body, applying [itself to it] carefully with its whole exten-
> sion, tirelessly forming with its hands the strange statue which in its
> turn gives everything it receives; the body is lost outside of the world
> and its goals, fascinated by the unique occupation of floating in Being
> with another life, of making itself the outside of its inside and the
> inside of its outside. And henceforth movement, touch, vision, applying
> themselves to the other and to themselves, return toward their source
> and, in the patient labor of desire, begin the paradox of expression.
> (VI 189/143–44)

With desire, expression is born such as it will complete itself in language, namely, as the inscription of the invisible in a flesh other than that of the world. In desire, the self is announced to itself through the other flesh, it lives their separation as a tearing of self, and then it attempts to reconcile itself in the other. Nevertheless, this appropriation that makes itself active in desire is at work on the sensible level as such; in originary sensibility, the self [309] already seeks itself even while it misses itself just as much, since it is separated from itself by the thickness of the world and remains errant vision. Only with the relation to the other is the "narcissism" at work in sensibility unfolded; if in the other the self still misses itself, it is in some sense as itself that it is missed, so that in the relation to the other, the horizon of unity is announced, a higher appropriation is primed. With the other, self-presence gains in proximity and expression gains in activity.

One cannot, therefore, oppose a layer of pure passivity, which would correspond to sensibility, and a properly active layer, which would appear with desire. There is a continuity between perception and desire; both must be conceived as moments of an expression which, beginning with the perceptual level, is already active to the degree that it unfolds dimensions—and which, on the plane of the relationship to the other, is still passive because, in desire itself, the other fails and the self does not know itself in it.

It is the case, then, that the perception of the other can give rise to desire. In desire, the other loses its constitutive distance, and the separation is suddenly lived as a lack of identity. In desire, self-absence attempts to make itself self-presence. Desire is therefore truly self-desire, fundamentally narcissistic. And yet, this self is not the negation of the other, because the act by which the self attempts to seize itself in the other is not distinguished from the act by which the other reaches itself, because the "entrance into self" is just as much "leaving of self." It is rather a matter of a unique advent where a single "self," a single sense, attempts to conquer itself, to possess itself in the element of a difference where it does not know itself. In desire, the two "consciousnesses" "seek a fulfillment which will be identically the same for the two of them, as the sensible world is for everyone" (S 24/17). The self joins back up with itself, therefore, not against the other, but *with* the other; it is together that they reach themselves. Also, there is no alternative between narcissism and the openness to the other, between a "concupiscent" and a "pure" love; the "identity" which I seek, by means of the other, to confer upon myself stops being mine to the degree in which it is fulfilled. It becomes just as much the identity of the other; or rather, when desire blossoms, there is a fulfillment common to both. To desire a flesh is not to ignore the other, because in this desire, the flesh surpasses itself as sensible flesh in the strict sense. Because the self is generality, by becoming itself it will pass into its other; by opening itself to the other in order to meet up with itself again, it will abandon itself just [310] as much to a life which is common to them both. There is therefore a fundamental reciprocity of desire or, at the very least, of its fulfillment; by remaining oriented toward itself, each one of the two participates without knowing it in a common work. By rising to itself through the mediation of the other, each one reaches a "self" which is neither its own nor other. The self is truly insular only to the degree that it is not itself; by being fulfilled, desire primes a surpassing of this insularity. It is here again a matter of understanding that desire, the dimension of the intersubjective inner frame, precedes the presence of me and the other; insofar as there is desire, neither one nor the other is itself, and it is rather in and by desire that they become themselves, that is, make themselves one alone. The "self," which existed only as the difference of consciousnesses present to each other as unpresentable, begins to be interiorized, to gather itself, to disincarnate itself; the exteriority of the other, where there is only a presentiment of my interiority, reaches transparency and, in desire, I possess myself a little better by getting a little closer to the other. In short, because individuality is veiled universality, the unveiling of self in the egoism of desire is raised to the universal and is thus just as much advent of the other as of itself. Thus, in desire, a new dimension is born, that of "sexualization." Desire does not proceed from a preexisting sexual difference; this sexual difference advents in desire, as the share of identity which is conquered in it. Each one surpasses itself in desire as strictly sensible flesh, without there being, nevertheless, any identification in the universality of sense; the advent of each one occurs as man or as woman. The dimension of intersubjectivity is unfolded according to another difference, at the heart of which its unity is made more pregnant, namely, as sexual difference. While difference in some way predominates on the "solipsistic" level, a difference which dissimulates identity—under the immediate form of the world—instead of unveiling it, sexual difference gives itself immediately as the reverse of an identity, as the condition of a fusion, and the sexual poles give themselves as necessary moments of a communication: "The I–other relation to be conceived . . . as complementary roles one of which cannot be occupied without the other being also: masculinity implies femininity, etc." (VI 274/220–21). Here Merleau-Ponty joins up with a discovery of psychoanalysis: sexualization cannot be considered an intrinsic determination. It is produced within a relation, as a role or place; it must be conceived [311] as becoming rather than as an acquired determination. There are no men and women, but a single axis of Desire within which these two poles are constituted, thus following out the divergence which is necessary to preserve its own life. Sexuality is a modality of access to the other, that is, to oneself; in this originary expression, the self gains an identity for the first time.

It is still the case that desire is nothing but the priming of expression or rather, strictly speaking, the articulation of a perceptual life and of an expressive life; in desire, the perception of the other begins to make itself language, but language that is still mute, the language of the body, within which the splitting of me and the other—that is, the splitting of each one in relation to itself—is ultimately maintained. In desire, I attempt to coincide with this me whose flesh is the imminent ordeal, to join back up with me where I miss myself, but I can reach myself again only through this invisible of which the other's body is, as it were, the place or the trace, so that I just as much escape myself. The self-appropriation through the mediation of the other opens out onto the experience of a body where the consciousness that I wanted to arouse in that body finally absents itself. In this way, as Sartre has shown, desire is indeed characterized, in Merleau-Ponty's opinion, by antagonism and failure. I thought I could find myself again, realize myself in the other and fulfill, thanks to it, this reflexivity that the relationship to the world did not allow me to realize. Yet I remain alone, facing a world where the other figures only as an object. In desire, the appropriation of the other as self, that is, the appropriation of me in the other, is still only imminent. Certainly desire realizes, in rare moments of intensity, a transparent self where we stop distinguishing ourselves and where, consequently, the world stops resisting. In the embrace, the other is disincarnated, and with the "resistance" of the other's body the opacity of the world disappears; thus is outlined the impalpable place of sense, and exteriority is fleetingly mutated into harmonious unity. At the heart of carnal contact, there can suddenly be the presentiment of the unity of a transcendental subject, the transparency of a world reconciled with itself. But this harmony is still contentless, bereft of a body which is its own; sense is still carried only by the thickness of fleshes. The promise of fulfillment in desire is finally disappointed; the other makes itself absence again, interposes between itself and me the thickness of its body, and the world regains its transcendence. If desire aims essentially at harmony, it is also and indissolubly the experience of disappointment. [312] Sartre, on the other hand, does not recognize the genuine meaning of this failure. It is not because the other is for me an object, nor because I cannot be myself except in being a pure subject, that desire fails, that the aim of possession which animates desire remains disappointed. It is, on the contrary, because expression in the relation of desire remains unfulfilled that the other remains incarnated, that is, invisible, and that the aim of possession turns out then to be unrealizable. The failure of desire in Sartre only confirms the antagonism which characterizes the relation between consciousnesses, each one of them being subjected to the abstract opposition of subject and object. Desire is not conceived on its own terms. Sartre always reconceives it either just short of itself, as the passivity of a seduced flesh, or truly beyond itself, where desire merges with an aim of mastery, because the activity can correspond only to the advent of a pure consciousness before which the other is doomed to be degraded to the rank of an object. In contrast, for Merleau-Ponty the antagonism and failure of appropriation are moments of a harmony which, insofar as it is still carnal strictly speaking, cannot realize itself fully. Desire is already speech addressed to the other, but silently. Just as in perception the self was unknown to itself in the world, so in desire it is unknown to itself and announces itself at the same time, through the common experience of corporeity. In the embrace, the body of the other is no longer entirely a body, as my body surmounts its own exteriority and rises back toward its source. At the contact of the two bodies, an interiority is sketched such that they are no longer entirely beside each other, *against* one another, but already one "in" the other, consequently already "consciousnesses." Thus there are not two bodies and two consciousnesses, with a body before a consciousness on each side. There is desire as inchoative expression, a common inner frame where at once each one is rejoined, reaches itself in the other, and remains flesh against the body of the other—where, correlatively, the dimensionality that remained still veiled in the other's immediate presence shows through for itself for an instant, thus sketching the future of a pure expression. Desire is in reality neither corporeal nor intellectual—which both boil down to the same thing, because the imprisonment of consciousness in one's body is a ruse of the will to mastery—but properly carnal; it is a modality of an irreducible intersubjectivity, already a work of meaning at the heart of corporeity, knowledge in sentiment, expression.

2. Psychoanalysis and Phenomenology

[313] This short passage from *The Visible and the Invisible* (VI 274/ 220–221) converges with Merleau-Ponty's declarations concerning the relation between phenomenology and psychoanalysis. In fact, throughout his work Merleau-Ponty never stopped returning to the genuine meaning of psychoanalysis to validate the importance of its discoveries, in opposition to a constrictive, that is, intellectualist, conception of consciousness. Especially in *Phenomenology of Perception*, at the level of the analysis of desire, he reaches the idea of an intentionality which is not the possession of a *cogitatum* but the immediate relation of a body to a body, "intentionality within Being" (VI 298/244; see also VI 291/238, PHP 283/245). By proposing, under the term *libido*, the irreducibility of this intentionality, psychoanalysis informs phenomenology and confirms what remains latent in Husserl by rejecting the idealist temptation. Also, as Merleau-Ponty

notes in his preface to Dr. Hesnard's book on Freud, "Freudian thought . . . confirms phenomenology in its description of a consciousness that is not so much knowledge or representation as investment; it brings to phenomenology a wealth of concrete examples that add weight to what it has been able to say in general of the relations of man with the world and of the interhuman bond."[1] Conversely, however, the Freudian discovery becomes fully significant only in the light of phenomenology, to the degree that phenomenology liberates it from the substantialism that marks psychoanalysis originally. In fact, a restrictive conception of desire as the ultimate substrate of existence, specific energy, drive, leads one to preserve intact the plane of pure consciousness rather than denouncing the opposition between what is and is not representation; characterized by its autonomy, the unconscious is the other of consciousness that does not call into question the validity of consciousness. Because Freud is still dependent on a Cartesian conception of consciousness, he is led to situate what exceeds the frame of representation as such outside of it, in a place that, though it is psychical, is no less dependent on an energetics. Psychoanalysis can then fully inform phenomenology only if informed by phenomenology in turn; we can conceive consciousness as "investment" only on the condition that [314] the latter be understood in a wider sense than the sexual drive as Freud understood it. In energetical and substantialist metaphors, through the conviction of a univocal determination by desire, psychoanalysis has a presentiment of the archaeological domain that phenomenology explores on its own account. Even though many of Freud's formulations give credit to the idea that sexuality would be the infrastructure of existence, that "every existence would have a sexual signification," his true intention, according to Merleau-Ponty, is to show that sexuality is enmeshed with the other dimensions of existence, is a modality of being-in-the-world— in short, that "every sexual phenomenon has an existential significance" (PHP 185/159). Because Freud did not have access to a sufficiently wide conception of consciousness, he fell short of the intuition that motivated him. Therefore, if psychoanalysis is truly a path toward the discovery of flesh, we can say that the philosophy of flesh represents the very truth of Freud, that is, "the condition without which psychoanalysis remains an-

---

1. M. Merleau-Ponty, preface to *L'œuvre de Freud et son importance pour le monde moderne,* by A. Hesnard (Paris: Payot, 1960), 5; trans. A. L. Fisher as "Phenomenology and Psychoanalysis: Preface to Hesnard's *L'Oeuvre de Freud,*" in *Merleau-Ponty and Psychology,* ed. K. Hoeller (Atlantic Highlands, N.J.: Humanities Press, 1993), 67.

thropology" (VI 321/267; see also 324/270). In fact, in Merleau-Ponty's eyes, desire must not be taken restrictively as the work of sexuality, of a specific energy, but as "search of the external in the internal, and of the internal in the external, that is, as a global and universal power of incorporation" (RC 178/198). In the same way, the true sense of the Freudian unconscious does not reside in the assignation of a place characterized by specific representations ruled by determinate laws; the unconscious merges with the carnal openness that makes something appear only by remaining unaware of what appears, only by misrecognizing itself in the form of an appearing world. Thus,

> a philosophy of the flesh finds itself in opposition to any interpretation of the unconscious in terms of "unconscious representations," a tribute paid by Freud to the psychology of his day. The unconscious is sensibility itself, since sensibility is not the intellectual representation of "what" is sensed, but a dispossession of ourselves in favor of it, an opening toward that which we do not have to think in order that we may recognize it. (RC 178/198)

By conceiving the unconscious as the other of consciousness, Freud oscillated between an organic approach—in order to preserve this alterity—and a psychical approach, in order to guarantee the signifying character of the manifestations [315] of the unconscious. The articulation between the drive and its representatives, between force and sense, would then remain incomprehensible. Now, the unconscious designates not a character affecting certain representations but what defines sensibility; it is not outside of consciousness but at the heart of it. It is only a matter of no longer understanding consciousness as an active power of representation but truly as a carnal openness, as the "indivision" of sensibility. Insofar as it opens onto *some thing,* perception remains necessarily blind to itself, "unconscious"; it is unaware of itself in the world to which it gives rise. If consciousness were conscious of itself throughout, if it did not carry any opacity, it would not be consciousness of anything and would then disappear into the unconscious, as the absence of all presence. The unconscious is the "*punctum caecum*" of consciousness, this level according to which the world is unfolded, in relation to which are measured divergences, differences, and which cannot then itself be perceived. The unconscious is on the side of the world rather than at the center of a psychism; it is between things as the pivot or the inner frame around which their phenomenality is constituted. It is synonymous with the dimension: "the unconscious is to be sought not at the bottom of ourselves, behind the back of our 'consciousness,' but in front of us, as articulations of our field" (VI 234/180; see also 243/189, 308/254). Unconscious because they give themselves only as the world they articulate, the dimensions represent not a negation of consciousness but truly its originary condition; around them, in them, the world appears. Precisely because they are crystallized in the thickness of the world, the dimensions do not need to be thought in order to be possessed; because they are well known, they remain unknown. As the structure of the openness to the world, the dimension is in some way too close to itself to possess itself, to become object; it is at the same time within flesh and far away in the depth of the world, at the same time familiar and strange. The unconscious is truly synonymous with the carnal opening, beyond the opposition between the organic and the psychical. It is organic, if you like, because no flesh is reached in transparency but rather remains invaded by the world. And yet the unconscious is meaningful because the flesh refers back to itself, because the world owes its consistency to the dimensions it articulates.

Throughout his analysis of desire, Freud demonstrates the originary character of the relationship to the other; it is on this ground that psychical identity is structured across a series of [316] identifications.[2] Nevertheless, because he depends on a psychology of Cartesian inspiration, Freud does not call into question the approach to the psyche understood as an insular entity, as a substance. Whereas the structure of desire could reveal to him what phenomenology discovers of its own accord at the level of the relationship to the world—namely, the originarily open and nonsubstantial character of consciousness—Freud does not reconsider his representation of the psyche as a reality closed on itself, where "*sites* can be circumscribed." Even while it is woven from the network of intersubjective relationships, the Freudian unconscious remains a solipsistic concept.[3] In

2. Even more than the Schelerian theory of psychical non-differentiation, Freudian psychoanalysis and its Lacanian developments feed Merleau-Ponty's approach to intersubjectivity as an originary reality irreducible to a relationship between insular subjectivities. See, for example, "The Child's Relations with Others."
3. As Erwin Straus remarks in *Vom Sinn der Sinne* (Berlin: Springer Verlag, 1956), 44; trans. J. Needleman as *The Primary World of Senses: A Vindication of Sensory Experience* (London: Free Press of Glencoe, 1963), 16.

short, we do not know if the unconscious should be understood as content or as relation—or rather, Freud's concepts do not allow the dimensions of content and relation to be articulated. Now, just when we reconceive it as dimension, this alternative turns out to be abstract; the unconscious is identically a mode of openness to the world and an axis of relationship to others. In every perception, insofar as a dimension is hidden there, the unity of a flesh which transcends the plurality of empirical subjects is sketched; the level according to which the world is unfolded outlines a modality of openness to others and carries perception away to the very place of the other. That by which objects are possible is also that by which a community is possible, a community that precedes the cleavage of insular subjects. The unconscious is between things "as the interval of the trees between the trees, or as their common level. It is the *Urgemeinschaftung* of our intentional life, the *Ineinander* of the others in us and of us in them" (VI 234/180); it is the hinge around which the reciprocal envelopment of self and others occurs.

This approach to the unconscious permits Merleau-Ponty to throw new light on certain central themes of psychoanalysis, and he leaves no room to doubt that *The Visible and the Invisible* would have laid the foundations for the "ontological psychoanalysis" he calls for in opposition to an existential psychoanalysis (VI 323/270). As soon as [317] the unconscious is reconceived on the basis of the indivision of sensibility, that is, as originary symbolism of the flesh, one cannot be satisfied with a determinist approach to its effects. These effects do not depend on a causal determination, and the unconscious could never be understood as a force blindly printing its mark on lived experiences or behaviors. One is led to this simplification only to the degree that one starts from its cleavage with representative life in the strict sense, from the cleavage that ultimately throws us back to the side of corporeal existence. In fact, if perception rests on an unconscious dimension, then the unconscious itself is perception; the blindness to itself that characterizes it does not imply a blind relation to the world and does not take back from it all signifying power. It is true that the dimension remains veiled and that, in this way, the articulation of the field, just like the modalities of behavior, is neither the object of a representation nor deliberate. But this does not mean that the subject depends on it as on a cause, since all carnal experience is precisely intuition of a level and not blind submission to nature. Within perception, the unconscious escapes, but the unconscious is there as a means for flesh to belong to itself and for the world to unveil itself as such. Merleau-Ponty demonstrates this in a note devoted to the status of "characters" in psychoanalysis:

> Superficial interpretation of Freudianism: he is a sculptor because he is anal, because the feces are already clay, molding, etc.
>
> But the feces are not the *cause:* if they were, everybody would be sculptors.
>
> The feces give rise to a character (*Abschau*) only if the subject lives in them in such a way as to find in them a dimension of being——
>
> It is not a question of renewing empiricism (feces imprinting a certain character on the child). It is a question of understanding that the relationship with feces is in the child a concrete ontology. . . .
>
> In other words to be anal *explains* nothing: for, to be so, it is necessary to have the ontological capacity (= capacity to take a being as representative of Being). (VI 323/269–70)

Thus, an authentic approach to fixation, to regression, to neurosis or psychosis cannot consist in exhibiting a univocal determination of representation or of behavior by a fragment of the obscurely deposited and insistent lived experience. It is rather a matter of showing each time how a being or a region of being is invested with an ontological power, is the bearer of a tacit symbolism, "*accentuated* as [318] an emblem of Being" (VI 323/270). It is a question of demonstrating, through the subjugations of the flesh, a work of phenomenalization. One can no longer maintain, then, the opposition between the normal and the pathological as the opposition between a life where the control of representation dominates and a life subordinated to the injunctions of the drive. If normality is not intellectual life, or rather if intellectual life is fed by the polymorphism of originary sensibility, then pathology does not conceal the reign of the drive but again represents a mode of putting the world into form. If, in pathology, a being is invested with a singular power, this does not mean that the subject becomes dependent on a biology or a mechanism, because this accentuation of a being is still a mode of openness to Being, of dimensionalization. Dimensions, Merleau-Ponty notes, "are the armature of that 'invisible world' which, with speech, begins to impregnate all the things we see—as the 'other' space, for the schizophrenic, takes possession of the sensorial and visible space" (VI 234/180). This proposition goes beyond comparison: in every experience, of which schizophrenic experience is in some way emblematic, the other world comes to haunt this world, the invisible impregnates the visible, and it does so even before speech occurs, from originary experience onward. *Every* experience is the articulation of the world according to a certain system of equivalences, the imminence of an invisible. As in the schizophrenic, the unconscious inhabits the world, situating itself outside. Moreover, from this perspective one could restore the genuine sense of unconscious associations on whose basis Freud was to make the work of the cure depend. That unconscious associations would appear gratuitous and incomprehensible to the eyes of an instituted thought does not mean that they would be genuinely arbitrary; it is not a choice between conventional symbolism and incoherence. It is simply a question of understanding that the different moments of the association belong to one same ray of the world and that, for this reason, its freedom is not without rules. The associative power does not consist in relating already constituted beings but in reconceiving in each of them the ray of the world that it crystallizes and which articulates them in relation to the others.[4]

[319] The flesh can truly be characterized, then, as desire and the relation to things or others as "coupling," but on the condition of understanding by desire this universal power of incorporation, this originary relation by virtue of which everything that can present itself is given only as absent, as "flesh open to a flesh" or once again as crystallization of a dimension. In this sense, to say that the flesh is desire is to recognize that it is just as much expression and that the relation to the other only completes a signifying power already at work in the simplest of perceptions. There is no meaning that is not incarnated and, in this measure, affection. There is no affection, particularly in the relation of desire, that is not already the advent of a sense, an attempt to carry the world's opacity to transparency. Merleau-Ponty also notes as a result of his reform of consciousness that

> immediately the non-objectifying intentionalities are no longer in the alternative of being *subordinate* or *dominant,* the structures of the affectivity are constitutive with the same right as the others, for the simple reason that they are already the structures of knowledge, being those of *language.* We must no longer ask why we have *affections* in addition to

4. On this point, we refer to Marc Richir's article "Merleau-Ponty: un tout nouveau rapport à la psychanalyse," *Les cahiers de philosophie,* no. 7 (1989): 155–88.

"representative sensations," since the representative sensation also (taken "vertically" to its insertion in our life) is affection, being a presence to the world through the body and to the body through the world, being *flesh*, and language is also. (VI 292/239)

One can account for desire as a modality of the relation to the other only by reconceiving it beyond the alternative between phenomenological consciousness and the Freudian libido, namely, as a moment of a universal flesh, as a moment of an expressive teleology. Flesh is nowhere submitted to determinations, and nowhere strictly unconscious, because all that enters into relation with it is already presentation of the invisible. But, correlatively, nowhere does the flesh possess itself in full clarity or attain a sense in the pure state, because at the heart of the visible, sense remains invisible.

16 The Flesh of Ideality

1. The Voice

[321] While we have at our disposal numerous texts from the period that separates *Phenomenology of Perception* from *The Visible and the Invisible,* there are very few passages dedicated to speech in the latter work. Merleau-Ponty broke off the writing of his work at the threshold of this question, which he considered to be "the most difficult" (VI 195/149). Thus we are committed, once again, to a reconstruction and are forced to draw on earlier texts, even if the vocabulary there is not yet that of *The Visible and the Invisible.* As we said, the "idea" appears only in transparency, in filigree in the flesh; it is not a being but a dimension. The law of perceived sense is the law of all meaning; it is manifested and dissimulated at the same time by the thickness of the sensible. Nonetheless, we have the experience of an ideal universe; we spontaneously distinguish ideas in the strict sense, those of "intelligence," from those that the sensible allows to appear in the hollow of its mass. The conviction that the idea would subsist as an autonomous being, that it would be based only on itself, must really have a root somewhere; this illusion must involve a truth. Because no idea is freed from the carnal condition, it is necessary to conclude that it is by means of a new flesh that the experience of pure ideality can be born; *the voice* is the element proper to expression and ideal significance. In fact, it manifests a particular reversibility, more "agile" than that to which the perceiving body bears witness:

> The reversibility that defines the flesh exists in other fields; it is even incomparably more agile there [322] and capable of weaving relations between bodies that this time will not only enlarge, but will pass definitively beyond the circle of the visible. Among my movements, there are some that go nowhere—that do not even go find in the other body their resemblance or their archetype: these are the facial movements, many gestures, and especially those strange movements of the throat and mouth that form the cry and the voice. Those movements end in sounds and I hear them. Like crystal, like metal and many other sub-

stances, I am a sonorous being, but I hear my own vibration from within; as Malraux said, I hear myself with my throat. In this, as he also has said, I am incomparable; my voice is bound to the mass of my own life as is the voice of no one else. (VI 189–90/144)

What defines vocal expression is in fact that it is heard at the same time that it is proffered, that it is heard "from the inside." The voice unfolds a body or a world that does not fall back outside of the "consciousness" of the one who proffers it, in pure exteriority; vocal flesh erases itself as body at the instant when it exteriorizes itself, it comes back to itself in the very movement by which it throws itself outside of itself. The voice is not a body which interposes itself within the self, but rather the element in which the self finds itself again; expression is present to itself and fulfills itself then in a meaning, in the very act by which it is exteriorized. Thus, the flesh makes itself world only to grasp itself again immediately in this alterity. It is the phenomenon of a pure auto-affection. This essential point, which Merleau-Ponty only evokes, is clearly demonstrated by Derrida:

> The "apparent transcendence" of the voice thus results from the fact that the signified, which is always ideal by essence, the "expressed" *Bedeutung*, is immediately present in the act of expression. This immediate presence results from the fact that the phenomenological "body" of the signifier seems to fade away at the very moment it is produced; it seems already to belong to the element of ideality. It phenomenologically reduces itself, transforming the worldly opacity of its body into pure diaphaneity. This effacement of the sensible body and of its exteriority is *for consciousness* the very form of the immediate presence of the signified. . . . When I speak, it belongs to the phenomenological essence of this operation that *I hear myself at the same time* that I speak. The signifier, animated by my breath and by the meaning-intention [323] . . . , is in absolute proximity to me. The living act, the life-giving act, the *Lebendigkeit*, which animates the body of the signifier and transforms it into a meaningful expression, the soul of language, seems not to separate itself from itself, from its own self-presence. It does not risk death in the body of a signifier that is given over to the world and the visibility of space.[1]

1. J. Derrida, *La voix et le phénomène* (Paris: Presses Universitaires de France, 1967), 86–87; trans. D. B. Allison as *Speech and Phenomena* (Evanston, Ill.: Northwestern University Press, 1972), 77.

In vision, the body makes itself world in order that the world make itself flesh; the seer meets up with itself by the mediation of the world which it unfolds, is reflected in the visible to which it gives rise. Nevertheless, this fulfillment ends only in the exteriority of a world. It is true that vision is turned back on itself, makes itself visible, but it is by unfolding an "outside" that it makes itself visible, so that it is not *as vision* that it reaches itself. The thickness of the world comes to insert itself at the heart of the vision and its visibility insofar as vision is then only imminent; its inscription in the visible remains an alienation, its visibility does not truly belong to it. The exteriority of the visible is, of course, not pure transcendence, objective spatiality, because it is the concretion of dimensions of visibility, because it already sketches a self. But it is still the case that the self is missed rather than being reached there. The perceptual self becomes itself by making itself other, but by making itself other it is not yet self. In other words, if the perceptual self is reached by passing through its other, it is nevertheless as other rather than as self that it is reached. In contrast, the reflectivity that is fulfilled in vocal expression is such that the flesh makes itself other only in order to find itself again. The alterity of the vocal matter corresponds to the minimal divergence necessary in order that the speaking subject be reflected and meet up with itself there; it allows for the arising of a meaning. Vocal expression is the erasure of its own corporeity, it is such that it cannot "take" in the form of the exteriority of a world; the moment of exteriority exists only as its own disappearance, that is, as the arising of a self, of a meaning. Whereas in perception interiority gives itself only in the form of exteriority, in verbal expression exteriority unfolds itself only as exteriority *for* an interiority, as held back in interiority. Speech is only, so to speak, the "weak" reverse side of a hearing, the divergence between corporeity and its significance or between speech and hearing, that tends toward its own cancellation. In short, the self is not alienated from itself in speech as in a foreign element; it reaches itself as [324] what it has that is most characteristic of it. Flesh can be characterized, as we have seen, as the identity of an identity and a difference, but we can nevertheless accentuate, at the heart of this first identity, the moment of difference—we are describing, then, perception specifically—or the moment of identity. The speaking self becomes itself only when making itself other, but in making itself other it is already self. It does not reach itself except by passing into its other, but it is as self rather than as other that it is reached.

If it seems, therefore, that the voice fulfills carnal reflexivity in the mode of a quasi-coincidence, one must nevertheless not forget the other half of the truth and sacrifice flesh under the pretext that the voice sublimates it. The one who touches seizes his own touch right up against himself in the form of a being-touched, in the form of a tangible corporeity. This is not the other of the touch but truly the imminence of a sensibility, the mode of being suited to this imminence. Touch functions only on the condition of remaining itself intangible; vision is realized only if it remains itself invisible; corporeity in the strict sense corresponds to this invisibility, which is not the negation of the touch or vision but the "zero degree" or power of sensibility. In the same way, the reflexivity of phonation and hearing essentially cannot be fulfilled in coincidence: "I do not hear myself as I hear the others, the sonorous existence of my voice is for me as it were poorly exhibited; I have rather an echo of its articulated existence, it vibrates through my head rather than outside" (VI 294/148). The corporeity of the voice is not gathered beyond itself: the auto-affection that characterizes it is not absolutely pure, or rather it is strictly auto-*affection*. In the voice, speech cannot coincide with hearing, cannot abolish the moment of exteriority; insofar as it is articulated, expression remains inaudible for itself. Even though it might be intimately linked to the mass of my life, my voice possesses a texture, a materiality through which my life continues to escape. Signifying speech remain imminent, therefore, in the voice, as vision was imminent in the visible body, touch in the tangible body. Speech is also endowed with a body, which is not the negation but the condition of its expressivity, the element that carries its imminence. By passing from sight to speech, one does not pass from a meaning that is only presumptive to its actual possession. On the contrary, the imminence of sense in [325] perceiving flesh remains an absolute distance in that it cannot in principle be rejoined, in that no flesh can make itself sufficiently diaphanous to give it in transparency. If that happened, then meaning would disappear with the body that carries it. In short, flesh cannot disincarnate itself. Like speech, that is, like the voice, sense is still carnal; simply put, everything happens as though this distance which flesh institutes, while remaining all the while insurmountable, accepted degrees of proximity. With voice, as with vision and touch, we remain in the flesh through and through, which nevertheless does not mean that the world shows itself or that the self reveals itself in the voice in the same way as in vision and touch.

Perception was already flesh, which means that it did not free an absolute exteriority, that the spatiality of the world was depth—that is, it is a unity not yet unfolded, a co-presence to every being, already significance. Speech corresponds to a surplus of "interiority," whereas in perception unity remains disjointed by the stature of visibles and looks then rather like a spatial relation. The voice determines a co-presence that is "tighter," such that each moment is distinguished only in order to unify itself with the others, to be gathered in the unity of the said. The exteriority in which verbal sense is acquired is disappearing exteriority, it is only its own disappearance; with the voice, carnal differentiation tends toward the imminence of a unique presence, and temporal unity tends to win out over spatial exteriority. It is true that just as visible space is ratcheted onto a temporal axis, just as it opens by its depth onto a beyond which is not only spatial, the temporal modulations of the voice are not, for their part, bereft of spatiality and still lay down the exteriority of a world. Nevertheless, at the heart of originary spatio-temporality, the voice corresponds to a predominance of the temporal moment, whereas with vision, the spatial moment wins out. Thus, insofar as speech affects itself immediately, it is not sensible in the strict sense, that is, in the sense of worldly exteriority; it is situated "higher" than the perceived in the strict sense, "higher" than the visible. The voice is always an interior voice. A spoken word that would pass through the visible would no longer be a spoken word; it would signify nothing other than the visible itself. Its significance would be erased behind the stability of a world, and it would border on silence. Because it is not the sign of a meaning possessed elsewhere, it is essential to the expression that it be verbal, that is, that it give itself a body which would not have the density of the visible world. But to [326] the very degree that speech is not sensible, it cannot be brought back to a pure intelligible, to a subsistent ideality. That it is interior cannot mean that it transcends the world, that it is free of all flesh. A "hollow" subsists "between speaking and hearing" (VI 300/246); if the voice is not strictly sensible, it does not go without a dispossession and is thus situated "lower" than the intelligible. Far from speech transcending the world, far from language "harboring the secret of the world, [it] is itself a world, is itself a being" (VI 132/96); and in the same way that *there is* the visible, one must recognize that *there is* speech. The description of the sensible as irreducible to pure spatiality— that is, as the secret exhibition of a sense—prepared us to understand that there are other modalities of the "there is." Because the thickness of the sensible allows ideas to show through at its jointures, because it is decompressed by the dimensions which it presents, nothing prohibits the recognition of a more "glorious" body across which the idea gives itself to be understood a little better. Because, starting with the sensible level, presence is not synonymous with facticity, the way is opened for other modalities of presence, and all that differs from the strictly sensible order must then no longer be pushed back into essentiality nor deprived of a specific worldly rootedness.

Such is the sense of linguistic expression: the self-proximity of the flesh, which situates the flesh beyond worldly spatiality, does not go without invisibility, that is, without unsayability. Speech does not let a pure meaning appear; it is the inscription of dimensions in an element that is lighter than the world. To the quasi-spirituality of the signified world corresponds the quasi-corporeity of the linguistic signifier. Speech does not add itself to a world that is perfectly circumscribed, that is, factual. Speech is itself a world, or rather, *of* the world, and one must instead say that it is the world itself that transforms itself in speech into an element other than that of visibility without, nevertheless, losing its fundamental opacity. Thus, as we have had occasion to observe in other areas, Merleau-Ponty's approach comes down to reconceiving *hearing* just short of the opposition instituted between understanding and hearing in the strict sense, that is, understood as the sense of hearing:

> in a sense, to understand a phrase is nothing else than to fully welcome it in its sonorous being, or, as we put it so well, to *hear what it says*. The [327] meaning is not on the phrase like the butter on the bread, like a second layer of "psychic reality" spread over the sound: it is the totality of what is said, the integral of all the differentiations of the verbal chain; it is given with the words for those who have ears to hear.
> (VI 203/155)

In fact, understanding is not the passive welcoming of a sensible event; when I listen, I slip immediately from sounds toward their sense; and in truth, the sounds are never posited for themselves, they are never given as sensible beings: "When I am listening, it is not necessary that I have an *auditory perception* of the articulated sounds but that the conversation pronounces itself within me. It summons me and I resound, it envelops and inhabits me to the point that I cannot tell what comes from me and what from it" (PM 28/19). This does not mean that I could actually hear the sounds themselves, that they are only separated [*écartés*] in favor of the transparent being to which they give birth; they give themselves in such a way that they cannot be strictly heard auditorially and are always already surpassed by their sense. It is only under cover of an abstraction that I can claim to separate the sound from its sense, an abstraction which comes down to substituting the sound for the voice—and, correlatively, substituting a quasi-spatial, mundane presence for the experience of an alter ego. In reality, even the noises of the world are first spontaneously heard as voice; we address them immediately as a spoken word that needs to be deciphered rather than as an event of objective space. Merleau-Ponty notes that language "is everything, since it is the voice of no one, since it is the very voice of the things, the waves, and the forests" (VI 204/155); but it is the spoken word of things only because things have a voice. Thus, every hearing is an understanding. But, correlatively, as revealed by the ambiguity of the French word *comprendre*—to understand, to comprehend, and to include—*comprendre* is always *entendre*, to hear and to understand. To the degree that the sound surpasses *itself* toward its sense, the latter cannot be posited apart from the vocal material; this would again be to distinguish the sound as a sensible entity. The sound itself is surpassed toward its sense, so that it is never surpassed completely, so that the sense itself exists in its turn only by remaining inscribed in this thickness, where it *gives* itself to be understood rather than presenting itself in all clarity. Thus, understanding is a hearing, contact with a phonetic [328] spoken word, and communication is a quasi-corporeal encounter of two spoken words; the other is understood "in a confrontation that repels his utterances as utterances, as events" (VI 229/175). Understanding is the "of course" [*bien-entendu*] that does without an intelligible presencing and is therefore always on the order of the implied [*sous-entendu*]. From then on, instead of the verbal expression corresponding to the intuitive presence of a meaningful entity in a sensible body, it must be understood as the very *body* of the invisible and, consequently, as an element that is just as irreducible as the visible was. Just as the analysis of the perceptual phenomenon has already confirmed, the invisible cannot itself appear; it gives itself only under cover of an experience, an encounter with another body, another flesh. "As the sensible structure can be understood only through its relation to the body, to the flesh—the invisible structure can be understood only through its relation to *logos*, to speech" (VI 277/224). Just as the sensible is the *medium* which Being needs to manifest itself without becoming positivity, in order to stay at a distance, the spoken word is the only means for it to offer a meaning. Thus, it is necessary to describe expression according to a modality parallel to that of the sensible. In the same way that the sensible phenomenon had to be reconceived beyond the opposition between fact and essence, as the crystallization of a dimension of visibility, the intelligible phenomenon must be situated beyond the opposition of sound and sense; it is the crystallization of a dimension of sayability which is finally nothing other than visibility itself. Speech is always beyond itself insofar as it is a sensible being—it is "on the side" of sense, on the axis of meaning; but, correlatively, there is speech only if sense itself remains absence, only if it remains something "to say" rather than something possessed, veiled in and as this element of expression that defines it. Speech expresses in such a way that in it nothing is ever *truly* said. There is then, if you will, an intelligible world. But this does not mean that the intelligible forms a world that is formed only of itself, which would be self-sufficient, which would by itself have the stability of the sensible world. The intelligible exists like the sensible, it has the form of the world, and it finally draws its own solidity only from the sensible from which it emerges and which it never completely transcends. That is why in *The Visible and the Invisible,* as in the texts coming shortly before it, the question of [329] the original motivation of the sign is abandoned. We can thus determine more clearly the limit of *Phenomenology of Perception:* the very posing of this question in the chapter devoted to speech presupposed the duality between the orders of the sensible and the intelligible, a duality which shifts the sensible onto the side of facticity and the intelligible onto the side of a specific positivity. The hesitation between the arbitrary character and the naturalness of the sign revealed to us that Merleau-Ponty was still under the sway of the theoretical configuration that he nevertheless was claiming to surpass; the explicit scission of the sign and meaning at the level of language responded to the general scission of fact and sense. To situate the linguistic sign on the side of the sensible gesture is inevitably to posit meaning outside of itself in the form of a positive being, and in this very way one shifts the sensible back onto the side of pure facticity. Indeed, this is why Merleau-Ponty returns at length to the phenomenon of expression after *Phenomenology of Perception,* and it is by means of the detour through this analysis that he is led to outline the way to an ontology. Expression reveals an original domain which does not fit the duality of fact and sense, a "there is" which escapes all positivity, so that in return the perceived world itself can be described as just such a "there is," as an element, a dimensionality exceeding the categories of reflective philosophy. The specific status of the world is first of all demonstrated at the level of expression before being fully unfolded and grounded in an ontology of the visible. In other words, the study of language takes the place of the phenomenological reduction. The natural attitude roots itself in a privileged manner in perceptual experience: "the natural being is at rest in its self, my look can stop on it" (VI 267/214). On its own, perception forgets the dimension of the phenomenon and appears to itself as relation to a positivity. On the contrary, "the Being of which language is the house cannot be fixed, looked at, it is only from afar" (VI 267/214). This means that an attentive analysis of language, which is not subjected to the presupposition of the autonomy of ideality, which would manage to seize language as an event, is a privileged access to the genuine meaning of sensible Being. The study of speech truly uncovers a presence at a distance, a thickness not resting on a positive being, a dissimulation constitutive of sense—all of which leads us to situate the sign "higher" than the pure [330] sensible and consequently to apprehend the sensible in general, of which the linguistic sign is only a particular case, outside of all reference to facticity. The genuine order of Merleau-Ponty's approach consists in demonstrating the genuine being of the visible, and thus of flesh, on the basis of the voice, in conceiving the perceived as the voice of silence rather than as a natural positivity.

2. Sense as Articulation

This analysis of expressive flesh, grounded on the reversibility of the voice, allows us then to put forward the genuine meaning of the diacritical dimension of the sign; ontology here converges with Saussurian linguistics by providing it with a foundation. Nowhere are we confronted with signs that are strictly vocal; they cannot be characterized as sensible, audible atoms, as individuals situated in exteriority. Most assuredly, I do not hear *anything other* than sounds, and yet it is not the sounds themselves that I hear. Their relationship escapes worldly exteriority; they are not situated side by side. Rather, they bear witness to a quasi-interiority corresponding to the quasi-reflexivity of the voice. Each sound already slips into the others, makes allusion there and, by this very relationship, sketches a meaningful unity. Nevertheless, this movement does not rest on the presence of a meaning possessed elsewhere; sense is nothing other than this lateral relation between the signs. It is implied in words and phonemes, as a coherent deformation, rather than being possessed by them. Sense remains, at the heart of expression, "organic" rather than pure meaning, a "matrix of ideas" (S 96/77) rather than an idea. Thus the incarnation of sense in the voice corresponds to the quasi-exteriority of signs. In other words, the signifying chain makes a specific type of multiplicity appear. The sounds are not foreign to each other, they do not have "enough world" to be separate from one another; as temporal, each sound cannot be punctually fixed, it slips toward the others, or rather it is itself this slippage, and in so doing it surpasses itself toward its "sense." But this quasi-unity, this complicity of signs, is not closed in on itself; it remains supported by their difference. Even as it is passing into its other [331] each sign remains itself, so that there is a differentiation of signs by their very unity, a difference which does not go as far as becoming a distinction, which is a quasi-identity—it is exactly the difference needed by identity in order to affirm itself as assignable identity, that is, as expressed. The ultimate reality consists of a certain relation between the signs which precedes them rather than bringing them into relation with one another, and sense is nothing other than this relation, this dimension: the principle of unity and of differentiation, of unity by differentiation. Sense does not merge with signs because it is the principle that organizes and unifies them, the principle which grounds their co-presence, the complicity of each to all. But it is nevertheless nothing other than signs, and these are not reabsorbed into it because this organization must be held back in what it gathers, disjunction in conjunction, *between* the terms which it nevertheless unifies, and they must animate it even when it gives them life. In short, the exchange of spoken words is exactly the "differentiation of which the thought is the integral" (VI 190n/145n5).

In other words, it is necessary to grasp expression as *articulation:* what defines the voice, as opposed to the cry, is that it is articulated. This property does not refer to the bringing into relation of terms posited elsewhere, since, conceived as strictly sensible, sounds would remain too distant to be articulated. Neither can this property conceal the positing of a principle of unity; reduced to their sense, sounds would lack the exteriority that allows them to *enter* into relation. Understanding the voice in its truth, namely, as this body of which the corporeity is erased in the very moment of its advent, comes down to conceiving it as articulation, that is, as a unity which is fulfilled only by being disjoined from itself, which mixes up the terms which it gathers in and by their very exteriority. To say that the spoken word is articulated is not to recognize in it the contingent power of putting positive sounds into relationship, but is rather to meet up with the essence of this power. And, there again, the identity of the sensible, in its turn, is being considered on the basis of this central idea: the principle of equivalence which characterizes the phenomenon, the dimension around which it had its advent, is a kind of "articulation before the letter" (VI 168/126). It is, however, necessary to distinguish degrees of articulation, and not to compromise the phenomenal difference of the sensible and the intelligible under the pretext that, on either side, one single [332] principle of equivalence is at work. It is not a question of starting with the atomic sensible in order to then discover modes of organization there; as a pure fact, the sensible would be incapable of unity, incapable of appearing. It is necessary, on the contrary, to treat the sensible *as* a mode of articulation, as a self-complicity that remains outside of self, and to treat its relative positivity as a "fall" of articulation into what it articulates. It is not because the sensible is a positive being that the unity that presides at its appearance remains veiled; it is because the articulation of the world lacks fluidity that each sensible tends to be based in itself. Far from the dismembering of unity in articulation, in dimension, being the tribute to pay to subsistent entities, exteriority is a weakness of articulation. The movement which carries each "this" toward all the others, the movement by which the world rises to meaning, has a tendency to congeal, to lack "fluidity"; such is what defines the perceptual order. On the contrary, speech is the place of a participation that, by means of the relative diaphanousness of its element, is not susceptible to congealing in exteriority but is capable of joining back up with itself, of outlining itself on its own. It is not because signs have a sense that they articulate themselves to each other. It is on the contrary because language is true articulation, dynamic co-presence, that the signs are signs, that is, rise up from their sensible thickness toward their sense. We have defined the sensible as "openness-opened,"[2] as the openness of each "this" to all the others, emblem of a world rather than spatial atom. Nevertheless, this openness remains allusive, distended, in some way *mens momentanea,* just as in Leibniz the material substance perceives the world only in the form of a distant murmuring. In this slack openness, the world is demoted to opacity, generality, and the "this" is demoted to facticity. Because articulation remains "weak," the signifying power of the thing is only latent, and perception is only contact in exteriority. In contrast, when sensible flesh is transformed into expressive flesh, perception makes itself tighter; each "this" is shifted from itself; it is no longer based on its calm identity but revives the co-presence that, on the sensible plane, remained blind. By this "ductility" of articulation, the sensible "this" becomes the sign that it has always been; and by this interiority of signs, the world lets

2. See part III, chapter 11.

appear the universality that it has always hidden. There is, then, no singular and universal, no sensible "this" and pure meaning that would transform every "this" into a sign, but degrees of articulation of generality. [333] Just as the exteriority of the world already conceals a co-presence—but one that is congealed, unfinished, and consequently veiled—the universality of sense is still only a mode of co-presence which, by its own dynamism, declares the participation of everything with every other, puts the general equivalence of the world on stage, and thus transforms the sensible atom into expressive sign. By virtue of this universal articulation, one must understand that nowhere is there full exteriority in the sense understood by realism, and hence the world is truly *logos;* but also that nowhere is there full interiority in the sense claimed by idealism, and hence language is still a world. In the same way, the moment of "for-itself" refers to a state of articulation, to a degree of continuity of the worldly fabric, instead of the articulation being based on a for-itself. And to an equal degree, instead of articulation presupposing positive terms, the ultimate facts between which it would be instituted, facticity itself refers to an inferior state of articulation, to a slackening of the worldly fabric. The sensible can be described, as we have said, as a mode of eidetic variation, that is, as a conquest or a sketch of a unique meaning across distinct exemplars. Nevertheless, there is a variation in some way congealed or realized which does not exhibit the theme's unity except in the form of individuals which concentrate and hide it. Already in filigree, essence nevertheless remains to be captured. This does not mean that it is necessary to oppose the individual to essence; it is simply because variation is only inchoative, and in some way lazy, that essence gives itself the aspect of the sensible individual. In contrast, language appears as the element proper to eidetic variation; and instead of language being only the instrument of variation, variation merges with the expressive work of speech. In fact, like speech, variation sublimates perception, frees the co-presence of the world, converts the sensible thing into its own sense, brings forth the unity of the theme. But there again, this is not to say that essence would be the other of the individual; there is no other theme than the world. Eidetic variation "does not make me pass to an order of separated essences, to a logical possible, the invariant that it gives me is a structural invariant, a Being in infrastructure which in the last analysis has its *Erfüllung* only in the *Weltthesis* of this world" (VI 282/229). The work of language does not consist in freeing essence from the individual; it realizes it in a new individuality, in a new element that permits it to appear more clearly.

[334] Of course, the insistence on articulation here is essentially valid in opposition to the positivist perspective, a perspective which, starting from sensible atoms, would be forced to articulate them by recourse to the symmetrical plenitude of essence, or which, giving itself autonomous essences, would be led to appeal to some obscure and indeterminate ground in order to account for the sensible moment. It is not, then, a matter of restoring under cover of the concepts of articulation or of dimension the positivism that they are supposed to uproot—that is, it is not a matter of conferring on them a sort of autonomy or life of their own, from which the sensible and intelligible would proceed as in a procession. If it is true that all positivity, all difference, are moments of a co-presence, it is just as true that co-presence would never be able to close upon itself beyond what it articulates; articulation or dimension are unities whose contents are exactly the negation of unity. Being is nothing other than the expressive teleology itself, and tends thus toward a completion; but this completion does not reach the autonomy of an organizing or directing principle. It is not distinguished from its own avatars, and it draws from them in some way the orientation that it breathes into them. In other words, it is not a matter of adopting an external point of view and of restoring, vis-à-vis the phenomenon of expression, the faults of reflective philosophies by reifying the universe of wild essence, by shifting the duality of fact and essence toward a new element which would give itself the figures of the phenomenon. It is incontestable that Merleau-Ponty aims at a wild world beyond the opposition of fact and essence, that flesh is an element "midway between the spatio-temporal individual and the idea" (VI 184/139), but *to this degree,* it is not a question of realizing this element and of understanding it, then, as the attestation of an ontological monism. This would still represent, in Merleau-Ponty's eyes, an avatar of the natural or positive attitude, that is, a non-phenomenological approach to the phenomena; this element that is the flesh has precisely no elementary consistency. *There is* diversity, particularly of the sensible and of language, and this diversity remains a unity precisely to the degree that it is not based on the reality of distinct worlds, to the degree that it is diversified within one same experience. It would be necessary, instead, to speak of a "phenomenological monism," whose sense would be essentially negative or regulative, against the risk of a surpassing of the phenomenal toward the plenitude of the in-itself or the autonomy of the idea. This would be a monism of the sensible, which does not express [335] the metaphysical positing of a principle of unity, because the sensible is characterized by the diversity of its phenomena and of its

modes of phenomenalization. In other words, it would be necessary to risk the idea of a chiasm *between the concept of flesh, that is, of chiasm, and the field of experience that it thematizes;* the flesh, as concept, does not join back up with a nature of things, it remains enveloped by the phenomenal diversity which it envelops. Insofar as it itself proceeds from expression, the concept that thematizes it cannot claim to possess it and make itself the mirror of a subsistent principle.

3. Speech and Intersubjectivity

The description of flesh at the perceptual level made it possible to account for the appearance of the other, as we have seen. Because I become seer only by making myself visible, I do not need to choose between the perception of the world and the openness to others; grounded on an ontological complicity with the world, my perception exposes me to others. Because by making itself world the self remains itself, its relation to the other does not call its perceptual life into question—on the contrary, the relation to the other is the counterpart to the perceptual life of the self. Nevertheless, at the level of perception there is an experience of the world rather than an openness to the other itself. The exteriority in which sensible flesh is fulfilled remains the negation, rather than the attestation, of another presence. Far from the world disclosing for me the interiority of the other, the latter flows back toward the exteriority of the world and is finally hidden there. The other and I vary together; in sensibility, as soon as I make myself world so that the world can make itself flesh, I reach the other as world rather than as "me." In vision, the other gives himself only as visible body; assuredly, this latter attests to a behavior and cannot, any more than any other perceived, degrade itself to the rank of pure object. But nevertheless, in it, the other still absents himself. Grounded on the anonymity of vision, that is, on visibility, the existence of the other can manifest itself only in an anonymous form: "the institutionalized conduct, of which I am the agent and witness, yields another only in general, diffused through my field, an anthropological or cultural space, a species-individual, so to speak, and finally a notion rather than a presence" (PM 195/140). [336] Thus, it is only at the level of expression that a true intersubjectivity can appear. Whereas in perception I am more concerned with the world than with others, through speech I gain access to the other rather than to the world. In fact, the unity between possession and dispossession, activity and passivity, makes itself more narrow there than it was on the plane of perception, where the reflexivity of flesh was fulfilled only as exteriority to a world. Within speech, there is no longer any opposition between becoming self and making oneself other, no difference for the speaking subject "between reaching oneself and expressing oneself" (PM 26/17), nor any distinction of priority between sense to be formulated and the element of its expression. There is no possessed meaning except to the degree that the speaking subject allows itself to be undone by its speech; it is not completed, does not return to itself, except by exposing itself in some way to itself in this speech. Or rather, speech is the place where the identity of self and its other is realized; the speaking subject makes itself other in becoming self, it reaches itself only by passing into its other. Expression, then, is not the unfolding of a meaning held in advance by a non-signifying matter; instead of being the source of speech, the speaking subject is spoken in and by its own speech, speech *speaks to itself* in the subject. Thus, "no locutor speaks without making himself in advance an allocutary, *be it only for himself*" (VI 202/154); or rather, there is speech only if, in it, the subject remains its own allocutary. Also, the act of expression can by itself outline the place of the interlocutor; insofar as it is spoken by its own speech, the speaking subject opens itself to an other. It is not the subject, the holder of its own speech, because insofar as speech is incarnate, it does not properly belong to it, and it is just as much speech of the other. Because understanding remains a hearing, in speaking I continue to receive my speech as if it were proffered by an other: "rather than imprisoning it, language is like a magic machine for transporting the speaking 'I' into the other person's perspective. . . . Language continuously reminds me that the 'incomparable monster' which I am when silent can, through speech, be brought into the presence of *another myself,* who re-creates every word I say and sustains me in being as well" (PM 29/19; see also S 121/96). In the same way, the experience of listening cannot be described in a univocal fashion. Speaking to me [337], the other does not offer me some signs in which the sense of what *the other* says would be lodged; the other relinquishes itself in order to join back up with itself and proposes its speech to me in order for this speech to become its own, so that the other's speech says itself in me at the same moment when the other says it. I discover that I think what the other seeks to say just as much as the other does; I discover that I had always known it—without, however, being able to formulate it; I express it at the same time as I receive it. In the experience of dialogue, the two perspectives slip into one another; the limit between the other and me becomes unassignable, because each of the two reaches itself in and as the other, so that, strictly speaking, one no longer knows who speaks and who listens: "When I speak and listen to the other, what I hear comes to insert itself in the intervals of what I say, my speech is intersected laterally by the other's speech, I hear myself in the other, while the other speaks in me. Here it is the same thing *to speak to* and *to be spoken to*" (PM 197/142; italicized words are in English in Merleau-Ponty's original). Because it proceeds from a more "glorious" body, speech completes what only sketched itself at the level of perception. Because signifying flesh does not deposit itself in mundane exteriority, this other, through the mediation by which it becomes itself, remains just as much a self; in speech, a genuine alter ego can manifest itself. The element of alterity in which speech is realized is at the same time a disappearing element, a vector of a reflexivity; therefore, it no longer comes to place itself between me and the other. In speech, the other is seized as itself, because in making myself other by speech I remain myself.

All the same, speech sublimates sensible intersubjectivity rather than suppressing it. As long as it does not raise itself to the transparency of meaning, as long as it has meaning by relying on the exteriority of the voice, it remains *my* speech, it maintains the scission between me and the other in the very moment when it opens me to the other. The other as such remains absent and is only the inaccessible reverse side of this body which meaning needs in order to constitute itself. Certainly the other announces itself otherwise and better in speech than it did in the visible world; but speech still veils the other's presence from me, and the other remains anonymous in it. Expression gives me access not so much to another "me" as to a neutral element where I am reflected—that is, once again, to a world which, as such, puts me face to face with myself and conceals no genuine interiority. Nevertheless, in contrast to the sensible world, this world carries [338] in filigree the consciousnesses from which it proceeds; it gives itself as animated by other presences rather than as resting in its place, as the element of a reciprocity rather than as the domain of a face-to-face. The self is concerned only with its speech, but speech, by opposition to the solipsistic sensible, passes beyond the circle of its singular identity and can people itself with other consciousnesses. In short, if speech does not free the other in person, it nevertheless unfolds a *cultural* world. Here again, it is not a question of starting from me and the other as positive existences in order then to wonder how their relationship is born; it is not a question of deriving a cultural universe from the insularity of consciousnesses. Instead of speech weaving a relationship *between* consciousnesses, it is on the contrary within speech, as irreducible reality, that others and myself are born, in agreement with their meaning—that is, at the same time multiple and one, as others and ego. In its order, speech completes this inner frame of intersubjectivity that ultimately characterized Being. In expression, sense returns to itself instead of being deposited in the form of the exteriority of a visible world, and that is why a quasi-identity with the other is realized; we penetrate into one another, and we recognize ourselves infinitely better than in silent perception. But nevertheless the carnal self does not reach itself fully there; it remains a stranger, other to itself, and its interiority remains subjected to the element of exteriority. To this degree, a scission subsists between me and the other; we remain absent from each other because insofar as our speech is still incarnate, we are absent to ourselves in speech. The cultural world is exactly the element of this scission that is also communication, the element of this absence which is also the presentiment of the other. To the degree that in speech the self reaches itself again only by missing itself, to the degree that it realizes its union with others only as separation, the self is fulfilled in speech in the form of a cultural world rather than as a full subjective identity. Speech is the genuine body of the other, that is, the element where its presence and absence are joined together, a mode of unveiling that is still dissimulation. Of course, insofar as expressive flesh never joins back up with the spatial exteriority of the world, insofar as it frees a sense, it truly institutes a co-presence, a unity of consciousnesses which perceptual life never allowed to be realized. But speech is expressed only to the degree that it does not possess what it nevertheless says, to the degree that it remains just short of itself as strictly signifying. Something is formulated only insofar as it is antedated, gives [339] itself as to be said, only insofar as it offers itself to another speech. Thus, although it would lack objective spatiality, speech is not without exteriority, and it is this exteriority of the flesh expressive to itself that determines the exteriority or the alterity of speaking consciousnesses. Hence, one must understand that it is not because consciousnesses *are* many that they speak; it is, on the contrary, because their speech remains incarnated, unfinished, that consciousnesses pluralize themselves in speech, or rather that the sayability separates itself from itself, makes itself multiple in itself. Nevertheless, sensible intersubjectivity completes itself at the heart of expression. Plurality has its advent in expression as the plurality of "consciousnesses"; their difference tends to annul itself in favor of a unique universe of sense. The difference of consciousnesses is not a subsistent difference; it does not refer to visible corporeities; it remains unstable, unassignable, a differentiation that is unification. The consciousnesses, then, are finally neither one nor many. They are not one, because then nothing else would motivate expression; but the consciousnesses are not many, because then communication would be impossible. In this inner frame of intersubjectivity, consciousnesses, as expressive subjects, gain access to themselves and consequently to each other. But insofar as expression is fulfilled in the exteriority of a spoken word, they remain just as much strangers to themselves, and therefore to each other; they join back up with each other only in the element of a culture. One must speak of a chiasm between expressive consciousnesses and the cultural world, just as there was a chiasm between sensible consciousnesses and the perceived world. In a sense, the cultural world is nothing other than what they formulate in common; insofar as the cultural world does not proceed from objective spatiality, it truly belongs to the "space" of consciousnesses. Nevertheless, it establishes itself by means of an expression whose light is inseparable from the darkness where it is reflected; in this way, it is not deprived of exteriority. No speech can gather itself, close itself on a definitive silence; every speech regains, in the very moment in which it illuminates it, the obscurity that animates its expressive effort. In other words, every speech, to the very degree that it expresses, makes itself delocutary[3] of another speech, becomes world or soil of another saying, inscribes itself in a culture: "it antedates itself by a retrograde movement which is never completely belied—because already in opening the horizon of the nameable and the sayable, the speech acknowledged that it has its place in that horizon" (VI 202/154). By signifying, [340] speech does not except itself from the world which it attempts to bring to transparency; it turns back on itself and constitutes itself as fragment of a universal Speech, it opens a horizon of interpretation. To this extent, speaking consciousnesses still belong to the world that they nevertheless unfold in common, and thus their community remains only presumptive. Speech signifies only by being enveloped by what it envelops, by being immersed in itself. To speak here of a chiasm is to recognize flesh's belonging to a universal sayability where a sense in the pure state nowhere appears— in this way, expression is still a world or of the world—but where nothing remains foreign to the saying, so that this world never falls outside of itself into a non-signifying exteriority.

Speech nevertheless represents a higher fulfillment vis-à-vis perception;

3. See IV 202/154 for Merleau-Ponty's use of this term.

it is truly a relationship with the other rather than with the world, and a difference does subsist between the natural world and the cultural universe. It is as if the universal, which in perception remains veiled in the form of the transcendence of a world, gave itself a body which suited it, and at the heart of which intersubjectivity, which remained presumptive of the level of the perceived, becomes predominant. It is as if the life of consciousnesses and their relationships, which had been latent in the depth of the world beforehand, suddenly became the very fabric of presence. One must in fact remember that individuality and generality are not opposed. Thus, to the degree that sensibility does not complete reflexivity, to the degree that the universal at which it aims remains veiled, perceptual flesh maintains an insular existence, cut off from others, separated from them by this world that it causes to appear. Objective transcendence itself refers to intersubjectivities that are still empirical. As generality or quasi-facticity, the world is this depth which places itself between sensible subjects, at the heart of which they encounter each other without knowing each other. Because there is a world, because they exist first of all only as the phenomenon of the world, sensible consciousnesses remain individual existences. In the experience of the world as objective transcendence, the sensible gains access to a certain universality, it truly makes itself object; but this universality remains unfulfilled, presumptive, and gives itself still as a fact of the world. Thus, sensible flesh refers to a self that, because it is not fully itself and dispossesses itself in favor of the world, is separated from others. In speech, by contrast, the flesh is at once a little [341] more itself and a little more other—not with the alterity proper to the world, where the self still remains foreign to itself, but as an alter ego where the universality of the world appears for itself. In speech, in a single movement, the individuality of what is sensed is transformed into "subjective" singularity and the generality of the world is transformed into universality: "it is as though the universality of sensibility . . . has finally ceased to be a universality for me and in the end redoubled itself through a recognized universality" (PM 197/141–42). By ascending to itself in speech, the sensible flesh does not distance itself from others, because by not distancing itself, the sensible flesh fulfills the latent universality of the world and thereby sketches the space of a community. Thus, the universe of culture is based entirely on language—even if, of course, it is prepared in non-vocal gestures—and truly represents a fulfillment in relation to nature. Nevertheless, one must not be mistaken about the sense of this distinction and infer from its descriptive validity that a dualism must be restored. With speech, one has not suddenly left the world of vision in favor of another universe of which speech would be the body; hearing would therefore come down to surpassing the specific order of culture toward an intelligible of which words would be the only trace. Vocal gestures are in no case signs turned toward themselves or toward an autonomous universe of meaning. These are still *gestures,* comparable to touch or vision; the sense that they exhibit is reached nowhere other than in the world. The sense is neither "in spirit" nor in them; rather, it merges with a certain transmutation of the visible. Insofar as it proceeds from the flesh, speech is still an *organ* in the sense that touch and vision are. It has the power to make me—and my interlocutor with me—slip toward the world, without the thickness of a living body interposing itself between it and us, and the power of offering to the world the fluidity and the transparency which characterize speech. Culture, therefore, is not a layer which would be added on top of that of the sensible conceived as nature; it designates the world itself, according to a certain coherent deformation, according to another mode of givenness, in which the dimensions would appear in some way for themselves rather than for the world. The advent of a culture—whose origin is of course unassignable, as it is already at work in originary expression—is still only a mode of appearance of the world, by whose aid the invisible comes to impregnate the visible that carries it. "Thought" is not "in us," or in [342] our words, but over there, in front of us. Culture does not hide the world; culture makes the world seen, but seen otherwise, namely, in such a way that the sensible stature of its moments is erased behind what articulates them. That is why Merleau-Ponty asserts elsewhere that there is no distinction to be made between the work of painting and that of language. Painting fulfills what speech effectuates on its side. It makes neither a mirror of the visible nor another imaginary world, but it shows the world according to dimensions which, at the level of perception, appear only in filigree. Painting offers to the world a fragment of its own flesh, seduces the world starting from a region of itself, in order to abandon a little of its own opacity and in order to give to sight, in the interstices of the canvas, the delicacy of its bonds. Painting and all of the mute arts allow us better to demonstrate the dimension of revelation, of "vision," which inhabits speech; instead of being its negation or its truth, intellectual intuition is only a modality of sensible intuition, that is, a modality of carnal intuition.

It is true that if we stick to incarnate speech, to voice, we do not take into account the universe of culture and the plenitude of its sense. What defines ideality is in fact that it gives itself as subsisting outside of all actual communication, that it seems to rest on itself, to be gifted with self-sufficiency. From there proceeds the conviction that extends the natural attitude, the conviction that spoken words join back up with a universe of truth and appropriate for themselves ideas whose existence owes nothing to the words. But that ideality transcends the fleeting body of the voice, the present of expression, does not mean that it is freed of all corporeity; the ideality of truth is only carried by another flesh, that of *writing*. Thus, its self-sufficiency

> does not place ideal being outside of speech, but merely obliges us to introduce an essential mutation in speech, namely, the appearance of writing. It is writing which once and for all translates the meaning of spoken words into ideal being, at the same time transforming human sociability, inasmuch as writing is "virtual communication," the speaking of *x* to *x*, which is not carried by any living subject and belongs in principle to everyone, evoking a total speech. (RC 166/187)

By passing into writing, speech does not close itself on pure ideality, and the becoming of truth is not terminated. It exposes itself and offers itself as interlocutor and delocutary of a virtual speech, and finally of all possible speech. Writing enlarges the [343] field of expression, but it does not transcend it completely. If expression is protected in writing from the threats of time and contingency, it is nevertheless not unburdened of its exteriority; if sayability and, finally, the dimensionality of the world themselves appear in writing better than in oral speech by giving the illusion of a finished and autonomous truth, written meaning does not stop being veiled, does not stop soliciting interpretation.

17 The Last Chiasm

[345] This analysis of the phenomenon specific to the invisible, the body of ideality, leads us to the last question, that of the relationship between the world of expression and the sensible world. "Is it the same being that perceives and that speaks? Impossible that it not be the same. And if it is the same, is this not to re-establish the 'thought of seeing and of feeling,' the Cogito, the consciousness of . . . ?" (VI 255/202). Such is truly the question around which *The Visible and the Invisible* is organized. It is the same being that perceives and speaks. The study of perception cannot ignore the fact of speech, the phenomenon of meaning, which forbids us to reduce the world to pure facticity. But the analysis of speech cannot cut itself off from that of the perceived; the one who speaks is the very one who opens onto a sensible world, and this forbids us from coming back to the *cogito* and a universe of essences. The philosophy of fact is overconfident in perception, ignoring the phenomenon of expression; it remains dependent on the natural attitude. But the philosophy of essence is overconfident in speech; and the transcendental attitude, insofar as it recognizes a universe of pure meaning, still proceeds from the natural attitude. Meaning is thus understood as a world whose ontological sense is not interrogated. For Merleau-Ponty, it is a matter of surpassing this double naiveté, of getting past these two antagonistic and interconnected attitudes by grasping the world and humanity at the point where perception and speech are articulated—beyond perception as contact with a fact, but just short of speech as intellectual adequation. Finally, the truth of perception and speech really lies on the level of their relationship. [346] This orientation oversees the development of the notion of flesh, which is intended to demonstrate the structural identity of perception and expression. The visible can be defined as the exploration of a universe of ideas, the presentation of an invisible; in this way, it is really speech, silent *logos*. Insofar as it lets the idea appear, insofar as it constitutes a mode of exhibition rather than opposing itself to the universe of essence, the visible can be conceived as an inchoative or originary speech—that is, always already sedimented, a

speech always already proffered, a "speech before speech" (VI 255/201). The visible cannot in fact be described as atomic multiplicity; it is gathered in itself, unfolds itself around dimensions, around structuring axes; it already sketches the interiority of sense. But expression can no more be opposed to the order of sensibility; expression is still a modality of sensibility, a modality characterized by Merleau-Ponty as "sublimation." If the sensibility is flesh, since in sensibility the world does not draw itself back into exteriority but comes from my side, then there is a body of expression. This is so because sense is born in expression only as the dimension or axis of a vocal articulated speech, because sense therefore remains on the side of the world. Insofar as it always proceeds from an expression, the universe of sense would never be able to be posited beside the visible in a relation of exteriority with it; it participates in the visible. Just as sensibility exhibited the idea only through its thickness, so expression makes it appear only in filigree, as the other side of a world. Sensibility is already expression, but expression is still a sensibility; it *shows* meaning rather than touching or possessing it. The sense of the novel, for example, "is perceptible at first only as a *coherent deformation* imposed on the visible" (S 97/78). The silence which characterizes the sensible, the mute *logos,* is definitive; no living spoken word can break it, as it again envelops the expression which envelops it (VI 224/170, 230/176, 233/179). The originary withdrawal of sense into the sensible renews itself on the plane of uttered speech; it does not fully possess itself there, it incarnates itself, antedates itself in offering itself to other expressive acts. Perception and speech appear, finally, as two modalities of the flesh insofar as it is institution; sense is synonymous there with its own concealment. It signifies only insofar as it calls for an appropriation. Thus, speech does not cease [347] being incarnated by ceasing to be "natural." Just as the perceptual "fact" already appeared as the exhibition of an idea, so the idea itself is offered as a "fact" for another body, for another flesh: "the Essences are *Etwases* at the level of speech, as the things are Essences at the level of Nature" (VI 273/220). There is no one place of language, no one universe of meaning distinguishable from the domain where sensible positivity reigns. Every perception is primordial expression, and the thing is a figurative sense, a stylization, the establishment of a secret equivalence. But for this reason there is no expression in which sense does not remain buried in a sensible depth, latent, figurative, offered to other expressive efforts.

It is therefore necessary to recognize an analogy or a parallelism between perception and expression, and the main point of Merleau-Ponty's analysis is developed at this level. But this does not mean that it is necessary to treat perception and expression as purely and simply identical. To say that perception is silent *logos* is to recognize that it is not of the order of facticity, that in this way it is on the side of language; it is not, however, to confuse it with language. In the same way, to assert that expression is always incarnate is to reject the principle of an opposition with perception, to rule out the possibility of a domain of positive essences; it is not to posit an immediate identity between perception and expression. Though they both proceed from flesh, they do not refer to the same flesh. Identifying perception and expression would bring back the difficulties that the notion of flesh was precisely intended to surmount; this would restore the pure positivity of fact by reabsorbing language into sensibility, or else it would restore the transparency of ideality by reabsorbing perception into language. It would be to reactivate the "to-and-fro" characteristic of reflective philosophies. Perception and expression cannot be confused, but neither can they be opposed, and for the same reasons: their opposition would be based on their positivity in such a way that the relationship could finally be understood only as the absorption of one term into the other. Therefore, language is distinguished from perception only if it does not differ radically from it, only if it does not go so far as the positivity of sense, only if it still roots itself in the perceived world at the very moment when it detaches itself from it. Correlatively, perception is distinguished from expression only if it is not completely distinguished from it [348], only if it does not go so far as pure facticity, only if it remains *logos*. In other words, their relationship, reconceived on the basis of an analysis of what gives each its specificity, must still be understood as a chiasm, as a modality of the reversibility "which is the ultimate truth" (VI 204/155):

> One can speak neither of a destruction nor of a conservation of silence (and still less of a destruction that conserves or of a realization that destroys—which is not to solve but to pose the problem). When the silent vision falls into speech, and when the speech in turn, opening up a field of the nameable and the sayable, inscribes itself in that field, in its place, according to its truth—in short, when it metamorphoses the structures of the visible world and makes itself a gaze of the mind, *intuitus mentis*—this is always in virtue of the same fundamental phenomenon of reversibility which sustains both the mute perception and the speech and which manifests itself by an almost carnal existence of the idea, as well as by a sublimation of the flesh. (VI 202–203/154–55)

It is a matter then of giving up the temptation of conferring a positivity on the visible. The positivity is only apparent, but is not based on a subsistent reality; it is only a modality of manifestation. It is not because the sensible is a positive being that it can be sensed. It is, on the contrary, because it is sensed that it gives itself as positive. The sensible does not therefore designate an ultimate layer, a "reality," but a certain mode of manifestation of Being, a milieu in which Being can remain what it is, namely, at a distance, which is the only means for it to manifest itself without becoming positivity. What is valid for the sensible is valid for expression, for the "intelligible." It is not a question, in fact, of grounding the intelligible on the sensible as on a solid soil, but on the contrary of seizing expression and the sensible as the two last "elements," as two modes of presentation of Being, by which its depth remains preserved differently. The sensible and the intelligible must be understood as "dimensions," in the sense that the sensible "thises" were sensible already, and their relation must be reconceived on the model that holds, within the sensible, between its "parts." The sensible and the intelligible are worlds in Merleau-Ponty's sense— namely, as what is closed on itself but nevertheless opens onto the others and makes itself their emblem, as "an organized ensemble, which is *closed* but which, strangely, is representative of all the rest, possesses its symbols, its equivalents for everything that [349] is not itself" (VI 277/323). Every tangible is visible, and every visible is tangible; here it is a question of two universes at once radically distinct but susceptible to being transposed into each other, of two total parts, identical but not superimposable. Likewise, the sensible and the intelligible function as emblems of each other; they are variants of an originary meaning or expression which cannot complete itself as pure sensible or as pure sense. There is not, strictly speaking, the sensible and the intelligible, but one sole presence which subsists only as the co-presence of every thing to every thing, as universal pregnancy and promiscuity. Insofar as both manifest Being, insofar as it is the same thing which perceives and which speaks, sensible and intelligible cannot be distinguished. But to the extent that it is precisely Being that they manifest, this non-distinction cannot be surpassed by a unity; sensible and intelligible join up with each other in the exhibition of a presence. Being, on which the "identity" of the sensible and the intelligible is based, has the negation of identity as its content, by which it distinguishes itself precisely from *what* is. The depth of Being rules out the possibility of its gathering itself into a unity, of its being susceptible to being possessed; it requires, on the contrary, that what manifests it still be exceeded by it, and this excess must occur at the very level of its ultimate modes of manifestation. Because it is based on their relation to Being, the unity of the sensible and the intelligible is at the same time their difference. The sensible and intelligible do not exist as factual positivity and ideal entity; that would entail being situated on the plane of the being and misunderstanding Being which, in them, comes to be manifested. Insofar as they are the expression of Being, they therefore communicate. But Being cannot be restituted beyond their difference; their communication cannot transform itself into identity. The "reality" that they manifest cannot be preserved in its depth except by not distinguishing itself from what manifests it. It is the character of these two orders, a character that is, so to speak, exhaustive and ultimate, which precisely guarantees their signifying power and which preserves their aptitude for continuity. *There is not* Being—a manifestation cannot present it in person. Thus, to distinguish the sensible and the intelligible would be the same thing as positing their object as a being; it would be the same thing as remaining ignorant of the Being that they manifest and at the heart of which they communicate. But to require that the principle of their communication be positively exhibited would be to fall once again to the plane of the being, such that in their very identity, the [350] difference of the sensible and the intelligible is maintained. Being could never be confused with beings, and that is why there is a unity of the intelligible and the sensible, a passage from one to the other, a nondifference. Because it presupposed a certain sense of Being, instead of gaining access to a true ontological interrogation, phenomenology reified the difference between the sensible and the intelligible by grounding it on realms that in the end are autonomous, thereby shifting the movement of phenomenalization back and forth from one side of itself to the other. Nevertheless, to respect the distinction between Being and beings is to recognize that their difference is itself not like that found between beings [*leur différence est elle-même non-étante*]; it is not a difference *between* different things. If we do not recognize this specific kind of difference, Being would again be projected onto the plane of the being; it is in the being or as the being that Being preserves its Being, and it is at the heart of this identity that the Difference of Being is guaranteed. Insofar as the Difference is the Difference of Being, the Difference must therefore defer differences at the heart of the being, and Being must not be *other* than the being. That is why the passage from the sensible to the intelligible cannot be thematized, why the principle of their articulation cannot be possessed in person, since, in order to unfold its signifying power, the principle of their articulation cannot be other than what it articulates. The risk run by a direct or immediate ontological interrogation lies in confusing the sensible and speech in a single advent of Being, that is, in misunderstanding the phenomenal diversity of what reveals the advent; this is a diversity that creates its being insofar as it hides its withdrawal. The sensible is itself only if it shifts itself toward the intelligible, and the intelligible remains itself only if it slips toward the sensible; each one maintains a reserve of being which permits it to exceed its own dimensionality and articulate itself to the other. But this reserve, this depth, in principle cannot itself be grasped; it has reality only if the sensible and the intelligible maintain between them a radical difference. Being, at the heart of which the sensible and intelligible are articulated, exists only as the terms that it articulates. Being truly appears as the universal dimension, the "dimension of all dimensions" (VI 319/265): "Each field is a dimensionality, and Being is dimensionality itself" (VI 280/227). Every fact is a dimension, but to that degree every dimension is itself a fact for another dimension: "there is no *hierarchy* of orders or layers or planes (always founded on the individual–essence distinction), there is a dimensionality of every fact and facticity of every dimension—[351] this is in virtue of the 'ontological difference'" (VI 324/270). Perception and expression, which are ultimate dimensions for the whole of the phenomenal field, are themselves facts for a final dimension of which they are still the crystallization, that of Being. Being must be conceived as the axis or the hinge around which perception and expression join back up with each other and are disjoined in a single movement; the unity of Being makes sense only as a unity which is not posited, only as a dimension, that is, only as an identity which is just as much difference. The dimensionality which is opened by the least sensible individual cannot be reclosed and cannot be based in itself; it proliferates in itself, makes itself different for other dimensions, indefinitely, right up to Being itself, which, far from corresponding to a principle of closure, is then only the very principle of this proliferation, the possibility of this openness. Being is everything because everything has its advent in it, because every thing, every organ, every field can, in it, communicate with the others; but to that degree it is nothing *itself* because this participation is the means for everything to preserve its difference and its determination. Such is the meaning of the last chiasm: the sensible world and the intelligible world envelop Being, in that Being is not other than they; but that is the means for Being to preserve its absolute depth, so that the sensible and the intelligible are just as much enveloped in it. By distinguishing itself from what manifests it, Being is demoted to the rank of a being where its absoluteness would be lost; it is therefore itself only by remaining included in what it contains. It is not distinguished from the phenomenality and expressivity which it nourishes; rather, these merge with the depth of Being, insofar as the depth is a depth that is held back and not unfolded. In other words, the absolute difference of Being and the being can be understood only as their absolute identity; by being *nothing* other than the being, Being preserves its alterity. One cannot ascend beyond. It is a matter of understanding that the absolute, instead of being able to be determinate itself as the transcendence of a transcendent, makes sense only as human contingency. One has to understand that the absolute can have its advent only as this contingency because it hides itself in this contingency. The flesh ultimately designates neither the perceiving body nor the expressive gesture, but rather the place where they come together as they differentiate themselves from each other. There is a flesh of this corporeal flesh and of this glorious flesh which is synonymous with Being.

[352] It is necessary, then, to picture the universe as intuited by Merleau-Ponty as a proliferation of chiasms that integrate themselves according to different levels of generality. Thus, we can distinguish four moments. First of all, sensible individuals appear and articulate themselves at the heart of a mode of determinate sensibility; vision is not given itself, present to itself, but it subsists only as dissimulated in the visibles which it institutes, crystallized in them. On the other hand, in its very difference, vision communicates with the other senses; even while they cannot be confused, every visible possesses an equivalent in the tangible order. Nevertheless, by virtue of its dimensionality—that is, its crystallization in diverse senses and thus in the thickness of each "this"—sensibility [*la sensibilité*] cannot be closed in on itself, cannot be assigned to a "self"; it appears, on the contrary, as a moment of a universal sensibility [*sensibilité*] which is intersubjectivity, the articulation between the sensible "consciousnesses," the inner frame at the heart of which they have their advent, at once as same and as other. With this dimension of universal sensibility [*sensibilité*], we pass from sensible "solipsistic" presence into objective transcendence. Nevertheless, this transcendence is not exhausted by the community of sensible consciousnesses; its transcendence subsists only on the condition of not closing itself on a transcendent, only on the condition of fulfilling itself in the form of rational objectivity. Lastly, the unity of the sensible universal is conceivable only if it is not closed on itself like a strictly sensible unity, like a subsistent unity. The intersubjective sensible articulates itself with

the world of expression, sublimates itself in speech; the sensible and the intelligible must themselves be apprehended as differentiations of an ultimate dimension which is Being.

Nevertheless, it is necessary to understand that everything resides in the point of departure, that Being is nothing other than sensible experience itself, reconceived according to all of its implications. Thus it is necessary to distinguish the sensible in the restricted sense—that is, in the sense of the visible, quasi-spatial exteriority—from the sensible world as synonymous with Being. In Merleau-Ponty's eyes, what defines sensible experience, insofar as it is a relation to an irreducible depth, is that it surpasses itself as experience of the visible world, that it carries in its thickness the destiny of meaning. Experience makes itself expression; that means not that it passes beyond itself, that it transcends itself in destroying itself, but truly that it differentiates itself, that it decelerates into itself. Experience envelops and appropriates what surpasses it, [353] closes itself around the hollows that break it, comes to weigh down with its depth that which breathes transparency into it. The sensible appears as the universal dimension, but only on the condition that we reconceive it beyond the traditional oppositions and understand it as a milieu of universal kinship and pregnancy. Everything that exists figures at the heart of the sensible, but a sensible which includes all that is, right up to the intelligible itself. Thus, "Being is the 'place' where the 'modes of consciousness' are inscribed as structuration of Being (a way of thinking oneself within a society is implied in its social structure), and where the structurations of Being are modes of consciousness" (VI 307/253).

It is possible, then, to respond to the question of the relationship between Being and the world raised by several commentators.[1] One must observe that Merleau-Ponty cared very little about clarifying the usage of these terms, which he even tends to confuse (e.g., VI 308/254–55). He nevertheless specifies in a note:

> World and Being:
>   their relation is that of the visible with the invisible (latency) the
> invisible is not another visible ("possible" in the logical sense) a positive
> only *absent*

1. Notably G. B. Madison in *The Phenomenology of Merleau-Ponty* (Athens: Ohio University Press, 1981).

It is *Verborgenheit* by principle i.e. invisible *of the visible*, *Offenheit* of the *Umwelt* and not *Unendlichkeit*. (VI 305/251)

In fact, the world and Being cannot be opposed or distinguished; to do this would be to disfigure them both. Being makes sense, is preserved in its absolute Difference, only if it does not possess its own positivity that would permit it to be separated from the world, that is, to fall back to the plane of the world. Its very depth requires that it not be distinguished from experience, from the world understood in the plenitude of its sense, namely, as the sensible and intelligible world. Being is the invisible of the world; it needs the world to remain what it is, namely, irremediably absent. Only the thickness of worldly texture allows the preservation of the invisibility of Being, because this invisibility is irreducible; it is not the promise of a visibility. But we must not conclude from this that world and Being merge. Because Being, insofar as it exceeds the being, can have its advent only in a world, and the world cannot be understood as positive reality. If the world hides Being, it is Being that it hides, so that it is just as much Being's [354] presentation, exactly the presentation of the unpresentable. Its own visibility is not the negation of Being: it is a mode of Being's manifestation. The world is the domain of all experience, the condition to which all that *there is* is subjected, and that is why it cannot be opposed to Being or close itself up on the positivity of the being. What defines the world is thus always to exceed itself, always to remain unassignable, ungraspable. Crystallizing every dimension, and finally Being as the ultimate dimension, the world is beyond all positivity: a point of passage, an openness to Being. Insofar as worldly experience is this element that Being needs in order to withdraw itself into invisibility, it is just as much expression, the speech of Being. Experience is the expression of Being, but because in this expression the expressed undoes all attempts at appropriation, it is just as much the experience of a world.

Conclusion

[355] "It is the experience, still mute, which we are concerned with leading to the pure expression of its own meaning." Following Husserl, this is the task that Merleau-Ponty assigned to philosophical reflection. In relation to this undertaking, the Husserlian meditation manifests an undeniable tension. If, on the one hand, Husserl is motivated by the concern for a return to things themselves, against the abstractions of naturalism and, in particular, against the abstractions of psychologism, nevertheless, on the other hand, the ontological sense of the world is reconceived as constituted-being within transcendental subjectivity and as appearance grounded on the presentation in person of what appears. He is still naive insofar as he does not recognize in the natural attitude a more fundamental ontological decision whose other form is eidetic intuitionism. To subordinate the appearing world to essence is still to determine the openness to Being on the basis of the being. To do this is to take as the very ground of experience what is really only a product of experience and is, because of this, unable to reabsorb experience's opacity. Certainly, as the paradoxes of the transcendental reduction gradually declare themselves, Husserl affirms the necessity of a return to the *Lebenswelt* as the soil of all idealizing production. He discovers the rooting of all speech in an originary silence, a rooting that stops it from realizing itself as completed speech, as intuitive exhibition of meaning. But it is still the case that Husserl maintains to the very end the necessity of a second reduction that leads the pregiven world back to the life of transcendental subjectivity. What is at issue first for Merleau-Ponty is to overcome this tension. Therefore, the point where Husserl's undertaking ends is Merleau-Ponty's starting point. What is at issue for Merleau-Ponty, as he said in relation to Leibniz, is to take the *Lebenswelt just as it is* instead of *explaining* it, instead of restoring the subjectivity which donates sense. Merleau-Ponty's ontology hides nothing other than the attempt to restore the "world of life" in itself, without presupposition. This requires [356] that we conceive together the possibility of signifying the world and the belonging of all meaning to the world; we have to conceive together the inscription of the world in the ledger of sense and the inscrip-

tion of sense in the ledger of the world: this inscription is *the ontology of the* Lebenswelt. That does not mean that Merleau-Ponty fails to go beyond the *Lebenswelt* toward Being: what is at issue rather is to reconceive the *Lebenswelt* as an ultimate mode of being. We must recognize, Merleau-Ponty says, "that the theoretically *complete,* full world of the physical explanation is not so, and that therefore it is necessary to consider as ultimate, inexplicable, and *hence as a world by itself* the whole of our experience of sensible being and of men" (VI 310/256). We must treat as definitive the stage that Husserl considered provisional: to describe *the* Lebenswelt *as Being.* Also, Merleau-Ponty's ontology does not break with phenomenology; it is rather phenomenology's most significant achievement. It aims to recognize what Husserl had foreseen, namely, "a type of being which contains everything"; it aims to make a return from "an objective world to a *Lebenswelt* in whose continual flux are borne Nature and the objects of perception, as well as the constructions through which we grasp them with Cartesian exactness; it is the source in general of all the historical structures which help us to analyze or model our relations with others and with the truth" (RC 151/176). While Husserl remains up to the end dependent on the primacy of the objective world, Merleau-Ponty's ontology develops a radical critique of objectivity, a critique that does not lead to the affirmation of an abyss of non-sense but which imposes, on the contrary, a genesis of the objective universe. Objectivity is not based on itself. It does not give us the ultimate ontological sense of the world, but nevertheless the world from which it proceeds is the world *for* objectivity: the archaeological approach is important only insofar as it is accompanied by the recognition of a teleology. Merleau-Ponty's ontology therefore does not come about from a break with classical interrogation. It claims only to take up its tension, that is, the tension between the horizon of science and the recognition of an "abyssal Being." It claims to restore the element within which objectivity and the pure "there is" no longer present a dichotomy. It wants to be "the science of pre-science, . . . the expression of what is before expression *and sustains it from behind*" (VI 221/167). Ontology therefore makes sense only as "*intra-ontology*" (VI 279/225, 280/227). It reverses the rationalist attempt to hang over [*surplomber*] the world of experience in order to determine its being. It is the rejection of the possibility of the overhang [*surplomb*], at least in a direct mode; it is the consciousness of the inscription of all speech, even those discourses which defy all belonging and which claim to join back up with an absolute in order to terminate the movement of reflection. Merleau-Ponty's ontology is the description of Being as the infinite mediation that sense needs in order to become itself. It is lucidity and humility in regard to philosophy, recognition of its share of non-philosophy, recognition of its dimension of pure interrogation, of its belonging to the very universe that it seeks to signify. This does not mean that this negation is militant, that philosophy returns to simple positivity, that it renounces itself in favor of the Fact. We are entirely within meaning itself, if, everywhere, meaning remains figurative, and if Being as the "world of life" harbors the entire destiny of expression. Every philosophy that claims to reabsorb the world of experience, to terminate reflection and thus verify its sovereignty, is naive and betrays its vow of radicality. For Merleau-Ponty, philosophy reaches the height of its demand for radicality only if it becomes conscious of its own rootedness and if it constructs itself around this realization. It is absolute only if it comes to contain itself (VI 221/167). It is "Being speaking in us," perceptual faith interrogating itself about itself. It is consciousness of what precedes it, an attempt to make the silence of the world resound in its speech, the renewal of silence in this speech. Far from asserting the sovereignty of Spirit, it describes on the contrary the passivity of our activity, a "body of the Spirit" (VI 274/221, 307/253). In this passivity, Spirit attempts to coincide with its carnal dimension; and instead of this being the renunciation of its sovereignty, Spirit is itself only in this humility. Philosophy is situated therefore in the hollow of a chiasm, at this "point of turning back" where the conversion of silence into speech and speech into silence happens. It wants to catch in the act the equivalence between the sense-being of the world and the world-being of sense, between the entering into oneself and the leaving of oneself; it wants to fix the place where teleology happens: "it cannot be total and active grasp, intellectual possession [358], since what there is to be grasped is a dispossession——It is not *above* life, overhanging; it is beneath. It is the simultaneous experience of the holding and the held in all orders" (VI 319/266). Ontology must be set up from two sides at once: from the side of the world while it speaks, and yet from the side of speech when it is plunging itself into the thickness of the world. In other words, it actively questions the possibility of distinguishing the two sides, the obverse and reverse of things, a subject and an object. It speaks of this "compound of the world and ourselves" (VI 138/102), which is deeper than the terms that intertwine there. While claiming to make its own account and to gather the universe that it names up into the nets of sense, philosophy puts naiveté to the test in relation to itself and, consequently, in relation to the world. An authentically philosophical speech must be an interrogation of its own possibility, an investigation of what is before speech, without however throwing this anteriority back into the domain of non-sense. The end of philosophy is really the account of its own beginning.

This task is not without difficulties. How can a word name what precedes it or mean that from which meaning itself proceeds? Does philosophical speech exile itself from the very world at which it aims as soon as it names this world? Holding ourselves to that position would amount to being dependent on the very opposition that Merleau-Ponty wants to criticize—the opposition between a universe of meaning, for which speech would be only the contingent *medium,* and a universe of actuality, which would be located just short of all speech. Then, in fact, as certain critics have asserted, there would be an insurmountable dichotomy between philosophical discourse, devoted to objectivism, and a return to the *Lebenswelt* whose price would be a call to silence. There would be a choice between philosophy, whose natal objectivism one would have to take up— since we can say it, the ultimate being of the world lies in the meaning —and a vow of fidelity to experience that only a silent coincidence would allow us to respect. Merleau-Ponty's ontology, and in particular his analysis of speech, is the actual rejection of this dichotomy. It is true that we speak, that lived experience is a "spoken-lived experience"; but it is also true that we speak of the world, that speech itself is the world, inscribed in the experience that it thematizes. On this condition, speech can be meaningful. [359] One has to start from this piece of evidence: we can speak only because the world speaks in us, makes itself language, and testifies about itself there in us. Philosophy can speak and express what precedes it

> because language is not only the depository of fixed and acquired signification, because its cumulative power itself results from a power of anticipation or of prepossession, because one speaks not only of what one knows, so as to set out a display of it—but also of what one does not know, in order to know it—and because language in forming itself expresses, at least laterally, an ontogenesis of which it is a part. (VI 139/102)

Thus, precisely because the world is entirely speech, *logos,* the claim that philosophical speech expresses the world itself becomes understandable. Like all speech, philosophy is the speech *of* the world—and what qualifies it as philosophy is that, like poetry, it knows itself to be of the world and takes this belonging as its theme. It is nothing other than speech becoming conscious of itself as speaking speech, inscribed in the ledger of the world. Is there, then, no dichotomy between philosophical speech and the wild world with which it wants to join back up? Philosophy is that speech at the heart of which, by virtue of this lucidity in regard to itself, the world comes to say itself. Philosophy is that infinite mediation through which the world can return to itself and become the *logos* that it has always been, through which it can accomplish its own genuine being; philosophy is not distinguished from what it mediates. Philosophy can coincide with the world that it thematizes and discover its secret only because it thematizes itself as a moment of the world, only because it makes itself such a moment. It can possess the world only by letting itself be possessed by it. In short, "between the *Lebenswelt* as universal Being and philosophy as a furthermost product of the world, there is no rivalry or antinomy: it is philosophy which discloses it" (VI 224/170). Philosophy's most extreme point is just as much the tranquillity of the origin. Philosophy is really creation, but "a creation that is at the same time a reintegration of Being: for it is not a creation in the sense of one of the commonplace *Gebilde* that history fabricates: it knows itself to be a *Gebilde* and wishes to surpass itself as pure *Gebilde*, to find again its origin. It is hence a creation in a radical sense: a creation that is at the same time an adequation" (VI 250/197). It is true that such a perspective [360] calls for a mutation of philosophical discourse, that Merleau-Ponty's project requires the elaboration of a kind of speech that would be susceptible to its own ontogenesis. Merleau-Ponty recognizes this at least once: "Hence it is a question whether philosophy as reconquest of brute or wild being can be accomplished by the resources of eloquent language, or whether it would not be necessary for philosophy to use language in a way that takes from it its power of immediate or direct signification in order to equal it with what it wishes all the same to say" (VI 139/102–103). It is clear that the description of brute Being cannot be brought about within a constituted language, satisfied with recalling meanings which are closed upon themselves, cut off from their signifying power, from their worldly rootedness. This justifies the new tone of *The Visible and the Invisible* and, in particular, of the working notes. But Merleau-Ponty never reverts to silence, nor even to poetic speech. *The Visible and the Invisible* attests, on the contrary, to the possibility of a philosophical speech in the strongest sense of the term, the possibility of a speech that names its inscription in Being without ever renouncing eloquence.

Must we conclude from this, as have certain commentators—perhaps a little too quickly—that in *The Visible and the Invisible* Merleau-Ponty ends up in agreement with Heidegger? It is true that the development of his thought leads him to overcome the viewpoint of transcendental subjectivity and brings him into the neighborhood of Heidegger, whose name appears several times in the working notes. But we must recognize that Merleau-Ponty never lays claim to such a relationship with Heidegger, and that, finally, the question of his relationship with Heidegger is not an issue for him. He recognizes in Heidegger only an echo of his own thought. He does not surrender himself to Heidegger's perspective; he reads it according to what he finds true in it, that is, from the viewpoint of its convergence with his own approach. Rather than his critique of Husserl proceeding from his connection to Heidegger, he grasps, across them both, a unique mode of interrogation whose ontology calls for clarification and completion. First and foremost, as we have said, Merleau-Ponty's ontology completes the Husserlian project of a return to the *Lebenswelt*, which proceeds by bringing the question of experience, the question of the phenomenon, into the foreground. In Merleau-Ponty, there is no question of Being as Being; there is a demand for fidelity to experience, to the being of the phenomenon. And if an ontological question [361] arises, if Being comes on the scene, it is as one moment, called for by the interrogation of the phenomenon. To pose the question of Being prior to that of the phenomenon makes no sense in Merleau-Ponty's eyes; the unconcealment of Being proceeds from a question bearing on the phenomenon. Being makes sense only as the Being of the being: "One cannot make a direct ontology. My 'indirect' method (being in the beings) is alone conformed with being—'negative philosophy' like 'negative theology'" (VI 233/179; cf. RC 125/156, 155/179). It is true that we cannot hold on to an approach to the being which would be cut off from its being. This was the limitation of realism and of objectivistic philosophies; in these philosophies, the domain of the being was in the end referred to one being, consciousness, with the result that in every phenomenon the appearing was based on the *eidos* and conceived as a present-being. However, the openness to the dimension of Being cannot be inaugurated by means of a rupture with the plane of the being. On the contrary, the openness to the dimension of Being is called for through an analysis of the being itself as soon as the latter is freed from objectivism. If the being can be reconceived only from a dimension which exceeds it and which carries its presence, this dimension does not lead us beyond the being. The dimension is rejoined only through a description of the being and of its different regions in the moment of their appearance. In other words, Merleau-Ponty's ontology is an *ontology of the visible* (VI 185/140). And if Merleau-Ponty essentially claims to follow Husserl, this is first of all because Husserl's philosophy "results in an ontological rehabilitation of the sensible" (S 210/166–67). It is not, therefore, the inaugural posing of the question of Being which leads to overcoming the plane of the sensible being; on the contrary, it is the rigorous consideration of the sensible "there is" insofar as this leads to the renunciation of consciousness and of the *eidos,* allowing a dimension of Being to be revealed in its heart. Instead of the ontological viewpoint proceeding from a questioning which breaks with the plane of the being, for Merleau-Ponty it is a question of understanding the sensible as Being and Being as the sensible—that is, as what, being based in itself and "containing everything," is nonetheless not distinguished from the modes of phenomenalization and thematization which advent in it and, in the end, from the indefinitely open set of beings. This is why Merleau-Ponty has been able to criticize, in Heidegger, the radical and consequently abstract character of his interrogation of Being. Husserl accentuates [362] the need to account for the world appearing as such, which leads him to apprehend phenomenality on the plane of the being instead of preserving in phenomenality a dimension of irreducible Being. But putting irreducible Being ahead by turning it into the object of a specific questioning, Heidegger still fails and splits Being off from the being whose presence it bears. Heidegger's growing silence stems from the fact that he "has always sought for a direct expression of what is fundamental at the very moment he is showing its impossibility, from the fact that he refused all the mirrors of Being" (RC 156/179–80). The phenomenon itself cannot be grasped or posited as present-being; its appearance refers, on the contrary, to an irreducible ground, and thus forbids all attempts to bring it into presence. But as for this ground, it cannot be made the object of a specific question, because its depth draws its support only from merging with the being which comes from it, only from passing into the phenomenon, only from being the soil for an appearing. This depth must be approached indirectly because it is just as much transparency. Every "there is" is, as we have said, the crystallization of a dimension. If, as mundane, it remains just short of the order of sense, it is not, however, anything other than it. It does not flow back toward an unsayable facticity. Being is the dimensionality itself, universal participation or kinship. And this is why it cannot be distinguished absolutely from meaning. Meaning can be conceived only on the condition of not being posited itself, as being-meaning; it preserves its fecundity only by crystallizing itself, only by turning itself into the opaque "there is," the world. For sense, the notion of dimensionality expresses only the necessity of being able to be itself only by staying in withdrawal. In other words, in Merleau-Ponty Being is synonymous with invisibility. The latter does not refer to an absolute invisibility—that would still be to refer itself, negatively, to an absolute vision. Invisibility is the very condition of vision; it merges with visibility. Thus, it is not Being which determines and maintains the fundamental invisibility of the being; on the contrary, it is because sense is essentially invisible that it presents itself as "there is." Being designates only "the inexhaustible richness" of the world "and therefore the absence that it conceals" (RC 155/179), the inexhaustible reserve of sense or, rather, the sense insofar as it is in reserve. It is not the ground but the horizon of the being. One would have to speak of a symmetry and therefore of a chiasm between Being and the being. It is true that every being is [363] included within Being in that its visibility requires a fundamental invisibility, in that it remains "there," at a distance, transcendent, so that no experience, no speech can claim to grasp it in person. Nevertheless, this invisibility is not something other than the visible; it is the very condition of its phenomenality. Being remains thereby a moment of the being, enveloped in the being that it envelops; this invisibility is depth *for* the being, the withdrawal that allows it to remain what it is. Everything sensible is; in other words, it is what *there is.* But its being is nothing other than *what* there is. Nothing in it escapes from phenomenalization, from expression, even if phenomenalization and expression require an infinite process. Thus, the difference between Being and the being cannot be understood as an absolute difference; the difference between Being and the being does not differ from their identity. The depth of Being is preserved only insofar as it merges with the indefinitely open field of phenomena and of expressivity; the being can detach itself only on the condition of not detaching itself completely, on the condition of remaining enclosed in what it nevertheless envelops and determines. The difference between Being and the being corresponds only to the infinite becoming of expression, to fundamental historicity, which is why it is equally identity. As de Waelhens notes, "The history of Being is therefore intrinsic to the *encounter* of man and things, without this implying in the least, of course, that reality is immanent to us. The distinction between Being and the being is not denied but limited; it is the history and the becoming of an understanding, *and it is only that.*"[1] If Merleau-Ponty's concern for fidelity to experience leads him to reject dialectical thought, which is devoted to thematizing itself and therefore to deteriorating into abstraction, it is still the case that some type of Hegelianism stops Merleau-Ponty from adopting Heidegger's radicality and abstraction. Even though, in Merleau-Ponty's eyes, the tension between consciousness and its other is abolished in the Hegelian notion of Spirit, Merleau-Ponty's notion of Being is traversed by a radical rending, by a difference which does not go as far as unity because it does not go as far as opposition. But if there is really a truth of difference that holds against opposition, there is, on the other hand, a truth of teleology that holds against the *absoluteness* of difference. And this is why the dialectic allows us to secure ourselves against a certain kind of phenomenology. [364] Thus, while in Heidegger Being gives itself to human understanding but withdraws itself absolutely before this understanding, what Merleau-Ponty understands by Being is *nothing other* than this very understanding. Correlatively, while in Heidegger Being remains a partner which gives itself or steals itself away *freely* from our understanding so that, in man, it is Being itself which comes to the point of questioning, for Merleau-Ponty Being responds to human freedom as the freedom of an understanding.

Thus, Merleau-Ponty's ontology in no way attests to an accord with Heidegger. It seems to us, on the contrary, that it is situated beyond Heidegger's interrogation insofar as it constitutes a critique in action of what the thought of Being as Being retains that is still abstract and unilateral. Merleau-Ponty's ontology allows us to recognize, as Richir has said, "in Heidegger's insistence to push interrogation in one sole direction—the direction of Being as such—a form of abstraction coming from classical philosophy, although here in Heidegger it is carried to a degree of necessity and subtlety never before attained." The humility of a philosophy of perceptual faith "commits us to yield the terrain of philosophy and of phenomenology less easily to the marvels of an intelligence of abysses; in other periods, we called this a sovereign Reason."[2] Being makes sense only as flesh, as universal pregnancy and parturition, beyond the opposition of

1. A. de Waelhens, "Situation de Merleau-Ponty," *Les temps modernes,* nos. 184–85 (1961): 392.
2. M. Richir, "Le sens de la phénoménologie dans *Le visible et l'invisible,*" *Esprit,* no. 66 (1982): 142.

the individual and the essence, of actuality and meaning. The aim of ontology is "not Being in itself, identical to itself, in the night, but Being that also contains its negation, its *percipi*" (VI 304/250–51). If, against idealism, Merleau-Ponty grasped Being as what recoils indefinitely under the look or speech, it is still the case that he reintegrates the possibility of our understanding into Being. If Heidegger's merit lies in having integrated "our power of error into truth" (RC 155/179), it is still the case that this errancy cannot be put in order by the proximity of an abyss; it draws a path. Thus Merleau-Ponty commits us to the patricide in relation to Heidegger that Plato carries out in relation to Parmenides. Just as Plato attempts to reintegrate the possibility of knowledge and discourse, [365] that is, the possibility of negation, into Parmenidean Being without compromising its purity, so Merleau-Ponty attempts to understand Heideggerian Being from or as the possibility of a phenomenalization and an expression. Merleau-Ponty attempts to reintegrate into it the viewpoint of the being without absorbing it back into ideality, without compromising its depth. It is this "Platonism" which in the end pulls Merleau-Ponty back to Husserl's side, even if what is at issue for him is also to free phenomenology from intuitionism, to free it from the Platonic naiveté from which Husserl never completely separated himself. Thus, it seems to us that one has to give to Merleau-Ponty's ontology the place that it deserves: a place beyond Husserl and Heidegger. For this very reason, phenomenology can read its own future in Merleau-Ponty's ontology.

Bibliography

Works by Maurice Merleau-Ponty

"La conscience et l'acquisition du langage." In *Merleau-Ponty à la Sorbonne: résumé de cours 1949–1952*. Grenoble: Cynara, 1988. Originally published in *Bulletin de psychologie* 18, no. 236 (November 1964). Translated by H. J. Silverman as *Consciousness and the Acquisition of Language*. Evanston, Ill.: Northwestern University Press, 1973.

Douze entretiens avec Maurice Merleau-Ponty, by G. Charbonnier. Recorded for the R.T.F. between May 25 and August 7, 1959.

"Husserl et la notion de Nature: notes prises au cours du 14 et 25 mars 1957 par X. Tillette." *Revue de métaphysique et de morale*, no. 3 (1965): 259–69. Translated by J. Barry, Jr., as "Husserl's Concept of Nature (Merleau-Ponty's 1957–58 Lectures)." In *Texts and Dialogues*, edited by H. J. Silverman and J. Barry, Jr., 162–68. Atlantic Highlands, N.J.: Humanities Press, 1997.

"Un inédit de Maurice Merleau-Ponty." *Revue de métaphysiques et de morale*, no. 4 (1962): 401–409. Translated by A. B. Dallery as "An Unpublished Text by Maurice Merleau-Ponty: A Prospectus of His Work." In *The Primacy of Perception*, edited by J. M. Edie, 3–11. Evanston, Ill.: Northwestern University Press, 1964.

Merleau-Ponty à la Sorbonne: résumé de cours 1949–1952. Grenoble: Cynara, 1988. Originally published in *Bulletin de psychologie* 18, no. 236 (November 1964).

L'œil et l'esprit. Paris: Gallimard, 1964. Translated by C. Dallery as "Eye and Mind." Revised by M. B. Smith. In *The Merleau-Ponty Aesthetics Reader: Philosophy and Painting*, edited by G. Johnson, 121–49. Evanston, Ill.: Northwestern University Press, 1993.

Phénoménologie de la perception. Paris: Gallimard, 1945. Translated by C. Smith as *Phenomenology of Perception*. Revised by F. Williams. London: Routledge and Kegan Paul, 1981.

Preface to *L'œuvre de Freud et son importance pour le monde moderne*, by A. Hesnard. Paris: Payot, 1960. Translated by Alden L. Fisher as "Phenomenology and Psychoanalysis: Preface to Hesnard's *L'Oeuvre de Freud*." In *Merleau-Ponty and Psychology*, edited by K. Hoeller, 67–72. Atlantic Highlands, N.J.: Humanities Press, 1993.

"Le primat de la perception et ses conséquences philosophiques." *Bulletin de la société française de philosophie* 41 (1947): 119–53. Translated by J. M. Edie as "The Primacy of Perception and Its Philosophical Consequences." In *The Primacy of Perception*, edited by J. M. Edie, 12–42. Evanston, Ill.: Northwestern University Press, 1964.

La prose du monde. Edited with preface by C. Lefort. Paris: Gallimard, 1969. Translated by J. O'Neill as *The Prose of the World*. Evanston, Ill.: Northwestern University Press, 1973.

Les relations avec autrui chez l'enfant. Paris: Centre de Documentation Universitaire, 1960. Translated by W. Cobb as "The Child's Relations with Others." In *The Primacy of Perception*, edited by J. M. Edie, 96–155. Evanston, Ill.: Northwestern University Press, 1964.

Résumé de cours, Collège de France 1952–1960. Paris: Gallimard, 1968. Translated by J. O'Neill as "Themes from the Lectures at the Collège de France, 1952–1960." In *In Praise of Philosophy and Other Essays*, 71–199. Evanston, Ill.: Northwestern University Press, 1988.

Les sciences de l'homme et la phénoménologie. Paris: Centre de Documentation Universitaire, 1951. Translated by J. Wild as "Phenomenology and the Sciences of Man." In *The Primacy of Perception*, edited by J. M. Edie, 43–95. Evanston, Ill.: Northwestern University Press, 1964.

Sens et non-sens. Paris: Nagel, 1948. Translated by H. Dreyfus and P. Dreyfus as *Sense and Non-Sense*. Evanston, Ill.: Northwestern University Press, 1964.

Signes. Paris: Gallimard, 1960. Translated by R. McCleary as *Signs*. Evanston, Ill.: Northwestern University Press, 1964.

La structure du comportment. Paris: Presses Universitaires de France, 1942. Translated by A. Fisher as *The Structure of Behavior*. Boston: Beacon Press, 1963.

L'union de l'âme et du corps chez Malebranche, Biran et Bergson, notes prises au cours de Maurice Merleau-Ponty à l'Ecole Normale Supérieure. Collected and edited by J. Duprun. Paris: Vrin, 1968. Translated by P. B. Milan as *The Incarnate Subject: Malebranche, Biran, and Bergson and the Union of Body and Soul*. New York: Humanity Books, 2001.

Le visible et l'invisible. Paris: Gallimard, 1964. Translated by A. Lingis as *The Visible and the Invisible*. Evanston, Ill.: Northwestern University Press, 1968.

Other Works

This list includes only those works that have contributed to our reflection. For an exhaustive bibliography of commentaries on Merleau-Ponty, see S. Delivoyatsis, *La dialectique des phénomènes* (Paris: Méridiens Klincksieck, 1987).

Alquié, F. "Une philosophie de l'ambiguité: l'existentialisme de Merleau-Ponty." *Fontaine*, no. 59 (1947): 47–70.

Aubenque, P. *Le problème de l'être chez Aristote*. Paris: Presses Universitaires de France, 1962.

Bannan, J. F. "The 'Later' Thought of Merleau-Ponty." *Dialogue* 5 (1966): 383–403.

Beaufret, J. *Dialogue avec Heidegger III*. Paris: Minuit, 1974.

Binswanger, L. *Analyse existentielle et psychanalyse freudienne: discours, parcours et Freud*. Translated by R. Lewinter. Paris: Gallimard, 1981.

———. "Daseinsanalyse und Psychotherapie." *Zeitschrift für Psychotherapie und medizinische Psychologie* 4 (1954): 241–45.

———. "Daseinsanalytik und Psychiatrie." *Der Nervenarzt* 22 (1951): 1–10.

———. "Traum und Existenz." *Neue Schweizer Rundschau* 9 (1930). Translated by J. Needleman as "Dream and Existence." In *Dream and Existence*, edited by K. Hoeller, 81–105. Atlantic Highlands, N.J.: Humanities Press, 1993.

———. "Vom anthropologischen Sinn der Verstiegenheit." *Der Nervenarzt* 20 (1949).

Brenna, G. L. *La struttura della percezione*. Milan: Vita e Pensiero, 1969.

Breton, S. *Conscience et intentionalité*. Paris: Emmanuel Vitte, 1956.

Caruso, P. "Il problema dell'esistenza altrui in Merleau-Ponty." *Aut aut*, no. 66 (1961).

Deleuze, G. *Le pli: Leibniz et le baroque*. Paris: Minuit, 1988. Translated by T. Coley as *The Fold: Leibniz and the Baroque*. Minneapolis: University of Minnesota Press, 1993.

Derossi, G. "Della percezione alla visione. L'ontologia negativa dell'ultimo Merleau-Ponty." *Filosofia* (April 1965).

———. "L'emergenza del percepito e del significato dal progetto intenzionale corporeo in Merleau-Ponty." *Filosofia* (January 1964).

———. "Maurice Merleau-Ponty. Dall' 'ambiguita' al transcendentalismo corporeo." *Filosofia* (April 1963).

———. "Tempo, soggetto, cogito e conoscenza intenzionale diretta (non-mediata) in Merleau-Ponty." *Filosofia* (October 1964).

Derrida, J. Introduction to *L'origine de la géométrie*, by E. Husserl. Paris: Presses Universitaires de France, 1962. Translated by J. P. Leavey, Jr., as *Edmund Husserl's Origin of Geometry: An Introduction*. 1978. Reprint, Lincoln: University of Nebraska Press, 1989.

———. "Violence et métaphysique." In *L'écriture et la différence*. Paris: Seuil, 1967. Translated by A. Bass as "Violence and Metaphysics." In *Writing and Difference*, 79–153. Chicago: University of Chicago Press, 1978.

———. *La voix et le phénomène*. Paris: Presses Universitaires de France, 1967. Translated by D. B. Allison as *Speech and Phenomena*. Evanston, Ill.: Northwestern University Press, 1972.

Fink, E. "Die phänomenologische Philosophie Husserls in der gegenwärtigen Kritik." *Kantstudien* (1933). Translated as "The Phenomenological Philosophy of Edmund Husserl and Contemporary Criticism." In *The Phenomenology of Husserl*, edited by R. O. Elveton, 73–147. Chicago: Quadrangle Press, 1970.

Franck, D. *Chair et corps. Sur la phénoménologie de Husserl*. Paris: Minuit, 1981.

Garelli, J. "Il y a le monde." *Esprit*, no. 66 (1982): 113–23.

———. "Le lieu d'un questionnement." *Les cahiers de philosophie*, no. 7 (1989): 107–44.

———. "Temps et phénoménologie: temporalité originaire, *ereignis* et jeu du monde." In *Ed. de l'Université de Bruxelles* (1989).

Granel, G. *Le sens du temps et de la perception chez E. Husserl*. Paris: Gallimard, 1968.

Heidegger, M. *Being and Time*. Translated by J. Stambaugh. Albany: State University of New York Press, 1996.

———. *Identity and Difference*. Translated by J. Stambaugh. New York: Harper and Row, 1969.

———. *On the Way to Language*. Translated by P. D. Hertz. New York: Harper and Row, 1971.

Henry, M. "Le concept de l'âme a-t-il un sens?" *Revue de philosophique de Louvain* 64
    (1966): 5–33.
Husserl, E. *Erfahrung und Urteil.* Edited by L. Landgrebe. Hamburg: Classen, 1938.
    Translated by J. Churchill and K. Ameriks as *Experience and Judgment: Inves-*
    tigations in a Genealogy of Logic. Evanston, Ill.: Northwestern University
    Press, 1973.
————. "Foundational Investigations of the Phenomenological Origin of the Spa-
    tiality of Nature." Translated by F. Kersten. In *Husserl: Shorter Works,* edited
    by P. McCormick and F. Elliston, 222–33. Notre Dame, Ind.: University of
    Notre Dame Press, 1981.
————. *Ideen zu einer reinen Phänomenologie und phänomenologischen Philosophie:*
    Erstes Buch. Edited by K. Schuhmann. Husserliana 3-1. The Hague: Martinus
    Nijhoff, 1976. Translated by F. Kersten as *Ideas Pertaining to a Pure Phenome-*
    nology and to a Phenomenological Philosophy, First Book: General Introduc-
    tion to a Pure Phenomenology. The Hague: Martinus Nijhoff, 1982.
————. *Ideen zu einer reinen Phänomenologie und phänomenologischen Philosophie:*
    Zweites Buch. Edited by M. Biemel. Husserliana 4. The Hague: Martinus
    Nijhoff, 1952. Translated by R. Rojcewicz and A. Schuwer as *Ideas Pertaining*
    to a Pure Phenomenology and to a Phenomenological Philosophy, Second Book:
    Studies in the Phenomenology of Constitution. Dordrecht: Kluwer Academic
    Publishers, 1989.
————. *Ideen zu einer reinen Phänomenologie und phänomenologischen Philosophie:*
    Drittes Buch. Edited by M. Biemel. Husserliana 5. The Hague: Martinus
    Nijhoff, 1971. Translated by T. E. Klein and W. E. Pohl as *Ideas Pertaining to*
    a Pure Phenomenology and to a Phenomenological Philosophy, Third Book:
    Phenomenology and the Foundations of the Sciences. The Hague: Martinus
    Nijhoff, 1980.
————. *Die Krisis der Europaischen Wissenschaften und die transzendentale Phänome-*
    nologie. Edited by W. Biemel. Husserliana 6. The Hague: Martinus Nijhoff,
    1962. Translated by D. Carr as *The Crisis of European Sciences and Transcen-*
    dental Phenomenology. Evanston, Ill.: Northwestern University Press, 1970.
————. *Logische Untersuchungen.* 2 vols. 2nd. ed. Halle: Max Niemeyer, 1913. Trans-
    lated by J. N. Findlay as *Logical Investigations.* 2 vols. London: Routledge and
    Kegan Paul, 1970.
————. *Méditations cartésiennes.* Translated by G. Peiffer and E. Levinas. Paris:
    Armand Collin, 1931. Translated by D. Cairns as *Cartesian Meditations.*
    The Hague: Martinus Nijhoff, 1960. For the original, see *Cartesianische*
    Meditationen und Pariser Vorträge. Ed. S. Strasser. Husserliana 1. The
    Hague: Martinus Nijhoff, 1950.
————. "The Origin of Geometry." Translated by D. Carr. In *The Crisis of European*
    Sciences and Transcendental Phenomenology, 353–78. Evanston, Ill.: North-
    western University Press, 1970.
————. "Universal Teleology." *Telos* 4 (1969): 176–80.
————. *Zur Phänomenologie des inneren Zeitbewusstseins (1893–1917).* Edited by
    R. Boehm. Husserliana 10. The Hague: Martinus Nijhoff, 1966. Translated

by J. Brough as *On the Phenomenology of the Consciousness of Internal Time*. The Hague: Martinus Nijhoff, 1992.

Jeanson, F. *Le problème moral et la pensée de Sartre*. Paris: Myrte, 1947. Translated by R. V. Stone as *Sartre and the Problem of Morality*. Bloomington: Indiana University Press, 1980.

Kelkel, A. "Le problème de l'autre dans la phénoménologie transcendental de Husserl." *Revue de métaphysique et de morale* 61 (1956): 40–52.

———. "Le problème de l'intentionnalité corporelle." In *Maurice Merleau-Ponty, le psychique et le corporel*. Paris: Aubier, 1988.

Lefort, C. *Sur une colonne absente*. Paris: Gallimard, 1978.

Leibniz, G. W. *De rerum originatione radicali*. Vol. 7 of *Die philosophischen Schriften*. Hildesheim: G. Olms, 1978.

Levinas, E. "Intentionnalité et sensation." *Revue internationale de philosophie* 71–72 (1965): 34–54.

———. *Théorie de l'intuition dans la phénoménologie de Husserl*. Paris: Vrin, 1978. Translated by A. Orianne as *The Theory of Intuition in Husserl's Phenomenology*. Evanston, Ill.: Northwestern University Press, 1973.

Madison, G. B. *La phénoménologie de Merleau-Ponty*. Paris: Klincksieck, 1973. Translated by G. B. Madison as *The Phenomenology of Merleau-Ponty*. Athens: Ohio University Press, 1981.

Maldiney, H. "Chair et verbe dans la philosophie de Merleau-Ponty." In *Maurice Merleau-Ponty, le psychique et le corporel*. Paris: Aubier, 1988. Translated by C. Katz as "Flesh and Verb in the Philosophy of Merleau-Ponty." In *Chiasms: Merleau-Ponty's Notion of the Flesh*, edited by F. Evans and L. Lawlor, 51–76. Albany: State University of New York Press, 2000.

Marini, A. "Psicologia e fenomenologia in Husserl e Merleau-Ponty." *Aut aut*, no. 66 (1961).

Paci, E. "Commento al manoscritto E III 5." *Tempo e intentionalita, Archivo di filosofia* (1960).

———. "Tempo e percezione." *Archivio de filosofia* (1958).

———. "Tempo e relazione intentionale in Husserl." *Tempo e intentionalita, Archivio de filosofia* (1960).

Patočka, J. "La doctrine husserlienne de l'intuition eidétique et ses critiques récentes." *Revue internationale de philosophie* 71–72 (1965): 17–33.

Pos, H. "Phénoménologie et linguistic." *Revue internationale de philosophie* (1939).

Richir, M. "Merleau-Ponty: un tout nouveau rapport à la psychoanalyse." *Les cahiers de philosophie*, no. 7 (1989): 155–88.

———. "Phénoménalisation, distorsion, logologie." *Textures*, nos. 4–5 (1972): 63–114.

———. *Phénomènes, temps et êtres: Ontologie et phénoménologie*. Grenoble: Jérôme Millon, 1987.

———. "Le sens de la phénoménologie dans *Le visible et l'invisible*." *Esprit*, no. 66 (1982): 124–45.

Ricoeur, P. *A l'école de la phénoménologie*. Paris: Vrin, 1986.

———. *Le conflit des interpretations*. Paris: Seuil, 1969. Translated by D. Ihde as *The Conflict of Interpretations*. Evanston, Ill.: Northwestern University Press, 1974.

——. *Du texte à l'action: Essais d'herméneutique II.* Paris: Seuil, 1986. Translated by
K. Blamey and J. B. Thompson as *From Text to Action: Essays in Hermeneutics, II.* Evanston, Ill.: Northwestern University Press, 1991.

——. *La métaphore vive.* Paris: Seuil, 1975. Translated by R. Czerny, with
K. McLaughlin and J. Costello, as *The Rule of Metaphor: Multi-disciplinary Studies of the Creation of Meaning in Language.* Toronto: University of Toronto Press, 1977.

——. "Par-delà Husserl et Heidegger." *Les cahiers de philosophie,* no. 7 (1989), 17–23.

Sartre, J. P. *L'être et le néant: essai d'ontologie phénoménologique.* Paris: Gallimard,
1943. Translated by H. Barnes as *Being and Nothingness.* 1956. Reprint, New York: Washington Square Press, 1966.

——. *La transcendance de l'ego.* Paris: Vrin, 1965. Translated by F. Williams and
R. Kirkpatrick as *The Transcendence of the Ego: An Existentialist Theory of Consciousness.* New York: Noonday, 1957.

Scheler, M. *The Nature of Sympathy.* Translated by P. Heath. New Haven: Yale University Press, 1954.

Schérer, R. "Clôture et faille dans la phénoménologie de Husserl." *Revue de métaphysique et de morale* 73 (1968): 344–60.

Schutz, A. "Le problème de l'intersubjectivité transcendentale chez Husserl." *Colloque de Royaument* (1959). Translated by F. Kersten with A. Gurwitsch and
T. Luckmann as "The Problem of Transcendental Intersubjectivity in Husserl." In *Collected Papers III,* edited by I. Schutz, 51–91. The Hague: Martinus Nijhoff, 1966.

Semerari, G. "Scienza e filosofia nella *Fenomenologia della percezione." Aut aut,* no. 66
(1961).

Sichère, B. *Merleau-Ponty ou le corps de la philosophie.* Paris: Grasset, 1982.

Simondon, G. *L'individu et sa genèse physico-biologique.* Paris: Presses Universitaires
de France, 1964.

Souche-Dagues, D. *Le développement de l'intentionnalité dans la phénoménologie
Husserlienne.* The Hague: Martinus Nijhoff, 1972.

Straus, E. *The Primary World of Senses: A Vindication of Sensory Experience.* Translated by J. Needleman. London: Free Press of Glencoe, 1963.

Thierry, Y. *Du corps parlant.* Brussels: Ousia, 1987.

Trân Duc Thao. *Phénoménologie et matérialisme dialectique.* Paris: Gordon and
Breach, 1971. Translated by D. J. Herman and D. V. Morano as *Phenomenology and Dialectical Materialism.* Dordrecht: Reidel, 1986.

Van Breda, H. L. "Maurice Merleau-Ponty et les archives Husserl à Louvain." *Revue de métaphysique et de morale* 64, no. 4 (1962): 410–30. Translated by Stephen Michelman as "Merleau-Ponty and the Husserl Archives at Louvain." In *Texts and Dialogues,* by Merleau-Ponty, edited by H. J. Silverman and
J. Barry, Jr., 150–61. Atlantic Highlands, N.J.: Humanities Press, 1992.

Waelhens, A. de. "Situation de Merleau-Ponty." *Les temps modernes,* nos. 184–85
(1961): 377–98.

Index

267–269, 274, 283, 289–290, 299, 305, 314–315; vital power, 47

Pradines, Maurice, xix

Presence, 21–25, 28, 36, 39, 55, 60–61, 84, 93–94, 97–98, 100, 102–103, 107, 123, 136, 140, 142–143, 149, 155–157, 160, 164, 166–173, 187, 211, 215–216, 220, 222–229, 249–250, 254, 257, 259–260, 262, 264–265, 268–269, 272, 274, 279, 281, 284–286, 288, 290–296, 298, 304, 307, 317; as mute presence, 109; as presence to world, xxviii, 126; as pure presence, 223; as self-presence, 14, 36, 55, 160, 239, 265, 268–269, 281

Presentability (*Urpräsentiertbarkeit*), 162–163, 201

Primordial, 55, 181, 207, 213, 217; as primordial experience, 207, 241; as primordial layer, 66; as primordial world, 66

Profile (*Abschattung*), 53–54, 175

Promise, 136, 254, 262, 271

Proximity, 102, 118–119, 124, 126, 160, 165, 175, 204, 206, 209–210, 212, 229, 244, 255, 268, 281, 283, 285, 320

Psychic, 7, 10, 34, 37, 248, 262, 285

Psychoanalysis, 270–278

Psychologism, 103, 105–106, 311

Psychology, 3, 7, 20, 58, 67–68, 70, 72, 135, 274; child psychology, 21, 34; Gestalt psychology, xxix, xxxiii–xxxiv, 3–5, 34, 44, 50, 70–71, 74, 179, 181, 186

Ravaisson, Jean Gaspard, xix

Realism, xxviii, xxxiii, 6, 13, 20, 23–24, 87, 92, 101, 103–104, 108, 113, 115, 143, 145, 149, 267, 291, 316; critique of realism, xxix–xxx, 3–5, 21–22, 25; transcendental realism, 89, 103

Reality, 13, 20, 22–23, 31, 54, 115, 122, 129, 170, 196, 211, 229, 252–253, 306, 309; formal reality, 48; objective reality, 23–24; perceived reality, 20; transcendental reality, 119

Reduction: phenomenological reduction, 27–29, 66, 70, 74, 76, 90, 104, 107, 110, 148, 288; transcendental reduction, 91, 104, 160, 311

Reflection, 14–17, 25–26, 32, 38, 48, 57, 65, 70, 87–88, 90, 106, 11–112, 116, 140, 153, 160, 313; critique of reflection, 125; phenomenological reflection, 68

Res cogitans, 106

Res extensa, 204

Richir, Marc, xxxi, 146n, 189–190, 286n, 319

Ricoeur, Paul, xxxi, 27–28, 196n, 197n, 218n

Robin, Léon, 183

Rupture, xxx, 61, 89, 101, 118, 122, 125, 197n, 234, 316

Sartre, Jean-Paul, xi, xxii, xxviii, 85, 113–128, 131–138, 149, 165–166, 241, 248–250, 257, 271; and *Being and Nothingness*, 114, 127; and *The Transcendence of the Ego*, 114. *See also* Subjectivity

Saussure, Ferdinand, x, 56

Scheler, Max, 4, 21, 34–37

Schelling, Friedrich, xx, 77

Science, xxxii, 3–4, 20, 25, 58, 72, 83, 111, 229, 312

Scission, 203

Sehen. See Vision

Sein, Sosein. See Being

Sense, xxxiv, 7, 9–10, 23, 25, 27, 32, 43, 46, 51–55, 59–65, 77–78, 90, 101, 109, 126, 144–145, 154, 159–165, 178–181, 194, 199, 203, 216, 236, 271, 279, 285–290, 299, 302, 313, 318; as self-sensing, 201

Sensible, xxxiv, 21–22, 26, 42, 49, 125–126, 143, 148, 162–165, 169, 175, 181, 187, 196, 198–201, 225, 236–244, 261–265, 280, 284–288, 290–295, 298, 304–309, 317; as sensibility, xxxiv, 48, 154–156, 199–202, 217n, 234, 239–240, 245–247, 251, 254, 268–269, 274, 276–277, 283, 293, 302–303, 307

Shame, 130, 134–135, 249

Sign, 22, 43, 35–36, 50–55, 65, 163, 179, 187, 209, 259, 266, 284, 287–291; artificial sign, 46; natural sign, 46

Signification, xxix, 50, 66, 158, 179–181, 187, 222, 259, 273, 314–315; as pure signification, 61; as signified, 281, 285; as signifying, 46, 66, 144, 162, 172, 180–181, 185n, 274, 289, 295–297; as signifying body, 47; as signifying operation, 50, 52; as signifying power, 180, 235, 276, 278, 290, 305, 315; as signifying speech, 283

Silence, 14, 45, 51, 55, 62, 66, 109–110, 132, 140, 164, 206, 219, 284, 288, 297, 302–303, 313–317; as originary, 311; as silent, 51, 67, 143, 164, 206, 264, 272, 294, 296, 301, 303. *See also* Mute

Singularity, 131, 200, 247, 251, 256–257, 298; as singular, 181, 216, 237, 256, 291, 295

RENAUD BARBARAS is Professor of Contemporary Philosophy at the Université de Paris I, Panthéon-Sorbonne.

TED TOADVINE is Assistant Professor of Philosophy and Environmental Studies at the University of Oregon.

LEONARD LAWLOR is Dunavant Distinguished Professor of Philosophy at the University of Memphis.